Awakening to Radical Islamist Evil

The Hamas War against Israel and the Jews

Awakening to Radical Islamist Evil

The Hamas War against Israel and the Jews

Monty Noam Penkower

Volume II

NEW YORK
2026

Library of Congress Control Number: 2024948276

ISBN 9798887197791 (hardback)
ISBN 9798887197807 (paperback)
ISBN 9798887197814 (adobe pdf)
ISBN 9798887197821 (epub)

Copyright © Touro University Press, 2026
Published by Touro University Press and Academic Studies Press.
Typeset, printed, and distributed by Academic Studies Press.

Touro University Press
Michael A. Shmidman and Simcha Fishbane, Editors
3 Times Square, Room 654,
New York, NY 10036, USA
press@touro.edu

Book design by Kryon Publishing Services
Cover design by Ivan Grave

Typeset, printed, and distributed by Academic Studies Press
1007 Chestnut St.
Newton, MA 02464, USA
press@academicstudiespress.com
www.academicstudiespress.com

To the innocent casualties of war

...but these poor sheep, what have they done?

(2 Samuel 24:17)

Contents

Preface	ix
1. Iran Enters the War	1
2. Into Rafah	35
3. Plus ça change …	77
4. … plus c'est la même chose	113
5. The War Grinds On	155
6. No End in Sight	197
Conclusion	237
Appendices	255
Index	279

Preface

The thought of visiting Auschwitz had never even occurred to Bella Haim, an Israeli Holocaust survivor who was born not far from the former Nazi death camp near Kraków, Poland. A founder of Kibbutz Gvulot near Gaza, eighty-six-year-old Haim arrived in Israel at the age of seventeen determined to make her patch of desert blossom, as the Zionist adage goes, and raise a family amid the multiple wars and crises that have shaped Israel's national story. She changed her mind about making the trip after she was once again traumatized on October 7, 2023, when Hamas terrorists abducted her twenty-eight-year-old grandson Yotam from Kibbutz Kfar Aza to Gaza's labyrinth of tunnels, leading to his death on December 15 at the hands of Israeli troops who accidentally killed him and two other Israelis who had escaped captivity.

This fresh trauma, she said, made her decide to visit Auschwitz for the first time. "I'm here to show we are alive, we have risen from the Holocaust, and we will rise again from October 7," she said ahead of the march, in which 8,000 Jews from all over the world slowly walked the two kilometers (1.2 miles) separating the Auschwitz compound from the gas chambers in the Birkenau part of the camp. Fifty-five Holocaust survivors joined in May 2024 on this March of the Living, including six survivors who were affected by the Hamas massacre in southern Israel on the "Black Sabbath" of October 7, 2023, the worst day of slaughter in Jewish history since the *Shoah*.[1]

Darkness once again cast its shadow over Jewish history. The October 7 bloodbath shattered Israel's sense of security. The brutal nature of the Hamas attack on the Jewish State, unprovoked and unprecedented, left its population traumatized in a way that previous wars did not. For a long time, the country was awash in grief, fear, and sorrow. How hitherto polarized citizens joined ranks behind the Israel Defense Forces (IDF) as it heroically responded to this existential threat to Israel's survival, strengthened by the US administration's vital aid and world Jewry's outpouring of support, is the subject of my book *Awakening to Radical Islamic Evil: The Hamas War Against Israel and the Jews*.[2] This daily account of the initial six months of the war explored its local, regional, and international significance. I am fully aware that, until primary archival files are available to scholars many years hence, mine is a first draft of history. Still, also cognizant that a war for the narrative would soon emerge, I felt obligated by offering a chronological survey committed to fact to counter the falsehoods and distortions that before very long flooded the media.

The present volume carries the story ahead another six months, bringing it near to the first anniversary of the outbreak of the war. I have once more relied on books, articles, and numerous internet sources, all the while seeking to bring the many actors involved in the drama onto the stage to play their parts. Appendices range from official statements to lamentation, eulogy, and song. For the multitude of innocents wherever they were, who are tragically casualties in war, the grief and pain will always be present to carry. These pages are dedicated to them, each a world cut short.

The project has been a draining endeavor, and I am especially grateful to those who provided encouragement while the effort went forward. Siblings, children, grandchildren, and great-grandchildren regularly remind me of what is most important in life. My cherished wife, Phyllis, provides a warm haven at all times. Touro University Press and Academic Studies Press are an inestimable union of forces. Professor Emeritus Michael Popkin, long-time academic colleague and dear friend, again read the text for clarity.

The outcome of Israel's battle with Iran and its Hamas, Hezbollah, and Houthi proxies remains far from clear. The Conclusion to this volume is peppered with questions awaiting resolution. Above all, if a recent assessment of the war in Gaza one year on, that it may now have driven "the proverbial final nail" in the coffin of the classic two-state paradigm for solving the Israeli-Palestinian conundrum, is correct,[3] is the Third Jewish Commonwealth fated not to enjoy the blessings of tranquility as it seeks to move ahead in the years to come? Is the Middle East's perilous landscape to be continuously bedeviled by hatred and strife?

One unique event shows the way. A chorus of Israeli and Palestinian teens won hearts, a standing ovation, and a chance at $1 million with a successful *America's Got Talent* audition that aired on the night of July 16, 2024. The Jerusalem Youth Chorus performed Phillip Phillips's version of *Home*, which envisions a safe and comfortable future after difficult times—with lyrics whose resonance in the post-October 7 climate are unmistakable. "Settle down, it'll all be clear. Don't pay no mind to the demons—they fill you with fear. The trouble, it might drag you down; if you get lost, you can always be found," sang twenty teens and young adults wearing jackets with the chorus's logo, featuring a peace dove. They went on, "Just know you're not alone, 'cause I'm gonna make this place your home."⁴

The Jewish nation whose anthem is *Hatikva* (The Hope) has always realized that peace cannot be imposed. It can only grow from the hearts of people. The message of tolerance and understanding is the clarion call for our troubled times. My prayer is that all sides will ultimately come to embrace this noble dream.

Jerusalem
Simchat Torah 5785

Endnotes

1. *Times of Israel*, May 6, 2024.
2. The first volume of this book has appeared as Monty Noam Penkower, *Awakening to Radical Islamic Evil: The Hamas War Against Israel and the Jews* (New York: Touro University Press, 2024).
3. Chuck Frerilich, "The War in Gaza One Year On: An Interim Assessment," *The Israel Journal of Foreign Affairs*, Oct. 22, 2024, 11. One Israeli historian's able summary of the first year of the war foisted on Israel by Hamas's savage attack on its southern communities near the Gaza Strip on October 7, 2023, suggests how to end the IDF's war with Hamas and Hezbollah while advising Iran to shut down its nuclear weapons project and stop supplying its proxies with weapons. He offers no solution to the Israeli-Palestinian imbroglio. Benny Morris, "The Shifting Sands of War," *Quillette*, Oct. 28, 2024. The same is true for another historian's excellent review of the years between the Oslo Accords of September 13, 1993, and the 2023 Hamas assault which sparked the war that followed. Efraim Karsh, "From Oslo to Be'eri: How the 30-Years-Long Peace Delusion Led to Hamas's 10/7 Massacres," *Israel Affairs* 30, no. 5 (2024): 1–49.
4. Jewish Telegraphic Agency (JTA), July 17, 2024. That song recalls *Goin' Home*, a poignant Afro-American spiritual which is based on Czech composer Antonin Dvořák's *New World Symphony* (Symphony No. 9, 1893), specifically the Largo movement. This was composed in 1922 by William Arms Fisher, who was one of Dvořák's students. Fisher arranged and adapted the Largo theme and wrote his own lyrics. The spirit of his work was meant to be applicable to many people. In *Goin' Home*, Fisher developed Dvořák's yearning for his own home into a universal message of hope for anyone searching for home. See Emily Stephenson, "William Arms Fisher's 'Goin' home': Somehow a 'Negro spiritual,'" *Music 345: Race, Identity, and Representation in American Music: Student Blogs and Library Exhibit Companion*, Oct. 24, 2017, https://pages.stolaf.edu/americanmusic/2017/10/24/william-arms-fishers-goin-home-somehow-a-negro-spiritual/.

CHAPTER 1

Iran Enters the War

On the first of April 2024, the Israel Defense Forces (IDF) declared an end to its two-week operation in Gaza's Al-Shifa Hospital, with about 200 terrorists killed and at least 500 arrested, including "very important officials" and participants in the October 7 Hamas savage attack on Israel. Several dozen patients were evacuated to the Al-Ahli Arab Hospital in Gaza City. Soldiers from the 7th Armored Brigade eliminated terrorist squads in the Kararat neighborhood of Khan Younis in cooperation with the Israeli Air Force (IAF). The IDF spokesperson also announced the death in the southern Gaza Strip of twenty-year-old Staff Sgt. Nadav Cohen, who fought with the 7th Brigade's 77th Battalion, marking the 600th fallen soldier since the beginning of the Hamas-Israel war. During the night, twenty-two suspects were arrested in the West Bank; since the start of the war, some 3,700 arrests had been made in the area. In the southern Israeli town of Gan Yavne, three Israelis were seriously wounded in a stabbing assault (one died later of his wounds); the attacker, nineteen-year-old Mumeen Al-Khalil from the West Bank village of Dura, was shot and killed. The same day, Israel's parliament by a vote of 71 to 10 passed a law allowing Prime Minister Binyamin Netanyahu to immediately close the Qatari-backed broadcasting of *Al Jazeera*, citing a "direct threat to the country's security" in the context of its pro-Hamas coverage since October 7.[1]

Six missiles from an Israeli F-35 jet fighter over the skies of Damascus eliminated senior Iranian Revolutionary Guard Corps (IRGC) commander Mohammad Reza Zahedi, who oversaw Iran's covert military operations in Syria and Lebanon, two more generals, and four other officers, the attack representing a possible escalation of the shadow war between Israel and Iran. The loss of Zahedi was being watched in the region. For instance, Al-Ain media in the United Arab Emirates (UAE) carried an article that examined a photograph on social media showing Zahedi, IRGC elite Quds Force commander Qasem Soleimani, Hezbollah leader Imad Mughniyeh, Hezbollah leader Hassan Nasrallah, and IRGC commander Ahmed Kazemi, noting that four of these men were now dead, and that Nasrallah "is the last of them." The Supreme Leader of Iran, Ali Khamenei, quickly responded that "Israel will regret the attack on the Iranian embassy in Damascus."[2]

Israel's Attorney General Gali Baharav-Miara sent a letter one day earlier instructing the legal advisers at the ministries of education and defense to start planning for the recruitment of haredi (ultra-Orthodox) yeshivah students to the IDF. This came after Israel's High Court of Justice had issued a temporary injunction prohibiting the government from continuing to provide funds to haredi yeshivot. Funds to those institutions were to be cut according to the number of their students under the age of twenty-six whose annual army deferments had expired and were thus eligible for the draft. In her opinion, all alternative methods of compensation would constitute a violation of the High Court's decision. The letter was sent because, by the end of the month, the attorney general was required to provide the High Court with details of the steps the state had taken to comply with its order.

Members of Netanyahu's government coalition took issue with Baharav-Miara's orders, which they considered high-handed, particularly after the High Court had granted Netanyahu's request for a thirty-day extension to resolve the haredi recruitment issue. Deputy Knesset Speaker Hanoch Dov Milwidsky of Netanyahu's Likud Party called for the attorney general's dismissal, adding that the subject should be off-limits in a time of war. The haredi parties (Shas and United Torah Judaism) warned Netanyahu that he had two weeks to find a solution or their communities' rabbinical leadership would force them to quit his coalition. Israel's ultra-Orthodox continued to frown on army service, considering it a distraction from Torah study and a threat to their way of life. However, October 7 had heightened the demands of the larger public that they contribute their share to the defense of the nation. The number of haredi men studying in yeshivot and eligible for IDF service was estimated at between 63,000 and 66,000. Since the war began, 1,140 haredim had enlisted, of whom 600 were over the age of twenty-six.[3]

On April 2, the World Central Kitchen declared that seven of its aid workers, citizens of Australia, Britain, and Poland, as well as Palestinians and a dual citizen of the United States and Canada, were killed on Monday night in an alleged Israeli drone strike in Gaza on one of its vehicle convoys, pausing future operations. An immediate IDF investigation revealed that faulty intelligence had reported a Hamas terrorist there. Israel took responsibility, Netanyahu calling the deadly strike "a tragic case of our forces unintentionally hitting innocent people." The UAE halted maritime corridor supply activities; Cypriot officials said ships carrying more aid were returning to Larnaca port. Consequently, Israel risked being left without any partners to provide and deliver humanitarian assistance to Gaza.

US and Israeli officials expressed concern that such a situation could force Israel to shift its war goals in the Strip, since Washington and other allies had made it increasingly clear to Jerusalem that continued support for the war on Hamas depended on Israel allowing and facilitating aid to Gaza's civilian population. The White House spokesman, National Security Council (NSC) advisor Jake Sullivan, expressed its "outrage" at the strike, and US President Joe Biden, saying he was "outraged and heartbroken," called the charity aid group's founder to share his condolences. The following night, he declared that Israel had "not done enough" to protect "brave and selfless" aid workers and Palestinian civilians. The prime ministers of Australia, Canada, the United Kingdom, and Poland issued similar rebukes.[4]

To mark Day 180 of the war, some twenty demonstrators gathered in the Knesset plenum visitors' gallery on Wednesday afternoon, demanding the Israeli government secure the release of the 134 captives still held hostage in Gaza. As Knesset members deliberated on climate change legislation, the protesters began splashing yellow paint on the windows separating the visitors' gallery from the Knesset plenum itself. Some dipped their hands in yellow paint and smeared it on the windows. Knesset ushers quickly intervened and removed them from the gallery, while several Opposition MKs raised their hands in solidarity with the group. This followed a demonstration the previous night in which hundreds of anti-government protesters broke through police barriers to get close to Netanyahu's Jerusalem residence, leading Israeli Security Agency (Shin Bet) chief Ronen Bar to warn that this went "beyond the accepted rules of protest, harm our ability to maintain civil order," and might lead to "violent friction with the security forces, prevent them from fulfilling their duties and even harm protected individuals." On the other hand, the Orthodox Union, representing more than 1,000 synagogues across the United States, delivered to the White House boxes with 180,000 letters claiming that Israel "is morally obligated to continue this war until it finishes the job of destroying Hamas," and urging the president to speak out against "the narrative fueling the domestic spike in antisemitism harming American Jews every day," and "to push relentlessly to achieve the unconditional and immediate release of each and every hostage."[5]

Responding to recent protests outside the Knesset and the Prime Minister's residence demanding new elections, Minister without Portfolio Benny Gantz (National Unity Party) declared in a press conference on April 3 that the Coalition and Opposition should reach a mutually agreed upon date for a Knesset election sometime in September. "In order for us to maintain unity, the public must know that we will soon come and ask for their trust," Gantz said.

"Let us not ignore October 7th. For this reason, we must agree on an election date sometime in September, roughly a year after the war started." "Setting such a date will allow us to continue the military campaign, while signaling to the citizens of Israel that we will soon renew their trust in us." Netanyahu dismissed his coalition partner's appeal as "petty politics," claiming that elections would harm the war effort; opposition head Yair Lapid said Israel could not wait six months.[6]

During a tour of the Middle East, Spanish Prime Minister Pedro Sanchez informed journalists that he intended to recognize a Palestinian state by July, according to reports by *El País* and *La Vanguardia*. Following a European Council meeting in late March, the Spanish Prime Minister had discussed with the heads of Ireland, Malta, and Slovenia plans to "take the first step" towards recognition of Palestinian statehood. He added that, considering elections in the European Parliament were scheduled to take place in June along with ongoing discussions in the United Nations, support for Palestinian statehood could reach a "critical mass" among nations. Israeli officials called the move by Ireland, Spain, Malta, and Slovenia tantamount to giving the Palestinians "a prize for terrorism" and could interfere with ongoing negotiations to secure the release of Israeli hostages from Gaza.

Riyad Mansour, the Palestinian Authority's envoy to the UN, told *Reuters* that he intended to apply for full UN membership at the Security Council. The PA sent a letter to Maltese diplomat Vanessa Frazier, who was currently serving as president of the fifteen-member council. That letter included the names of 140 countries that had recognized a Palestinian state. In late March, nearly one-third of the Democrats in the US Senate had signed an open letter to President Joe Biden urging him to take "bold" steps towards establishing a Palestinian state. The White House spokesman hinted, however, that the administration believed this was to be achieved through direct negotiations between the parties involved in the matter, and not the United Nations.[7]

With Iran vowing to retaliate for the recent strike on one of its consular buildings in Damascus, killing IRGC commander Zahedi and other army officers, which it blamed on Israel, the IDF on Thursday said it had halted home leave for all combat troops following a fresh assessment. Israel also withdrew its ambassadors and evacuated its embassies in multiple locations around the world, and certain ambassadors were requested not to arrive at public events. Israeli officials said they foiled a plot by a group of Palestinians and Arab Israelis to kill rightist National Security Minister Itamar Ben-Gvir, as well as a plan to place explosives at a soccer stadium in Jerusalem. Asad Issam Kanbari, wanted by Israel for his association with the Jenin Battalion armed group, was killed by the IDF in a village southwest of Jenin. Israel's High Court of Justice demanded that the state provide answers by next Wednesday regarding the necessary scope of aid to Gaza, efforts made to increase aid access, and the difficulties faced in delivering it, in response to a petition by five Israeli human rights organizations. Many Muslim leaders declined Biden's invitation to an Iftar dinner at the White House to break the Ramadan fast because of tensions over Israel's military operations in Gaza. Nonetheless, CNN reported that the administration had authorized the transfer of military aid to Israel, including 1,000 500-pound bombs and over 1,000 smaller-diameter bombs.[8]

Lobby 1701, created to inform the public about the Iranian proxy Hezbollah's activities in Lebanon, summarized the terrorist organization's efforts in the past month. Its name came from a United Nations resolution passed at the end of the Second Lebanon War in 2006, when a cease-fire between the different parties was reached and the UN Security Council issued Resolution 1701. It called for a full cessation of hostilities between Israel and Hezbollah, the withdrawal of Israeli forces from Lebanon to be replaced by Lebanese and UNIFIL forces deploying to southern Lebanon, and the disarmament of armed groups including Hezbollah. According to the Lobby's report, at least 700 rockets towards Israel and some 40 missiles were launched. Two Israeli citizens were killed, and sixteen civilians and soldiers were wounded. From the beginning of the war, more than 750 buildings and businesses had been struck. On the other side of the political divide, Lebanon's president announced that since October 7, 313 were killed in Lebanon, with more than 1,000 wounded.[9]

After "a tense call" earlier on Thursday between Biden and Netanyahu, during which the US president said that the situation in Gaza was "unacceptable" and that he "hinges support" on the protection by Israel of civilians there, the prime minister's security cabinet authorized increased aid for Gaza. This "will prevent a humanitarian crisis and is necessary to ensure the continuation of the fighting and to achieve the goals of the war," Netanyahu's office declared. To help facilitate the delivery of aid, Israel would temporarily allow goods for Gaza to land at the port in Ashdod, a step which had been halted after the Hamas-led attack on October 7. Israel also planned to temporarily open the Erez Crossing by northern Gaza and close to Ashdod for the entry of humanitarian assistance. In addition, more Jordanian aid would enter Gaza through the Kerem Shalom Crossing. Quickly responding, a White House spokesperson welcomed the decision, adding that these steps "must now be fully and rapidly implemented." The next morning, as Muslim pilgrims to Jerusalem's Al-Aqsa compound on the last Friday of Ramadan continued to chant support for Hamas, the lead editorial in *Haaretz* made the position of that liberal-left newspaper, long an opponent of Jewish settlement in the West Bank and of Netanyahu's right-wing coalition government, crystal clear: "Israel must end its war in Gaza now."[10]

The UN Human Rights Council adopted a resolution on April 5 calling for Israel to be held accountable for possible war crimes and crimes against humanity committed in Gaza. Twenty-eight countries voted in favor, thirteen abstained, and six were opposed, including the United States and Germany. The State Department declared that the resolution did not contain a specific condemnation of Hamas for the October 7 attacks, nor "any reference to the terrorist nature of those actions." It did, however, add that Israel had not done enough to mitigate harm to civilians. Israel dismissed the resolution's text as "distorted."[11]

President Biden wrote to the leaders of Egypt and Qatar, calling on them to press Hamas for a hostage deal with Israel, according to the Associated Press. Some thirty Israeli embassies across the world were closed on Friday amid fears of an Iranian attack in retaliation for a suspected Israeli strike that killed IRGC General Zahedi earlier that week in Syria, Tehran declaring that Israeli embassies "are no longer safe." Hezbollah leader Hassan Nasrallah said that the Iranian response "will undoubtedly come but will not adhere to a time frame." Even as Friday Ramadan prayers in the Al-Aqsa compound proceeded without disturbance, eight East Jerusalem residents were arrested for pro-terrorism incitement. That night, thirteen suspects throughout the West Bank were taken for interrogation and considerable weaponry was uncovered.[12]

The IDF announced that its fighter jets on Wednesday had struck and eliminated Akram Abd Al-Rahman Husein Salamah, a senior terrorist operative of Hamas's Internal Security. He had served as Deputy Head of the Khan Younis District and was responsible for planning and executing significant terror attacks in Israeli territory. The Israeli army said it had retrieved the body of Elad Katzir, who was kidnapped from Nir Oz during Hamas's October 7 attack, and returned it to Israel. IDF intel showed that Katzir was killed in January while in Palestinian Islamic Jihad captivity, and his body was found buried in Khan Younis. Israeli strikes that killed seven World Central Kitchen workers in Gaza were "carried out in serious violation" of the military's procedures and were a "grave mistake stemming from a serious failure due to a mistaken identification" of vehicles as carrying Hamas operatives, according to the findings of an Israeli military investigation. Forty House Democrats, including former House Speaker Nancy Pelosi, urged Biden to withhold pending arms transfers to Israel after the seven aid workers were killed, as well as to place conditions on future weapons assistance. In a related fashion, the campaign to protest Biden's support for Israel at the ballot box declared victory in Wisconsin the same week following the Democratic primary as more than 47,000 people voted "uninstructed" rather than supporting the party's presumptive nominee for the US presidency.[13]

On April 7, Day 184 of the war and six months since it began, the IDF announced that the 98th Commando Division had left the Gaza Strip in order "to recuperate and prepare for future operations," leaving no troops actively maneuvering in southern Gaza. The Nahal Brigade, made up of ground troops stationed along a corridor that divided northern and southern Gaza as a buffer zone, would continue to operate. Its official report stated that 604 soldiers had been killed to date, 260 of these in combat since the ground op in Gaza began; 3,193 soldiers were wounded, 1,552 of these in the ground op. The IDF also listed forty-one soldiers killed due to "friendly fire" in Gaza and other military-related accidents.[14] More than 13,000 Hamas operatives and members of other terror groups had been killed by the IDF in the Gaza Strip since the beginning of the war, in addition to some 1,000 terrorists inside Israel on October 7. The IDF's data said the military had killed five Hamas brigade commanders and those of equivalent rank, as well as more than twenty battalion commanders. More than 100 Hamas company commanders and operatives with a similar rank had been killed. The number included thirty commanders in the Iran-backed group. Some 32,000 targets had been struck in the Strip since the beginning of the war, including more than 3,600 that were discovered as Hamas sites during the fighting. The IDF added that its Military Intelligence Directorate's Unit 504 had interrogated some 4,600 Palestinian suspects in the Gaza Strip, many of whom were arrested and brought to Israel for questioning.

In Lebanon, the IDF said it had killed more than 330 terror operatives, mostly members of Hezbollah. Around 4,700 Hezbollah positions had been hit, according to the IDF's data. Since the war began, some 9,100 projectiles fired from Gaza had crossed the border into Israel, alongside 3,100 from Lebanon and around 35 from Syria. The figures did not include rockets—said by Israel to be at least in the hundreds—launched by Gazan terror groups that misfired and landed inside the Strip. In the West Bank, since October 7 troops had arrested more than 3,700 wanted Palestinians, including more than 1,600 affiliated with Hamas. Another 420 gunmen had been killed by troops in the West Bank. The IDF added that seventy brigade-level raids had been carried out in the West Bank, and nineteen homes of Palestinians accused of terrorism demolished.[15]

In a statement delivered on Sunday at the start of the weekly cabinet meeting, Netanyahu reiterated his commitment to the goals of the war: "To return all our hostages, to complete the elimination of Hamas in the entire Gaza Strip including Rafah, and to ensure Gaza will no longer constitute a threat to Israel." "I made it clear to the international community: There will be no cease-fire without the return of the hostages. It just won't happen," Netanyahu said. "This is the Israeli government's policy, and I welcome the fact that the Biden administration made it clear the other day that this is still its position as well." Turning to the ongoing negotiations for a temporary truce and hostage release deal, Netanyahu declared that "Israel is not the one preventing a deal. Hamas is preventing a deal." "Its extreme demands were intended to bring about an end to the war and leave it intact. To ensure its survival, its rehabilitation, its ability to endanger our citizens and our soldiers," the prime minister continued. "Surrendering to Hamas's demands will allow it to try to repeat the crimes of October 7 again and again, as it promised to do." Hamas had so far stuck to its demands for a complete cease-fire and pullout of Israeli troops from Gaza in exchange for a hostage deal—demands that Jerusalem had so far rejected.

"This is the time for unity," Netanyahu went on, "but, precisely at this time, an extreme and violent minority is trying to drag the country into division," in an apparent reference to ongoing anti-government protests that called for an immediate election. "There is nothing our enemies want more." "Let our enemies make no mistake—the absolute majority of the people are united in the need to continue fighting until victory," Netanyahu asserted. "The majority of the people, and I am among them, condemns any manifestation of violence within us—riots and violations of the law, trampling on demonstrators or attacking policemen, wild incitement and murderous violence on social media," he said, seeming to refer to the violence at a protest in Tel Aviv on Saturday night, including a car ramming a crowd of demonstrators. Netanyahu also pointed the finger at Iran, stating that the war had "shown the world what we always knew—Iran stands behind the attack against us through its proxies." "Since October 7 we have been attacked on many fronts by Iran's proxies—Hamas, Hezbollah, the Houthis, militias in Iraq and Syria, and other attacks," he said.[16]

"The defense system finished preparations for a response against any scenario that may develop with Iran," said Defense Minister Yoav Gallant during an operational situation assessment on Sunday. Despite the announced troop withdrawal from Gaza's south, leaving a single brigade, the military was also preparing for "follow-up missions" that included Rafah. "We will reach a point when Hamas no longer controls the Gaza Strip and does not function as a military framework that poses a threat to the citizens of the state of Israel," he declared. However, the IDF's primary war objectives—eliminating Hamas and freeing the hostages—had not yet been attained. Further, two people were wounded, including a nineteen-year-old female soldier in serious condition, in a terrorist shooting attack in Samaria that morning on Route 55 between Azzun and Nabi Ilyas. As part of a joint operation by the IDF and Shin Bet last night in Shechem (Nablus), two wanted men suspected of carrying out a shooting attack on a military post were arrested several hours after the attack. During another operation in Nur Shams in the Tulkarm Governate, the IDF and Border Police arrested Omar Abu Halal, identified as a Palestinian Islamic Jihad terrorist, who was suspected of being involved in shooting attacks and preparing explosives for attacks on Israeli soldiers and civilians. An Israeli airstrike eliminated Ali Ahmed Hassin, the commander of Hezbollah's Radwan forces in the Hajir region of southern Lebanon, and two others near As-Sultaniyeh.[17]

British Prime Minister Rishi Sunak spoke for many when declaring on Saturday that the "terrible" war between Israel and Hamas "must end." Unfortunately, six months since it began, Israel's war with Hamas in Gaza appeared, in the *New York Times*'s phrase, to have "reached an impasse" that analysts and diplomats said had no resolution in sight, even as experts warned of famine and Gaza's health system's collapse, and the death toll on both sides continued to climb. Although Israel had routed Hamas in much of Gaza, and fighting seemed to have slowed, mediators found it difficult to advance negotiations for a truce there. Israel was reluctant to agree to a cease-fire that allowed Hamas to regroup in parts of Gaza, while Hamas rejected proposals that did not ensure its long-term survival. sticking to a proposal that it submitted in mid-March, including a total IDF withdrawal from Gaza, which Israeli officials vehemently rejected. The outpouring of global sympathy for Israel after October 7 had dwindled, replaced by images of starving and dead Palestinians in Gaza. Images projected across the world showed swaths of the Gaza Strip turned into rubble. The Gazans who now returned to Khan Younis, for example, found a city devastated beyond recognition. More than 33,000 Palestinians had been killed, according to the Gaza Health Ministry, whose numbers did not distinguish between combatants and civilians, including those killed as a consequence of terror groups' own rocket misfires.[18]

And many hostages taken by Hamas on October 7 were still in Gaza, their fate unknown. Reminding a demonstration on Sunday afternoon of more than 1,000 people in front of UN headquarters in New York City that these 133 innocents were not a homogenous group, Rachel Goldberg-Polin noted that their diversity included eight Arab Muslims, eight Thai Buddhists, and two black African Christians, whose identities should not be erased. Eight US citizens were somewhere held in the labyrinth of Hamas tunnels; Mexico, Nepal, Germany, and France, besides native Israelis, were represented as well, Christian and Hindu alongside Jew. Among them, her twenty-three-year-old son Hersh, born in Berkeley, California, who was kidnapped at the Nova music festival, his left arm from the elbow down blown off by an RPG as terrorists lobbed grenades into a field shelter; Hersh managed to fashion a tourniquet around his own arm. The reality was "unfathomable, unimaginable," she said while wearing the number 184 to mark the days since his abrupt disappearance. Her "torment too deep," her "sorrow too sharp" for words in this time of darkness, she read a poem urging "the boys in the room" to imagine their own loved ones in these horrific circumstances and to redeem their failure in negotiations so far by bringing these hostages home.[19]

Iran informed Washington that it would refrain from responding to the airstrike a week earlier in which senior IRGC commanders were killed in Damascus if a cease-fire in Gaza were reached, reported the Jadeh Iran news outlet on April 8. Yet a forum of local emergency security teams was raising the alarm on a scenario of terrorists infiltrating Jewish communities along the seamline in the Sharon region, using motorized paragliders as they had in attacking southern Israel on October 7, *Yisrael Hayom* reported. The Hineni Forum, which united over 360 emergency security teams consisting of thousands of volunteers across Israel, warned that the idea that a wall or checkpoint could stop a terrorist infiltration had collapsed, and the lessons and possible threats of this had yet to have been learned. The local authorities in the Sharon region, in the meantime, were taking steps to prepare for a scenario of aerial infiltrations from nearby Arab towns and villages. Last week, local authorities in the region which bordered Samaria set up radar systems to alert residents of attempted terrorist infiltration.[20]

Concurrently, signs of a civil conflict between Hamas and its Palestinian rivals were beginning to build, raising far-reaching questions about what a postwar government in Gaza might look like—and how long it might prevail. Hamas late last month detained several Palestinian Authority (PA) officials in Gaza and tried to prevent an aid convoy overseen by PA staff from traveling in the enclave, accusing them of working with Israel in the first standoff between the two groups since October 7. Meanwhile Fatah, the party controlling the West Bank-based Palestinian Authority, last week issued a rare public rebuke of Iran, one of Hamas's primary funders and supporters. It said it rejected Tehran's attempts to dictate what happened in the region while also criticizing the creeping influence of other foreign powers in Palestinian affairs.

While the United States and other Western powers were looking to a reformed Palestinian Authority to take a significant leadership role in Gaza and prevent a power vacuum from forming that could allow Hamas to continue in some form, Israeli security officials had quietly been developing a plan to distribute aid in the Gaza Strip that could eventually create a Palestinian-led governing authority there, enlisting Palestinian leaders and businessmen who had no links to Hamas, as well as the PA's top intelligence official, Majed Faraj. Hamas was stepping up its own efforts to ensure it would still play a future political role by limiting the Palestinian Authority's access to the narrow strip of land. It accused PA intelligence agents of plotting to sow chaos and division in Gaza, echoing its longstanding practice of labeling anyone who worked with Israel as a traitor. Fatah's spokesman in Gaza, Munzer Al-Hayek, said Hamas was trying to eliminate any control on the ground outside of its own. "They are focused on attacking the PA, accusing it of being a foreign power," he charged in an interview.[21]

In a video published on April 8, Netanyahu announced that the IDF must enter Rafah to achieve complete victory and return the hostages while also claiming that Israel had decided on a date for entry. Even as Hezbollah significantly escalated tensions by launching several drones into northern Israel, the vast majority of Israelis still wanted to keep the war going until Hamas was completely destroyed, a poll commissioned by *Channel 14* showed Sunday. Fully 83 percent of the public thought the fighting should continue until nothing was left of the terror organization and all the hostages were returned. Although 133 hostages remained in Gaza, the Israeli government believed that only 60–70 were still alive. The definitive support for the war came despite the drop in confidence reflected in the answer to whether Israel could win it. A significantly lesser majority of seventy percent answered positively, while fully twenty-seven percent responded in the negative.[22]

Six months after the Hamas onslaught on southern Israel, seventy percent of those who departed the affected area had returned, with only a handful of locales remaining uninhabited, according to data published by the government on Sunday. Northern evacuees, however, remained evacuated indefinitely. In the south, Kissufim, along with Be'eri, Kfar Aza, Netiv HaAsara, and Nir Oz, were among thirteen so-called "red locales" that were either too severely damaged in the Hamas October 7 massacre or deemed to be too risky to be repopulated for the time being. These communities would take at least eighteen months to repopulate.[23]

King Abdullah II of Jordan, French President Emmanuel Macron, and Egyptian President Abdel Fattah El-Sisi wrote an opinion piece on Monday for *New York Times*, in which they called for an immediate cease-fire in Gaza while warning that an Israeli operation in Rafah would have "dangerous consequences." "Violence, terror, and war cannot bring peace to the Middle East. The two-state solution will. It is the only credible path to guaranteeing peace and security for all and ensuring that neither the Palestinians nor the Israelis ever have to relive the horrors that have befallen them since the Oct. 7 attack," wrote the three leaders. At the same time, US Senator Roger Wicker (R., Miss.), the ranking member of the Senate Committee on Armed Services, charged that

Biden's recent call for a cease-fire "plays directly into Hamas's hands and the priority should be the release of the hostages and victory for Israel." That day, the IDF announced that 419 humanitarian aid trucks had passed through the Kerem Shalom and Nitzana border crossings into Gaza, the largest number of humanitarian aid trucks since the beginning of the war, and about 258 food packages were also airdropped across the Gaza Strip. The IDF stated that it "will continue its efforts to facilitate the entry of humanitarian aid to the Gaza Strip by land, air, and sea in accordance with international law."[24]

Speaking to new military recruits at the Tel HaShomer base on Tuesday, Netanyahu highly praised the unique motivation of Israeli youth, their desire to mobilize, defend, and fight in the war. He then added this: "We will complete the elimination of the Hamas brigades, including in Rafah. We are committed to doing it, and each and every one of you now . . . will contribute in one way or another to the completion of the goal. After they did something like this to our country, they won't do it again." The IDF announced that its fighter jets eliminated Hatem al-Am'ari, the chairman of Hamas's Emergency Committee in the Central Camps in Gaza who was also active in its military wing. The 146th Division successfully held a joint exercise in cooperation with the Israeli Air Force, Israel Navy, Israel Police, and search and rescue units to increase readiness against aggression from Israel's northern border. As for the Palestinians' received application for complete entry into the UN, Washington, which held veto power as one of the five permanent members. poured cold water all over their hopes. "Our position is that the issue of full Palestinian membership is a decision that should be negotiated between Israel and the Palestinians," deputy US ambassador to the UN Robert Wood told reporters. "It was a final-status issue under Oslo. They need to work out an agreement and that's how full membership should come about."[25]

"Our commitment to Israel's security against Iran is ironclad" and the hostage negotiations were "now up to Hamas," Biden declared on April 10, even as he criticized Netanyahu's approach to the war in Gaza as a "mistake" and called for a six- to eight-week cease-fire for total access to humanitarian aid for Gaza. US National Security Council Advisor Sullivan said the United States "still hasn't seen a credible and executable plan to account for Rafah evacuation and civilian care." During a press conference with UK Foreign Secretary David Cameron, US Secretary of State Antony Blinken said "it remains astounding to me that the world is almost deafeningly silent when it comes to Hamas." Concurrently, support among Democratic voters for a deal between Israel and the Palestinian Authority plunged from seventy-three to forty-three percent following revelations of the PA's alignment with Hamas according to a recent poll by Gideon300, a public affairs agency, and RMG Research. Hamas political head Ismail Haniyeh, three of whose sons, together with four grandchildren, were killed in an IAF airstrike that day, called his sons "martyred on the road to liberating Jerusalem and the Al-Aqsa Mosque" and said their deaths would not affect Hamas's negotiations with Israel. The terrorist organization declared that it did not have forty hostages who met the US-proposed criteria for their release in exchange for 900 Palestinians during a cease-fire, CNN reported.[26]

The next day, Biden administration Middle East envoy Brett McGurk called the foreign ministers of Saudi Arabia, UAE, Qatar, and Iraq to ask them to deliver a message to Iran urging it to lower tensions with Israel, which they did, a source with knowledge of the situation informed *Reuters*. A senior US official told *Al Jazeera* that Washington was not ruling out the possibility of launching a joint attack on Iran with Israel if the Islamic Republic would respond to the assassination of a senior IRGC general last week by attacking Israel. The official also said that "if Israel comes under attack by missiles or drones, we will not rule out the possibility of helping the Israelis intercept them." The Kremlin, *per contra*, said that Israel's airstrike on the Iranian consulate in Damascus was a violation of all principles of international law, and called on all countries in the region to exercise restraint.

The IDF announced that its forces killed a key financial operative of Hamas's military wing in Rafah, and that its forces had been operating in the Shejaiyah neighborhood in eastern Gaza City. It had also successfully deployed the "Naval Iron Dome" missile defense system for the first time, using it to intercept a hostile aerial target over the Red Sea. That morning, soldiers and Israel Police forcefully removed dozens of Israeli protesters, including families of hostages and terror victims, who blocked aid trucks entering Gaza at the Nitzana Crossing.[27]

Still, as the year's Ramadan came to an end, US officials told CNN that Biden made light of Netanyahu's claim about a "date" for the Rafah operation, calling it "bluster" and "bravado." On the same day, Blinken took the opportunity to mark the Muslim religious holiday by comparing the "plight of Palestinians in Gaza and the West Bank" to "civilians in Syria, women suffering under the Taliban in Afghanistan, Uyghurs in the People's Republic of China [and] Rohingya in Burma and Bangladesh." At the same time, worried at the apparent shift in the administration's stand towards Israel in a presidential election year and at former House Speaker Nancy Pelosi joining forty Democrats in urging Biden to halt the transfer of US armaments to Israel, the *Wall Street Journal* weighed in. "Denying weapons to an ally in the middle of a war is the definition of betrayal," the newspaper's editorial board wrote. "Democrats claim to be looking out for Israel's best interests," its members added, "but that's for Israelis to decide. The threats to withhold weapons from an ally must overjoy Hamas, whose strategy of hiding behind civilian deaths is the real source of Gaza's humanitarian tragedy."[28]

President Biden remarked on Friday that he expected Iran would strike Israel "sooner [rather] than later" in retaliation for an April 1 attack that killed seven Quds Force operatives in Damascus, US intelligence saying that the strike could happen within twenty-four to forty-eight hours. Biden's message to Tehran was simple: "Don't." While the United States rushed warships into position to protect Israel and American forces in the region, hoping to head off a direct attack from Iran on Israel and avoid a wider conflict in the Middle East, the Iranians responded through the Swiss, as recently as Wednesday, that they did not want a confrontation with the United States. Tehran sent the same message through China and other nations. Blinken informed the foreign ministers of Egypt and Jordan that an "escalation by Iran would not benefit anyone in the region." Defense Minister Gallant met with US CENTCOM head Gen. Michael Kurilla amid preparations for a possible Iranian strike. US Secretary of Defense Lloyd Austin expressed to his Israeli counterpart the Pentagon's frustration that the United States was not informed of the attack in Damascus last week, the *Washington Post* reported. The Pentagon later said Austin assured Gallant that Israel could count on full US support to defend Israel against Iranian attacks.[29]

Referring on Saturday to the Iranian seizure of an Israeli-linked vessel, IDF spokesperson Rear Adm. Daniel Hagari declared that "Iran will bear the consequences for choosing to escalate the situation any further," and that "Israel is on high alert. We have increased our readiness to protect Israel from further Iranian aggression. We are also prepared to respond." The same day, the IDF found the body of Binyamin Achimeir, a fourteen-year-old Israeli from Malachei Shalom who went missing on Friday after he went out to herd sheep in the West Bank, confirming the death as a terrorist murder. Clashes erupted in Al Mughayyir near Ramallah during searches for the missing boy, in which three Israeli soldiers, the army, and Border Police intervening after Jewish settlers nearby entered the village with guns and stones, were shot and lightly wounded. A Palestinian was killed and six were wounded in the incident. The Red Crescent reported, in addition, the deaths of two Palestinians in fighting with the IDF at the Al-Fara refugee camp near the city of Tubas.[30]

That evening, family members of Gaza hostages issued an emergency statement outside the Kirya military headquarters in Tel Aviv, declaring thus: "If in order to receive our loved ones quickly and alive, the price is a ceasefire, agree to end the war and return all the hostages in a deal now." It went on: "Then, you will be free to deal with the threats from Gaza. First, save lives. The lack of coordination that leads to decisions that endanger the lives of the abductees is carelessness and a crime." The *New York Times* editorial board went further, calling on the United States to condition military aid to Israel on these grounds: "Netanyahu has turned his back on America and its entreaties," and "The United States cannot remain beholden to an Israeli leader fixated on his own survival and the approval of the zealots he harbors." Yet the United States Treasury Office of Foreign Assets Control announced that it was targeting leaders of Hamas's offensive cyber and drone units with sanctions, and the European Union (EU) imposed sanctions on Hamas's and Palestinian Islamic Jihad's military wings over the sexual violence committed on October 7, 2023.[31]

The same day, *Haaretz* reported an interview with Brig. Genl. Yuval Biton, former head of the Intelligence Division of the Israeli Prison Service. In the course of his interviewing for countless hours Yahya Sinwar, then serving a long sentence for murdering several Israelis, Biton had asked Sinwar a question: "Is it worth 10,000 innocent Gazans dying?" The reply from the future mastermind of Hamas's brutal invasion of Israel's communities near the Gaza border on October 7, which included the murder of Biton's nephew, thirty-eight-year-old Tamir Adar of Kibbutz Nir Oz, came without hesitation: "Even 100,000 is worth it." One week earlier, reports emerged that Sinwar's novel *The Thorn and the Carnation* was being sold on the Amazon website. It was supposedly written while he was serving four life sentences, in which he served twenty-two years until his release among 1,026 other Palestinians in a 2011 prisoner exchange for the Israeli soldier Gilad Shalit. Proudly claiming Sinwar's responsibility for the October 7 attacks, dubbing him the "architect of the Flood of Al-Aqsa" invasion that day, the book's description on Amazon declared that "his narrative offers a profound window into the resilience and the ethos of a man who has played a pivotal role in shaping the discourse of resistance within the Palestinian context."[32]

On April 14, 2024, at 1:43 a.m. Israel time, sirens began to wail in the central Negev region, shortly followed by other regions across the country including the Jerusalem and Dead Sea areas, Golan Heights, Gush Etzion, Hebron, and Samaria. For the first time in the State of Israel's history, Iran began a direct attack on Israel in operation "The True Promise" after years of a shadow war.[33] The Islamic Republic launched a heavy barrage of more than 300 UAVs, ballistic and cruise missiles carrying approximately 60 tons of warheads and explosive materials toward the Jewish commonwealth. To thwart the attack, Israel used two primary defensive weapons systems, the Iron Dome and the Arrow 3. Five hours later, the IDF declared that not a single drone or cruise missile launched in the Iranian barrage had penetrated Israeli territory, and most of the targets were shot down outside the country's borders. One casualty was reported, Amina al-Hassouni, a seven-year-old girl in southern Israel from a Bedouin town near Arad, wounded by shrapnel following the interception of an Iranian drone over the area, who was taken to Beersheba's Soroka Hospital in critical condition. The Nevatim air force base in the Negev desert in southern Israel suffered light damage from the attack and was functioning. Shortly thereafter, US sources said that Biden told Netanyahu during their conversation overnight Saturday that, while the United States shot down dozens of drones and missiles launched from Iran, Lebanon, Iraq, Syria, and Yemen, he opposed any retaliatory Israeli attack on Iran and would not take part in it.

One hour later, IDF spokesman Hagari issued the following statement:

> Last night, for the first time in Israel's history, Iran launched an attack against the Jewish State with 170 advanced drones, 120 ballistic missiles, and 30 cruise missiles. The Iranian threat met the aerial and technological superiority of the IDF combined with a strong fighting coalition that together intercepted 99 percent of the threats launched against the territory of the State of Israel. This is a very significant strategic achievement. Of the approximately 170 unmanned aerial vehicles that Iran launched, zero penetrated Israeli territory. Dozens of them were intercepted by Air Force fighter jets, Israel's air defense system, and the defense systems and aircraft of its partners. Of the cruise missiles that Iran launched, zero penetrated Israeli territory. Twenty-five of them of them were intercepted by Air Force fighter jets outside the country's borders.

Netanyahu wrote on X, "We intercepted. We blocked. Together we will win." At 8:38, twelve minutes after Jordan (whose F-16 fighter jets had intercepted some drones) reopened its airspace, the Israel Aviation Authority announced the reopening of Ben-Gurion Airport. Iraq and Lebanon followed. President Isaac (Yitzhak) Herzog wrote on X: "Bless you dear soldiers and commanders of the IDF and IAF. Bless the coalition of nations led by the US and @POTUS. Bless my sisters and brothers, the people of Israel, for their exceptional show of resilience. Together, the forces of good will overcome the forces of evil. *Am Yisrael Chai!*" (The nation of Israel lives!)

At 9:47 a.m. the Chief of Staff of the Iranian military, Major General Mohammad Bagheri, warned that "our response will be much larger than tonight's military action if Israel retaliates against Iran," adding a threat against the United States if Washington supported Israel's retaliation. "Our operations are over, and we have no intention to continue them," Bagheri said before claiming that Iran's attack had successfully targeted two Israeli military bases. Iran's President Ebrahim Raisi advised Israel and its allies "to appreciate this responsible and proportionate action," a strike of unprecedented magnitude that was even more powerful than the Russian opening strike against Ukraine in 2022. Addressing Iranian state TV, the commander of the Islamic Revolutionary Guard Corps, Major General Hossein Salami, declared that Tehran had entered "a new equation" in which any Israeli attack on its interests, assets, officials, or citizens would be reciprocated from its own territory.[34]

Speaking to Netanyahu after the attack, Biden said that Israel "demonstrated a remarkable capacity to defend against and defeat even unprecedented attacks—sending a clear message to its foes that they cannot effectively threaten the security of Israel." Britain, France, Canada, Argentina, Japan, South Korea, the European Union, and the UN secretary-general also condemned Iran's attack. Ukrainian President Volodymyr Zelenskyy joined, saying: "We know very well the horror of similar attacks by Russia, which uses the same Shahed drones and Russian missiles, the same tactics of mass air strikes . . . the obvious collaboration between the two regimes in spreading terror must face a resolute and united response from the world." Spain, Turkey, Saudi Arabia, Egypt, Jordan, Qatar, India, Pakistan, Russia, and China expressed concern over a possible escalation in the Middle East and called for restraint. Hamas, on the other hand, like Lebanon and Yemen, defended Iran's attack on Israel, calling it "a natural right," even as it again rejected a hostage/cease-fire deal proposed by the United States, Qatar, and Egypt, with Israel showing flexibility. This prompted the Mossad, Israel's intelligence agency, to declare that Sinwar "has proved he doesn't want a humanitarian deal and to return the hostages."[35]

The next day, the *Wall Street Journal* revealed that Israeli and US forces were able to intercept most of the Iranian drones and missiles in part because Arab countries quietly passed along intelligence about Tehran's attack plans, opened their airspace to warplanes, shared radar tracking information or, in some cases, supplied their own forces to help. The operation was the culmination of years of US effort to break down political and technical barriers that thwarted military cooperation between Israel and the Sunni Arab governments. That evening, a senior Israeli official said that Hamas's response to the mediators' latest proposal for a deal included agreeing to release only twenty of its 133 hostages in exchange for a six-week cease-fire. This was because, among other things, Hamas claimed that a number of the hostages included in this part of the deal—women, men over the age of fifty, and men with serious medical conditions—were no longer alive or were held captive by others. At the same time, Hamas demanded the release of terrorists serving higher sentences in Israeli jails, such as murderers, for each hostage who was handed over to Israel. The terrorist organization also demanded international guarantees for a complete stop to the war in the first stage of the deal. The UN Security Council debated, but did not condemn, Iran's missile and drone attack against the Jewish State, as the United States and Israel had called on it to do so.[36]

On April 16, US Defense Secretary Austin held calls with Israeli Defense Minister Gallant, as well as leaders across the Mideast and Europe, expressing support for Israel's defense while stressing regional stability to prevent the conflict from spreading. The leaders of Germany, France, and the United Kingdom made the same point, as did Blinken with the foreign ministers of Jordan, Saudi Arabia, Turkey, and Egypt. Iran's President Raisi declared that his country would respond to any action against its interests, while he told Russian President Vladimir Putin that after its "limited" strikes, Tehran was not interested in escalating. Protesters tried to block the passage of aid trucks from Jordan to Israel on their way to Gaza, the Tzav (call up notice) 9 movement saying they blocked the Allenby Bridge crossing—now declared a closed military area—for six hours before security forces contained them and allowed the trucks to pass around 4 a.m. The IDF announced it had assassinated Ismail Yusef Baz (also known as Abu Ja'far al-Baz), who had served for decades with Hezbollah in a variety of posts before managing both rocket and anti-tank missile attacks from the coastal region into Israel and masterminding various terror operations against Israel. Also in Lebanon, the Mossad was suspected in the killing in a local villa of Mohammad Sarur, sanctioned by Washington in 2019 for funneling "tens of millions of dollars" from Iran's Revolutionary Guard Corps to Hamas for terror attacks.[37]

Iran said on Wednesday that its military was ready to confront any attack by Israel on its soil "with a severe response," with the Iranian air force saying it was prepared for action. The *Wall Street Journal* reported that Iran's Revolutionary Guard Corps had enacted "emergency measures" for their facilities across Syria, according to a Syrian government adviser and an activist who was briefed by the Guards' Syrian proxies. Turkish President Recep Tayyip Erdogan said that Israel was trying to provoke regional conflict and added that Netanyahu and Israel's leadership were solely responsible for recent Middle East tensions. European Commission President Ursula von der Leyen asserted that Iran's attack on Israel was the latest signal of intent of a "new league of authoritarians," mentioning Russia and North Korea as well. IDF forces continued to operate in central Gaza to deepen control over the Netzarim Corridor, the dividing line between north and south Gaza. As for the Hezbollah threat, eighteen people, including fourteen IDF reservists, were wounded by Hezbollah rocket fire in the northern Israeli town of Arab al-Aramshe; Maj. (res.) Dov Zimel, set to wed on June 7, would succumb to his wounds.[38]

On April 18, the Qatari newspaper *Al-Araby Al-Jadeed* reported that Washington had approved a potential Israeli Rafah operation in exchange for the Jewish State not conducting counterstrikes on Iran. Overnight, an Israeli Air Force (IAF) strike killed senior Hamas intelligence officer Yussef Rafik Ahmed Shabat, who had served as a security officer in the military intelligence wing of Hamas's Beit Hanoun Battalion. The IDF said that it carried out an airstrike against a site belonging to Hezbollah's air defense unit in northeastern Lebanon's Baalbek area. In response to Iran's unprecedented attack on Israel, the US Treasury announced that it was taking sweeping actions against several actors involved in Iran's unmanned aerial vehicle (UAV) program, suppliers and customers of one of Iran's largest steel producers, and Iranian automobile companies with connections to US-designated entities IRGC and the Ministry of Defense and Armed Forces Logistics.[39]

The same day, the United States blocked the UN Security Council from moving forward on a Palestinian bid to be recognized as a full member state at the United Nations, quashing an effort by Palestinian allies to get the world body to back the effort. The vote was twelve in favor of the resolution and one—the United States—opposed, with abstentions from Britain and Switzerland. The Palestinian envoy to the UN, Riyad Mansour, had described the bid for full-member status as an effort "to take our rightful place among the community of nations." After the vote, a visibly upset Mansour delivered a passionate address asserting "Our right to self-determination is a natural right—a historical right—to live in our homeland Palestine as an independent state that is free and that is sovereign." Israel's foreign minister, Israel Katz, reacted: "The shameful proposal was rejected. Terrorism will not be rewarded." Although the Security Council had consistently called for a two-state solution to the Palestinian-Israeli conflict, a result that failed to materialize during negotiations between the two sides, US Ambassador to the UN Linda Thomas-Greenfield said that the new resolution would not have brought a two-state solution closer: "Right now, the Palestinians don't have control over a significant portion of what is supposed to be their state." Referring to Hamas, she added "It's being controlled by a terrorist organization."[40]

Early Friday morning, long-distance IAF missiles struck Iranian air force assets at Isfahan in central Iran, right next to the Islamic Republic's top-secret

Natanz nuclear site, using a radar-evading missile to hit Russian-made S-300 defenses at the Eighth Shekari Air Base. The message was unmistakable, sources told *the Jerusalem Post:* to make it eminently clear how vulnerable to attack Iran's nuclear sites were. At the same time, by not attacking the actual nuclear sites at Natanz and Fordow, the attack signaled to Iran that Israel was not seeking a spiraling and escalating regional war—a very nuanced, middle-of-the-road attack. Tehran media and officials later described a small number of explosions, which they said resulted from Iran's air defenses hitting three drones over the city of Isfahan. Notably, they referred to the incident as an attack by "infiltrators," rather than by Israel, obviating the need for retaliation. Iran's Foreign Minister Hossein Amir-Abdollahian told *NBC News*, "What happened last night was no attack. It was the flight of two or three quad-copters, which are at the level of toys that our children use in Iran." An Iranian official told *Reuters* there were no plans to respond against Israel for the incident. Another report that Israeli warplanes destroyed a radar installation in southern Syria at the same time, deep in the territory of its adversaries, reflected a necessary step toward rebuilding Israeli deterrence, which Hamas's savage, methodical attack on October 7 had put into serious question.[41]

On Saturday, the IDF announced that one member of Iraq's pro-Iranian Popular Mobilization Forces was killed and eight were wounded in an explosion at a military base south of Baghdad. It added that there were no drones or fighter jets detected in the area's airspace before or during the blast. Three Hezbollah operatives were reportedly killed in an Israeli strike, the IDF saying its planes attacked Hezbollah military infrastructure in southern Lebanon, striking sites from which three rockets had been launched earlier on Friday with artillery. The IDF on Saturday continued a counter-terrorism operation in the West Bank's Nur Shams refugee camp near Tulkarm, the military said that afternoon, lasting more than forty hours. Amid the operation, the IDF said troops killed at least ten gunmen and detained another eight wanted Palestinians. US officials announced that the UN World Food Programme agreed to help deliver aid to Gaza once the pier project was completed, officials working on how to deliver the humanitarian assistance "in an independent, neutral, and impartial manner." According to a *Wall Street Journal* report, Hamas's leadership was considering moving its political base out of Qatar, which had been mediating ceasefire talks. A source said, "talks have already stalled again with barely any signs or prospects for them to resume any time soon, and distrust is rising between Hamas and the negotiators."[42]

The US House of Representatives voted resoundingly to provide Israel with $26 billion in emergency assistance, including nearly $14 billion in unconditional military aid. The bill passed by a total of 366–58, with 37 Democrats and 21 Republicans voting against. Netanyahu thanked Congress for passing the emergency aid bill, saying it "demonstrates strong bipartisan support for Israel and defends Western civilization." He also declared that "in the coming days, we will increase military and political pressure on Hamas, this is the only way to free the hostages and achieve victory." Iran's Supreme Leader Khamenei thanked his country's armed forces for the strike against Israel, Tehran's official news agency reported. "How many missiles were launched and how many of them hit their target is not the primary question, what really matters is that Iran demonstrated its willpower during that operation." Iran will receive the first delivery of the latest generation of Russian Sukhoi SU-35 fighter jets in the next few days, Iranian media reported. Head of Hamas's political bureau, Haniyeh said that Israel refused to accept Turkey and Russia as guarantors of any agreement between the Israelis and Hamas, and he accused Israel of being unwilling to compromise on a complete cease-fire.[43]

The next day, while 357 trucks carrying humanitarian aid entered Gaza, three people were slightly injured in a double Jerusalem terror attack; police located a Carlo submachine gun along the attackers' escape route. The terrorists, two teenagers from Hebron, were arrested following a manhunt. In honor of the approaching Passover holiday, Biden reiterated the United States' obligation for the security of Israel and the Jewish people. Maj.-Gen. Aharon Haliva, the IDF Military Intelligence Directorate head, retired from the IDF on Monday, stating that he would like to take responsibility for what happened on October 7 and promised to do his best to complete as many of the war's goals as possible. These included reestablishing military dominance in the north and south of the Gaza Strip, deterring further threats from Iran and other foreign enemies, and returning the hostages. In his letter to the Chief of Staff, Haliva said he carried the weight of "that black day" with him day and night, "and I will always carry the terrible pain of the war." *Yediot Achronot* soon speculated that this first resignation of a senior officer on the General Staff could "trigger a domino effect" in which Chief of Staff Herzi Halevi and other senior officers would follow suit. However, the army was still expected to carry out a ground operation in Rafah in the southern Gaza Strip or Deir Al-Balah and Nuseirat in the center," the daily added.[44]

The *New York Times* reported the same day that Israel had abandoned plans for a much more extensive counterstrike on Iran after concerted diplomatic pressure from the United States and other foreign allies. The second factor, according to three senior officials, was because the brunt of an Iranian assault on Israel soil had been thwarted. The original strike plan included several military targets, some near Tehran, and would signal that Israel had developed the capacity to attack Iran without violating its airspace, the report said. A detailed investigation by the *Wall Street Journal* added considerably to this revelation by showing how, over the course of nineteen days, US officials raced to contain escalating tensions between Israel and Iran. Based on sources in the White House, the newspaper described the "frantic scramble" to avert "a full-blown Middle East War."[45]

With Passover recalling Jewry's release in the thirteenth century BCE from slavery under the Egyptian Pharaoh Ramesses II, the unclear fate of the Israeli hostages kidnapped to Gaza was not forgotten. Hundreds calling for the release of the hostages held by Hamas, among them relatives of twelve hostages, demonstrated in Caesarea on the eve of Passover with a "Protest Seder" in front of Netanyahu's residence. Homes across Israel placed an empty chair at Seder tables to signal their long absence in captivity, with special prayers said for their quick release. UK Foreign Secretary Cameron called on Hamas to "send the hostages home." Yet Qatar was disappointed that Israeli ministers attacked its mediation efforts in negotiations for a deal between Israel and Hamas, and it was examining the seriousness of the parties involved in the talks. A Qatari Foreign Ministry spokesperson added that all countries must "act to curb the expected Israeli aggression in Rafah," and that Doha was coordinating with Turkey "in order to increase the pressure to stop the war." Hamas had informed those involved in truce negotiations that it would not agree to a mediator other than Qatar, the Hezbollah-affiliated *Al Mayadeen* reported, citing a senior Palestinian source.[46]

On the morning of April 23, the first day of the Passover holiday and day 200 of the war, IAF aircraft struck and eliminated Hussein Ali Azkul, a significant terrorist operative in Hezbollah's Aerial Defense Unit, and Hezbollah's elite Radwan Force senior member Mohammad Khalil Atiyeh, Additionally, overnight, Sajed Sarafand, a major Hezbollah member of the Radwan Force's Aerial Unit, was eliminated in the area of Arzoun, while the terrorist who carried out the attack that murdered young shepherd Binyamin Achimeir was found and arrested. At the same time, two rockets launched from Lebanon were intercepted above Israel's northern coast. The third rocket was intercepted above the Israeli city of Acre, the furthest south hit by Hezbollah to date; rocket sirens sounded across northern Israel all throughout the day. In Gaza, the Hamas-controlled health ministry reported that at least 34,183 Palestinians had been killed in the war. The organization's spokesman, Abu Obaida, called on Palestinians in the West Bank to increase their resistance to Israel and termed the area "the most significant front" of the war. In a speech commemorating two hundred days of war, he also called for more unrest in Jordan.[47]

Secretary of State Blinken declared that Hamas's attacks on October 7 and the loss of civilian life in Gaza "as Israel exercises its right to ensure that those attacks never happen again" had "raised deeply troubling concerns." Washington was looking into allegations of human rights violations by Israel in Gaza, particularly where US weapons were involved, he noted. Blinken ended by remarking that "what is important in Israel's case is that Israel has demonstrated the capacity to look at itself . . . this is what separates democracies from other countries." Tehran sharply disagreed. The sanctions announced by the European Union following Iran's attack against Israel were "regrettable," Iran's Foreign Minister Amir-Abdollahian insisted, because the country was acting in self-defense.[48]

On Tuesday evening, the US Senate approved a major aid package for Ukraine, Israel, and Taiwan. The bill included $60.8 billion for Ukraine; $26.4 billion for Israel and humanitarian aid for civilians in conflict zones, including Gaza; and $8.1 billion for the Indo-Pacific region. It also included sanctions against Iranian and Russian officials. The 79–18 vote provided Biden another legislative accomplishment to point to, even in the face of an obstructionist House of Representatives. "Congress has passed my legislation to strengthen our national security and send a message to the world about the power of American leadership. We stand resolutely for democracy and freedom, and against tyranny and oppression," Biden said on Tuesday evening, just minutes after the Senate vote. Signing the bill, he announced that "shipments will start in the next few hours." Declaring that "the security of Israel is critical," and that the aid would "help replenish Israel's air defense," he added that the legislation "significantly increases humanitarian assistance to Gazans," and called on Israel to "ensure aid gets to Palestinians in Gaza without delay."[49]

Hamas chief in Gaza, Sinwar, briefly exited the terrorist movement's tunnels and met with the movement's forces aboveground recently, a senior source in Hamas told *Al-Araby Al-Jadeed* on Wednesday. Sinwar "recently inspected areas that witnessed clashes between the resistance and the occupation army, and he met some of the movement's fighters on the ground and not in the tunnels," said the source. The source also denied reports that Hamas had changed its demands to only being willing to release twenty hostages instead of the forty originally discussed in the first phase of any agreement. The source stated that, while it was not possible to "accurately determine the number of living hostages," it was "certain" that the number was higher than the number being cited in some media reports. The source further claimed that Hamas had about thirty IDF and Shin Bet officers and that these hostages were being kept in "highly secured places, far from the hands of the occupation, and it is impossible to reach them under any circumstances."

The Israeli Hostage and Missing Families Forum announced in response that intelligence sources had found the report that Sinwar emerged from the tunnels under Gaza was "reliable." "The picture of Sinwar in the streets of Gaza, while the hostages languish in basements, is the picture of Israeli failure," the group said. Micah Kobi, a former senior Shin Bet officer who had interrogated Sinwar when the Hamas leader was still in prison in Israel, told *Ma'ariv* that "theoretically, there is a possibility that Sinwar is taking advantage of the IDF's shuffling and the withdrawal of most of the forces from the Strip, for his freer movement while commanding his fighters." "Hamas's discourse in the media, and especially the report on Sinwar's exit from the tunnels, is nothing more than media spin," insisted Kobi. "They now know that the highest probability is that the IDF will enter Rafah, and therefore, through false information, they are trying to confuse us and divert us from our main goals there."[50]

IDF fighter jets and artillery struck approximately forty Hezbollah terror targets on Wednesday in the area of Ayta ash Shab in southern Lebanon. This after Hezbollah had launched a barrage of missiles, anti-tank missiles (ATGMs), and UAVs at Israel's western Galilee yesterday and that morning. In one attack, Hezbollah fired into the northern village of Margoliot, damaging the electrical grid and knocking out power in neighboring Kiryat Shmona. In Gaza, the IAF struck targets in Rafah, Khan Younis, Gaza City, and camps in the center, including rocket launchers located in a humanitarian aid area in the south. Announcing that he would retire in the summer, Maj. Gen. Yehuda Fox, head of the IDF's Central Command who took a strong stance fighting terrorists in the Jenin and Tulkarm areas, had told those close to him in recent months that he saw himself as part of the General Staff that failed on October 7 and that he must take accountability and end his tenure as others did.[51]

The IDF concluded all necessary preparations to enter the southern city of Rafah, seeking to remove an estimated four brigades from Hamas's last major redoubt in the enclave. Israeli forces could launch an operation the moment it received government approval, a senior defense official told *Reuters* on April 24. Two reserve brigades, the 679th "Yiftah" Armored and the 2nd "Carmeli" Infantry, had been mobilized to return from the northern border to southern Gaza in order to "continue the mission of defense and attack" in the Strip. The move would free up Nahal Brigade troops currently holding the central corridor to join the rest of the 162nd Division in preparing for future operations, including planned offensives in Rafah and central Gaza, military sources said. Chief of Staff Halevi and Shin Bet Director Bar visited Cairo, where they met senior Egyptian military and intelligence officers to discuss Israel's plans for continued fighting in Gaza and efforts to renew negotiations to secure a hostage deal.

Images from the satellite company Maxar showed multiple tent camps on Khan Younis land that had been vacant on April 7. Citing Israeli and Egyptian officials, the *Wall Street Journal* reported earlier that Israeli plans envisioned that the first two to three weeks of the operation in Rafah would consist of evacuating civilians, in coordination with the United States, Egypt, and other Arab countries.[52]

The IDF informed the government on April 25 that its forces had completed their preparations for an upcoming military operation in Rafah, and that the start date for such an operation would be decided by the cabinet. Egyptian President Abdel Fattah El-Sisi reiterated his country's firm stance against the displacement of Gazans into the Egyptian-controlled Sinai as Israel prepared for this operation. Biden released a statement alongside the leaders of seventeen other countries—all with citizens held captive in Gaza—calling upon Hamas to release the hostages in order to bring an immediate and prolonged cease-fire. Dozens of people, some of them family members of hostages held in Gaza, protested outside the Defense Ministry headquarters in Tel Aviv, where the war cabinet was meeting. In Jerusalem, hundreds participated in prayers for hostage Hersh Goldberg-Polin, one day after Hamas released a video showing him alive with an amputated arm, looking thin, dour, and scared. John Polin, Hersh's father, said that he expected the world leaders to do more to secure the release of the hostages. "There are hostages that come from twenty-five countries around the world, and we are asking ourselves: where are all the leaders?" he told Israel's Channel 12 News.

Top Hamas official Khalil al-Hayya informed the Associated Press that his organization was willing to agree to a truce of five years or more with Israel, and it would lay down its weapons and convert into a political party if an independent Palestinian state were established along pre-June 1967 borders. Hamas wanted to join the Palestine Liberation Organization (PLO), headed by the rival Fatah faction, al-Hayya said, in order to form a unified government for Gaza and the West Bank. Al-Hayya, who represented Hamas in cease-fire negotiations, also said that Israel presented the mediating countries maps which showed its intent to take over twenty percent of Gaza when the war ended. As for Iran, the European Parliament voted to condemn Tehran after its attack against Israel on April 13. The decision, passed with a majority of 357–20, included a call to add the Iranian Revolutionary Guard Corps to the European Union's list of terror groups, expanding sanctions on Iran, recognizing Iran's disobedience in keeping nuclear law, and recognizing Iran's role in destabilizing the Middle East. Iranian forces had pulled out of bases in Damascus and southern Syria, which would potentially be replaced by Iraqi militants, the London-based *Asharq Al-Awsat* reported, citing a source close to Hezbollah. According to the source,

Hezbollah forces had replaced the Iranians in areas around Damascus, Daraa, and Quneitra.[53]

Israeli officials told their Egyptian counterparts on Friday that Israel was ready to give hostage negotiations "one last chance" to reach a deal with Hamas, but, if there were not progress soon, it would move forward with a ground invasion of Rafah. Overnight, terrorists fired anti-tank missiles toward the area of Har Dov in northern Israel. As a result, Israeli Sharif Suad, a resident of an Arab village in the Galilee who was doing IDF infrastructure work, died of his wounds. In response, IAF jets struck Hezbollah terror targets in southern Lebanon. Blinken said it could be possible to roll out a framework for Israel-Saudi Arabia normalization along with a two-state solution proposal for Israel and the Palestinians before a Gaza cease-fire was implemented. Dozens protested in front of war cabinet minister Benny Gantz's home on Friday, including the families of hostages, demanding that he resign from the government, as they believe there are no signs that a new hostage deal was being considered.[54]

The United States began the initial stages of constructing a temporary pier to deliver humanitarian aid from the Gaza coast, a Pentagon spokesperson confirmed. A senior US military official said that Israeli forces would dedicate a brigade to protect the US forces building the pier. As for Hamas, Israel agreed to allow UK-appointed observers to visit the detention facilities holding the organization's members who were arrested on October 7, following reports that the conditions in these facilities constituted a breach of international law. Meanwhile, Hamas fired mortars at the artificial pier the US military was building off the coast of the Gaza Strip, making it clear to many that the improvement of conditions for civilians in Gaza could only come after Hamas was defeated. The Israeli government allocated $400 million to the rehabilitation of Gaza border communities, funding the renovation of homes up to seven kilometers from the Gaza border. Surveying Gaza, Pehr Lodhammar, a senior officer at the UN Mine Action Service, said that the vast amount of rubble left by Israel's war there could take about fourteen years to remove.[55]

Across the Atlantic, police clashed with US students critical of the war and the Biden administration's support for Israel's war in Gaza. Nearly 550 arrests were made over the protests in the past week. Blinken declared that the protests, including Gaza Solidarity Encampments on campus lawns, were a hallmark of democracy, adding that he decried their "silence" on Hamas. Virulent antisemitic calls and harassment of Jewish students on campuses from the East Coast to the West Coast were common, chants such as "We are Hamas!" and "Al-Qassam [in reference to the Izz ad-Din al-Qassam Brigades, Hamas's military wing], you make us proud, kill another soldier now!" Yad Vashem Chairman

Dani Dayan sent a letter to Columbia University President Minouche Shafik, asking her to take a stand against calls for "the destruction and elimination of the Jewish state" amid the ongoing pro-Palestinian campus protests.

Four days earlier, Biden had remarked "I condemn the antisemitic protests," but then he felt compelled to add: "I also condemn those who don't understand what's going on with the Palestinians." An unfortunate example of moral equivalence, critics pointed out, recalling the joint statement by eighteen countries—after six months—about Hamas's illegal kidnapping of hostages holding dual citizenship. Most of the statement focused on the Gazans, not the abductees. It emphasized the rewards that the international community was offering Hamas, such as a cease-fire and a "surge of humanitarian assistance," in exchange for freeing the kidnapped hostages.[56]

Aid shipments to Gaza from Cyprus resumed after a pause following Israel's killing of seven World Central Kitchen aid workers. A small cargo vessel left Larnaca's port on Friday night with aid donated by the United Arab Emirates. US Joint Chiefs of Staff General C. Q. Brown Jr. said the IDF was creating "a buffer zone or bubble" around the temporary pier currently being built to facilitate aid to Gaza in order "to keep the threat away from our forces and to allow the distribution of the aid." The Israeli army said it had killed Mosab Khala, a senior member of the al-Jama'a al-Islamiya terror group, in an airstrike in Lebanon. It also announced that two Palestinians were shot and killed after they had opened fire at the IDF's Salem military outpost in the West Bank near Jenin. US Defense Secretary Austin declared that Iran's attack on Israel earlier in the month, in which Israel and its allies intercepted the bulk of projectiles, "should give [Iran] pause, and they should be questioning the effectiveness of their weapons systems and their planning." China announced that Beijing will host Palestinian unity talks between Hamas and Fatah.[57]

In a statement following a telephone call on Sunday between Biden and Netanyahu, the White House said Biden "reaffirmed his ironclad commitment to Israel's security following the successful defense against Iran's unprecedented missile and drone attack earlier this month." The two "also reviewed ongoing talks to secure the release of hostages together with an immediate ceasefire in Gaza. The president referred to his statement with seventeen other world leaders demanding that Hamas release their citizens without delay to secure a cease-fire and relief for the people of Gaza." The United States and Egypt had in recent days increased pressure on Hamas to accept a hostage deal with Israel to prevent an IDF operation in Rafah, the London-based *Asharq Al-Awsat* newspaper reported. The Egyptian mediators made it clear to Hamas that this was the best deal they could get, and, if it was not met, Israel would have the legitimacy to enter Rafah. Israeli war cabinet minister Gantz said that the government would have no right to exist if it blocked a hostage deal, adding that the return of the hostages was of greater importance than a military operation in Rafah. PA President Mahmoud Abbas demanded an end to the fighting in Gaza, adding that more aid must be delivered. According to Abbas, only the United States could halt Israel's planned operation in Rafah, which he said could lead to "the biggest catastrophe in the Palestinian people's history."[58]

Blinken said Hamas received a truce proposal that was "extraordinarily generous," and that it needed to decide quickly. He told Turkey's Foreign Minister Hakan Fidan that Hamas's refusal to accept a deal was responsible for the continuation of the conflict in Gaza, and urged that all efforts be made to convince Hamas to accept the current proposal. The *New York Times* reported that Israel had reduced the number of hostages it would accept to be released by Hamas in the first phase from forty to thirty-three, prompted partly by the fact that Israel now believed that some of the initial forty had died while in Hamas captivity. Parents of 400 IDF soldiers urged ministers Gantz and Gadi Eisenkot to stop plans to enter Rafah, saying "We will not stand idly by and allow our children to risk their lives." As for the anti-Israel protests that led to 275 police arrests on four US university campuses over the weekend, White House spokesman John Kirby declared that, while Washington certainly respected the right of peaceful protests, "we absolutely condemn the antisemitic language that we've heard of late and certainly condemn all the hate speech and the threats of violence out there." Foreign Minister Israel Katz told Israeli missions abroad to prepare for "a wave of severe antisemitism, anti-Jewish, and anti-Israeli outbreaks" amid the possibility of arrest warrants issued by the International Criminal Court against senior Israeli officials.[59]

Netanyahu once again pledged on Tuesday to launch a ground invasion into the southern Gazan city of Rafah "and obliterate all the Hamas battalions there—with or without a deal," a move that could undermine efforts to negotiate a cease-fire agreement after seven months of war in the Palestinian enclave. "The notion that we will stop the war before achieving all of its goals is out of the question," said the prime minister during a meeting at his office in Jerusalem with the Heroism Forum, which represents bereaved IDF families, and the Tikva Forum for Families of Hostages endorsing the invasion. They could take encouragement from a recent Harvard-Harris poll of American voters showing that seventy-two percent of respondents said they supported an IDF operation in Rafah, while eighty percent supported Israel in the war in general. Two-thirds of respondents said that Israel was attempting to avoid causing civilian casualties in Gaza, and sixty-eight percent of respondents said they opposed the imposition of a permanent cease-fire without the return of all of the hostages still held by Hamas in Gaza.[60]

President Biden told Egypt's President Abdel Fattah El-Sisi and Qatar's Emir Sheikh Tamim bin Hamad Al Thani to "to exert all efforts to secure the release of hostages held by Hamas, as this is now the only obstacle to an immediate cease-fire and relief for civilians in Gaza." An Israeli official stated on Tuesday that no delegation will depart for negotiations with Hamas in Cairo, as Jerusalem was awaiting Hamas's response to the Egyptian proposal, expected Wednesday evening, after which a decision would be made regarding the delegation's departure. Chairman of the Religious Zionist Party, Finance Minister Smotrich, attacked the Egyptian outline for a deal to release the hostages in exchange for a cease-fire that would prevent Israeli military entry into Rafah, saying that Israel was "conducting negotiations with those who should no longer exist" and that "the Egyptian proposal is a terrible defeat."[61]

Qatar was supposed to announce that, if Hamas did not progress towards a hostage/prisoner swap deal, its leaders should have been removed from Doha by the local authorities, but Qatar failed to keep its commitment on this, *Yisrael Hayom* reported. Qatar was also supposed to freeze some of the Hamas leaders' bank accounts. These steps were agreed on by Qatar and US representatives, as part of efforts to pressure Hamas to agree to the Egyptian proposal for a swap and cease-fire deal.[62]

Qatar's stance may be related to an article that appeared in July 2020 by Najat Al-Saeed, a researcher from the UAE, in the *Al-Hurra* newspaper describing the alliance formed between the radical American left and Muslim Brotherhood activists in the United States with funding by Qatar. She cited figures from the US Department of Education indicating that in 2019, American educational institutions received funds exceeding $1.3 billion from external sources, predominantly Qatar. Al-Saeed further exposed that Qatar routinely spent $405 million annually to support activities at six American universities that maintain branches in Doha, Qatar's capital. Rich in oil and natural gas, the country used the initiatives it sponsored and the research it financed to disseminate Islamist ideology reflective of an extremist Wahhabi religious school that was profoundly influenced by the ideology of Sheikh Yusuf Al-Qaradawi, one of the leaders of the Muslim Brotherhood who operated in Qatar until he died in 2022. Two months ago, Raymond Ibrahim, an American Christian academic of Egyptian origin, revealed that Qatar had invested $5.6 billion in eighty-one American universities since 2007, including Harvard, Yale, Cornell, and Stanford. His reports also mentioned the funding of academic activities in the United States by other countries, albeit in much smaller amounts, led by

Saudi Arabia, Oman, and Turkey. Further investigation should disclose if Qatar funding was directly connected to the current violent pro-Hamas protests taking place on university campuses across the United States.[63]

After finding five IDF units guilty "of gross violations of human rights," the US State Department announced on April 30 that it would not block aid to Israel as "four of these units have effectively remediated these violations," with a decision on the fifth pending following the submission of new information by Israel. As for the Columbia University protesters, including their unfurling of Palestinian flags, including an "intifada" banner, and barricading themselves in Hamilton Hall, the White House said Biden "condemns the use of '*intifada*'" (the Arabic term for uprising), and that "forcibly taking over buildings is not peaceful—it is wrong. And hate speech and hate symbols have no place in America." Speaking about news that the International Criminal Court at The Hague might issue arrest warrants against senior Israeli officials, the White House declared: "We've been really clear about the ICC investigation—we don't support it and don't believe they have the jurisdiction." Concurrently, the ICC rejected a request by Nicaragua to order Germany to halt aid to Israel and renew funding to the UN aid agency in Gaza. The Court said that legal conditions for making such an order were not met.[64]

The month ended with a startling report that Saudi Arabia had decided to normalize relations with Israel. This came on the heels of yet another Blinken visit there to discuss Gaza's future and other regional issues. The kingdom's rulers were debating the timing of the announcement, a foreign diplomat familiar with the details told *Haaretz*. According to the source cited in the article by the Israeli daily's diplomatic correspondent, Jonathan Lis, Riyadh was discussing whether to make the move in the coming weeks or after the US presidential election come November, in which either Democrat Joe Biden will continue to lead the country or his challenger Republican Donald Trump will return to the White House. While the Biden administration had been pushing to connect a pathway to Palestinian statehood as part of the Saudis joining the Abraham Accords, the source said that the kingdom would only demand guarantees on progress towards achieving that goal in return for establishing diplomatic ties with Jerusalem. Blinken spoke about progress toward a Jerusalem-Riyadh detente at the World Economic Forum special meeting in the Saudi capital on Monday, emphasizing the importance of a Palestinian state despite former Israeli foreign minister Eli Cohen saying last August that it was not a major obstacle for Crown Prince Mohammed bin Salman, who met with Blinken on the sidelines of the summit. So closed day 207 of the Hamas-Israel war, uncertainty on several crucial matters by now to be expected.[65]

Endnotes

1 *Times of Israel*, Apr. 1, 2024; IDF News, Apr. 2, 2024; *Haaretz*, Apr. 1, 2024. Blocking *Al Jazeera* "marks an alarming escalation, and Israeli efforts restrict the freedom of the press and further limit the access that citizens of the world have to the daily realities in Israel and Palestine," Human Rights Watch's Israel and Palestine Director Omar Shakir told CNN. The White House also called reports of the move to shutter *Al Jazeera* "concerning." "The United States supports the critically important work journalists around the world do. And that includes those who are reporting in the conflict in Gaza," White House press secretary Karine Jean-Pierre said Monday during a press briefing. CNN, Apr. 2, 2024. Yet also see Gil Hoffman, "The Case Against *Al Jazeera*," *Jerusalem Post Magazine*, Apr. 26, 2024.

2 *Jerusalem Post*, Apr. 2, 2024; *Haaretz*, Apr. 1, 2024. According to the Bloomberg TV network, the entire command hierarchy responsible for the activities of the Revolutionary Guard Corps in Syria and Lebanon was killed in the consulate building next to the Iranian embassy. *Jerusalem Post*, Apr. 21, 2024.

3 JNS, Apr. 1, 2024.

4 *Haaretz*, Apr. 2–3, 2024; *New York Times*, Apr. 2, 2024; *Times of Israel*, Apr. 2, 2024; *Washington Post*, Apr. 3, 2024. World Central Kitchen founder chef José Andrés wrote in the *New York Times*: "We know Israelis. Israelis, in their heart of hearts, know that food is not a weapon of war. Israel is better than the way this war is being waged. It is better than blocking food and medicine to civilians." *Haaretz*, Apr. 3, 2024.

5 *Times of Israel*, Apr. 3, 2024; Israel National News, Apr. 33, 2024; alerts@ounetwork.org, Apr. 3, 2024. A new poll found a broad consensus among American Jews, including those who supported the current president, endorsing an Israeli military operation in Rafah to eliminate Hamas. The March edition of the monthly *Kol Ha'am: Voice of the People Survey*, by the Jewish People Policy Institute, found that, among respondents intending to vote for Biden, seven out of ten believed that Israel should enter Rafah. The only cohorts with a significant percentage against entering Rafah were those who identified as "strong liberal" (twenty-six percent) and Jews who had never visited Israel (twenty-one percent). Israel National News, Apr. 3, 2024.

6 World Israel News, Apr. 3, 2024; *Times of Israel*, Apr. 3, 2024.

7 World Israel News, Apr. 3, 2024; IDF News, Apr. 4, 2024.

8 *Times of Israel*, Apr. 4, 2024; *Forward*, Apr. 4, 2024; *Haaretz*, Apr. 4, 2024.

9 IDF News, Apr. 4, 2024.

10 *New York Times*, Apr. 5, 2024; *Washington Post*, Apr. 5, 2024; *Jerusalem Post*, Apr. 5, 2024; Israel National News, Apr. 3, 5, 2024; *Haaretz*, Apr. 5, 2024.

11 *Haaretz*, Apr. 5–6, 2024.

12 *Haaretz*, Apr. 6, 2024; Israel National News, Apr. 6, 2024; IDF News, Apr. 5, 2024.

13 Israel National News, Apr. 6, 2024; *Washington Post*, Apr. 7, 2024; *Haaretz*, Apr. 6, 2024; *The Forward*, Apr. 4, 2024. In Michigan's Democratic primary in March, 101,457 (13.2 percent of voters) chose "uncommitted," for a gain of two delegates.

14 On troops killed by error from their own forces—"friendly fire," see the conclusion by Israel's former ambassador to the United States: "No matter how frequent, friendly fire incidents have never stood in the way of pursuing justified wartime goals. Neither the death by American anti-aircraft fire of US Army pilot John L. Dains, the first to shoot down a Japanese bomber over Pearl Harbor, nor the unintended massacre of 7,000 POWs in a British bombing raid on a German harbor just days before the end of World War II prevented the Allies from completing the Axis's defeat. . . . Notwithstanding the exquisite pain involved, Israel must not let friendly fire consume our will and determination to defend ourselves against an enemy sworn to annihilate us." Michael Oren, "'Friendly Fire,' That Horrific Oxymoron," *Times of Israel*, Dec. 17, 2023.

15 *Haaretz*, Apr. 7, 2024; *Times of Israel*, Apr. 7, 2024.
16 *Times of Israel*, Apr. 7, 2024.
17 *Jerusalem Post*, Apr. 7 and 8, 2024; *New York Times*, Apr. 8, 2024; Israel National News, Apr. 7, 2024.
18 *New York Times*, Apr. 7, 2024; *Times of Israel*, Apr. 7, 2024; *Washington Post*, Apr. 9, 2024.
19 "To the Boys in the Room," bring.hersh.home, Instagram, Apr. 7, 2024, https://www.instagram.com/bring.hersh.home/reel/C5eUy0CNbWC.
20 *Jerusalem Post*, Apr. 8, 2024; Israel National News, Apr. 8, 2024.
21 *Wall St. Journal*, Apr. 8, 2024; Reuters, Apr. 3, 2024.
22 *Jerusalem Post*, Apr. 8, 2024; World Israel News, Apr. 8, 2024.
23 Of some 57,000 people who had been classified as evacuees from the south on February 29, at least 40,150 residents, including some 23,000 from Sderot alone, were now living in their municipalities situated within seven kilometers (4.3 miles) of the border, declared the Tekuma Authority for rehabilitating the affected Gaza-adjacent area. A group of some 6,350 evacuees, still living in state-funded hotels, were waiting to join the approximately 2,000 evacuees who had already left hotels in favor of temporary housing in communities, such as residents of Kibbutz Nir Oz, who were living in an apartment complex in Kiryat Gat, and the population of Nahal Oz, which had been absorbed by Kibbutz Mishmar HaEmek near Haifa. Approximately 60,000 people were living as evacuees, mostly in hotels, from Israel's north. Evacuees were not allowed to host guests overnight in the hotels, including their own children. The Tekuma Authority had spent roughly $600 million of its budget of $4.7 billion for rehabilitating the southern border area over the next five years. *Times of Israel*, Apr. 8, 2024.
24 *New York Times*, Apr. 8, 2024; Israel National News, Apr. 8, 2024.
25 Israel National News, Apr. 9, 2024; *Jerusalem Post*, Apr. 9, 2024; JNS, Apr. 9, 2024.
26 *Times of Israel*, Apr. 10, 2024; *Jerusalem Post*, Apr. 9, 2024; CNN, Apr. 10, 2024; *Haaretz*. Apr. 10, 2024.
27 *Haaretz*, Apr. 9, 11, 2024; *Times of Israel*, Apr. 11, 2024.
28 JNS, Apr. 11, 2024; *Wall St. Journal*, Apr. 10, 2024.
29 *Wall St. Journal*, Apr. 12, 2024; *Washington Post*, Apr. 12, 2024; *Haaretz*, Apr. 12, 2024.
30 *Haaretz*, Apr. 12, 2024; BBC. Apr. 12, 2024.
31 *Jerusalem Post*, April 13, 2024; *New York Times*, Apr. 13, 2024; *Haaretz*, Apr. 12, 2024.
32 *Haaretz*, Apr. 13, 2024; *Jerusalem Post*, Apr. 9, 2024.
33 In its shadow war with Iran, Israel had launched a series of attacks including killing the chief of Iran's nuclear program, Mohsen Fakhrizadeh Mahabadi, in 2021, and assassinating in broad daylight the Revolutionary Guard Corps secretive Quds Force Unit 840 deputy commander, Col. Hassan Sayad Khodaei, in 2022. In April (and later in July) 2018, Netanyahu publicly revealed details on how IDF commandos smuggled out a huge trove of secret nuclear documents and CDs, going back to 2003, from a nuclear facility in Tehran the previous January. He then gave US President Donald Trump a briefing at the White House, and argued that it was another reason Trump should abandon the July 14, 2015, nuclear deal endorsed by then President Barack Obama as an historic document "that will verifiably prevent Iran from obtaining a nuclear weapon." In May, Trump withdrew from the deal. Tehran has always claimed its nuclear program was only for peaceful purposes. Radio Free Europe-Radio Liberty, July 16, 2018. In September 2018, Netanyahu showed photographs at the UN General Assembly to assert that Iran had another secret facility in its capital city, an atomic warehouse for storing equipment for Iran's secret nuclear weapons program. UN News, Sept. 27, 2018.
34 Israel National News, Apr. 14, 2024; *Jerusalem Post*, Apr. 14, 2024; *Times of Israel*, Apr. 14, 2024; *Haaretz*, Apr. 14, 2024; *New York Times*, Apr. 14, 2024; Eado Hecht, "The Gaza Terror Offensive—9 March–14 April 2024," BESA publication, Bar-Ilan University, April 14, 2024; Uzi Rubin, "Operation 'True Promise', Iran's Missile Attack on Israel," BESA publication, Bar-Ilan University, June 18, 2024. The United Kingdom and France were reported to have

aided in thwarting Iran's barrage of drones and missiles. Seven-year-old Amina al-Hassouni, who suffered serious head wounds from shrapnel during the Iranian drone and missile attack on Israel in April, was discharged from Soroka Medical Center at the end of July to continue her rehabilitation from home. *Haaretz*, July 28. 2024.
35 *Haaretz*, Apr. 14, 2024; *Al Jazeera*, Apr. 14, 2024. Following his traditional Sunday prayer in Saint Peter's Square at the Vatican, Pope Francis made a "pressing appeal" against a "spiral of violence," warning of a potential regional conflagration. "I am praying and following with concern, but also pain, the news that has come in recent hours about the worsening situation in Israel due to Iran's intervention," he told worshippers. "No one should threaten the existence of others. All countries must, however, side with peace and help Israelis and Palestinians to live in two states, side by side and in security," the pope said.
36 *Wall St. Journal*, Apr. 15. 2024; *Jerusalem Post*, Apr. 15, 2024; *Israel National News*, Apr. 15, 2024.
37 *Haaretz*, Apr. 16, 2024; *Jerusalem Post*, Apr. 16, 2024; *Times of Israel*, Apr. 16, 2024.
38 *Haaretz*, Apr. 17, 21, 2024.
39 *Jerusalem Post*. Apr. 18, 2024.
40 *New York Times*, Apr. 19, 2024.
41 *Jerusalem Post*, Apr. 19, 2024; *New York Times*, Apr. 19–20, 2024; *Times of Israel*, Apr. 19, 2024.
42 *Haaretz*, Apr. 20, 2024; *Times of Israel*, Apr. 20, 2024.
43 *Haaretz*, Apr. 21, 2024.
44 IDF News, Apr. 22, 2024; *Israel National News*, Apr. 22, 2024; *Jerusalem Post*, Apr. 22, 2024; *Middle East Monitor*, Apr. 24, 2024.
45 *New York Times*, Apr. 22, 2024; *Wall St. Journal*, Apr. 22, 2024.
46 *Haaretz*, Apr. 23, 2024.
47 *Israel National News*, Apr. 23, 2024; *Haaretz*, Apr. 23, 2024.
48 *Haaretz*, Apr. 24, 2024.
49 *New York Times*, Apr. 24, 2024.
50 *Times of Israel*, Apr. 25, 2024; *Jerusalem Post*, Apr. 24, 2024.
51 *Israel National News*, Apr. 24, 2024; IDF News, Apr. 24, 2024; *Haaretz*, Apr. 24, 2024.
52 *Haaretz*, Apr. 24, 2024; *Times of Israel*, Apr. 24, 2024.
53 *Haaretz*, Apr. 25, 2024. Hamas had periodically published videos of hostages in an attempt to increase pressure on the Israeli government to agree to its terms and as a form of psychological warfare. In the past, hostages were forced to read from scripts prepared by the terrorist organization. Hersh's parents released this statement on Wednesday: "Seeing the video of Hersh today is overwhelming. We are relieved to see him alive, but we are also concerned about his health and wellbeing, as well as that of all the other hostages and all of those suffering in this region. We are here today with a plea to all of the leaders of the parties who have been negotiating to date. This includes Qatar, Egypt, the United States, Hamas, and Israel: be brave, lean in, seize this moment, and get a deal done to reunite all of us with our loved ones and end the suffering in this region. Hersh, we heard your voice today for the first time in 201 days and if you can hear us, we are telling you we love you, stay strong, survive." *Jerusalem Post*, Apr. 24, 2024.
54 *Israel National News*, Apr. 26, 2024.
55 *Israel National News*, Apr. 26, 2024; *Haaretz*, Apr. 26, 2024.
56 *Times of Israel*, Apr. 27, 2024; *Haaretz*, Apr. 26, 2024; *New York Times*, Apr. 24 and 28, 2024; ADL, Apr. 22, 2024; *Washington Post*, Apr. 24, 2024. The fullest account of what transpired at Columbia University was gathered by students on the staff of the *Columbia Spectator*, published as "The Takeover," *New York Magazine*, May 4, 2024.
57 *Haaretz*, Apr. 27, 2024.
58 *Israel National News*, Apr. 28, 2024; *Haaretz*, Apr. 28, 2024.
59 *Haaretz*, Apr. 29, 2024; *Times of Israel*, Apr. 29, 2024.

60 *New York Times*, Apr. 30, 2024; Israel National News, Apr. 30, 2024.
61 *Haaretz*, Apr. 30, 2024; Israel National News, Apr. 30, 2024.
62 Israel National News, Apr. 30, 2024.
63 *Jerusalem Post*, Apr. 30, 2024. Additional investigation uncovered that the encampment at Columbia University, the epicenter of the nationwide protest movement, was principally organized by Students for Justice in Palestine (SJP), Jewish Voice for Peace (JVP), and Within our Lifetime (WOL). JVP, favoring the Boycott, Divestment and Sanctions movement against Israel, has received substantial funding from the George Soros and Kaphan Foundations, and the Rockefeller Brothers Fund, the latter instrumental in selling former US President Barack Obama's Iran deal to the public. SJP is a subsidiary of American Muslims for Palestine, which is sponsored by the WESPAC Foundation (also the fiscal sponsor for WOL, perhaps "the most notorious antisemitic group" in the United States and listed as a "field organizer" on the website of MPower Change, a fiscal sponsorship of NEO Philanthropy and NEO Philanthropy Action Fund, which have received millions of dollars from the Soros' Open Society Foundations, the Rockefeller Brothers Fund, and the Tides Foundation). Tides has become "tightly integrated" with the ascendant Obama faction of the Democratic Party and with left-wing major donors. It is connected as well to pro-Palestinian radical organizations, such as the Arab Resource and Organizing Center, Palestine Legal, the Adalah Justice Project, and Samidoun. Park MacDougald, "The People Setting America on Fire," *Tablet*, May 12, 2024.
64 *Haaretz*, Apr. 30, 2024.
65 JNS, Apr. 30, 2024; *Times of Israel*, Apr. 30, 2024. The Abraham Accords declaration begins as follows: "We, the undersigned, recognize the importance of maintaining and strengthening peace in the Middle East and around the world based on mutual understanding and coexistence, as well as respect for human dignity and freedom, including religious freedom." Having secured the historic agreement, President Donald Trump hosted the signing on the Truman Balcony of the White House, Netanyahu standing on his right, together with Bahraini foreign minister Abdullatif bin Rashid Al-Zayani and Emirati foreign minister Abdullah bin Zayed Al-Nahyan. Not long thereafter, Morocco (December 22, 2020) and Sudan (January 6, 2021) endorsed the Accords. In exchange for Morocco's recognition of Israeli sovereignty, the United States recognized Moroccan sovereignty over Western Sahara.

CHAPTER 2

Into Rafah

On the first day of May, Blinken met with Israeli President Isaac Herzog in Tel Aviv, urging a cease-fire and prisoner swap deal between Israel and the Hamas terrorist group. "We're determined to get a cease-fire that brings the hostages home, and to get it now," Blinken said, "and the only reason that that wouldn't be achieved is because of Hamas." (He repeated this in a post on social media platform X, adding that Hamas was "the only obstacle" to "relief for civilians in Gaza.") At the same time, the US Secretary of State added that Israel must do yet more to help the people of Gaza, "who are suffering in this crossfire of Hamas's making." Hearing the same points later that day, Netanyahu made clear to Blinken that he "would not accept a deal that includes an agreement to end the war in the Gaza Strip." Further, Netanyahu said that Israel saw the importance of a military operation in Rafah, and it would move forward with an invasion of Hamas's last redoubt if that organization continued to condition a hostage deal on ending the war. Blinken reiterated that Washington objected to an operation without an executable plan to protect the civilian population and evacuate civilians.[1]

The Israel Defense Forces (IDF) will establish a humanitarian safe zone in the central Gaza Strip as part of preparations for the evacuation of noncombatants from Rafah, Army Radio reported that Wednesday. It would be located south of Wadi Gaza and north of the central camps, Nuseirat and Bureij, near the Netzarim Corridor which the IDF recently created to split the Strip into two parts. Additionally, the current shelter area near the southern coastal town of Al-Mawasi would be expanded eastward towards Khan Younis. (Before Israel's unilateral disengagement from the Gaza Strip in 2005, Al-Mawasi was a Bedouin enclave within the Katif Bloc of Israeli communities.) However, intense international opposition to a full-scale offensive was manifest, Blinken himself saying in Riyadh two days earlier that "we have not yet seen a plan that gives us confidence that civilians can be effectively protected."[2]

Senior Hamas official Sami Abu Zuhri responded that Blinken was unfairly blaming Hamas for delays in reaching a truce. "It is not strange for Blinken, who is known as the foreign minister of Israel, not America [sic], to make such a statement," Abu Zuhri told *Reuters*. Senior Hamas official Osama Hamdan signaled that same day, in an interview with the Hezbollah-backed Lebanese channel Al-Manar, that "if the enemy launches an aggressive ground operation in Rafah the negotiations will be stopped because the resistance does not negotiate under fire." Referring to the fighting in Gaza, he said that "the resistance capabilities [of Hamas] are still high and the resistance is still fine, this while the Zionist elite brigades have collapsed in the Gaza Strip."[3]

The *Wall Street Journal* proposed a separate reason for Blinken's stance, the Biden administration needing Netanyahu to "deliver a halt in fighting" that could ease the pressure of violent, often antisemitic protests, followed by more than 2,000 police arrests, across US college campuses against Israel's war in Gaza. (More than half of those arrested in New York City were not affiliated with the schools, and in some cases "professional outsiders" trained students in "unlawful protest tactics," declared Police Commissioner Edward Caban.) For UN aid chief Martin Griffiths, warning that an Israeli ground operation in Rafah "is on the immediate horizon," Israeli improvements to aid access in Gaza "cannot be used to prepare for or justify a full-blown military assault" on the southernmost city in the Strip. In fact, the wording of the Egyptian proposal for a cease-fire, as delivered to Hamas, did not include an Israeli commitment not to return to Gaza, the Lebanese newspaper *Al-Akhbar* reported.[4]

Saudi Arabia sent a warning to Israel via the Americans that a military operation in Rafah would be a great mistake and would further delay the normalization of ties between the two nations, Kan Reshet Bet TV reported the next day, citing a source in the Saudi royal family. The source stated that such an operation would only serve Iran, which did not want the situation in Gaza to calm down. According to the Saudi source, Israel must make sacrifices for peace to create a regional alliance with the Arab nations based on the already existing partnership in order to fight Iran and Hezbollah. The Saudi source further stated that if there will not be a Palestinian state, Israel would not be able to establish ties with Riyadh. Saudis see themselves as the leaders of the Muslim and Arab worlds and therefore believe they must advocate for the Palestinians. Agreeing to normalization with Israel without the foundation of a Palestinian state would damage that status. Remarkably, Bloomberg News reported that Saudi Arabia had launched a wave of arrests of citizens who attacked Israel and identified with Hamas on social networks amid the war in Gaza.[5]

In an unscheduled press conference at the White House on May 2, Biden called on those taking part in university protests to respect the rule of law while exercising their freedom of speech, asserting that there was "no place for antisemitism on any campus or anywhere in America." A widely circulated statement by 600 Columbia University students went much further, asserting that "We proudly believe in the Jewish People's right to self-determination in our historic homeland as a fundamental tenet of our Jewish identity." Hamas senior official in Lebanon Hamdan told local television that the organization's "position on the current negotiating paper is negative," the *New York Times* reported. Hamas later clarified Hamdan's comments, saying that "while the group would not accept the current Israeli proposals without changes, they were willing to keep negotiating." Protesters, including family members of hostages held in Gaza, blocked Tel Aviv's Ayalon highway in both directions, holding up signs that read: "It's either the hostages or Rafah." Simultaneously, a women's protest group calling for the return of the hostages set up photos of women hostages in front of Netanyahu's home in Jerusalem. As for Colombia's decision to break off diplomatic relations with Israel, Foreign Minister Israel Katz responded by calling its leader, Gustavo Petro, a "hate-filled, antisemitic president" who, referring to Hamas, "decided to side with the most despicable monsters known to mankind."[6]

On May 3, day 210 of the war, Israel notified Hamas that it would launch an offensive on Rafah if a cease-fire and hostage release deal was not achieved within a week, the *Wall Street Journal* reported, citing Egyptian sources. Senior Israeli officials were weighing a postwar plan for Gaza in which Israel would offer to share oversight of the Strip with "an alliance of Arab countries, including Egypt, Saudi Arabia and the UAE, as well as the United States," the *New York Times* reported. In return, Israel would ask for "normalized relations between itself and Saudi Arabia." Netanyahu's office declined to comment. Saudi normalization with Israel would likely only happen if Israel agreed to "get out of Gaza, freeze the building of settlements in the West Bank, and embark on a three- to five-year 'pathway' to establish a Palestinian state in the occupied territories," Biden confidant Thomas Friedman wrote in the *New York Times*, adding it was clear to US and Saudi officials that Netanyahu was unlikely to agree to such terms. The same day, Hamas's Hamdan, denying that civilians were killed during the October 7 massacre, responded thus to an interviewer's question if he was willing to accept a two-state solution: "There was no and there will be no Israel!" Nor did he recant Hamas's earlier promises to carry out multiple future "October 7ths."[7]

President Biden issued a statement ahead of Holocaust Remembrance Day, speaking out against an "alarming surge in antisemitism at home and abroad" and calling to "push back [against] attempts to ignore, deny, distort, or revise the history of Nazi atrocities during the Holocaust or Hamas's murders and other atrocities committed on October 7."[8] International Criminal Court (ICC) Prosecutor Karim Khan issued an unusual warning that the court's "independence and impartiality are undermined" when "individuals threaten to retaliate," after Netanyahu on Tuesday had called the possibility that Israeli military and political officials would face arrest warrants a "scandal" and an "antisemitic hate crime." A French draft proposal for a cease-fire between Israel and Hezbollah included the withdrawal of Hezbollah forces to ten kilometers north of the Litani River and the dismantling of Hezbollah facilities near the border, the Hezbollah-affiliated daily *Al-Akhbar* reported. The United Arab Emirates (UAE) had informed the United States in February that it would no longer permit American warplanes and drones based at Al Dhafra air base in Abu Dhabi to carry out strikes in Yemen and Iraq. That prompted United States commanders to send the additional aircraft to Al Udeid air base in Qatar, which had not imposed similar restrictions. As regional tensions rose, the UAE grew increasingly nervous that it could be targeted by Iranian proxies in the region if it were seen to be publicly aiding American military operations, US officials said.

In Gaza, the Hamas-controlled Health Ministry claimed that 34,622 Palestinians had been killed and 77,867 wounded since the start of the war. At least 370,000 housing units in Gaza had been damaged, including 79,000 destroyed completely, according to the new report by the UN Development Programme (UNDP) and the Economic and Social Commission for Western Asia, which estimated that even if Israel allowed a five-fold increase of construction material to enter Gaza, it would take until the year 2040 to rebuild the destroyed houses, without repairing the damaged ones. As for an Israeli incursion in Rafah, that would put the lives of hundreds of thousands of Gazans at risk and be a huge blow to the humanitarian operations in all of Gaza, the UN humanitarian office declared.[9]

The next day, an Israeli official announced that a delegation would not leave Jerusalem for Cairo until a response from Hamas was received on a possible hostage deal, KAN TV stated. Netanyahu was reportedly opposed to the departure of the delegation and would not accept any offer that would see the end to the Israel-Hamas war, even to achieve a hostage deal. The *Washington Post* reported that the United States told Qatar Hamas's leadership should be "expelled" from Doha if they continued to refuse a cease-fire deal. IAF fighter jets eliminated in southern Gaza Aiman Zaarab, a senior Islamic Jihad commander who had led a number of infiltration attempts into Israeli territory over the last few years, including the Islamic Jihad forces' attack on Kibbutz Sufa and the Sufa military post during the October 7 massacre. In the West Bank, five terrorists of a cell in Tulkarm were killed, and many arrested. Cindy McCain, executive director of the UN World Food Programme (WFP), said that based on what her organization had seen and experienced on the ground, northern Gaza was in a "full-blown famine." Armed groups in Gaza, including one with presumed Hamas links, robbed last month the Bank of Palestine of some $70 million, the French daily *Le Monde* reported. Israel's foreign ministry said it would contact international forums about sanctioning Turkey for violating export agreements after Ankara halted trade with Israel. The ministry said it would act toward reducing financial ties between Turkey, the Palestinian Authority, and Gaza.[10]

In a Sunday letter penned to mark Israel's *Yom HaShoah* (Holocaust Remembrance Day) on the 27th of the Hebrew month of Nisan, Chief of Staff Herzi Halevi wrote the following message: "The State of Israel was established, among other things, thanks to the soldiers from across generations, who were willing to sacrifice their lives for it." He continued:

> These days, we are in a war where, at its onset, we failed in our mission and lost many—civilians, soldiers, civilian rapid response team members, and security and rescue personnel. Entire lives were cut short in their prime in a war that was also thrust upon us by a wicked enemy who rose up to destroy us. But this time, we are different. A transformation has occurred in the Jewish people. From a voiceless and defenseless people, rose up a people who take responsibility for their destiny, to fight, and promise—never again.[11]

Nine people were wounded and four soldiers killed on Sunday by mortars and rockets launched from Rafah at the area of the Kerem Shalom border crossing. Hamas claimed responsibility for the attack, prompting Israel's Foreign Ministry to write on X: "While the IDF is facilitating humanitarian aid to the people of Gaza through the Kerem Shalom Crossing, terrorists fire rockets into the same area. Israel remains committed to providing life-saving aid while Hamas remains committed to destroying lives." Just moments before, a heavy Hezbollah barrage of about thirty rockets was fired from Lebanon toward Kiryat Shmona and the surrounding area. In Kiryat Shmona, a rocket hit a building and a vehicle, causing damage to the site. An IAF aircraft eliminated the terrorist Saleh Jamil Muhammad Amad, responsible for combat support within Hamas's Bureij Battalion, alongside a number of other terrorist operatives who were with him inside Hamas terror infrastructure. During an additional strike, IAF aircraft also eliminated three Hamas elite Nukhba terrorists, some of whom had taken part in the October 7 slaughter.[12]

Speaking that evening at Yad Vashem's memorial ceremony for the *Shoah*, Israeli President Herzog recalled how Eliakim Hollanders, a Holocaust survivor at ninety-six and a reservist in the IDF, embraced grandson Uri, a reserve soldier who went out for his first deployment. As tears flowed down his cheeks, Eliakim whispered: "Blessed be God who allowed me to see you, armed, with a medal," then added: "You are my victory." "On this holy day," Herzog went on, "we must commit together to return and rebuild ourselves, relying on three foundations, weakened before the October massacre—the foundation of self-defense. the foundation of partnership and unity, and the foundation of faith and hope." He concluded thus:

> Our beloved Holocaust survivors—you are our eternal heroes. Your legacy is a legacy of resilience, of pride, of hope. You are the source of my unwavering belief that our people can overcome anything. Everything! We will continue to plant, to build and to rebuild, we will keep the eternal flame, we will continue to produce new generations, as you have done—in the name of the past and for the sake of the future, and we will prove to the whole world that the eternal people is here—forever. *Am Yisrael Chai!*[13]

According to a report on Sunday by two Israeli officials to Axios and Walla, the Biden administration had frozen a planned arms shipment to Israel, raising concerns among Israeli leaders of a major shift in American policy vis-a-vis the Jewish State. If confirmed, this marked the first time that the United States had suspended arms shipments to Israel since Hamas's October 7 invasion of Israel's southern communities. The White House, Pentagon, and State Department all declined to comment, as did Netanyahu's office. During his visit last week to Jerusalem, Blinken had conveyed to Israeli leaders the Biden administration's continued opposition to the planned Rafah operation as it was currently drafted, including during a conversation with Netanyahu which two sources described as "tough." Blinken had warned the prime minister that a "major military operation" in Rafah would jeopardize Israel's relations with the United States. Meanwhile, the IDF was encouraging residents of eastern Rafah to move northward towards an expanded humanitarian area, saying its forces "were expected to operate in Rafah with extreme power," even as it expanded the humanitarian area in Al-Mawasi town to accommodate the increased levels of aid flowing into Gaza. Netanyahu issued a statement marking Holocaust Remembrance Day in which he vowed that Israel would "stand alone" if necessary. "In the terrible

Holocaust, there were great world leaders who stood by idly; therefore, the first lesson of the Holocaust is: If we do not defend ourselves, nobody will defend us. And if we need to stand alone, we will stand alone," he declared.[14]

On Monday, the same day that two IDF reservists in the 6551st Patrol Battalion of the 551st Paratroopers Brigade were killed by a Hezbollah explosive drone in Metula, the *Wall Street Journal* reported that the White House had delayed the sale of thousands of precision weapons to Israel, raising questions about whether the United States was deliberating slowing the delivery of weapons to its top Middle East ally amid growing domestic political pressure with a presidential election some months away. At issue was the sale of up to 6,500 Joint Direct Attack Munitions, kits that enable unguided bombs to be steered to a target. Congress first learned in January about the proposed sale, which was worth as much as $260 million, but the administration since that time had not moved forward with the deal. A US official, speaking on the condition of anonymity, described the move as a "shot across the bow" intended to underscore to Israeli leaders the seriousness of US concerns about an offensive in Rafah, National Security Council (NSC) spokesman John Kirby declined to comment on whether any arms sales to Israel had been put on hold. "Our security commitments to Israel are ironclad," he said during the White House briefing.[15]

That evening, Hamas announced after many delays that it had decided to agree to a cease-fire proposal. A Hamas source said the group received guarantees that Israel would not renew operations in Gaza after the deal. The United States continued "to believe that a hostage deal is the best way to preserve the lives of the hostages, and avoid an invasion of Rafah, where more than a million people are sheltering. Those talks are ongoing now," NSC's Kirby remarked. In a telephone phone call with Biden, Netanyahu stated he would ensure that the Kerem Shalom Crossing would be open for humanitarian aid. Biden reiterated his opposition to a Rafah operation, the White House announced. Mossad intelligence agency chief David Barnea declared "We are obligated to return the hostages from the tunnels of death in Gaza. The Mossad—and I, as its head—will turn over every stone to bring them back home." Concurrently, in a call with US counterpart Secretary of Defense Lloyd Austin, Israel's Defense Minister Yoav Gallant said Hamas left Israel no choice but to begin an offensive in Rafah.

Israeli orders to relocate Palestinians from Rafah were "inhumane" and risk exposing them to further danger, UN High Commissioner for Human Rights Volker Türk declared. French President Emmanuel Macron reiterated his "firm objection" to an Israeli assault on Rafah in a telephone call with Netanyahu. Senior Hamas official Sami Abu Zuhri told *Reuters* that Israel's Rafah evacuation order ahead of an expected offensive was a "dangerous escalation that will have consequences." Hamas later remarked that any military operation in Rafah "will not be a picnic" for the IDF. Israel must renounce a ground offensive in Rafah, European Union (EU) foreign affairs chief Josep Borrell said, adding that the EU and the international community "can and must" act to prevent such a scenario. Saudi Arabia's Foreign Ministry cautioned Israel against targeting Rafah as part of what it called a "bloody and systematic campaign to storm all areas of Gaza and displace its people." Egypt's Foreign Ministry also warned against such an offensive and called on Israel to show restraint "at this sensitive point in time." For its part, the Jordanian government dispatched veteran diplomat Ziad Majali to quickly pour cold water on a possible move by Hamas's political bureau from Qatar to Amman, saying "Jordan has closed the book on Palestinian cells—and we do not intend to reopen it."[16]

Late on Monday night, the Israel Defense Forces began operating in what was termed "a targeted manner" against Hamas sites in the eastern part of Rafah. The military announcement came minutes after Israel's War Cabinet decided unanimously to "continue the operation in Rafah to exert military pressure on Hamas in order to promote the release of our hostages and the other goals of the war." According to a report by Israel's *Channel 12 News*, which cited Arab media, IDF ground forces entered eastern Rafah accompanied by heavy airstrikes, including so-called "Belt of Fire" barrages, which entailed setting off circular explosions around terrorist infrastructure. The next morning, exactly seven months since Hamas's brutal attack on Israel, the IDF confirmed that its forces had gained full control of the Gazan side of Rafah Crossing. During the operation, the IDF's Division 162, 401st Armored Brigade, and Givati Brigade took control with the aid of other forces. Thus far, twenty terrorists had been eliminated, and three operational tunnel shafts located. No troop injuries were reported. IDF ground troops and IAF fighter jets also struck and eliminated Hamas targets in the Rafah area, including military sites, underground infrastructure, and additional terrorist infrastructure. Dozens of Gazans attempting to flee were blocked from crossing into Egypt by Egyptian soldiers. The IDF stressed that it was providing ongoing updates to Egypt regarding its operations in Rafah.[17]

On Tuesday, Minister of Defense Gallant visited an artillery battery that provided fire support to IDF troops operating in Rafah. He then made the following statement:

> I toured the Rafah area today and met the commanders and soldiers operating there. I want to remind everyone something crucial—the murderers who went to [the Israeli communities of] Sufa, to Holit, and also targeted Yated, Yevul, and other local

communities, came from the Rafah area. We are targeting [the terrorists] who murdered our children. This operation will continue until we eliminate Hamas in the Rafah area and the entire Gaza strip, or until the first hostage returns.

In fact, the limited action at this point indicated that Netanyahu was taking seriously Biden's warnings against moving on Rafah.[18]

Hamas declared that Israel's seizing of the Rafah Crossing aimed to undermine efforts to reach a cease-fire agreement. For their part, sixty-two percent of Israelis believed that a deal to release the hostages held in Gaza should be prioritized over additional military action in Rafah, a poll from the Israel Democracy Institute found. Actually, sources familiar with Hamas's counteroffer for a cease-fire and prisoner swap deal reported that there were significant discrepancies between the agreed-upon deal and the counteroffer. One of the major changes was that under the new offer, Hamas would not commit to releasing only living hostages, and would instead release thirty-three hostages "living or dead" from the "humanitarian" group of hostages. The terror group would also release the first hostages only on the third day of the deal each week, instead of at a rate of three hostages every three days, as previously agreed. Hamas was also demanding thirty convicted terrorists for every civilian hostage, instead of twenty, and fifty convicted terrorists for every female soldier, instead of forty. The new deal also removed Israel's right to veto the release of any terrorists who Hamas demanded be released, and did not allow for the released Hamas terrorists to be released into exile, as Israel demanded. In addition, under the new agreement, Israel would commit to discussing a permanent cease-fire starting from the sixteenth day of the agreement.[19]

The same day, Biden declared that hatred of Jews "continues to lie deep in the hearts of too many people," saying there had been a "ferocious surge of antisemitism" in the United States following the October 7 assault by Hamas on Israel. Speaking at the US Holocaust Memorial Museum's Days of Remembrance commemoration after weeks of pro-Hamas campus protests that included rhetoric spewing Jew-hatred, Biden demanded that Americans learn the lessons of what he called one of the "darkest chapters in human history" by opposing attacks on Jews. "People are already forgetting, are already forgetting that Hamas unleashed this terror," Biden said from Emancipation Hall on Capitol Hill. "It was Hamas that brutalized Israelis. It was Hamas that took and continues to hold hostages. I have not forgotten." The president vowed that his commitment to the security of Israel "and its right to exist as an independent Jewish state is ironclad—even when we disagree," a reference to the arguments his administration has had with Israel's right-wing government about the death of tens of thousands of people in Gaza. Focusing on the need for Americans to push back against what he called an "ancient desire to wipe out the Jewish people off the face of the Earth," Biden stated that that desire was the driving force behind the October 7 attack.[20]

On day 215 in the war. Israel reopened the Kerem Shalom Crossing for aid into Gaza. That afternoon, Hamas launched eight rockets from Rafah on the area. Biden told CNN that he would halt shipments of 2,000-pound and 500-pound bombs to Israel if Netanyahu ordered a major invasion of the city of Rafah. During a March interview with MSNBC, he had warned that an Israeli offensive on Rafah would be a "red line," saying (accepting Hamas casualty figures) "we cannot have another 30,000 more Palestinians dead." Now he declared "Civilians have been killed in Gaza as a consequence of those bombs and other ways in which they go after population centers." The United States would continue to provide defensive weapons to Israel, including for its Iron Dome air defense system, he added, but other shipments, including artillery shells, would end should a major ground invasion of Rafah begin.[21]

"Israel will continue to fight Hamas until its destruction," Foreign Minister Katz wrote on X. "There is no war more just than this." Bezalel Smotrich, the far-right finance minister, declared that Israel would achieve "complete victory," despite what he described as the American president's "pushback and arms embargo." Blasting Defense Secretary Austin on this "disastrous, obscene, absurd" decision, rather than giving Israel "what they need to fight the war they can't afford to lose!" when Iran, Hamas, and Hezbollah openly sought its destruction, Senator Lindsey Graham (R., S.C.) asked Austin pointedly in a congressional hearing "Are you worried that if you make a decision to deny weapons that Israel says they need that it would send a signal to Hamas and Iran to keep pushing?" On the other hand, the UAE strongly condemned Israel's takeover of the Rafah border crossing and warned of the consequences of military escalation. Qatar also lambasted Israel's actions and called for "urgent international action" to prevent the "commitment of a genocide." This from a country whose legislative Shura Council member Essa Al-Nassr attacked Israel's very existence at an Arab League meeting in April, praised Hamas's "Al Aqsa Flood" of October 7 as only a "prelude to the annihilation" of "the second Zionist entity" upon earth, and threatened, to an ovation, "we will murder the Jews—who are killers of prophets, and there will never be peace."[22]

Israel saw no sign of a breakthrough in Egyptian-mediated talks on a cease-fire and hostage release deal with Hamas but was keeping its delegation of mid-level negotiators in Cairo for now, an Israeli official told *Reuters*. Netanyahu was rolling back truce negotiations to their starting point, a senior Hamas official told Qatar's *The New Arab*, adding that "the hostages' families need to know that the latest round of talks is the last chance to bring their sons back." Family members of abductees, together with protesters calling for a hostage release deal, blocked Tel Aviv's Ayalon highway. Israel Police issued fines to fourteen protesters for obstructing drivers on the road.[23]

Throughout the past day, while the IDF limited a Rafah incursion to the eastern sector, its fighter jets and aircraft struck over 100 terror targets throughout the Gaza Strip. In Gaza City, Israeli forces killed Ahmed Ali, the commander of Hamas's naval force who in the past weeks had masterminded attacks that targeted IDF soldiers operating in the central Netzarim Corridor which split the Strip. IDF spokesperson Daniel Hagari told the Israeli daily *Yediot Achronot* that the military had accepted responsibility for the failures that led to October 7, saying "we will not deceive the public. Even after we take care of Rafah, there will be terrorism. Hamas will move north and regroup. We will return and operate wherever it does." Defense Minister Gallant visited soldiers near the Lebanese border and said, "The mission here is not completed—this could be a hot summer." According to him, "an agreement or operational process is needed" to allow residents of Israel's north to return to their homes. Down south, the Tekuma agency, responsible for rebuilding the Israeli communities along the Gaza border ravaged by Hamas on October 7, said that residents of Kibbutz Be'eri would not be able to return for two to three years.[24]

Ahead of Israel's Memorial Day (*Yom HaZikaron*) three days hence, the Ministry of Defense published the number of Israeli casualties of war, registered since 1860, which stood at 25,035. Since the last Memorial Day, 760 servicemen and women had been added to the number of fallen, and another 61 wounded veterans who died as a result of their wounds were recognized as Israeli casualties of war. 711 servicemen and women fell during the Swords of Iron War, 637 of them IDF soldiers, 39 members of local security response teams, 68 police officers, and 6 ISA agents. As a result of the current war, there were 1,294 new bereaved parents, 248 new military widows, 520 new bereaved children, and 2,174 new bereaved siblings, for a total of 6,236.[25]

Late on May 9, Hamas said it was sending its delegation back to the Qatari capital, Doha, and remained committed to the cease-fire proposal it received last week, blaming Israel for trying to scuttle truce talks by entering Rafah. Declaring that the proposal Hamas agreed to differed from the version it reviewed, the Israeli team left Cairo that evening. In a later interview on US television, Netanyahu said he hoped that he and Biden could overcome their disagreements, adding that in his vision of a post-Hamas Gaza there would need to be "continuous demilitarization" in the Strip, with a civilian government that was not committed to Israel's destruction. Following the interview, Netanyahu shared his recent Holocaust Remembrance Day speech on X, in which he stressed, "If Israel has to stand alone, Israel will stand alone." The White House, recalling CIA director William Burns from the Cairo talks, declared that Israel "smashing into Rafah" with a major operation would strengthen Hamas in cease-fire negotiations. Gallant remarked: "Whatever the cost, we will ensure the existence of the state. I turn and say to our enemies and our best friends—Israel cannot be subdued." Israel's far-right national security minister, Itamar Ben-Gvir, tweeted "Biden loves Hamas," evoking in turn President Herzog's response that saying "baseless, irresponsible, insulting statements" must be avoided as they "damage Israel's national security interests." Herzog then thanked the United States and Biden specifically for aiding and supporting Israel.[26]

In the United States, while some left-wing and progressive Jewish organizations backed Biden, normally non-partisan groups had harsh criticism for the president's decision. Thus the Jewish Federations of North America: "Israel is fighting an existential war against a terror army that has entrenched itself in a civilian population. Israel has always and will always take enormous care in its military actions to protect the civilian population, but the only way to stop the killing of innocent people in Gaza is to defeat Hamas." Thus the Conference of Presidents of Major American Jewish Organizations on Biden's announcement: his "counterproductive" remarks and public rebuke "serves to fuel domestic antisemitism as well and will likely invigorate the divisive, vitriolic rhetoric we see on many college campuses today." The Israel Policy Forum, a group that dedicates itself to advancing a two-state outcome to the conflict and has a board replete with donors to the Democratic Party, announced "We are disheartened by the partial withholding of US military support from Israel while the threats from Hamas and other actors hostile to Israel are acute, and when the US-Israel partnership should be at its strongest." Going far further, Senator Tom Cotton (R., Ark.) called on X for Biden's impeachment over withholding arms from Israel in order "to help with reelection." He pointed to the Democrat-led impeachment of then President Donald Trump in 2019, in which Trump was accused of withholding aid to Ukraine to pressure Ukrainian President Volodymyr Zelenskyy to cooperate with his campaign against Biden. "Only with Biden, it's true," wrote Cotton.[27]

In Israel, families of deceased hostages whose bodies were still being held by Hamas in Gaza carried an empty coffin through Jerusalem on Thursday to raise awareness of their plight and call for the return of their loved ones. Concomitantly, protesters from the Tzav 9 group, who vowed to block humanitarian aid until all the remaining hostages were released, blocked the passage of forty trucks carrying aid headed to Gaza at the entrance to Mitzpeh Ramon; twenty-six were arrested by police. The Mossad, which had been involved primarily in the flow of Qatari funds to Hamas, admitted for the first time "we were surprised on October 7." In southern Gaza, about 110,000 people had fled Rafah; food and fuel supplies in the area were critically low. All crossings into the area remained closed, cutting off supplies and preventing medical evacuations and the movement of humanitarian staff, said Georgios Petropoulos, an official for the UN Office for the Coordination of Humanitarian Affairs working there. In Malmö, Sweden, chants of "Sinwar, we will not let you die," could be heard among thousands of protesters in multiple locations calling for the destruction of Israel and the deportation of Jews back to Poland (referencing the Holocaust), this ahead of Israeli entry Eden Golan's performance at the Eurovision Song Contest semi-finals.[28]

Hamas demanded a twelve-week cease-fire in the recent round of negotiations, instead of the six-week pause that Israel had agreed to, CNN reported. Israeli officials were "staunchly opposed" to the longer pause, the report said, "as they believe it would be no different than agreeing to an effective end to the war." In an interview with TV talk show host Phil McGraw, Netanyahu admitted for the first time that "there were failures, obviously" on October 7, adding that "the government's first responsibility is to protect the people . . . and the people weren't protected, we have to admit that." The prime minister said he had disagreements with Biden before, and that "we've been able to overcome them. I hope we can overcome them now, but we will do what we have to do to protect our country," adding "there will probably have to have a [post-war] civilian government" in Gaza "with Gazans that are not committed to our destruction" supported by the UAE, Saudi Arabia, "and other countries who want stability and peace." At the UN, the General Assembly backed a Palestinian bid to become a full member by recognizing it as qualified to join and recommending the UN Security Council "reconsider the matter favorably." The resolution was adopted with 143 votes in favor and nine against—including the United States and Israel—while twenty-five countries abstained.[29]

Israel ordered tens of thousands of people to leave Rafah on Saturday, signaling an imminent push by Israeli forces into the city's most urban districts, a move that could trigger the White House to freeze offensive weapons shipments. The evacuation orders included crowded neighborhoods, a hospital, and two refugee camps in central Rafah. In the north, the IDF ordered residents of Jabaliya and Beit Lahia to also evacuate, warning that it would act with "great force" against Hamas militants grouping in those areas. More than 150,000 people had already fled Rafah this week, the United Nations said, after Israeli troops staged a lightning offensive east of the city to capture the border crossing with Egypt. According to Israeli military analysts, armored brigades in eastern Rafah were encircling the city.[30]

Arms deliveries would continue as the Biden administration said it accepted Israel's assurances to use US weapons in accordance with the law as "credible and reliable," given a lack of complete information to verify that US weapons were definitely used in specific cases, and that Israel was currently seeking accountability for possible violations. The administration also did not find that Israel had intentionally obstructed humanitarian aid into Gaza. According to the IDF, 300,000 Palestinians had evacuated Gaza's southernmost city of Rafah for the humanitarian zone of Al-Muwasi near Khan Younis. IDF spokesperson Hagari stated on Saturday night that "The Israel Defense Forces is continuing its precise operation against Hamas in Rafah as part of our efforts to achieve an enduring defeat of Hamas and bring all our hostages home. Our operations against Hamas in Rafah remain limited in scope . . . and have avoided densely populated areas." He continued: "Since the start of our precise operation against Hamas in Rafah we have eliminated dozens of terrorists, exposed underground terror tunnels and vast amounts of weapons. Prior to our operations we urge civilians to temporarily move towards humanitarian areas and move away from the crossfire that Hamas puts them in." Hagari concluded: "Over the last few days we facilitated the entry of 200,000 liters of fuel through the Kerem Shalom Crossing; we facilitated and coordinated the opening of a new field hospital in Central Gaza; and we are operating to enable the flow of humanitarian aid to Rafah through the Salah Al-Din Road."[31]

On the eve of May 12, marking the start of *Yom HaZikaron* at Jerusalem's Western Wall Plaza, Herzog, wearing a torn shirt in Jewry's traditional sign of mourning, hailed the heroes who died since the war began, and concluded "I believe with all my heart: a new dawn will rise over all of Israel. By their merit, for their sake, and for ours." Shin Bet internal security chief Ronen Bar admitted at the Memorial Day ceremony held in the organization's headquarters that "We all feel that the same security blanket we have always been proud of—we failed to provide the people of Israel on October 7." Israel was in an existential war in which defeat was not an option, Netanyahu said during the next morning's ceremony at the Mt. Herzl Military Ceremony to mark the annual Remembrance Day. It was announced that 826 members of the security forces and 834 victims of terrorist attacks had been added to the list of the fallen during the past year. Not surprisingly, protesters disrupted several ceremonies by heckling government ministers. For hundreds of families since October 7, their pain was unfathomable.[32]

Chris Coons (D., Del.), Biden's top ally in the Senate, told ABC News that Netanyahu's "legacy is the huge strategic and defensive failure of October 7." The Biden administration had reportedly offered Israel intelligence on the location of Hamas leaders in exchange for avoiding a major Rafah offensive. Egypt announced it was joining South Africa's petition against Israel at the International Court of Justice (ICJ) due to the military operation in Rafah. As for Hezbollah, it was reportedly planning to gradually withdraw most of its combatants from the Lebanon border with Israel, deciding to rely more on attack drones that would be launched from areas near the Israeli border. IDF Chief of Staff Halevi tore into Netanyahu during security consultations over the weekend for failing to develop and announce a so-called "day after" strategy for who will rule Gaza after the war, according to a Channel 13 TV evening report. "We are now operating once again in Jabaliya," he said. "As long as there's no diplomatic process to develop a governing body in the Strip that isn't Hamas, we'll have to launch campaigns again and again in other places to dismantle Hamas's infrastructure." He concluded, "It will be a Sisyphean task."[33]

In apparent agreement, Blinken remarked on CBS's "Meet the Nation" that Israel had not shown the United States a "credible plan" to prevent Hamas from re-establishing its presence in areas of Gaza the IDF has left, warning that Israel could face an "enduring insurgency." "We want to make sure that Hamas cannot govern Gaza again," he claimed, despite the administration's pushing for a cease-fire that would preserve Hamas's military and political power in Gaza. "We want to make sure it's demilitarized. We want to make sure that Israel gets [Hamas's] leaders.... We have a different way, and we think a more effective, durable way of getting that done. We remain in conversation with Israel about exactly that." According to Sky News Arabic, the United States was pressuring Israel to reopen the Rafah Crossing and transfer control of it to the Palestinian Authority, and Israel offered the PA control of the crossing prior to the end of the war. The PA conditioned its agreement on Israel's acceptance of a plan which would lead to the creation of a Palestinian state, and it told Israel that it would not accept the Rafah Crossing under Israeli military control nor accept control over parts of Gaza.[34]

On day 220 of the war, US Ambassador to Israel Jack Lew told Israeli Channel 12 News that "it's a mistake to think that anything has fundamentally changed in the relationship" between the two countries, and that Israel's recent actions in Rafah had not "crossed over into the area where our disagreements lie." He added that the United States "concluded in the national security memorandum review that there will be no interruption in US aid for Israel.... You look at that in the context of one shipment of heavy bombs, you have to look at it in the broader context." The White House denied reports that the United States had withheld intelligence from Israel on the whereabouts of Hamas's leaders. Washington was working with Israel "day and night to hunt the senior leaders of Hamas, who were the authors of the brutal terrorist assault of October 7," a White House official told the Jewish Telegraphic Agency. Hamas chief Sinwar was not hiding out in Rafah, and most likely never left the tunnel network under Khan Younis in northern Gaza, the *New York Times* reported, citing American officials who quoted Israeli and US spy agencies. Hamas's armed wing claimed it had lost contact with the militants guarding four Israeli hostages in Gaza, including Hersh Golberg-Polin.[35]

Palestinians were stuck between an Israeli blockade and a repressive security force, the *New York Times* reported on May 13 based on Hamas documents seized by the IDF. Sinwar had created and oversaw a secret police force, the General Security Service, which monitored and created files on ordinary Gazan civilians. The documents showed that Hamas leaders, despite claiming to represent the people of Gaza, would not tolerate "even a whiff of dissent." Security officials trailed journalists and people whom they suspected of immoral behavior. Agents got criticism removed from social media and discussed ways to defame political adversaries. Political protests were viewed as threats to be undermined. The secret force was used to quash any and all dissent in Gaza, the newspaper reported. Journalists were often followed, criticism of Hamas was removed from social media, and all efforts were made to suppress anti-Hamas protests.[36]

Yet another dramatic development surfaced when the UN Office for the Coordination of Humanitarian Affairs (OCHA) sharply revised downward the number of "identified" female and child fatalities in the Hamas-Israel war in Gaza. The data now differentiated between the total number of deaths reported by Hamas (over 34,000) and the number of "identified" fatalities (over 24,000). The new figures reported by OCHA reduced by more than half the number of women and children that it previously said had been killed during the war, although other "unregistered" deaths might be pending. The Jewish News Syndicate (JNS) asked Farhan Haq, deputy spokesman for UN Secretary-General António Guterres, at a press conference why the math did not add up. "The revisions are taken... you know, of course, in the fog of war, it's difficult to come up with numbers," Haq responded.[37]

As Israel ushered in its seventy-sixth Independence Day on Monday night, the most somber since the nation's establishment, Israeli tanks pushed further into Jabaliya in the northern Gaza Strip while tanks and troops crossed a key highway on the outskirts of Rafah in the south. Yet the traditional evening torch-lighting ceremony, marking the start of *Yom HaAtzmaut* (Independence Day) and the end of *Yom HaZikaron*, Israel's Memorial Day for the Fallen Soldiers and Victims of Terrorism, was a muted commemoration. Due to the security situation, this year's ceremony was filmed in advance without a live audience, the first time since the COVID world epidemic. Of the standard twelve torches, symbolling the tribes of Israel, the last burned without bearers to symbolize the hostages in Gaza. The traditional fireworks that would regularly follow were cancelled, and the Israeli Air Force flyover, which annually took place the following morning of *Yom HaAtzmaut*, was canceled due to the military's focus on the war. The *Chidon HaTanakh*, the international Bible contest for Jewish youth, which had always been held that morning, did take place in the Jerusalem Theatre. Two Israeli yeshiva high-school students, Evyatar Bar-Gil, an eleventh-grader at Jerusalem's Ort Pelech High School, and David Shasha, a twelfth-grader at the Amit Yeshiva in Kfar Ganim, Petah Tikva, shared the top prize.[38]

In greetings sent to Herzog for Independence Day, Biden declared that "the United States is proud of its enduring relationship with Israel," and that its "commitment to Israel's security is ironclad. . . . I look forward to our nations continuing to work together to forge a brighter future for all our people." As for Rafah, almost 450,000 people left the city in the space of one week to escape the heavy fighting, the UN said. Cairo was considering downgrading its diplomatic ties with Israel because of its decision to launch an operation in Rafah, Egyptian officials told the *Wall Street Journal*. Talks over a hostage release and cease-fire deal had reached a stalemate due to Israel's operations there, Qatar's Prime Minister Mohammed Al Thani announced. At the same time, thousands of Israelis, including Netanyahu government ministers, participated in a march calling to resettle Gaza. After a group of far-right Israelis set fire to aid trucks bound for the Strip on Monday evening, the IDF secured the passage of an aid truck through the Tarqumiyah border crossing near Hebron in the West Bank. In the northern Strip, IDF Division 98 killed dozens of Hamas terrorists in Jabaliya in the largest Gaza battle since mid-March and the largest battle in Jabaliya itself since January. It was also revealed that Hamas planned to establish a base in Turkey and use it to plan attacks against Israeli targets in neighboring countries, shown in documents seized by Israeli forces from the home of a senior Hamas official in Gaza and published in Britain's *Times*.[39]

Netanyahu quickly responded to Gallant's unprecedented call on May 15 for him to declare that Israel will not exercise governing control of the Gaza Strip following the ongoing war with Hamas: "I am not ready to replace Hamastan with Fatahstan. The first condition for the day after is to eliminate Hamas and do it without excuses." He did not reply to Gallant's most damning sentence that "national priorities," rather than "all other considerations, even with the possibility of personal or political costs," should govern "tough decisions for the future of our country." Fourteen months earlier, the defense minister had urged Netanyahu to stop the judicial reform plan because the breach it created in the nation had penetrated the IDF—"a clear, real, and immediate danger to the security of the state." Now Gallant gave voice to what many in the army and heads of the security services had been saying privately and in anonymous briefings to reporters.[40]

Hamas was in talks with Egypt, and both sides believed that Israel should immediately withdraw from the Rafah Crossing, announced Hamas political leader Ismail Haniyeh. He accused the White House of providing political support to the "war of extermination that Israel is waging against the Palestinian people." Regarding the scenarios for the "day after" the war in Gaza, Haniyeh said that Hamas and the other Palestinian Arab organizations were the ones who would determine the future of the Strip. The Biden administration was urging Arab states to join a "peacekeeping" force which would control Gaza once the war ends, the *Financial Times* reported. At the same time, the US president was unwilling to send American troops into Gaza. Three Arab states, it was reported, had had initial discussions, namely, Egypt, the UAE, and Morocco, but they would want Washington to recognize a Palestinian state first. EU diplomat chief Borrell urged Israel to end its military operation in Rafah "immediately" to "refrain from further exacerbating the already dire humanitarian situation," adding that continuing the offensive "would inevitably put a heavy strain on the EU's relationship with Israel."[41]

A senior official in Biden's administration said on Wednesday that Washington shared Gallant's "concern that Israel has not developed any plans for holding and governing territory the IDF clears, thereby allowing Hamas to regenerate in those areas." "This is a concern because our objective is to see Hamas defeated," added the official. The same day, after a visit to the headquarters of the IDF's Division 162, then operating in the Rafah area, Gallant declared: "This operation will continue as additional forces will enter the area. Hamas is not an organization that can reorganize, it does not have reserve troops, it has no supply stocks and no ability to treat the terrorists that we target. The result," he concluded, "is that we are wearing Hamas down. Hamas's faucets are running dry." In northern Gaza's Jabaliya, two IDF tanks killed five IDF soldiers and wounded seven more in a "friendly fire" incident. IDF confirmed Hezbollah's announcement regarding the assassination by a drone strike in

Tyre of Hussein Ibrahim Makki, describing him as a senior field commander on the southern front. In retaliation, a heavy barrage of sixty Hezbollah rockets followed on northern Israel.[42]

While the ICJ heard South Africa's request to issue emergency orders against Israel's offensive in Rafah, Egypt rejected an Israeli proposal for the two countries to coordinate to re-open the Rafah Crossing between Egypt's Sinai Peninsula and the Gaza Strip, and to manage its future operation. The Arab League called for an international force to operate in Gaza and the West Bank until the implementation of a two-state solution for Israel and the Palestinians. In the thirty-third Arab Summit, held in Bahrain, the League called on the UN Security Council to present a timetable for promoting the creation of a Palestinian state along the 1967 borders prior to the Six Day War. Netanyahu insisted that the majority of Israelis supported his war strategy, but a recent poll published by *Ma'ariv* found that his Likud Party would earn just seventeen seats, a steep drop from the thirty-two seats it currently held in the Knesset. Additionally, when asked who would be a better prime minister, forty-seven percent of respondents said that Benny Gantz, former IDF Chief of Staff and Minister Without Portfolio since 2023, would be the better option, while thirty-four percent chose Netanyahu. Right-wing ministers Ben-Gvir and Smotrich had made clear that they would leave the ruling coalition if Netanyahu capitulated to US demands—a move that almost certainly would cause the government to collapse and force new elections. Michael Oren, former Israeli ambassador to the United States under Netanyahu, said the prime minister had come to think that Israel's survival was intrinsically linked to his own. That belief, he added, "enables him to withstand tremendous pressure."[43]

Gallant put forward a plan which would provide weapons—under international supervision—to the Gazans who took charge of the Strip "on the day after" the war, *Yisrael Hayom* announced. According to this report, Gallant was proposing that the population in Gaza be concentrated in "humanitarian" bubbles, and, for each bubble like this, a civilian system be set up comprised of local Gazans who would take charge of its management. At the same time, UN Secretary-General Guterres appeared on Thursday to equate between Hamas's October 7 attack on Israel and the humanitarian situation in the Gaza Strip. In a post on social media, he wrote, "Nothing can justify the 7 October terror attacks by Hamas" but then added, "Nothing can justify the collective punishment of the Palestinian people." Guterres then declared, "It's high time for a humanitarian cease-fire, the immediate and unconditional release of all hostages, and unimpeded humanitarian access throughout Gaza." At the International Court of Justice, Israeli representative Gilad Noam asserted "This war, like all wars, is a tragedy, and it takes a terrible toll on both Israelis and Palestinians, but it is not a genocide." Noam added that South Africa's case made "a mockery" of the "heinous charge of genocide," that Israel "didn't want a war in Gaza" and that it attacked Gaza "to defend itself and its citizens."[44]

Gadi Kedem, who lost his daughter, his son-in-law, his son-in-law's mother, and his grandchildren in the October 7 Hamas bloodbath, lodged a police complaint after being assaulted by right-wing activists on Saturday evening during a protest calling for the release of hostages. Several of the activists carried Likud Party flags and signs that read "Leftist traitors." Kedem suffered head injuries in the attack. Over 1,000 Israeli academics and administrative staff signed a petition calling on the Israeli government to immediately end the war in Gaza and return the hostages held by Hamas. Finance Minister Smotrich, on the other hand, asserted that the IDF should invade and take control of southern Lebanon if Hezbollah refused to withdraw from the Israel-Lebanon border, and that Israel's security cabinet should order a permanent military presence "in all of the Gaza Strip." The IDF ordered residents of additional Beit Lahia neighborhoods in northern Gaza to evacuate their homes, saying it intended to operate in the neighborhoods due to Hamas activity in the area. Nearly 800,000 Palestinians had evacuated Rafah since Israel launched its ground operation on May 6, the head of UNRWA announced. Jordanian Foreign Minister Ayman Safadi said that the Hashemite kingdom demanded an international investigation into what he said were "many war crimes" committed during Israel's military campaign in Gaza.[45]

At an 8:30 p.m. press conference that night, Gantz gave Netanyahu a deadline until June 8 to come up with a clearer war program or he would withdraw from the government. He listed six objectives that Netanyahu must adopt or face this withdrawal: the return of the hostages; the demobilization of Hamas and the demilitarization of the Gaza Strip; determining a governing alternative in the Strip; the return of the residents of the north by September 1; promoting normalization; and adopting an outline for creating a standardized Israeli national service. "If you choose to lead the nation to the abyss, we will withdraw from the government, turn to the people, and form a government that can bring about a real victory," Gantz declared in his statement. "For many months, the unity [government] was indeed real and meaningful. It prevented serious mistakes, led to great achievements, and returned home over a hundred hostages. Together, we faced the hardships of the campaign, protected the nation with a good and strong spirit—and gave the fighters on the front a feeling of being backed by a shared destiny." "But lately, something has gone wrong. Essential decisions were not made," he continued, "A small minority has taken over the command bridge of the Israeli ship of state and is steering her toward the rocks." "I came here today to tell the truth. And the truth is hard: while Israeli soldiers show supreme bravery on the front, some of the people who sent them into battle behave with cowardice and irresponsibility."[46]

The Prime Minister's Office lost little time in replying to Gantz's statement:

> While our heroic soldiers are fighting to destroy the Hamas battalions in Rafah, Gantz chooses to set an ultimatum to the prime minister instead of setting an ultimatum to Hamas. The conditions set by Benny Gantz are whitewashed words that clearly mean ending the war and a defeat for Israel, abandoning most of the hostages, leaving Hamas intact, and establishing a Palestinian state. Our soldiers did not fall in vain and certainly not for the sake of replacing "Hamasstan" with "Fatahstan."

It went on:

> If Gantz prefers the national interest and is not looking for an excuse to overthrow the government, he should answer the following three questions: 1. Is he willing to complete the operation in Rafah to destroy the Hamas battalions, and if so, how is it possible that he threatens to dismantle the emergency government in the midst of the operation? 2. Does he oppose civilian control of the Palestinian Authority in Gaza, even without Abbas? 3. Is he willing to accept a Palestinian state in Gaza and the West Bank as part of the normalization process with Saudi Arabia?

Prime Minister Netanyahu "is determined to eliminate the Hamas battalions, he opposes the entry of the Palestinian Authority into Gaza and the establishment of a Palestinian state which will inevitably be a state of terror. The Prime Minister thinks the emergency government is important for achieving all the war's objectives, including recovering all our captives, and expects Gantz to clarify his positions to the public on these issues."

In response, Gantz's office shot back:

> 1. If the Prime Minister had listened to Gantz, we would have entered Rafah months ago and completed the mission. We need to complete it and create the necessary conditions for it.
> 2. The Palestinian Authority will not be able to govern Gaza,

other Palestinian factions might—but only if we create backing from moderate Arab countries and American support. It would be advisable for the Prime Minister to focus on this and not sabotage these efforts. 3. As Gantz said in a speech—there is no intention to establish a Palestinian state, and this is not the demand of the Saudis. Gantz, unlike Netanyahu, did not return Hebron nor announce support for a two-state solution. 4. If the emergency government is important to the Prime Minister, it would be wise to conduct the required discussions, make the necessary decisions, and not drag his feet for fear of the extremists in his government.[47]

Over the weekend, the IAF eliminated Azmi Abu Daqqa, an operative in Hamas's Procurement Department who was actively involved in the smuggling of weapons and terror funds into the Gaza Strip. The IAF also struck dozens of terror targets, including two tactical-level Hamas commanders who were preparing to attack IDF troops in the Rafah area. It also eliminated a significant Islamic Jihad terrorist operative who was the Head of Logistics of its Rafah Brigade. preparing the terror organization for operations against IDF ground troops in the area. In addition, IAF aircraft eliminated Zaher Huli (also known as "Abu Hamed"), who held roles in Hamas's Military Wing and the Hamas Police in the Central Camps. During an additional operation, Rami Khalil Faki, who operated in Hamas's Military Wing and Hamas Police in the area of Nuseirat, was targeted in an aerial strike. Faki's deputy and four additional Hamas terrorist operatives were eliminated together with him. The IDF said that several "significant terrorists" were also killed who had been involved in shooting attacks in the Jenin area. Most notable among those eliminated by an IAF strike was Islam Khamayseh, a senior Islamic Jihad operative in the refugee camp. He was responsible for a series of terror attacks in the area, including a shooting attack that took place in the community of Hermesh in May 2023, in which Meir Tamari, a thirty-two-year-old father of two, was murdered. A leader of the Jenin Battalion, Khamayseh was also responsible for another drive-by shooting attack in the area which had injured four Israelis in June 2023.[48]

Ebrahim Raisi, Iranian president since 2021, was killed on Sunday in a helicopter crash in the country's northwest, along with the death of Iranian Foreign Minister Hossein Amir-Abdollahian, who was close to the country's paramilitary Revolutionary Guard, among others. The hardline Shiite cleric, adamantly opposed to the Zionist enterprise and a denier of the Holocaust, was seen as a possible successor to Iran's supreme leader, the aging Ayatollah

Ali Khamenei. A conservative who was known as "the butcher of Tehran" for his hand as a member of the Council of Death in signing the execution sentences of at least 4,000 political prisoners in 1988 during a crackdown on opponents of the Islamic Republic of Iran and who led a bloody repression of Mahsa Amini protests in 2022, Raisi was a protege and long-time ally of Khamenei's and a devoted upholder of religious rule in the country. Israeli officials quickly denied any hand in the crash. Former Foreign Minister Mohammad Javad Zarif told state media that the US embargo on aviation parts caused the American-made Bell 212 helicopter to crash. The impact of Raisi's death on Iran's future policies, threatening a smooth transition to a new supreme leader, was unclear. Still, Rafael Mariano Grossi, head of the International Atomic Energy Agency (IAEA), the world's center for cooperation in the nuclear field which seeks to promote the safe, secure, and peaceful use of nuclear technologies, stated that Iran might be mere weeks away from developing nuclear weapons. He flew to Iran last week to strengthen the UN's supervision of Iranian nuclear activities.[49]

The International Criminal Court's Chief Prosecutor, Karim Khan, was seeking warrants of arrest for both Sinwar and Netanyahu on charges of "war crimes and crimes against humanity" over the October 7 attacks on Israel and the subsequent war in Gaza, he told CNN's Christiane Amanpour on May 20. Khan also said that the ICJ was seeking warrants for Gallant, as well as two other top Hamas officials: Haniyeh and leader of the Al Qassem Brigades' Mohammed Deif. Khan announced that the charges against Sinwar, Haniyeh, and Deif included "extermination, murder, taking of hostages, rape and sexual assault in detention." He added: "The world was shocked on the 7th of October when people were ripped from their bedrooms, from their homes, from the different kibbutzim in Israel. People have suffered enormously." As for the Israeli officials, Khan said the charges included: "Causing extermination, causing starvation as a method of war, including the denial of humanitarian relief supplies, deliberately targeting civilians in conflict." A panel of ICJ judges would now consider Khan's application for the arrest warrants, including the first-ever for a leader of a Western democratic state.[50]

Herzog called the decision by the prosecutor of the International Criminal Court "beyond outrageous." He also dismissed potential arrest warrants for Hamas and Israeli leaders, stating that "any attempt to draw parallels between these atrocious terrorists and a democratically elected government of Israel . . . cannot be accepted by anyone." In an historic bipartisan statement, the Israeli Knesset declared: "The scandalous comparison by the Hague prosecutor between Israel's leaders and the heads of terror organizations is an unerasable historic crime and a clear expression of antisemitism. We reject this with revulsion. Eighty years after the Holocaust, no one will block the Jewish state from defending itself." The petition was signed by all the members of Knesset save for those from the Hadash-Ta'al, Ra'am, and Labor parties. Biden concurred, issuing this statement: "The ICC prosecutor's application for arrest warrants against Israeli leaders is outrageous. And let me be clear: whatever this prosecutor might imply, there is no equivalence—none—between Israel and Hamas. We will always stand with Israel against threats to its security." Hamas, for its part, denounced the ICC, saying "it equates the victim with the executioner and encourages the occupation to continue its war of extermination." It argued that the Palestinian people and all those living "under occupation" have a "right to resist ... with all their might, including armed resistance."[51]

The IDF had succeeded in evacuating around 950,000 Palestinian civilians in only two weeks since May 6, the military revealed on Monday. In addition, around 30–40 percent of Rafah was now under IDF control, and about 60–70 percent of Rafah had been completely evacuated. The remaining Rafah civilians, estimated at around 300,000–400,000, were almost all near the Gaza coast Tel al-Sultan area. This occurred despite US predictions that the civilian population could not be evacuated without a huge death count or without leaving around four months to do so. Of those evacuated, the overwhelming majority moved northwest to Al-Muwasi, while a smaller number moved to central Gaza. Given this reality, Gallant told US National Security Council advisor Jake Sullivan that Israel was committed to expanding its ground operations in Rafah to dismantle Hamas and release the hostages. The IDF said it assessed that the fighting in Gaza would last at least another six months to completely end Hamas's military and governance body in Gaza.[52]

Israeli leaders had reached final consensus on an operation in Rafah, and the United States was not expected to oppose it, the *Washington Post*'s David Ignatius reported on May 20. Instead of a heavy attack with two divisions, Israel would conduct a more limited attack, which US officials believed would result in fewer civilian casualties. He also noted that "Hamas will retain a presence in Gaza," and that the terror group had chosen to "melt into the population as a guerrilla force" instead of fighting the IDF in open warfare. The IDF therefore planned to continue conducting anti-terror raids in Gaza, where the status quo may become like that in Judea and Samaria. The article also confirmed that Israel's plans for "the day after" included a Gazan security force drawn from the Palestinian Authority's system, which would be overseen by "a governing council of Palestinian notables" and backed by moderate Arab states. Israel was divided on whether this entity should have ties in Ramallah. Meanwhile, Hamas had confirmed that this entity could be part of a "transitional agreement" included in a cease-fire and prisoner swap deal. According to Ignatius, US officials believed that talks on such a deal could resume as early as this week.⁵³

The same day, speaking at a celebration of Jewish Heritage Month, Biden said flatly that Israel's military assault in Gaza in the wake of the Hamas-led October 7 attacks "is not genocide." "We reject that," he said, telling an audience of Jewish leaders and activists that Americans "stand with Israel." Elsewhere, the director-general of the World Health Organization, the president of the European Council, the EU representative for foreign affairs, the NATO spokesperson, and the US State Department all expressed their condolences to Iran for the death of its president and foreign minister. Meanwhile, an American diplomat stood solemnly at attention while the UN Security Council—at the request of Iran, China, and Algeria—held a moment of silence for Iran's Raisi, a man who had launched his political career by presiding over the execution of some 10,000 dissidents. Asked to explain why the United States sent official condolences to Tehran, White House spokesperson Matthew Miller acknowledged that the deceased president was "a brutal participant in the repression of the Iranian people for nearly four decades," but "that said, we regret any loss of life. We don't want to see anyone die in a helicopter crash."⁵⁴

France, the Czech Republic, and Poland echoed UK Prime Minister Rishi Sunak's criticizing ICC prosecutor Khan thus: "There is no moral equivalence between a democratic state exercising its lawful right to self-defense and the terrorist group Hamas." Israel urged "nations of the civilized world" to oppose the prosecutor's request and to declare they would not honor any such warrants, a government spokesperson said. If the court did issue the warrants, it would make it difficult for leaders and foreign ministers of countries that recognize its authority to meet with the Israeli officials, several diplomats told *Haaretz*. Netanyahu remarked on ABC's "Good Morning America" that he rejected ICC prosecutor Khan's assessment of Israel's conduct in Gaza. "We have supplied half a million tons of food and medicine with 20,000 trucks. This guy is out to demonize Israel. He's doing a hit job."

On the other hand, Steffen Hebestreit, a senior spokesman for the Berlin government and head of the country's press information office, announced that Netanyahu could face immediate arrest as per the ICJ warrant if he were to travel to Germany: "Of course. Yes, we abide by the law." Oman's foreign minister, Sayyid Badr al Busaidi, welcomed the ICJ's "clear-eyed judgment," and said "history will remember the real criminals committing genocide and war crimes against humanity." Qatari Foreign Ministry spokesperson Majed Al-Ansari declared that while it was too early for Doha to directly comment on the prosecutor's recommendation, all states and organizations should be "held responsible for the killing of civilians." He added that cease-fire and hostage release talks between Israel and Hamas remained "close to a stalemate."[55]

A disturbing CNN News exclusive revealed that Egypt had altered cease-fire terms before handing agreements to Hamas, three anonymous sources informed CNN as published on May 21. According to the report, Egypt changed the details of the deal submitted to Hamas after it had been signed by Israel and before reaching the terrorist organization. It was also reported that this move led to great anger among Israel, the United States, and Qatar against the Egyptians. One source even claimed that the Egyptians "deceived us all." Qatari Prime Minister Mohammed bin Abdulrahman bin Jassim Al Thani assured the Mossad that Egypt had acted alone in making the changes, two of the informants told CNN. As for Gaza's future, Israelis would not be able to rebuild settlements there and the Palestinian Authority will not be able to control the enclave, Netanyahu told CNN that night: "Resettling Gaza, that was never in the cards." Just last week, National Security Minister Ben-Gvir had called for the construction of Israeli settlements in Gaza and the voluntary emigration of Palestinians from the enclave.[56]

On Wednesday morning, Norwegian Prime Minister Jonas Gahr Støre, Irish Prime Minister Simon Harris, and Spanish Prime Minister Pedro Sanchez announced that their countries would formally recognize the Palestinian Authority as the State of Palestine, to take effect on May 28. "There cannot be peace in the Middle East if there is no recognition," Støre declared. He added, "The terror has been committed by Hamas and militant groups who are not supporters of a two-state solution and the state of Israel." According to Harris, Ireland will recognize Palestine "because we believe in freedom and justice." In response, Israeli Foreign Minister Katz ordered the immediate return to Israel of Jerusalem's ambassadors to Norway and to Ireland "for urgent consultations", declaring that Dublin and Oslo "intend to send a message to the Palestinians and the whole world today: Terrorism works.... The twisted step of these countries is an injustice to the memory of the victims of October 7. It also harms the efforts to recover the 128 hostages—this is a reward to the jihadists of Hamas and Iran, which distances the chance for peace and undermines Israel's right to self-defense." He then declared: "If Spain realizes its intention to recognize a Palestinian state, a similar step will be taken against it. The Irish-Norwegian march of folly does not deter us. We are determined to achieve our goals: restoring security to our citizens, defeating Hamas and returning the hostages. There are no more just goals than these."[57]

Hamas immediately expressed its appreciation, saying that the three governments' announcement will be a "turning point in the international position on the Palestinian issue." In a statement to Agence-France Presse, Bassem Naim, a senior Hamas figure, opined that the "brave resistance" of the Palestinian people was behind the move. The Palestinian Authority said that Norway, Ireland, and Spain had demonstrated their "unwavering commitment" to "delivering the long overdue justice to the Palestinian people." (The three European dignitaries did not explain where this state will be located, who will govern it, or why now might be an auspicious time to take such action.) Israeli Finance Minister Smotrich responded by announcing that "until further notice" he would not transfer tax funds collected by Israel for the Palestinian Authority. Saudi Arabia's Foreign Ministry announced that it supported the recognition, and it called on other countries to follow suit in order to guarantee a "just and broad peace" in the Middle East. Jordan's Foreign Minister, Ayman Safadi, said his country "values the decision" made by Spain, Norway, and Ireland, and condemned "the radical Israeli government," which, according to him, "announced more illegal measures" that "kill all prospects" of a Palestinian state.

Per contra, French Foreign Minister Stéphane Séjourné stated that officially recognizing the Palestinian state "is not a taboo for France," but any such decision "must come at the right time and is not just as a matter of political positioning." Biden still believed a Palestinian state "should be realized only through direct negotiations with Israel," a US National Security Council spokesperson told CNN, "not through unilateral recognition." He added that the president "is a strong supporter of a two-state solution and has been throughout his career." A German spokesman agreed. Critics noted, at the same time, that according to Palestinian polls, 89 percent of Palestinians supported establishing a government that included or was led by Hamas. Only around 8.5 percent said they favored an authority controlled exclusively by PA chief Mahmoud Abbas's ruling Fatah faction.[58]

Concurrently, the IDF approved the return of Israelis to live in the three localities Sa-Nur, Ganim, and Kadim. The move followed a vote in the Knesset Plenum in March 2023, which approved the law amending the 2005 "disengagement law" in the northern West Bank. "The Jewish hold on Judea and Samaria guarantees security, the application of the law to cancel disengagement will lead to the development of settlement and provide security to residents of the area," Gallant remarked. Egyptian officials said the Israeli military now controlled around seventy percent of the strategic Philadelphi Corridor, land around 100 yards wide that runs nearly nine miles from Israel's border to the Mediterranean. That new border, which divided the city of Rafah, was set up under the Egypt-Israel peace treaty of 1979. that divided Gaza from Egypt. Israel declared that taking control of the corridor was critical to its goal of defeating the Hamas group holding out in Rafah; analysts pointed out that doing so could jeopardize the country's forty-five-year-old peace treaty with Egypt, which limited the number of troops both countries could deploy in the area. In Khan Younis, the IDF killed Hamas commander Ahmad Yasser al-Qara in an airstrike, along with another Hamas member and a member of the Palestinian Islamic Jihad. Two days earlier, an IAF strike eliminated Qassem Saqlawi, commander of the Rocket and Missile Array in Hezbollah's Coastal Sector. The UN announced it had planned new routes within Gaza to transport aid from a US-built floating pier, begun operating on May 17, after crowds of Palestinians intercepted eleven trucks, causing a halt to deliveries.[59]

The same day, in a bombshell accusation, Senators Chuck Grassley (R., Iowa) and Ron Johnson (R., Wis.) presented unclassified emails from the FBI, obtained from whistleblowers, showing that the US State Department had blocked multiple arrests of Iranian terrorists and agents in 2015 and 2016 so as not to jeopardize the Joint Plan of Action. That 2015 nuclear deal was an agreement about the Iranian nuclear program, reached in Vienna on July 14, 2015, between Iran and the P5+1 (the five permanent members of the UN Security Council—China, France, Russia, the United Kingdom, and the United States—plus Germany), together with the European Union. It stipulated that Iran's nuclear activities would be limited in exchange for reduced economic sanctions against Tehran. President Donald Trump announced the US withdrawal from the Joint Plan of Action during a speech at the White House on May 8, 2018, saying, "the heart of the Iran deal was a giant fiction: that a murderous regime desired only a peaceful nuclear energy program." He added that there was "definitive proof that this Iranian promise was a lie." The previous week, Israel had published intelligence documents—long concealed by Iran—conclusively showing the Iranian regime and its history of pursuing nuclear weapons. Netanyahu demonstrated this at the UN, concluding that "Iran lied."[60]

That night, Israel's War Cabinet decided unanimously to restart negotiations under new guidelines after the talks stalled some two weeks ago. A proposal presented by IDF Maj. Gen. Nitzan Alon to renew negotiations had been rejected by Netanyahu on Saturday night at the end of that War Cabinet meeting, but this time the prime minister gave the green light. The decision occurred after the families of some of the five IDF female border monitors who had been filmed by Hamas body cameras during their capture on October 7 released to the cabinet and the public a harrowing three-minute video of their daughters (they had apparently gotten the video from IDF authorities some time back), wanting to wake up the nation, and especially the leadership, to work more urgently to secure the hostages' release. One terrorist tells the bloodied, terrified soldiers they are "women who can get pregnant." (Hamas declared, in turn, that Israel had doctored the video.) The next day, the *Daily Mail* featured the confession of two Hamas members, a father and son, to raping Israeli civilians before killing them on October 7. In the report, Jamal Hussein Ahmad Radi, a forty-seven-year-old Palestinian from Gaza, and his eighteen-year-old son Abdallah described, during a videoed IDF interrogation, murdering civilians in their Kibbutz Nir Oz homes and kidnapping and raping women before murdering them.[61]

The IDF pressed on. The Palestinian Health Ministry in Ramallah said that Israel's two-day operation in the city of Jenin left twelve Palestinians dead and twenty-five wounded. According to Palestinian reports, seven of those killed were members of Fatah's Al-Aqsa Martyrs Battalion, and another was a member of Hamas. An air strike eliminated Deya Aldin Alsharafa, deputy commander of Hamas's national security forces in the Gaza Strip, who had prevented the civilian population from evacuating combat zones. IAF special forces and the Yahalom Unit eliminated the terrorist Hussein Fiad, commander of Hamas's Beit Hanoun Battalion, during special operational activity in Jabaliya; Yusuf Alshubaki, in charge of the operation and advancement of Hamas's weapons production, was killed in Gaza City. About thirty projectiles were fired from Lebanon at Israel's northern towns, some sparking a bush fire in the Huleh Valey region, after a senior Hezbollah member, who the IDF said had procured "strategic and unique weapons" for the terror group, was eliminated in an Israeli air strike. At the same time, an IDF investigation found that Israeli forces had fired at a UN vehicle in the Rafah area last Monday, leading to the death of a UN aid worker. Further, several human rights organizations petitioned Israel's High Court of Justice to demand the closure of the Sde Teiman detention center in the Negev that held arrested Gazans. The petition included testimonies accumulated over recent months regarding abuses of detainees at the facility.[62]

Pentagon Press Secretary Patrick Ryder told Channel 13 News that the Biden administration had not yet decided whether to transfer to Israel the weapons shipment that was recently delayed. He stressed, however, that "the United States, since the October 7 attack, has literally rushed billions of dollars' worth of security assistance to Israel. We're going to continue to provide Israel with the munitions it needs to defend itself."[63] The United States was discussing the possibility of appointing an American representative to serve as a senior civilian advisor to the peacekeeping force that will be established in Gaza the day after the war, *Politico* reported, secret discussions recently held between the

White House, the Pentagon, and the State Department on the question of what the powers will be of the senior official appointed to the Gaza position.⁶⁴

Agreeing with the Biden administration, German Chancellor Olaf Scholz told a press conference after talks with Portuguese Prime Minister Luis Montenegro, "We have no reason to recognize the Palestinian Authority as a separate state now." "There is no clarity about the territory of the state and other questions related to it," he added. "What we need is a negotiated solution between Israel and the Palestinians that amounts to a two-state solution... but we are still a long way from there," Scholz said. As for the kidnapped Israelis still in Gaza, IDF spokesperson Hagari, announcing on Friday the recovery in Jabaliya of the bodies of Hanan Yablonka (42), Michel Nisenbaum (59), and Orión Hernández Radoux (30), who were murdered and kidnapped by Hamas terrorists on October 7, declared "We won't stop fighting for the hostages' freedom from living hell."⁶⁵

That Friday afternoon, the International Court of Justice, in the context of the case brought by South Africa accusing Israel of committing genocide in Gaza, ordered Israel by a vote of 13–2 to "immediately halt" its offensive in Rafah in southern Gaza but stopped short of ordering a full cease-fire. The court cited "exceptionally grave" developments for the already "extremely vulnerable" population in Rafah since its previous orders, and said it was "not convinced that the evacuation effort" for Palestinian civilians in Gaza is sufficient to "alleviate the immense risk." It also ordered Israel to keep the Rafah Crossing open for "urgently needed" aid, and to ensure the "unimpeded access into Gaza Strip of any commission of inquiry, fact-finding mission or other investigative body" mandated by the UN to investigate allegations of genocide. A fourth order required Israel to submit a report to the court on the ruling's implementation and its operational response within a month. In addition, the ICJ called for the "immediate, unconditional" release of the hostages held by Hamas. While the ruling by the ICJ was a blow to Israel's international standing, the court does not have a police force to enforce its orders. In another case on its docket, Russia had so far ignored a 2022 order by the court to halt its full-scale invasion of Ukraine.⁶⁶

Hamas welcomed the ICJ ruling to halt Israel's Rafah operation, but said it was not enough, and called for an end to Israel's offensive on all of Gaza. Hamas also said it would cooperate with the ICJ plan to send an investigation committee into Gaza. Palestinian Authority spokesman Nabil Abu Rudeineh said the ruling "represents an international consensus on the demand to stop the all-out war on Gaza." Jordan's Foreign Minister Ayman Safadi responded, "Once again, the ICJ exposes Israel's war crimes in Gaza," and he called on the UN Security

Council to "put an end to Israel's impunity." South African official Zane Dangor welcomed the ruling as "ground-breaking, as it is the first time that explicit mention is made for Israel to halt its military action in any area of Gaza." Spain's Foreign Minister José Manuel Albares called on Israel to obey the ICJ ruling, adding that "the suffering of the people in the Gaza Strip and the violence must end." Referring to the ICJ ruling, German Vice Chancellor Robert Habeck said, "The famine, the suffering of the Palestinian population and the attacks in the Gaza Strip are—as we are now seeing in court—incompatible with international law."[67]

Netanyahu's office, on the other hand, called South Africa's genocide accusations "false, outrageous and disgusting. Israel has not and will not carry out a military campaign in the Rafah area that creates living conditions that could lead to the destruction of the Palestinian civilian population, in whole or in part." "It is completely unacceptable that Hamas and Israel are put on the same level," Italian Foreign Minister and Deputy Prime Minister Antonio Tajani said in an interview with the *Corriere della Sera* newspaper, adding: "Be careful not to legitimize anti-Israeli positions that can fuel antisemitic phenomena." "Your bias is outrageous," editorialized the *Wall Street Journal* in condemning the ICJ ruling against Israel: "The inversion of international law is something to behold. Hamas slaughters Israeli civilians and hides behind its own so that Israel stands accused."[68]

Reacting to the ICJ arrest warrants sought against Israeli officials, Biden declared: "We don't recognize the jurisdiction, the way it's being exercised. It's that simple. We don't think there's an equivalence between what Israel did and what Hamas did." Speaking next at the West Point Military Academy on Saturday, he declared that the United States was engaging in "urgent diplomacy to secure an immediate cease-fire that gets hostages home." Protests were held across Israel that night, including in Tel Aviv, Haifa, Caesarea, Jerusalem, and Beer Sheva, many thousands calling for the release of hostages and new elections. The PA agreed with Egypt to temporarily send humanitarian aid to Gaza through Israel's Kerem Shalom Crossing until an agreement were reached to reopen the Rafah Crossing. G7 finance leaders called on Israel to release clearance revenues to the PA in view of its urgent fiscal needs, and to ensure that correspondent banking services between Israeli and Palestinian banks remain in place.[69]

The IDF's Division 162 continued to press its offensive in Rafah over the weekend, with Israeli officials insisting that military operations in the enclave were being conducted in conformity with Friday's International Court of Justice ruling. Sunday also saw a twelve-rocket barrage fired by Hamas in Rafah at central Israel, triggering sirens in Tel Aviv and surrounding areas for the first time in four months and reaching further north to the Sharon region. Referring to the rocket barrage after visiting a few southern communities and the Urim SIGINT Base, Gantz declared, "The launches from Rafah today prove that the IDF must operate everywhere Hamas is. And that's what will be. The world must know that the ones who hold hostages, the ones who fire at our cities, the ones who spread terror—they're responsible. The Hamas murderers are war criminals. We will settle the score with everyone—sooner or later." For its part, Hamas leader Khaled Mashal tweeted on X his organization's thanks to "the Great 'Student Flood' at American universities," and called for "a 'Legal Flood' in the Hague," asserting that "annihilating the Zionists is good for humanity; being far away doesn't absolve us from Jihad and resistance." In Brussels, the EU's Josep Borrell, after meeting with Mohammad Mustafa, prime minister of the Palestinian Authority, and Norwegian Foreign Minister Espen Barth Eide, alongside donors to the PA, called for "an immediate end of the hostilities."[70]

An IAF aircraft on Sunday evening eliminated the terrorist Yassin Rabia, commander of Hamas's leadership in Judea and Samaria, as well as Khaled Nagar, a senior official in Hamas's Judea and Samaria wing, in northwest Rafah. Twenty-one civilians in a tent camp perished in the fires that followed. The IDF declared that it had carried out "several operations" earlier to ensure that there were no Palestinian civilians in the area. Netanyahu admitted it was a "tragic mistake," then added. "For us, every uninvolved civilian who is hurt is a tragedy. For Hamas, it's a strategy. That's the whole difference." Hamas, for its part, told the countries mediating in cease-fire negotiations that it will not participate in talks for a hostage deal because of the IDF's "massacre" in Rafah. It also issued a statement: "In light of the horrific Zionist massacre this evening committed by the criminal occupation army . . . we call on the masses of our people in the West Bank, Jerusalem, the occupied territories, and abroad to rise up and march angrily against the ongoing Zionist massacre against our people in the sector."[71]

French President Emmanuel Macron said he was "outraged" by Israel's strike and called for an immediate cease-fire in Gaza. Italy's Defense Minister Guido Crosetto declared "Palestinian people are being squeezed without regard for the rights of innocent men, women, and children who have nothing to do with Hamas and this can no longer be justified." Egypt's Foreign Ministry condemned "Israeli forces' deliberate bombing of displaced people's tents . . . in a new and blatant violation of the provisions of international law." Qatar called the strike a "grave violation of international laws" that will aggravate the humanitarian crisis in the besieged Strip. Jordan and Kuwait condemned "war crimes" committed by Israel in Gaza, and urged the international community to compel

Israel to adhere to the recent decision of the ICJ ordering Israel to stop any operation in Rafah that could threaten civilians. EU chief Borrell added that "from now on I will never say Israel. I will say 'the Netanyahu government', because it's this government who is making the decisions that could kill the Palestinian Authority."[72]

Troops of the 146th Division and the reserve 205th Armored Brigade carried out exercises simulating maneuvers in Lebanon, the IDF said on Monday. IDF troops destroyed an 800-meter-long and 18-meter-deep underground tunnel in the Gaza Strip. Near Rafah, Israeli and Egyptian forces exchanged fire, with sources in the IDF saying that Egyptian soldiers had fired at Israeli soldiers who returned fire, according to *Ma'ariv*. The military said that the incident, where an Egyptian soldier was killed, was under investigation, and that a dialogue was taking place with the Egyptians. Some Israeli settlers expanded their attacks on aid trucks passing through the West Bank this month, blocking food from reaching Gaza while humanitarian groups warned that the enclave was sinking deeper into famine. Still, 126 trucks from Egypt containing food, fuel, and other necessities entered the Gaza Strip through the Kerem Shalom Crossing under a new US-brokered agreement to reopen a vital conduit for humanitarian relief.[73]

On Tuesday. IDF spokesperson Hagari stressed that Sunday's airstrike which killed many Gaza civilians was nearly a mile away from a protected civilian zone established by Israel to shield Palestinian civilians, and that the attack had utilized small, precision munitions which were not capable of causing the deadly conflagration. The IDF released the recording of a conversation between two Gazans who said that the deadly blast was in fact caused by a Hamas ammunition warehouse. White House National Security Council spokesperson Kirby told reporters that Sunday's air strike in Rafah did not cross Biden's "red line." KAN reported that four IDF brigades began expanding the ground maneuver into new areas, including central Rafah. Canada said it would issue visas to 5,000 Gazans, more than it had originally pledged, and stated that it was "horrified" by Israel's strike in Rafah. The US military suspended aid deliveries into the Strip by sea after its $320-million floating pier system off Gaza's coast suffered damage in bad weather.[74]

On Wednesday, the same day that Staff Sgt. Eliya Hilel, 20, from Tel Zion, and Staff Sgt. Diego Shvisha Harsaj, 20, from Tel Aviv, both infantrymen in the Kfir Brigade's Nahshon Battalion, were hit in a car ramming attack in the West Bank (they would succumb to their wounds the next day), Ireland, Spain, and Norway formally recognized a Palestinian state. The moves by the three European nations were largely symbolic, but served as a rebuke to the Jewish State. Israeli Foreign Minister Katz quickly lashed out at Spain on X, saying it was "being complicit in inciting genocide against Jews and war crimes." Concomitantly, Denmark's parliament voted down a bill to recognize a Palestinian state. This came one month after Foreign Minister Lars Løkke Rasmussen said Denmark "cannot recognize an independent Palestinian state, for the sole reason that the preconditions are not really there." The Australian Parliament would reject the Green Party's proposal to unilaterally recognize a Palestinian state by a large majority of 80 to 5.[75]

Come Thursday, the IDF achieved total control over the Philadelphi Corridor separating the Egyptian side from Gaza. Some of the twenty discovered tunnels there led to Egyptian territory, estimated for smuggling weapons and materials for weapon production. In addition, investigations by CNN and the *New York Times* confirmed that the bombs Israel used in Sunday's strike near Rafah that killed numerous Palestinian civilians were GBU-39s, a US-manufactured bomb intended for precision strikes to minimize civilian casualties. Yet Saudi Arabia, while eschewing Turkey president Erdogan's vilifying Netanyahu as a "maniac, psychopath, a vampire that feeds on blood," echoed many others in calling on Israel to "stop the genocidal massacres" in Gaza. Israeli National Security Adviser Tzachi Hanegbi said he expected fighting in Gaza to continue throughout 2024 at least. While evacuees were slowly returning to southern communities, at least 60,000 Israelis who left their homes near Lebanon in October were still displaced. Only hours after Hamas terrorists fired shots at Bat Hefer from the West Bank city of Tulkarm, shots were fired on Wednesday at the town of Gan Ner in the Gilboa region of northern Israel for the fourth time in a week. The hostage release and cease-fire talks in Cairo remained deadlocked. Moreover, the Biden administration was pressing European allies to back off plans to rebuke Iran for advances in its nuclear program, the *Wall Street Journal* reported, as it sought to keep tensions with Tehran from escalating before the autumn's US presidential election.[76]

Following a statement by Israeli National Security Adviser Hanegbi that the war in Gaza will last at least another seven months, senior US officials called on Jerusalem to prioritize a hostage release deal immediately. "The hostages in Gaza can't wait seven more months. Every passing day increases the likelihood that they won't come back alive," a senior US official told *Haaretz* on Thursday. IDF Arabic spokesman Lt.-Col. Avichay Adraee revealed a Hamas document which showed how the organization planned to rob bank safes following its financial hardships during the war. One month later, its operatives broke into Bank of Palestine branches in Gaza and stole over $100 million. As for Iran, the Mossad said Tehran had been inciting crime organizations across Europe to carry out terror attacks on Israeli targets. One such attack, according to the spy agency, took place when two grenades were thrown at the Israeli embassy in Belgium last week, and in Sweden in January. A dramatic letter from Iran's Supreme Leader, Ayatollah Ali Khamenei, to American university students, praising their "defense of the Palestinian people," declared that "as the page of history is turning," "you are standing on the right side of it." He lambasted the US government's support for Israel and framed the students' actions as part of a broader "Resistance Front" against Zionist treatment of Palestinians—"the continuation of extreme oppressive behavior which has been going on for decades."[77]

During three-week operations in the Rafah area, IDF troops of the 162nd Division located many weapons in huge stockpiles, among which were long-range rockets, RPGs, and explosives. In central Rafah, troops of the Givati, Nahal, and 401st Brigades found tunnel shafts, weapons, and rocket launchers, and destroyed a Hamas weapons storage. After rescuing the bodies of seven hostages, destroying ten kilometers of tunnels, and killing 500–600 terrorists, troops of the 98th Division and engineering forces exited Jabaliya on Friday. In parallel, forces of the 679th Brigade operated in central Gaza, where an aircraft eliminated terrorists who were in the vicinity of the troops. The IDF also reported that the three soldiers who were killed Tuesday in Gaza were hit by an explosive device that went off inside a civilian clinic found in an UNRWA school in Rafah. As for humanitarian aid to Gaza, the US-built pier meant to help provide this was so damaged by high seas that it became inoperable and was being sent to the Israeli port of Ashdod for repairs that would take at least a week. Overall, the amount of aid entering Gaza had dropped by two-thirds since Israel began its operation in Rafah, the UN Office for the Coordination of Humanitarian Affairs said.[78]

On May 31, day 238 of the war, President Biden announced from the White House what he described as an Israeli plan to end the war with Hamas and urged the terror group to take it up, although he expressed concern that pressure from right-wing leaders in Israel's government could still scupper the deal. The deal would start with a six-week cease-fire and the release of women, wounded, and elderly hostages, as well as a withdrawal of Israeli forces from population centers, and the acceleration of the entry of humanitarian assistance into Gaza, where the food crisis was believed to be cascading into a state of famine. Israel would release hundreds of Palestinian prisoners in exchange. The second phase of the deal would see the release of Israeli troops held by Hamas and did involve a permanent ceasefire, but talks were needed for the start of that phase. "There are a number of details to negotiate to move from phase one to phase two. Israel will want to make sure its interests are protected," Biden said in his Friday speech, but he did not outline what those were. The final phase would release the bodies of hostages who were killed by Hamas or who died in captivity and the full withdrawal of Israeli forces. According to the Hamas-run Gaza health ministry, more than 36,000 people had been killed in Gaza. Israel said more than a third of that number were combatants, and had itself lost close to 300 soldiers in the war.

Netanyahu's office released a statement that seemed to affirm the contours of the deal as described by Biden. "The government of Israel is united in the desire to bring home the hostages as soon as possible and is working to that goal," it said. "Therefore, the prime minister authorized the negotiating team to present an outline to that end, with the position that the war will not end until its goals are achieved, including the return of all our captives and the destruction of the military and governing capacity of Hamas." "The exact outline that was proposed by Israel, including conditional phases, allows Israel to preserve these principles." Yet Hamas political chief Haniyeh declared that "those who speak of 'the day after' must understand, the Palestinian people won't have Hamas replaced," adding that "a national Palestinian plan must be promoted based on a unified leadership under the framework of the Palestinian Liberation Organization's institutions which will rule both Gaza and the West Bank." How would Hamas, which always made a full hostage deal contingent on a permanent cease-fire and the IDF's complete withdrawal from Gaza, respond now?[79]

Endnotes

1   Israel National News, May 1, 2024; *Haaretz*, May 1, 2024.
2   JNS, May 1, 2024.
3   *Haaretz*, May 1, 2024; *Jerusalem Post*, May 2–3, 2024.
4   *Haaretz*. May 1, 2024; *Wall St. Journal*, May 1, 2024. The recent wave of pro-Palestinian protests on US college campuses came on suddenly and shocked people across the nation. But the political tactics underlying some of the demonstrations were, according to extensive investigation, the result of months of training, planning and encouragement by longtime activists and left-wing groups. *Wall St. Journal*, May 3, 2024.
5   Israel National News, May 2, 2024.
6   *Haaretz*, May 2, 2024. For the full Columbia University students' statement, see the Appendices.
7   *Haaretz*, May 3, 2024; Israel National News, May 3, 2024; World Israel News, May 3, 2024.
8   A recent report published by Tel Aviv University and the Anti-Defamation League showed a near-quadrupling of antisemitic incidents in France, the highest increase recorded of any country, from 436 in 2022 to 1,676 in 2023 (74 percent since October 7). It also highlighted antisemitism on US campuses, which the head of the ADL called the "most alarming" aspect of the surge of Jew-hatred in the United States. In the US, the tally more than doubled, from

3,697 incidents in 2022 to 7,523 last year, with 52 percent of the 2023 total occurring after October 7. In Canada, the increase was from 65 to 132; in the United Kingdom from 1,662 to 4,103; in Germany from 2,639 to 3,614, and in Italy from 241 to 454. The new findings warned that current trends could threaten the very "ability to lead Jewish lives in the West." *Times of Israel*, May 5, 2024.
9 *Haaretz*, May 2–3, 2024.
10 *Jerusalem Post*, May 4, 2024; *Haaretz*, May 4, 2024; *Times of Israel*, May 4, 2024.
11 *Jerusalem Post*, May 5, 2024.
12 Israel National News, May 5, 2024.
13 i24 News, May 5, 2024. "*Am Yisrael Chai!*" translates as "The Nation of Israel Lives!"
14 Israel National News, May 6, 2024; IDF News, May 6, 2024; World Israel News, May 6, 2024.
15 Israel National News, May 7, 2024; *Wall St. Journal*, May 6, 2024; *Washington Post*, May 7, 2024.
16 *Jerusalem Post*, May 6, 2024; *Haaretz*, May 6, 2024.
17 JNS, May 6, 2024; Israel National News, May 7, 2024; World Israel News, May 7, 2024.
18 Israel National News, May 7, 2024; *Jerusalem Post*, May 7, 2024.
19 *Haaretz*, May 7, 2024; Israel National News, May 7, 2024. Israeli officials disclosed that the Biden administration had withheld key information on Hamas's plans to adopt an Israeli-Egyptian draft of a ceasefire agreement, while adding numerous clauses of its own. This allowed the terror group to lay "a political ambush" against Israel. The White House was aware of Hamas plans to "endorse" the hostage deal hammered out by Israel and Egypt, even as Yahya Sinwar, Hamas's chief in Gaza, made significant changes to the proposal, adding numerous clauses which could be used to force an end to the Gaza war. World Israel News, May 8, 2024.
20 *New York Times*, May 7, 2024.
21 IDF News, May 9, 2024; *Wall St. Journal*, May 8, 2024; *New York Times*, May 9, 2024. Critics blamed Biden's decision on the influence of two White House staff members, Jonathan Finer, Deputy Advisor on the National Security Council (NSC), who called assistance to Israel after October 7 a "misstep," and Maher Bitar, former leader at Georgetown University of the anti-Israel Students for Justice for Palestine who also worked at UNRWA, and the current Coordinator for Intelligence and Defense Policy at the NSC. United With Israel, May 14, 2024. Some have also noted that Ariane Tabatabai, chief of staff to the US Assistant Secretary of Defense for Special Operations and Low-Intensity Conflict, was part of an "Iran Experts Initiative," created by the Iranian Foreign Ministry to bolster Tehran's position on global security issues, particularly its nuclear program. She also runs the office overseeing hostage negotiations. Her father, Iranian dissidents claimed in March 2021, was part of Iranian President Rouhani's circle, and she parroted the Iranian regime's position at multiple public appearances. Melanie Phillips, "Buried Facts About the Gaza War," JNS, May 16, 2024. Netanyahu's office and Israeli military declined to comment on the Biden declaration, the clearest public rebuke to date by that administration of the IDF's response to the October 7 Hamas massacre. Michael Oren, a former Israeli ambassador to the U.S., said to Fox News that Biden was sending "a mixed message" to Israel, and he concluded: "It's a pressure tactic. We might have a certain amount of reserve left, but it's sending a message." *Wall St. Journal*, May 8, 2024.
22 *New York Times*, May 9, 2024; *Washington Post*, May 9, 2024; *Jerusalem Post*, Apr. 23, 2024; May 10, 2024. A prominent US military figure publicly stood at this time in support of Israel's war against Hamas. Retired General Mark A. Milley, who served as the Chairman of the Joint Chiefs of Staff from October 1, 2019, to September 29, 2023, hit back at those in the United States who had been critical of Israel's operation in Gaza. Speaking at the Ash Carter Exchange on Innovation and National Security in Washington, D.C., Milley said, "Before we all get self-righteous about what Israel is doing, and I feel horrible for the innocent people in

Gaza that are dying, but we shouldn't forget that we the United States killed a lot of innocent people in Mosul and Raqqa [during the war against ISIS, the Islamic State of Iraq and Syria, in 2016–2017], that we, the United States, killed 12,000 innocent French civilians [during the 1944 Normandy Invasion] and here we are on the 80th anniversary of Normandy . . . we destroyed 69 Japanese cities, not including Hiroshima and Nagasaki. We slaughtered people in massive numbers—innocent people who had nothing to do with their government—men, women and children." "War is a terrible thing but if it's going to have meaning, if it's going to have any sense of morality, there has to be a political purpose and it must be achieved rapidly with the least cost and that you do by speed," he added.

Firing back at so-called "peace activists" who were criticizing Israel's conduct in Gaza, Milley added, "They're out there supporting a terrorist organization, whose very written charter calls for the death of all Jews—not just in Israel, worldwide. I mean, come on now. If you're going to support that, you're on the wrong side." Israel National News, May 10, 2024. The same day, eighty former US generals and admirals called in an open letter for a reaffirmation of the US-Israeli bond, declaring "A strong Israel is vital to the United States national security, and it is imperative that America unequivocally stand by this indispensable ally." JNS, May 12, 2024.

23 *Jerusalem Post,* May 8, 2024; *Haaretz,* May 8, 2024.
24 Israel National News, May 8, 2024; JNS, May 8, 2024; *Haaretz,* May 7–8, 2024.
25 Israel National News, May 9, 2024. The year 1860 was chosen to mark the first modern Jewish settlement beyond Jerusalem's Old City walls thanks to British philanthropist Moses Montefiore's building new housing on a hill overlooking the Old City, This was done to help relieve the congestion and poverty in the Jewish Quarter. The first of several developments was called *Mishkenot Sha'ananim* (peaceful dwellings).
26 *Washington Post,* May 10, 2024; *Haaretz,* May 9, 2024.
27 *Jerusalem Post,* May 10, 2024; JTA, May 9, 2024; *Times of Israel,* May 9, 2024.
28 JNS, May 9, 2024; *Haaretz,* May 9–10, 2024; AP News, May 10, 2024; Ynet News, May 9, 2024. The original Israeli entry for the Eurovision Song Contest, *October Rain,* was rejected as political in nature alluding to the Hamas massacre on October 7, 20232. *Hurricane* was finally accepted and sung by Eden Golan in the final on May 11. It was later revealed that Israel placed first out of the sixteen participating countries in the semi-final with 194 points. In the final, Israel performed in position 6 and placed fifth out of the twenty-five participating countries, scoring 375 points. For the full text of *October Rain,* see the Appendices.
29 *Haaretz,* May 10, 2024.
30 *Washington Post,* May 11, 2024; Israel National News, May 11, 2024.
31 Israel National News, May 12, 2024. The IDF's statement notwithstanding, tens of thousands clashed with the police when protesting against the government on Saturday night, charging that "the hostages won't return under Netanyahu's rule." *Haaretz,* May 11, 2024.
32 *Haaretz,* May 12–13, 2024; *Jerusalem Post,* May 13, 2024. For the full text of Herzog's address, see the Appendices.
33 *Haaretz,* May 12, 2024; *Times of Israel,* May 12, 2024.
34 *Haaretz,* May 12, 2024; Israel National News, May 13, 2024.
35 *Haaretz,* May 13, 2024; JTA, May 13, 2024.
36 *New York Times,* May 13, 2024.
37 *Times of Israel,* May 13, 2024; JNS, May 12, 2024.
38 *Haaretz,* May 13, 2024; JNS, May 13, 2024; *Times of Israel,* May 14, 2024.
39 *Haaretz,* May 14, 2024; *Jerusalem Post,* May 14, 2024.
40 *Jerusalem Post,* May 15, 2024; Herb Keinon, "Gallant's Second Stand," *Jerusalem Post,* May 17, 2024.
41 Israel National News, May 15, 2024; *Haaretz,* May 15, 2024.
42 Israel National News, May 16, 2024; *Jerusalem Post,* May 16, 2024; *Haaretz,* May 16, 2024.

43 *Haaretz*, May 16, 2024; *Jerusalem Post*, May 16, 2024; *Wall St. Journal*, May 17, 2024. The sister of Gilad Arye Boim, who was killed in that "friendly fire" incident, addressed the soldiers who accidentally had caused her brother's death and assured them that the family held no anger for what occurred. Israel National News, May 16, 2024.
44 Israel National News, May 17, 2024; *Haaretz*, May 17, 2024.
45 *Haaretz*, May 19, 2024.
46 *Jerusalem Post*, May 18, 2024.
47 Israel National News, May 18, 2024.
48 Israel National News, May 19–20, 2024; World Israel News, May 19, 2024.
49 *New York Times*, May 20, 2024; Israel National News, May 20, 2024; *Jerusalem Post*, May 19–20, 2024; Ali Deilani, "The Ayatollah of Execution: My Memories of Ebrahim Raisi," Times of Israel," May 21, 2024. The Bell 212 is a civilian version of a Vietnam War-era UH-1N "Twin Huey," developed in the 1960s by an American company. With Iran not having ties with the United States for over forty years, many wondered why the state's leadership continued to use American aircraft and not ones developed by its allies, such as Russia or China. Twenty-two-year-old Mahsa Amini died in police custody on September 26, 2022, after being arrested three days earlier for allegedly violating rules requiring women to wear the hijab headscarf. The death of this Iranian Kurdish woman sparked protests led by women and girls unlike any the country had seen before then. Following the protests, which lasted many months, a UN fact-finding mission concluded on March 8, 2024, that Iran was to blame for the "physical violence" that killed Amini. The mission's report also found that Iran committed crimes against humanity in its violent repression of the protests in 2022 and 2023, including "murder, imprisonment, torture, rape and other forms of sexual violence, persecution, enforced disappearance, and other inhumane acts." NBC News, Mar. 8, 2024.
50 Israel National News, May 20, 2024.
51 *Washington Post*, May 20, 2024; *Jerusalem Post*, May 20, 2024.
52 *Jerusalem Post*, May 20, 2024; *Haaretz*, May 20, 2024.
53 *Washington Post*, May 20, 2024.
54 *New York Times*, May 21, 2024; *Mosaic Daily*, May 21, 2024; World Israel News, May 26, 2024.
55 World Israel News, May 21–22, 2024; *Haaretz*, May 21, 2024.
56 *Jerusalem Post*, May 22, 2024.
57 Israel National News, May 22, 2024. Norway's decision was a "reaction" to the policies of the Netanyahu government, Norwegian Foreign Minister Espen Barth Eide told *Haaretz* hours after the announcement, saying it was "clear" that Israel's government "has no intention to negotiate with the Palestinian side, and has been so accepting and even supportive of new illegal settlements." *Haaretz*, May 22, 2024. Not long thereafter, Irish Foreign Minister Micheál Martin told CNN that "The integrity of that two-state solution has been undermined in recent years by the strategy of the Israeli government and, particularly, Prime Minister Benjamin Netanyahu, who has declared opposition to it." He also claimed that Netanyahu "hasn't really dealt with the violent settlers" in Judea and Samaria. Israel National News, May 23, 2024.
58 BBC, May 22, 2024; *Haaretz*, May 22, 2024; JNS, May 22, 2024. Saudi Foreign Minister Prince Faisal bin Farhan Al Saud told reporters in Brussels that the unilateral recognition of a Palestinian state would "reinvigorate the two-state solution independent of Israel's position because Israel doesn't get to decide whether or not the Palestinians have a right to self-determination." "I firmly believe," he went on, "that a two-state solution with the establishment of a credible Palestinian state serves . . . the interest of the Palestinians and delivers [on] their right to self-determination. It is also in the interest of Israel and delivers the security that Israel needs and deserves." World Israel News, May 27, 2024.
59 *Jerusalem Post*, May 22, 2024; *Wall St. Journal*, May 22, 2024; *New York Times*, May 17, 2024. Of 569 metric tons of humanitarian aid that had been delivered into Gaza via the temporary

pier, not a single one had yet been distributed to Gazans in need, Air Force Maj. Gen. Pat Ryder, the Pentagon press secretary, admitted on May 22. According to Israeli estimates, Hamas had been stealing up to sixty percent of the aid entering the Strip, and an Israel TV Channel 12 report the previous week revealed that Hamas had made at least $500 million in profit off humanitarian aid since the start of the war on October 7. United With Israel, May 22, 2024.

60 Israel National News, May 23, 2024.
61 JNS, May 23, 2024; *Jerusalem Post*, May 23, 2024.
62 Israel National News, May 23–24, 2024; IDF News, May 23, 2024; *Haaretz*, May 23, 2024.
63 In the largest US airlift to Israel since the Yom Kippur War (1973), dozens of US C-17s and 747 cargo planes shuttled in and out of Israel from American bases around the world: Dover in Delaware, and bases in Germany, Qatar, Spain, Italy, and Greece. More than half of the munitions in this war came from the United States. Looking ahead, Congress appropriated $14 billion in special military aid to Israel. Concluded one historian regarding Netanyahu's rhetoric: "It's time for its leader to stop talking like a Holocaust survivor and act like what he is: the head of a sovereign but small state whose job is to leave Israel's enemies in no doubt that the Jewish state will never stand alone. To even suggest that "the gentiles" might shun it is an invitation to ceaseless aggression. Any leader who errs there should be left by the Israeli people to fight for his own political survival—alone." Martin Kramer, "Israel Must Never Stand Alone," *Times of Israel*, May 16, 2024.
64 Israel National News, May 24, 2024.
65 *Times of Israel*, May 24, 2024.
66 *Washington Post*, May 24, 2024. *New York Times*, May 24, 2024. In a dissenting opinion, Israel's Judge Aharon Barak criticized the Court's tendency to "act every time there is a development in the hostilities," and in response to "public opinion," not international law, saying these kind of rulings would make the ICJ "become the micromanager of an armed conflict . . . a dangerous [road that] weakens the régime of the Genocide Convention by using it (or misusing it) to arbitrate an armed conflict." Uganda's Julia Sebutinde, the ICJ Vice President, asserted this in her dissent: "Israel's ongoing military operations in Rafah are part of the broader conflict initiated by Hamas on October 7, 2023, when Hamas attacked Israeli territory, killing citizens and abducting others. To maintain its judicial integrity, the court must avoid reacting to every shift in the conflict and refrain from micromanaging the hostilities in the Gaza Strip, including Rafah."
67 *Haaretz*, May 24, 2024; *Wall St. Journal*, May 24, 2024.
68 *Haaretz*, May 25, 2024.
69 *Haaretz*, May 25, 2024; *Times of Israel*, May 21, 2024. The fiscal situation of the Palestinian Authority, which runs the West Bank, had worsened in the last three months, "significantly raising the risk of a fiscal collapse," the World Bank announced. *Reuters*, May 24, 2024.
70 JNS, May 26, 2024; *Jerusalem Post*, May 26, 2024; *Times of Israel*, May 26, 2024; World Israel News, May 26, 2024; *Haaretz*, May 26, 2024.
71 Israel National News, May 27–28, 2024; World Israel News, May 27, 2024; *Forward*, May 28, 2024.
72 *Haaretz*, May 27, 2024; *Times of Israel*, May 27, 2024.
73 *Jerusalem Post*, May 27, 2024; *Washington Post*, May 27, 2024; *New York Times*, May 27, 2024.
74 World Israel News, May 28, 2024; Israel National News, May 29, 2024.
75 *Times of Israel*, May 30, 2024; *Jerusalem Post*, May 28, 2024; *Haaretz*, May 28, 2024; Israel National News, May 30, 2024.
76 IDF News, May 29, 2024; *Haaretz*, May 29, 2024; *Wall St. Journal*, May 27, 2024; Israel National News, May 29, 2024. US officials said that Iran's current material could be converted into weapon-grade enriched uranium in a matter of days. It would then be enough to fuel three nuclear weapons. Alarmed by this development, the UK, France, and Germany prepared a resolution of censure against Iran for next week's IAEA board meeting. For the

last eighteen months, as the Foundation for Defense of Democracies noted, Washington refused to support a fresh IAEA censure of Iran. Instead, the United States unfroze Iranian assets and helped Tehran evade sanctions through waivers that funneled billions into its coffers. Iranian oil exports consequently surged to 1.82 million barrels a day, the highest total since the Trump administration reinstated sanctions in 2018. In an article in *Tablet* in 2021, Michael Doran and Tony Badran asserted that this was a continuation of the Obama doctrine of "realignment" aimed at establishing a new regional order in the Middle East. America's allies, then President Barack Obama had said, needed to learn "to share the neighborhood" with Iran. Their hostility was preventing Washington from exploiting the "more pragmatic dimensions" of the Iranian regime. Melanie Phillips, "America's Double Game on Iran," Israel National News, May 30, 2024.

77 *Haaretz*, May 30, 2024; *Jerusalem Post*, May 30, 2024.
78 *Jerusalem Post*, May 31, 2024; Israel National News, May 31, 2024; *Haaretz*, May 31, 2024.
79 *JTA*, May 31, 2024.

CHAPTER 3

Plus ça change...

On June 1, Netanyahu posted on *X* that "Israel's conditions for ending the war have not changed: The destruction of Hamas military and governing capabilities, the freeing of all hostages, and ensuring that Gaza no longer poses a threat to Israel. Under the proposal, Israel will continue to insist these conditions are met before a permanent cease-fire is put in place." Hamas leaders outside Gaza expressed support for the proposal announced by Biden on Friday, but sources emphasized that Hamas's official answer would depend on the position of its leaders in Gaza, Yahya Sinwar and Mohammed Deif, who must implement the details of the deal, including releasing the hostages. French President Macron expressed his support for the US cease-fire proposal for a "durable peace," declaring on *X* in English, Hebrew, and Arabic that "the war in Gaza must end." UK Foreign Secretary David Cameron said Hamas "must accept" the cease-fire deal announced by Biden, adding that "a stop in the fighting can be turned into a permanent peace if we are all prepared to take the right steps." The Hostages and Missing Families Forum in Israel announced protests outside all ministers' homes, declaring that its members will reach "every member of the cabinet, government, and Knesset in the coming hours" to demand the approval of a cease-fire deal.[1]

The wide, seemingly unbridgeable gap between Hamas and Israel remained. According to a Hamas statement on Friday, the Biden administration's stance and the approach that had taken root in the world regarding the need to bring an end to the war in the Gaza Strip were a result of the steadfastness of the "Palestinians" and the fighting organizations. Abu Hamza, the spokesman for the Al-Quds Brigades, the military wing of Palestinian Islamic Jihad, echoed this in a message to the Israeli public, declaring that the return of the hostages would not take place except after the end of the "aggression," the complete withdrawal of the IDF from the Gaza Strip, and the implementation of a swap deal. At the same time, fully forty percent of Israeli respondents in the most recent survey said that "Israel should control the Gaza Strip after the war," while only fourteen percent believed that "Gaza's residents should decide who will control" the area. Only six percent would like to see the Palestinian Authority (PA) under Mahmoud Abbas's control in Gaza, while twelve percent would prefer to see the PA but without Abbas. (Last year, thirty-five percent of Israelis who participated in a similar survey had said they supported a Palestinian state. In the current survey, only twenty-six percent said they still supported it.) However, seventy-four percent of Israeli Arabs claimed that "the Israeli response went too far" after the Hamas October 7 massacre, while only three percent claimed that "Israel should control Gaza after the war."[2]

On Saturday, Netanyahu said there would be no cease-fire until Hamas was completely defeated. "In any process of ending the war, we will not accept Hamas rule," Defense Minister Gallant declared at the Southern Command the next day. Rather, he stated, Israel would remove Hamas operatives from isolated areas and "introduce other forces that will enable a different governance." Tens of thousands of Israelis had protested on Saturday night against the government and in support of Biden's proposal in several locations across the country, including Tel Aviv, Jerusalem, Haifa, Caesarea, and Be'er Sheva. The next morning, dozens of hostages' family members joined the more than 100,000 participants and observers in the New York Jewish Community Relations Council's Israel on Fifth Avenue parade in midtown Manhattan. Forty thousand marched through London on Sunday, asking that the hostages being held by Hamas in Gaza be brought home as the top priority without further delay. Three days later, a *Jerusalem Post* editorial granted that the cease-fire agreement did not provide an alternative to Hamas and wrongly assumed that Hamas was no longer capable of inflicting damage on Israel. Yet it would assert "with a resounding 'yes'" that the president's proposal did create a mechanism to free some hostages and provide some relief to the North, assuming that Hezbollah would refrain from attacking Israel during the implementation of the cease-fire plan.

Per contra, bereaved families from the Gevura (valor) Forum, representing hundreds of families whose children fell in battle and "an overwhelming majority of the people," sent an urgent letter on Sunday to the members of the War Cabinet calling for the destruction of the Hamas terrorist organization, the return of all the hostages, and "ensuring there is no threat to the citizens of Israel from the Gaza Strip, in one word—victory." Critics pointed out that Biden's proposal was similar to one Israel had offered Hamas weeks ago but did not require Hamas to be ousted from power in the Strip—which remained one of Israel's stated aims of the war. Israeli President Herzog noted that "We must not forget, as mentioned by the Sages, that there is no greater commandment than the commandment of redeeming captives, and I add—especially when it comes to Israeli citizens whom the state did not guard and protect." "It is imperative to bring them home as part of a deal that maintains the security interests of the State of Israel," he declared.³

In the meantime, the IDF continued precise, intelligence-based targeted operations in the area of Rafah, with Israeli Air Force (IAF) fighter jets hitting more than thirty terror targets. The Israeli army said its airstrikes killed key Hamas operatives in Gaza over the past few days: Mansur Adel Mansur Kashlan, involved in planning attacks in Israel and the West Bank; Walid Abd Abu Dalal, from Hamas's internal security apparatus; and Tariq Darwish, whom the IDF called "a key figure in the Nuseirat battalion's air defense command." The IDF also killed Salame Baraka, who was a Hamas operative in the eastern Khan Younis Battalion and Head of Finance in the Hamas Police. Six suspects were arrested in the West Bank. Concurrently, 1,858 humanitarian aid trucks were inspected and transferred into the Gaza Strip through the Kerem Shalom and Erez West Crossings over the last week, 764 on Sunday alone through the Rafah Crossing. In the north, Hezbollah escalated attacks during the same weekend, causing twelve Israeli firefighting crews to work on Sunday in several locations after several missiles and drones landed near Katzrin in the Golan Heights and Yiftah in the Galilee. In addition, two unmanned aircraft launched by Hezbollah were not intercepted and exploded near Akko (Acre) and Nahariya on Israel's northern-western coast.⁴

Minister of National Security Ben-Gvir announced on Monday that he would bring the government down if Israel accepted the Biden proposal. Following a meeting with Ben-Gvir, Netanyahu said that the Biden deal will not end the war but would lead to a temporary cease-fire to release the hostages held by Hamas. Far-right Finance Minister Bezalel Smotrich threatened to "replace the failed leadership" of Israel if the Biden proposal were adopted, adding that Israel's green light "was given by the war cabinet, without authority and in violation of the law." US National Security Council (NSC) spokesperson John Kirby said mediators were "awaiting an official response" from Hamas—"the ball is in their court," asserting that "this gives them what they've been looking for, which is a cease-fire, and over time and through the phases the potential withdrawal of Israeli forces from Gaza." He added that Biden made the proposal public "to try to energize the process and catalyze a different outcome." Iran's Supreme Leader Ali Khamenei took the moment to assert that Hamas's October 7 attack on Israeli communities was executed "at the right time," as it stopped normalization efforts between Israel and other Mideast states. PA President Abbas fired back at Khamenei thus: "Iran aims to sacrifice Palestinian blood."⁵

On Monday, NSC advisor Kirby remarked that the White House agreed with Netanyahu that Israel had the right to destroy Hamas's capabilities, but that "now was the time to move to the next stage, to begin the first stage of freeing some of the hostages and start discussing the second stage. We will not give up on total victory." The United States also said it wanted the UN Security Council to adopt a resolution backing the Biden proposal. Kirby's statement came after Netanyahu participated in a discussion of the Knesset Foreign Affairs and Defense Committee and declared: "I will not be ready to stop the war. Despite what President Biden said, it has not yet been agreed how many hostages will be released in the first phase. We can stop the fighting for forty-two days in order to return the hostages. We cannot stop the war. The Iranians and all our enemies are looking at us and want to see if we surrender." Biden omitted "one crucial detail regarding the second stage" of the deal, Netanyahu added. "Israel didn't agree to end the war, but only to 'discuss' its end," he asserted, adding that such a discussion would occur after the hostages were returned and "only on our terms." He concluded with "there are many more details in the deal and the war will not end without achieving all of our objectives."[6]

Both warring parties appeared lukewarm toward Biden's peace plan for separate reasons, argued an analysis by Alan Cullison in the *Wall Street Journal*. Netanyahu's government had not yet achieved its goal of destroying Hamas militarily, and far-right members were threatening to quit the governing coalition rather than accept a halt to the war. Hamas seemed to be in no rush to end the war either, believing it was "drawing Israel into a quagmire" that was turning the country into an international pariah while reviving the Palestinian national cause. For Biden, the continuing war in Gaza was a political liability before presidential elections in the fall, dividing his base, which had criticized him for supporting Israel "too much or too little." His peace plan appeared to be a gambit to end the dilemma, one that closely paralleled Israel's own ceasefire proposal, to make it harder for Netanyahu to reject. To bridge the divide, concluded Cullison, Biden was seeking to recast the goal of the conflict, arguing that degrading Hamas so it was no longer capable of carrying out large-scale attacks should be Israel's goal, instead of Hamas's destruction. As if to confirm this, when asked by *TIME* magazine if it were possible that Netanyahu was prolonging the war for his own political considerations, Biden said "there is every reason for people to draw that conclusion." When asked if Israel had committed war crimes in Gaza, the president replied: "It's uncertain."[7]

All the while, the combatants in this war enjoyed no respite. Israeli airstrikes near Aleppo, Syria, in the early hours of Monday killed General Sayeed Abyar of Iran's Islamic Revolutionary Guard Corps, who had been deployed to that country as an adviser. In the afternoon, undercover Israeli Border Police agents in Shechem killed Adam Faraj, considered one of the highest-ranking members of Fatah's Al-Aqsa Martyrs' Brigades, in the Balata refugee camp. The Shin Bet (Israel Security Agency) thwarted a terror attack that Hamas had planned to carry out in Israel under the direction of one of its headquarters in Turkey. Hamas was paying Palestinian civilians in the Gaza Strip up to $19 a day to watch over Israeli hostages taken on October 7, testified freed captive Ada Sagi (75) of Kibbutz Nir Oz. Syrian army sources said that an Israeli air strike killed sixteen Iranian-affiliated militia members. Overnight, an IAF drone struck a Hamas compound in Gaza embedded inside UNRWA's "Abu Alhilu" school in Bureij; eight members of Hamas's police force were eliminated and several civilians wounded in an Israeli strike in Deir al-Balah. Two Palestinians were killed overnight near Tulkarm after they approached the West Bank separation barrier with the aim of firing at adjacent Israeli communities. It took several hours to extinguish the fire that had erupted at the Valley of the Cross in Jerusalem, damaging the Israel Museum; arson was suspected.

Falling rocket debris and strikes from Hezbollah UAVs that were not intercepted caused massive fires in significant areas of northern Israel, taking twenty hours to control most of the blazes. Civilians were evacuated; six reservists and five civilians were injured. All told, rocket fire decimated 10,000 dunams of nature reserves, agricultural fields, and pastures in northern Israel. Responded Ben-Gvir: "Now it's the army's duty to destroy Hezbollah.... They are burning our areas, we need to burn all the Hezbollah strongholds, destroy them. War!" In an interview with *Al Jazeera*, the media network funded in part by Qatar, Hezbollah deputy secretary general Naim Qassem said the organization had chosen not to expand the war with Israel, but warned "If Israel chooses a full-out war, we are ready."[8]

As for the hostages, Israel believed that more than a third of the remaining abductees in Gaza were dead, a government tally showed on Tuesday. The tally stated that 120 remained in captivity, 43 of whom had been declared dead in absentia based on various sources of information, including intelligence tip-offs, CCTV or bystander videos, and forensic analysis. Hamas, which threatened at the outset of the war to execute hostages in reprisal for Israeli air strikes, had since alleged that such attacks caused hostage deaths. Israel did not rule this out in all cases, but said that some recovered hostage bodies showed signs of execution.[9]

On June 5, the fifty-seventh anniversary of the IDF's reunification of Jerusalem on 28 Iyar in the Hebrew calendar, the government approved expanding the number of IDF reservists to 50,000 in the framework of the war, bringing the total number to 350,000 by the end of August. The IDF also unveiled a new Lotar elite unit for Gaza border communities, created in the aftermath of and in response to the October 7 massacre. It was further revealed that the Defense Ministry had signed a deal with the Biden administration for the procurement of the third squadron of F-35 jets. These reports coincided with IDF chief Herzi Halevi stating that Israel was ready to transition to an offensive in Lebanon, aiming to prepare the public for a broader conflict. Visiting the North after many fires caused by Hezbollah rockets that were finally brought under full control after forty-eight hours, Netanyahu said Israel was prepared for "very intense action" against Lebanon. In recent weeks, Hezbollah had escalated its drone and rocket attacks, hitting important Israeli military installations. Israel, too, had stepped up attacks, targeting Hezbollah sites deep into southern Lebanon's Beqaa Valley, as well as senior military officials in the group. Without a cease-fire in Gaza and subsequent deal with Hezbollah that met Israel's requirements, Israeli officials said an offensive was inevitable. Minister Benny Gantz declared that Israel would return residents to northern Israel by September 1—when the new school term begins—either "through a deal or through an escalation."[10]

As for its war against Hamas, IDF troops begin a division-wide operation above and below ground in Bureij and eastern Deir al-Balah simultaneously, while continuing operations in central and southern Gaza. They destroyed a large tunnel in Rafah that reached the Philadelphi Corridor and destroyed ready-to-fire rocket launchers that were hidden in a UN post. World media indicated that deep divisions would limit progress at reconciliation talks in China between Hamas and the Palestinian Authority's Fatah, scheduled for mid-June. Yet the meetings highlighted that the radical Islamist group was likely to retain influence after the Gaza war ended. "We are speaking about political partnership and political unity to restructure the Palestinian entity," Hamas's Basem Naim, who attended the previous round of China talks, said in an interview. "Whether Hamas is in the government or outside it, that is not a prime demand of the movement, and it doesn't see it a condition for any reconciliation," he declared.[11]

An attack drone by Hezbollah, which had launched some 4,000 projectiles on Israel in the last eight months, exploded in a soccer field in Hurfeish, a Druze town in northern Israel. IDF reservist Refael Kauders was killed and ten others wounded in the attack, three in serious condition, stoking calls in Jerusalem for escalated retaliation in Lebanon. The IDF said that it would start presenting to the Chief of Staff next month the findings of its probe into the events of October 7 and the war. The first issues to be presented will be the battles in

Kibbutz Be'eri during Hamas's October 7 attack and the defense strategy on the Gaza border, starting from 2018. As for Iran, the UN International Atomic Energy Agency's thirty-five nation Board of Governors passed a resolution on Wednesday condemning Tehran for its lack of cooperation with the watchdog and for its barring of some top IAEA inspectors. The resolution, proposed by Britain, France, and Germany, was passed with twenty countries in favor, Russia and China against, and twelve abstentions, *Reuters* reported. Iran called it "hasty and unwise."[12]

IAF fighter jets early Thursday morning conducted a precise strike on a Hamas compound embedded inside an UNRWA school in the Nuseirat refugee camp, the fifth time the IDF engaged terrorists operating within a UNRWA facility. The attack killed forty people, including fourteen children and nine women, and wounded seventy-three, Hamas officials told *Reuters*. An IDF spokesperson retorted that twenty-seven Hamas and Islamic Jihad terrorists who belonged to the Nukhba Forces and took part in the murderous attack on October 7, who used the school as a forward operating base to direct attacks on IDF forces, were killed in the pinpointed strike. At the same time, the Israeli military warned the Netanyahu government that its policy of cutting off funds to the Palestinian Authority could push the West Bank, home to 2.8 million Palestinians and 670,000 Israelis, into a third "intifada," Kan Radio reported. The warning underlined the increasingly dire state of the West Bank economy, where hundreds of thousands of workers had lost their jobs in Israel and public servants had been unpaid or on partial pay for months. According to estimates from the Palestinian finance ministry, Israel was holding back a total of around $1.61 billion in tax revenues.[13]

"Hamas will not surrender its guns or sign a proposal that asks for that," Arab mediators said Hamas leader Sinwar told them in a brief message they received Thursday, as two top US officials, including CIA director William Burns, held talks in the region aimed at jump-starting long-stalled negotiations. This from a terrorist organization that never released a list of hostages nor permitted International Red Cross visits to the abductees. "The Israeli documents speak of open-ended negotiation with no deadline, and it speaks of a stage during which the occupation regains its hostages and resumes the war. We had told the mediators that such a paper wasn't acceptable to us," senior Hamas official Sami Abu Zuhri said. Confronted with Hamas's about 9,000–12,000 terrorists remaining in the entire Gaza Strip, compared to the 20,000–25,000 it had in the enclave before October 7, with between 7,000–8,000 entrenched in Rafah, an IDF spokesman for foreign media told *Reuters* that "Israel cannot eliminate all Hamas terrorists or destroy all its tunnels; this is not a realistic goal. Destroying Hamas as a governing authority is an achievable military goal. There is no quick solution after seventeen years of them building their capabilities." Hamas fighters were now largely avoiding sustained skirmishes with Israeli forces, instead relying on ambushes and improvised bombs to hit targets often behind enemy lines.[14]

On the same day, Maj. Gen. Ori Gordin, chief of Northern Command, said the IDF had completed preparations for an attack in the north over the last week. "We are prepared and ready and when we command so, the enemy will meet an army that is strong and ready," said Gordin in a ceremony marking eighteen years since the Second Lebanon War. A few days after Hamas's savage October 7 assault, the combination of US pressure, the entry of former IDF chiefs of staff Benny Gantz and Gadi Eisenkot into the war cabinet, and the "burning need" to strike back at Hamas had led the government to stand down from attacking Hezbollah, the stronger enemy, and send the IDF into Gaza. Now, with Hamas's forces and capabilities diminished, a campaign in Lebanon appeared conceivable; Gordin's announcement reflected this change. "Hezbollah has suffered severe blows. About 420 terrorists and senior operatives were eliminated. The terror infrastructure built over the years has been destroyed and is attacked every day. We have been doing this for eight months, with the understanding that this time too, like eighteen years ago, we have no choice but to continue fighting, together, until the mission is completed," Gordin asserted. Addressing residents of Israel's north, he concluded: "Our mission is clear—change the security reality, so we can return you to your homes as soon as possible – safely and securely."[15]

Qatar and Egypt told Hamas leaders that they faced possible arrest, freezing of their assets, sanctions, and expulsion from their haven in Doha if they did not agree to a cease-fire with Israel, threats made at the behest of the Biden administration, which was searching for a way to cajole the US-designated terrorist group into striking a deal that the president needed amid a "political maelstrom" over the war. It had the opposite of the desired effect, however. On Thursday, after the threats were made, Hamas political chief Ismail Haniyeh, bearing a message from Sinwar, said Biden's current proposal was unacceptable because, in the group's eyes, it did not guarantee an end to the war. The same day, Israel, Hamas, and the Palestinian Islamic Jihad were added to the United Nations' so-called "list of shame" of countries that harm children in conflict zones, attached to an annual report released by UN Secretary-General António Guterres's office. Netanyahu immediately called it "preposterous," adding that "the UN has put itself today on the blacklist of history, when it joined those who support the Hamas murderers. The IDF is the world's most moral army."[16]

Netanyahu will address a joint session of Congress on July 24, Punchbowl News reported on Friday, six weeks after the originally intended date. The prime minister declared he was "very moved to have the privilege of representing Israel before both houses of Congress and to present the truth about our just war." As for calls from Israel's attorney general to establish a state commission of inquiry into the events of October 7 and the war in Gaza, Netanyahu's cabinet secretary said "the time is not yet ripe" to do so. The Israeli military now reportedly had total control over the Philadelphi Corridor from the Kerem Shalom Crossing to the shore of the Mediterranean Sea. The proportion of Palestinian women and children being killed in the Israel-Hamas war appeared to have declined sharply, an Associated Press (AP) analysis of Gaza Health Ministry data found, a trend that both coincided with Israel's changing battlefield tactics and contradicted the ministry's reports. In the West Bank, dozens of Israelis entered a Palestinian village near the city of Nablus, fired shots in the air, torched cars and olive trees, and attempted to set fire to houses, an IDF source told *Haaretz*. Palestinian reports also said settlers set fire to houses and cars near the village of Beitin. The same day, Arab rioters from the village of Burqa lit fires in several locations which began to spread toward homes in the Oz Zion hilltop community. Residents and volunteers from the area who rushed to the scene battled the flames and managed to extinguish the fire before it reached the homes.[17]

The same day marked the forty-third anniversary of Operation Opera, when eight Israeli F-16 fighter jets destroyed the Osiraq nuclear reactor, then still under construction, in Tuwaitha, Iraq. Thirty-eight years later, pilots recalled how Iran had inadvertently enabled the reactor raid. On February 11, 1979, the Islamic Revolution led by Ayatollah Ruhollah Khomeini overthrew the Shah of Iran, Mohammad Reza Pahlavi, a staunch US ally. The transformation of a 1,300-year-old monarchy into a country ruled by Sharia law and the subsequent detaining of more than fifty Americans (for 444 days) led the United States to cancel a massive deal to supply Iran with seventy-five top-of-the-line F-16 fighter jets, a stroke of luck for Israel, which quickly purchased the jets when the United States offered them for sale. That was "one of the greatest ironies in history," said Col. (Ret.) Ze'ev Raz, who had led the raid on June 7, 1981. Now the Islamic Republic of Iran, which regularly called for Israel's destruction, posed a far more ominous threat, having enriched its uranium stockpile by at least sixty percent, a degree of purity that no country without an atomic weapon had ever pursued. The IAEA's condemnation of Tehran on May 29 was "too little, too late," asserted Israeli Brig-Gen. (res.) Yossi Kuperwasser, former head of the IDF's Military Intelligence, who warned that Iran might seek nuclear breakout ahead of the US presidential elections.[18]

Israelis enjoyed a rare moment of collective joy amid a grim war upon hearing that on Saturday morning, aided by US intelligence, a joint IDF, Shin Bet, and Yamam (the Border Police's elite national counter-terrorism unit) force freed four Israeli hostages in Gaza. Noa Argamani (25), Almog Meir Jan (21), Andrey Kozlov (27), and Shlomi Ziv (40), all kidnapped from the Nova music festival on October 7, were rescued simultaneously from two buildings several hundred feet apart in the heart of the Nuseirat refugee camp, the mission taking place in broad daylight to surprise the terrorists. The Israeli undercover operatives (known as *mista'arvim*—a Hebrew moniker borrowed from an Arabic term for people steeped in Arab culture) drove a pair of battered white trucks—one displaying a soap advertisement, the other bearing a mattress and furniture on the roof. They were armed, but their main weapon was disguise, blending into a Hamas stronghold until the guns started firing. In the days leading up to the rescue, the Yamam unit had drilled on various models of the extraction from Nuseirat, which military officials said were similar to the Entebbe raid of July 3–4, 1976, when Israeli commandos rescued 103 hostages in Uganda. As they brought the four captives to two CH-53 Sea Stallion helicopters on the beach, the officers announced by radio that "the diamonds are in our hands," using an assigned code word.

The rescue team had come under intense fire from Hamas operatives when a truck in the operation broke down, which necessitated calling in an air force strike. Thirty-six-year-old Lt. Col. Arnon Zamora of Sdeh David, the Yamam Chief Inspector who led the daring operation, was critically injured while freeing the three men and later died of his wounds. On October 7, he had led the battle at the Yad Mordechai Junction, eliminating dozens of terrorists and preventing the terrorists from infiltrating northwards. He then went on to fight in the battle at Kibbutz Nahal Oz and Kibbutz Be'eri. In his honor, the original name Operation Seeds of Summer was changed to Operation Arnon.

Gaza's Health Ministry claimed that the raid in Nuseirat killed at least 274 Palestinians and wounded 698. The mainstream media, accepting the Hamas-controlled ministry's numbers, accused Israel of "war crimes." Responding to the news, Haniyeh said that Israel could not force its choices on Hamas, and that the group would not surrender to the Israeli "criminal enemy" which "continues the massacres against our people, children and women." Later, Hamas put out another statement saying that the Israeli rescue operation would "not change its strategic failure in the Gaza Strip," as the terrorist organization still held the bulk of the hostages and could capture more hostages.

Egypt, Jordan, and the PA likewise condemned the Nuseirat operation. The EU's Borrell referred to the operation as "another massacre of civilians," noting that his organization "condemns this in the strongest terms." "We know about under 100 (Palestinian) casualties. I don't know how many [of] them are terrorists," IDF spokesperson Hagari said in a briefing. He added that Hamas had fired at Israeli forces during the rescue mission from streets filled with civilians, deeming "the cynical way" that Hamas was using the population "tragic."

After celebrations that erupted across Israel, hearts returned to the 120 hostages still held in captivity, although the army said 43 of them were dead. Thousands demonstrated that night in Tel Aviv, calling for the toppling of the government and the promotion of a deal for the release of the remaining abductees. Police used a water cannon on the crowds in Tel Aviv, with thirty-three protestors arrested. It was noted that Saturday's IDF operation was only the third such success since the start of the war; common to all three was that the seven rescued hostages were not held in tunnels but in civilian apartments. Minister Gantz scraped his anticipated resignation announcement following news of the hostages' rescue. Welcoming the return of the four abductees, who were in a "state of severe malnutrition—physically and mentally abused for a long time," according to a doctor who treated them upon their return to Israel, Blinken said "The only thing standing in the way of achieving this cease-fire is Hamas. It is time for them to accept the deal." Announcing over $90 million in humanitarian aid for Palestinians in Gaza, the US Agency for International Development (USAid), also called on Hamas to accept the latest cease-fire proposal.[19]

Minister Gantz, Netanyahu's chief political rival, then announced on Sunday that he and Gadi Eisenkot, together with their National Unity Party, would be leaving the emergency government which they had joined at the onset of the war. "Months after the October tragedy . . . Netanyahu and his partners have turned unity into a moving call, without real-world action. Fateful strategic decisions are met with hesitancy and procrastination due to political considerations," Gantz stated. He claimed that "Netanyahu prevents us from proceeding to true victory. Therefore, today, we are leaving the emergency government with a heavy heart, but with a full heart." According to Gantz, "In the fall, a year after the tragedy, we need to go to elections that will eventually establish a government which gains the trust of the people and can stand up to the challenges. I call on Netanyahu: set an agreed-on date for the elections. Don't let our nation be torn apart."[20]

At a protest in northern Israel, former IDF chief and later Defense Minister Moshe ("Bogie") Ya'alon also called for elections and said Netanyahu was responsible for "the growth of Hamas and the appointment of messianic ministers." He then declared: "Total victory is a concept borrowed from dark dictatorships." On the other hand, Netanyahu on Sunday declared that "the majority of the Israeli public" will not tolerate ending the war before Hamas is dismantled, adding that "this situation requires internal unity, if not by the entire nation, then most of it." This did not prevent Brig. Gen. Avi Rosenfeld, the IDF's Gaza division commander, from announcing his resignation, saying he had failed in "his life's mission to protect the lives of residents of Gaza border communities" on October 7.[21]

Hamas was the only one not accepting the proposal for a three-phase deal involving the release of hostages and talks toward an end to fighting, Blinken said on Monday as he departed to the Middle East, adding that he was urging leaders in the region to press Hamas to say yes to the proposal. The Biden administration had discussed examining the possibility of securing a deal with Hamas that would lead to the release of the five US citizens being held hostage in Gaza if the current cease-fire talks involving Israel failed, NBC News reported. Responding to this, Netanyahu's office said "Israel welcomes any attempt to free our hostages." Hamas members had standing orders to kill hostages if they suspected a new IDF rescue operation was coming, reported the *New York Times*. The same day, Senior Hamas official Sami Abu Zuhri urged the United States to pressure Israel to end the war in Gaza, adding that "the Hamas movement is ready to deal positively with any initiative that secures an end to the war." Washington was close to finalizing a defense treaty with Saudi Arabia, but the move depended on Israel's commitment to a two-state solution and ending the war in the Gaza Strip, the *Wall Street Journal* reported.[22]

The day after four soldiers from the Givati Brigade died in a booby-trapped building in Rafah that collapsed on them and seven were wounded, the *Wall Street Journal* published correspondence revealing Sinwar's discontent with Hamas officials meeting other factions in December to debate reconciliation after the war, which he labeled "shameful and outrageous." He added, "As long as fighters are still standing and we have not lost the war, such contacts should be immediately terminated. We have the capabilities to continue fighting for months." "In dozens of messages," the newspaper went on, Sinwar "has shown a cold disregard for human life and made clear he believes Israel has more to lose from the war than Hamas." In a recent message to Hamas officials seeking to broker a prisoner swap agreement, Sinwar wrote, "We have the Israelis right where we want them." In another message to Hamas members in Doha, Sinwar described civilian deaths in Gaza as "necessary sacrifices." In an April 11 letter to Hamas leader Haniyeh, following the killing of three of Haniyeh's sons, Sinwar wrote that those deaths and others "infuse life into the veins of this nation, prompting it to rise to its glory and honor."

Sinwar's "ultimate goal appears to be to win a permanent cease-fire that allows Hamas to declare a historic victory by outlasting Israel and claim leadership of the Palestinian national cause," the newspaper concluded. "Even without a lasting truce, Sinwar believes Netanyahu has few options other than occupying Gaza and getting bogged down fighting a Hamas-led insurgency for months or years." Sinwar himself, meanwhile, was willing to die fighting: "We have to move forward on the same path we started," he had written, "or let it be a new Karbala."[23]

On June 11, the UN Security Council approved a resolution backing Biden's three-phase hostage deal in a 14–0 vote, with Russia abstaining. "Today we voted for peace," US Ambassador to the UN Linda Thomas-Greenfield declared after the vote. "Hamas can now see that the international community is united behind a deal that will save lives and help Palestinian civilians in Gaza start to rebuild and heal," she said. Hamas welcomed the resolution, stating it was ready to cooperate with mediators over implementing the principles of the plan, even though it had yet to formally accept the deal Biden had first unveiled on May 31. Sometime later, a Hamas official told *Reuters* the group accepted the UN cease-fire resolution, and was ready to negotiate over the details.[24]

On June 12, day 250 of the war, Hamas leaders told Arab mediators that they want Israeli forces to withdraw from territory alongside Egypt by the end of the first week after a deal is signed, and to completely withdraw from Gaza and announce a permanent cease-fire before the group released additional hostages in a second phase. Hearing this, Blinken blamed Hamas for prolonging the war, noting that Hamas waited nearly two weeks and then proposed more changes, a number of which went beyond positions it had previously taken and accepted. As a result, he declared, "the war that Hamas started on October 7th, with its barbaric attack on Israel and on Israeli civilians, will go on. More people will suffer. More Palestinians will suffer; more Israelis will suffer." Concomitantly, a UN report accused Israel and Hamas of committing war crimes and crimes against humanity on and since October 7. The report was published by a commission formed in 2021 by the UN Human Rights Council to investigate human rights violations in Israel and the Palestinian territories.[25]

He same day, the IDF announced that overnight a Hezbollah command and control center in southern Lebanon, which was used to direct terror attacks against Israeli territory from southeastern Lebanon in recent months, was struck by the IAF. As part of the strike, Sami Taleb Abdullah, the commander of the Nasr Unit in the Hezbollah and one of Hezbollah's most senior commanders in southern Lebanon, was eliminated. Hezbollah fired 215 rockets, the most it had launched at Israel in a single day since cross-border hostilities broke out eight months ago, as part of its retaliation for an Israeli strike which killed Abdullah and three others of its operatives. The US military urged a de-escalation in rising tensions between Israel and Lebanon, and noted that US Defense Secretary Lloyd Austin had raised the matter in a call with his Israeli counterpart on Tuesday." "We don't want to see a wider regional conflict and we do want to see a de-escalation of tensions in the region," Pentagon spokesperson Sabrina Singh told a news briefing. Yet, the next day, the IDF declared that over forty rockets and five explosive drones were launched by Hezbollah across the Galilee as far south as Safed and in the northern and central Golan Heights, triggering multiple warning sirens during the day and igniting fifteen fires in several locations.

The reaction of those Israelis suffering the massive, relentless barrage was swift and harsh. Moshe Davidovich, head of the Mateh Asher Regional Council, charged, "The North is attacked continuously and non-stop. The residents of the north are used as cannon fodder for Nasrallah's whims, and the Israeli government is falling asleep while standing." Lobby 1701, a group representing thousands living in the north, responded "The residents of the north are all awed by the government's abandonment, neglect, and cowardice. If Israel is burning, Lebanon should be burning. This is the only equation that should concern the government."[26]

A far larger issue of contention in Israel surfaced as the result of the Knesset vote on Monday night granting wholesale IDF exemptions for ultra-Orthodox men (haredim) from military service. Hundreds of parents whose children serve as combat soldiers in the IDF sent an open letter to Defense Minister Gallant and IDF Chief of Staff Halevi, criticizing the Knesset's decision by a vote of 63–57 along strict coalition-opposition lines to approve the law, proposed in a draft bill from 2022. "We are letting our fighting children know they must stop the fighting right now, put down their weapons and return home immediately," they wrote, adding that "We will not sacrifice our children on the altar of public corruption." On June 13, a *Jerusalem Post* editorial endorsed this view, thundering "Talk about parliamentary tone deafness! Talk about being out of step with the mood of the country!" It then emphasized the critical impact of October 7:[27]

> With the country engaged in its longest war since the War of Independence, the morale of soldiers, reservists, and their families needs to be bolstered.
>
> October 7 imposed the realization that a fence with state-of-the-art hi-tech bells and whistles was not enough, that it neither deterred the enemy nor protected the country's civilians. Soldiers, lots of them, were needed for that.

As a result, what seemed like a workable option in 2022 to enable recruitment of a minimum number of haredim is completely outdated and obsolete in 2024 as the needs of the army, and the country, have dramatically changed. What in the past was necessary for the creation of a more equitable society—that everyone carry the burden of defense—is now an existential matter.

As for Hamas, it staunchly refused the Israeli demand to exile the terrorists, not even to the Gaza Strip, and demanded that they be returned to their place of origin, including Judea and Samaria. Perhaps not surprisingly, the *Wall Street Journal* reported that support for Hamas as rulers in Gaza fell from fifty-two to forty-six percent over the past three months, according to a survey at the end of May by the Palestinian Center for Policy and Survey Research of more than 700 residents of the enclave. In the West Bank, the trend was reversed, with seventy-one percent of Palestinians surveyed supporting Hamas's continued rule in Gaza, up from sixty-four percent in the previous poll. Mkhaimar Abusada, associate professor of political science at Al-Azhar University in Gaza and now based in Cairo, said the current level of public criticism, including on social media, of Hamas was unprecedented, stemming from the perception that Hamas was detached from the everyday suffering of Gazans. "Maybe 80 percent of Palestinians in the West Bank and diaspora love Hamas, something that gave them honor or dignity, but for someone who lives in Gaza and is paying the price, it's a totally different story," he said. Nonetheless, despite Hamas's waning popularity in Gaza, it was still by far the most popular Palestinian political party in Gaza and the West Bank. More than two thirds of those polled said they supported the October 7 attacks.[28]

Hamas spokesperson and political bureau member Osama Hamdan claimed on Thursday that "no one has an idea" how many of the 120 hostages still being held by the group were alive, and that any deal to release them must include guarantees of a permanent cease-fire and the complete withdrawal of Israeli forces from Gaza. He also called the October 7 terror attacks "a reaction against the occupation." When Hamdan was asked about the abuse the hostages faced while in captivity, he directed the blame to Israel's bombing in Gaza. He also falsely claimed that released hostages, after looking at photos of before and after their release, "were better than before."

IDF Southern Command chief Maj. Gen. Yaron Finkelman, however, declared to troops of the Givati, 401st, and Commando Brigades in a situation assessment in Rafah, that "the [Israeli army's] plan is clear," and he vowed to "continue to move forward until we obtain all our objectives." Up north, with dozens of rockets fired in the third day of Hezbollah barrages, Gantz responded on Friday, "If Hezbollah doesn't stop attacking, Lebanon should burn."[29]

During the last week, Commando Brigade Combat Team, operating under the 162nd Division, raided terrorist infrastructure, eliminated terrorists, and located many weapons above and below ground in the area of Rafah, the IDF reported Saturday. In cooperation with the Yahalom Unit, soldiers located large quantities of weapons including RPG missiles, arms, explosives, grenades, and other military equipment. The cost continued to be heavy, with eight soldiers of Combat Engineering Corps's Battalion 601 killed early that morning near Rafah, after their Armored Personnel Carrier (APC) drove over an explosive device and caught fire, two reservists killed in northern Gaza, and another who succumbed to his wounds. As for the northern front, CBS News reported that US officials feared tensions between Israel and Hezbollah could erupt into a full-scale war. Some said they interpreted the recent further-reaching Israeli strikes as "preparing the battlefield for a sweeping assault" into Lebanon by the Israeli army.[30]

The IDF Spokesperson's Unit announced on June 16 that, as part of ongoing efforts by Israel to increase the volumes of humanitarian aid entering the Gaza Strip and following additional related discussions with the UN and international organizations, a local, tactical pause of military activity for humanitarian purposes would take place starting yesterday from 8:00 a.m. until 7:00 p.m. every day until further notice along the road that led from the Kerem Shalom Crossing to the Salah al-Din Road and then northwards. Just over an hour later, after Netanyahu called it "unacceptable" and ordered for the decision to be reversed, IDF spokesman Hagari clarified that "there is no cessation of fighting in the southern Gaza Strip, and the fighting in Rafah continues." In addition, he emphasized: "The axis carrying the goods will be open during the day, in coordination with international organizations, for the transportation of humanitarian aid only."[31]

Brig.-Gen. (res.) Moshe Edri, the director of the Tekuma (Revival) Authority which had overseen the return of many residents to their homes or intermediate dwellings, received government authorization to extend to August 15 the state-funded stay in hotels for residents evacuated from their homes in the "Gaza Envelope." "Approximately 70 percent of the residents of the area have returned to their homes in recent months," the prime minister's office said. On April 17, the Israeli government had unveiled a five-year $5 billion strategic plan to "rebuild the communities in the western Negev." Edri added: "The Hamas terrorists sought to uproot us. We will uproot them and deepen our roots. We will build the Land of Israel and safeguard our state." As for the draft of haredim into the army, IDF chief Halevi, calling it a "clear need," announced the future creation of an ultra-Orthodox battalion defending a sector of the Jordan Valley and a sector in Judea and Samaria. "Every such battalion that we establish, an ultra-Orthodox battalion, decreases the need for the deployment of many thousands of reservists thanks to the mandatory service people," Halevi said. These steps did not halt anti-government protesters from blocking major highways across central Israel on Sunday morning, part of a "week of resistance" against the Netanyahu coalition. Another demonstration took place in a branch of the Interior Ministry in Tel Aviv, where protesters called for the public to stop paying taxes as an act of protest.[32]

Netanyahu announced to his ministers on Sunday that he decided to dissolve the War Cabinet and to hold the relevant discussions in the broader Security Cabinet instead. However, those close to him predicted that he would hold consultations with a smaller forum, similar to the War Cabinet, while decisions would be made in the Security Cabinet. By doing this, Netanyahu absolved himself of National Security Minister Itamar Ben-Gvir's demands to join the War Cabinet after the National Unity Party left the government. That evening, Israel's Diplomatic Security Cabinet voted eight to one, with one abstaining, to adopt Netanyahu's proposal concerning strengthening the Palestinian Authority, "while demanding that it cease its anti-Israel activity in the international legal-diplomatic arena, the incitement in its media and education system, the payments to the families of terrorists and murderers, and the illegal construction in Area C."[33]

The IDF, taking control of the Philadelphi Corridor, declared on Monday that its Division 162 had defeated half of Hamas's battalions in Rafah, including killing at least 550 terrorists, as well as destroyed around 200 tunnel shafts and eliminated the terror group's last major rocket inventory. Further, the IDF said that within a couple of weeks it would likely be in control of all of Rafah and that the final battles with the remaining two Hamas battalions in parts of Tel al-Sultan and the eastern part of Shabura were already underway. It also eliminated Muhammad Mustafa Ayoub, a key operative in the Rocket and Missile Department of Hezbollah's Nasr Unit. Nonetheless, thousands of Israelis took to the streets of Jerusalem to call for elections and the immediate return of hostages held in Gaza in a demonstration that followed Netanyahu's decision to dissolve his war cabinet.[34]

Up north, intensified cross-border fire from Lebanon's Hezbollah into Israel could trigger serious escalation, IDF spokesman Hagari said, adding that such an escalation "could have devastating consequences for Lebanon and the entire region." Biden's Mideast special envoy Amos Hochstein met in Israel with senior Israeli officials before heading to Lebanon in an attempt to de-escalate tensions between Israel and Hezbollah. Meeting with Netanyahu and Herzog, he claimed that the solution did not have to be based on the UN Resolution 1701,[35] but could be resolved if Hezbollah moved ten kilometers from the Lebanon border with Israel. Further, he warned that war with Hezbollah could lead to a wide-scale Iranian attack on Israel of a kind that would be difficult for Israel's defense systems to repel, in concert with possible wide-scale fire by Hezbollah from Lebanon. Arab media reported that Hochstein brought the Lebanese president and other government officials a sharp message from Israel that they must "get a move on" and enter negotiations before escalation develops. In the last forty-eight hours, however, Hezbollah launched no rockets or drones from Lebanon to Israel, a rare quiet which the IDF attributed to the Muslim Eid al-Adha holiday and Hochstein's visit.[36]

As the Biden administration increased pressure on Israel to avoid an all-out war with Hezbollah, displaced residents of the northern border region said they would not return to their homes unless the terror group's military capabilities are crippled by an IDF operation. About 56,000 northern Israelis had evacuated their homes after the Hamas terror attack and the war it spawned in Gaza, as Hezbollah intensified its strikes. That included nearly all of Kiryat Shmona's 24,000 residents. Some one thousand residents of northern cities and towns, who had been evacuated from their homes for more than eight months, signed an open letter to Netanyahu on June 18 urging him to take decisive military action against Hezbollah. For his part, Netanyahu expressed astonishment at moves from the White House to hold up munition shipments to Israel during the war against Hamas. "Secretary Blinken assured me on his recent visit that the administration was working day and night to remove these bottlenecks. I certainly hope that's the case. It should be the case." The same day, a Biden administration plan to sell $18 billion worth of F-15 fighter jets to Israel moved forward once two top Democratic holdouts in Congress signed off on the deal after facing intense pressure from the administration and pro-Israel advocates.[37]

Two revelations that Tuesday regarding the period before Hamas's assault on October 7 against Israel's southern communities near Gaza merited further attention. First, sources in Gaza said that Hamas had prepared a plan before that attack in which two of its battalions would be a governing force in Gaza after the war. One battalion in Deir al-Balah in central Gaza and another one in Khan Younis in the south were reportedly given orders not to participate in fighting as much as possible during the war. The Khan Younis battalion moved south to Rafah under civilian cover during the Israeli incursion there with terror operatives assimilating into the local populace. With the end of the Israeli military's operations in Khan Younis, the terrorists came back from Rafah. More worrisome to the IDF, a document based on information from its military intelligence 8200 unit, including details of Hamas's plan for a massive cross-border attack on Israel and taking 200–250 hostages, had been brought to the attention on September 19 of at least some senior intelligence officials in the Southern Command but apparently ignored. Responding to the Kan News broadcaster, the IDF did not acknowledge the document, but said it was investigating the failures that led to the massacre and would present them "transparently to the public."[38]

Despite publicly pledging that Washington's commitment to Israel's security was "ironclad," the Biden administration, according to a *Wall Street Journal* exclusive on June 19, was reportedly holding up a critical sale at $18 billion of 50 F-15 fighter jets to the Israeli Air Force, one of the largest in recent history. This, even though issues potentially holding up the transfer had already been resolved. Presumably connected, the White House canceled a critical, high-level US-Israel strategic meeting on Iran's nuclear capacities that was scheduled for Thursday after Netanyahu released a video on Tuesday claiming the United States was withholding military aid, two American officials told Axios's Barak Ravid. Biden's top advisers were enraged by the video, a message US envoy Hochstein delivered personally to Netanyahu in a meeting hours after it was published, saying that the prime minister had "exaggerated" and caused anger at the top levels of the administration.[39]

In Gaza, Israeli tanks supported by the air force pushed deeper into the western part of Rafah, killing eight people, local residents and Palestinian medics told *Reuters*. The UN Environment Programme estimated that the war to date had destroyed over sixty percent of the Strip's water infrastructure, creating some forty million tons of building debris, which contained toxic materials. Separately, alongside investigations from the UN's own Famine and Review Committee and two Columbia University professors that there was no mass starvation in Gaza, Haim Goldich, Kan 11 News reporter in Jerusalem, published footage from the Zaytun area proving that much of the humanitarian aid products which entered Gaza ended up in the hands of terrorists. "At the end of the day," US Assistant Secretary for Near Eastern Affairs Barbara M. Leaf spoke of Sinwar to reporters, "there's one guy ten stories below the ground: a psychopath, messianic in his own belief that he has established himself in history, and [he believes that] there's a sunk cost of having lost thousands of fighters and carnage in Gaza." In an interview with Israel's Channel 13 News, IDF spokesman Hagari went further: "The idea of destroying Hamas is simply throwing sand in the eyes of the public... Hamas is an idea, Hamas is a political party... whoever thinks we can eliminate Hamas is mistaken."[40]

Still, Hezbollah remained the far greater threat. Since October 8, it had fired more than 5,000 rockets, anti-tank missiles, and suicide drones at Israeli border communities. Unlike Hamas, Hezbollah possessed a wide range of sophisticated, Iranian-made missiles, estimated at over 150,000, capable of striking anywhere in Israel with deadly precision. Following a two-day lull in hostilities, Hezbollah resumed its attacks on Tuesday afternoon, launching three "suspicious aerial targets" toward towns in the Upper Galilee, the IDF declared. The same day, Hezbollah published a video captured by a surveillance UAV of the Haifa Port, one of Israel's most important commercial shipping gateways. On Wednesday, the IDF said more than ten rockets were launched from Lebanon at Israel's Upper Galilee region, two anti-tank missiles were fired at the northern city of Metula, and fifteen rockets were fired at the northern Israeli city of Kiryat Shmona. Hezbollah Secretary-General Hassan Nasrallah, who had declared after IDF forces left southern Lebanon in May 2000 that Israel was "weak as a spider's web" despite its nuclear weapons, stated in a televised address that "an invasion of the Galilee [in Israel's north] remains on the table if the fighting escalates"; Hezbollah was not seeking a major confrontation but would fight it with "no rules" and "no ceilings." In turn, head of the IDF's Northern Command Maj. Gen. Ori Gordin and Operations Directorate Chief Maj. Gen. Oded Basiuk approved offensive battle plans should Israel engage in an all-out war with Lebanon if diplomacy between Israel and Lebanon failed. The IDF announced that it was "accelerating the readiness of the forces on the ground" even as it continued to strike Hezbollah targets and launch sites in southern Lebanon.[41]

IDF aircraft continued to conduct precise and targeted strikes, eliminating in northern Gaza Ahmed Hassan Salame Alsauarka, a squad commander in Hamas's Nukhba Forces who carried out attacks on communities in southern Israel on October 7. In southern Lebanon, a strike killed Fadel Ibrahim, commander of Hezbollah operations in the Jouaiyya area. Jim Risch (R., Ida.), a senior member of the Senate's powerful Foreign Relations Committee, took to the Senate floor to lambaste the White House for interfering with Israel's ongoing war against Hamas, most recently the reported freezing of a planned sale of F-15 fighter jets, and demanded it "get out of the way." *Per contra*, White House Advisor John Kirby responded to Netanyahu's accusatory video of June 18: "Those comments were deeply disappointing and certainly vexing to us given the amount of support that we have and will continue to give." As for the Israeli hostages still held in Gaza, the *Wall Street Journal*, citing US officials and based partly on Israeli intelligence, stated on June 20 that the number still alive was potentially just fifty. If true, it would mean that sixty-six of the hostages yet in Gaza may be dead—a full twenty-five more than the fifty-one hostages who Israel had publicly acknowledged as dead. Most of the Palestinians wishing to leave besieged Rafah for Egypt found it nearly impossible, a *New York Times* investigation revealing that the Hala organization had charged most Gazans older than sixteen years $5,000, and most of those younger than sixteen half that, $2,500, to coordinate their exit.[42]

Biden envoy for the Israeli-Lebanese conflict Hochstein raised the alert level in Israel on Wednesday when he announced that his efforts toward agreement between Israel and Hezbollah had reached a dead end. Hezbollah continued to carry out their plans despite having more than 350 of their terrorists killed, over twenty-five rockets fired from Lebanon at northern Israel in the last day. Israel was utterly unprepared for a war with Hezbollah and for the toll such a conflict could take on the country's power infrastructure, the CEO of a company that manages and oversees Israel's electrical systems on behalf of the government declared on Thursday. The country's Religious Services Minister Michael Malkieli said his ministry was preparing itself for cases of mass burial due to possible war in northern Israel. US officials had raised concerns that Israel's air defenses in northern Israel, including the Iron Dome system, would be overwhelmed if there were a full-blown war between Israel and Hezbollah, according to a report by CNN. Netanyahu warned in closed conversations with senior American government officials that a delay in American arms shipments to Israel would lead to a situation where an all-out war with Hezbollah would be imminent, *Yisrael Hayom* reported on June 21. According to the report, in the last three months, senior officials in the Israeli defense system had been warning of a significant slowdown in arms shipments.[43]

Gaza residents and Israel's army said Friday that the IDF attacked areas across the Strip and engaged in close-quarter combat with Hamas fighters. Israel's advance was now said to be focusing on two areas: Rafah and the area surrounding Deir al-Balah in central Gaza. According to the Palestinian Red Crescent, eighteen Palestinians were killed and thirty-five were wounded in an Israeli strike on tents for displaced people in Rafah. The Israeli army said it destroyed a Palestinian Islamic Jihad rocket launch site on Thursday in the humanitarian zone in Khan Younis and killed a Hamas drone operator. The US military's floating pier off Gaza, following repairs to the $230 million structure, resumed bringing in humanitarian aid, the Pentagon announced. According to US Central Command, 656 tons of aid had been unloaded since the temporary pier was re-anchored. In Washington, nearly seventy Democratic lawmakers urged the Biden administration to consider opening pathways for Palestinians to obtain refugee status in the United States, particularly those with family already in the country.[44]

On day 260 of the war, the IDF attempted to eliminate Ra'ad Sa'ad, considered to be Hamas's fourth-highest commander who served as head of the terror group's operations division. Sa'ad, also known as Abu Ma'ad, was struck when the building where he was hiding in Gaza City's Al-Shati refugee camp exploded. Hamas's Information Ministry said at least forty-two people were killed in two separate air strikes, one in the al-Shati camp and one in the Tuffah neighborhood in the city's center. Up north, an IDF drone strike in the Beqaa Valley killed Ayman Ghatma, a weapons supplier to Hamas and Jamaa Islamiya, a branch of the Muslim Brotherhood in Lebanon which was involved in several attacks against Israel since the beginning of the war. CNN reported US officials raised concerns that Israel's air defenses in the north, including the Iron Dome system, would be overwhelmed if a full-blown war with Hezbollah erupted. At the same time, a senior Biden administration official who spoke with CNN said US officials told an Israeli delegation in Washington that, in the event of a full-out war with Hezbollah, the United States was prepared to back Israel and offer security assistance. Meanwhile, as on past Saturday evenings, tens of thousands protested in Tel Aviv and in several other locations across Israel, including Jerusalem, Caesarea, Haifa, and Be'er Sheva, against the Netanyahu coalition and for a deal that would release the hostages still held in Gaza.[45]

The same day, a sixty-seven-year-old Israeli named Amnon Muchtar was killed in the West Bank city of Qalqilya, where he regularly visited to buy vegetables and visit friends. Even more significant, Moshe Phillips pointed out in *Yisrael Hayom*, last week Hamas terrorists standing within the municipal boundaries of Tulkarm, a Palestinian Authority-governed city, unleashed a barrage of gunfire aimed at the nearby Israeli town of Bat Hefer, less than twelve miles from the coastal city of Netanya. Then they posted a video of the shooting on social media. It was the third such shooting attack on Bat Hefer in two weeks. Similar attacks recently targeted Kibbutz Meirav, which is next to the PA city of Jenin. Once again, terrorists within the boundaries of the city were able to shoot into an Israeli community without ever having to go beyond the borders of their PA-ruled area. Palestinian terrorists of Tulkarm also remotely detonated explosives near the Samaria security fence, intending to draw IDF forces to the scene, where they could be ambushed, according to the military.

Although the PA, with a huge police and security force of 60,000 men, was mandated by the Oslo Accords to combat terrorists, it continually refused to do so; consequently, the shooters in Tulkarm and Jenin went on their way unscathed. At present, with the PA not a sovereign state, the IDF has entered when needed to counter terrorists. If, however, terrorists shooting at nearby Israeli areas did so from an independent Palestinian state, Israel would be crossing an international border if it attempted to capture enemy forces. This growing reality in the West Bank has led a clear majority of Israelis to oppose a two-state solution.[46]

Overnight, Hezbollah released a psychological warfare video in which leader Nasrallah threatened that "in case an inclusive war is imposed on Lebanon, the resistance will fight without restraints, without rules, without limits." It published a second video claiming to show satellite footage of Israeli military and strategic facilities such as the Haifa oil refineries, Ben-Gurion Airport, and the Ashdod Port. Hezbollah was storing "huge quantities" of Iranian weapons inside the International Airport in Beirut, the *Telegraph* reported on Sunday, increasing residents' fear that the airport would become a legitimate military target. Several drones crossed into Israel from Lebanon, one close to a facility owned by Israeli weapons manufacturer Rafael. In response, the IAF struck Hezbollah targets in southern Lebanon. Thousands of fighters from Iran-backed groups in the Middle East were ready to come to Lebanon to join Hezbollah in its battle with Israel if the simmering conflict escalated into a full-blown war, the AP reported. More than 100,000 Lebanese residents were fleeing the country over anxiety that a war between Israel and Hezbollah could lead to the collapse of the state, as the country was already mired in a deep political and economic crisis. For its part, the Israeli Embassy in the United States published a video stating: "Since October 7, thousands of rockets, missiles, and explosive drones have been launched from Lebanon toward Israel. Make no mistake: We will not allow Hezbollah to terrorize the people of Israel."[47]

On other fronts, the IDF said that its 162nd Division captured munitions, destroyed tunnel shafts, and demolished a Hamas training complex in Rafah, while the 99th division continued to operate in the central Gaza Strip. Israeli tanks advanced to the edge of the Muwasi refugee camp in the northwest of Rafah in fierce fighting with Hamas, Gazan residents told *Reuters*. An IAF strike eliminated Muhammad Salah, who commanded a number of Hamas terrorist squads that worked on developing weapons. An Israeli source familiar with the hostage release and cease-fire talks told *Haaretz* that Hamas leader Sinwar "wants a war in the north, which is why he won't lead any moves for reaching a cease-fire." In Judea and Samaria, the IDF arrested thirteen suspects. The Israeli government extended for three months the temporary order raising the exemption age from army reserve duty by one year. (The temporary order was supposed to expire at the end of June, four months after it had been first approved.) Defense Minister Gallant headed to Washington on Sunday for a whirlwind visit whose main aim was to get the United States to unfreeze a shipment of heavy-duty bombs it had been withholding from Israel. "The meetings with the senior government officials are critical for the future of the war," he said before departing. "During these meetings, I plan to discuss developments in Gaza and Lebanon. We are prepared for any action that may be required in Gaza, Lebanon, and in additional areas."[48]

Early in the war, Gallant had publicly outlined a three-phase battle plan for Gaza. That included intense airstrikes against Hamas targets and infrastructure; a period of ground operations aimed at "eliminating pockets of resistance"; and a third phase that would create "a new security reality for the citizens of Israel." He said over the weekend that his meetings in Washington would feature discussion of "the transition to 'Phase C' in Gaza" and the intensive phase of Israel's war against Hamas is "about to end."

Echoing that line, Netanyahu said in a rare Sunday night interview on Israeli television that after the operation in Rafah, Israel would keep "mowing the lawn"—a term long used in Israeli security circles to denote the use of force aimed at curtailing the re-growth of militant organizations. He was willing to accept a partial deal with Hamas, during which some hostages held in Gaza would be released but was committed to carrying on with the war after the pause in fighting. (Following a backlash from some hostage families, Netanyahu said in the Knesset that he was "committed to the Israeli proposal laid out" by US President Biden for a deal.) The prime minister added that he would not agree to any deal that involved Hamas's survival as the ruling party in Gaza. Polls showed strong support among Israel's right-wing for re-establishing Israeli settlements in Gaza, which were evacuated by Israel in 2005, but Netanyahu said the idea was "not realistic and doesn't serve the aims of the war." Netanyahu's remarks, following Gallant's, were the latest suggestion by senior Israeli officials that the war could soon enter a period of change.[49]

The day Gallant landed in Washington, US Air Force General Charles Brown, chairman of the Joint Chiefs of Staff, warned publicly that Washington would have a hard time aiding Israel in the event of a war against Hezbollah. According to Brown, Iran will provide significantly more support to Hezbollah than it provided to Hamas, "particularly if they felt that Hezbollah was being significantly threatened." He also warned that due to the type of weapons Hezbollah uses, the United States would not be able to provide the same level of assistance to Israel during the war. Moreover, triggering a broader war could put US forces in the region in danger. "From our perspective, based on where our forces are, the short range between Lebanon and Israel," Brown asserted, "it's harder for us to be able to support them in the same way we did back in April" when Iran launched a major missile and drone barrage at Israel. *Jerusalem Post* senior military correspondent Yonah Jeremy Bob found the statement shocking, "publicly undermining the viability of a military threat which could get Hezbollah to agree to a diplomatic deal seems to do little right now."[50]

The Biden administration in recent months removed emergency procedures that were in place to fast-track weapons to Israel in the early months of the war, an American official familiar with the matter told the *Times of Israel* on Sunday. The revelation helped explain the claim Netanyahu began making the previous week that the United States had been withholding weapons shipments to Israel. Washington denied the assertion, explaining that it had only withheld one shipment of heavy bombs because it was concerned Israel would use them in the densely populated city of Rafah. In recent months, the United States resumed its normal procedures for weapons transfers, including various Congressional authorizations. The American official added on condition of anonymity that the move coincided with a significant slowdown in the IDF's operations in Gaza, along with concern in Washington about a potential Israeli preemptive offensive against Hezbollah in Lebanon that could lead to a regional war.[51]

In a statement published after Gallant's meeting on Monday with Blinken, State Department spokesperson Matthew Miller said the two "discussed ongoing efforts to achieve a ceasefire in Gaza that secures the release of all hostages and alleviates the suffering of the Palestinian people. The Secretary emphasized the need to take additional steps to protect humanitarian workers in Gaza and deliver assistance throughout Gaza in full coordination with the United Nations." Blinken also "updated Minister Gallant on ongoing diplomatic efforts to advance security, governance, and reconstruction in Gaza during a post-conflict period and emphasized the importance of that work to Israel's security," said Miller. "He also underscored the importance of avoiding further escalation of the conflict and reaching a diplomatic resolution that allows both Israeli and Lebanese families to return to their homes. Secretary Blinken reaffirmed the United States' ironclad commitment to Israel's security," concluded the State Department spokesperson. Gallant said to Blinken: "The eyes of our enemies and our friends are looking at the relationship between Israel and the United States—we must quickly resolve our issues, that's how we get our goals and weaken our enemies."[52]

Meanwhile, a spike of antisemitic attacks, many related to pro-Hamas protests, took place across the globe. A twelve-year-old Jewish boy and his two-year-old sibling were victims of an attempted kidnapping in London's

Stamford Hill on June 13. A twelve-year-old girl was raped on June 15 by adolescent boys in a Paris suburb because she was Jewish and reportedly said "disparaging things about Palestine." On June 23, ISIS launched simultaneous attacks in Dagestan, Russia, against a church—where the pastor had his throat slit—and a synagogue that was burnt to the ground; more than a dozen police were killed or wounded. A pro-Hamas mob on Sunday, with many faces masked by keffiyehs, assaulted Jews outside the Adas Torah synagogue in western Los Angeles who were attending an Israeli Real Estate Seminar. The attackers used pepper spray and bear spray; some of their victims required medical treatment. "Intimidating Jewish congregants is dangerous, unconscionable, antisemitic, and un-American," Biden said in a statement posted on Monday on social media. "Americans have a right to peaceful protest. But blocking access to a house of worship—and engaging in violence—is never acceptable." A group tracking antisemitism in Germany said on June 25 that it had recorded an overall increase of more than eighty percent in incidents last year, with well over half of the total coming after the Hamas October 7 attack.[53]

New York City witnessed a pronounced escalation. On June 12, people purporting to be pro-Palestinian activists hurled red paint at the homes of top leaders at the Brooklyn Museum, including its Jewish director, Anne Pasternak, whom they damned as a "white-supremacist Zionist." The paint attacks came the same week that pro-Palestinian groups held a large demonstration outside a New York City exhibition memorializing victims of the October 7 Hamas attack on the Tribe of Nova music festival. The violently anti-Israel group Within Our Lifetime called the memorial tribute to the victims "Zionist propaganda" and dismissed the music festival, where hundreds died, as "a rave next to a concentration camp." One group of protesters riding a subway train to the demonstration outside the Nova exhibit chanted "Raise your hands if you're a Zionist," at their fellow passengers, followed by "This is your chance to get out." Late last May, hundreds of protesters had marched on the Brooklyn Museum, briefly setting up tents in the lobby, defaced the iconic OY/YO sculpture on the plaza with pro-Palestinian graffiti, and unfurled a "Free Palestine" banner from the roof before police moved in to make dozens of arrests. Within Our Lifetime said the museum was "deeply invested in and complicit" in Israel's military actions in Gaza through its leadership, trustees, corporate sponsors and donors—a claim museum officials denied. Similar protests had occurred since October at other New York City museums.[54]

On the morning of June 25, a full, extended nine-judge panel of Israel's High Court of Justice ordered a full draft of haredim into the IDF and the freezing of all funds for institutions that did not comply starting April 1. The court ruled that a government decision from June 2023 instructing the army not to begin drafting eligible ultra-Orthodox men—issued after the law allowing for blanket military service exemptions expired—was illegal, and therefore no grounds existed to continue the decades-long practice of granting them blanket exemptions from army service. The historic ruling could lead to new elections or, if not, a change in the political landscape on the issue of haredim in the IDF. Part of what had been so surprising about the hearing was that three of the most conservative voices, all religiously Orthodox—Justices Noam Sohlberg, Alex Stein, and Yael Wilner—were among the most aggressive critics of the government, joining their colleagues in asserting: "In the midst of a grueling war, the burden of inequality is harsher than ever and demands a solution." Their conclusion reflected the cataclysmic October 7 Hamas attack and its aftermath, which threw into sharp relief the IDF's need for more manpower. Within hours of the ruling, Deputy Attorney General Gil Limon called for immediate implementation of the ruling with the drafting of 3,000 haredim above and beyond the 1,000 plus haredim who have been drafted in recent years, the number which the IDF said it could be immediately prepared to absorb at a hearing earlier in June before the court.[55]

The same day, IAF fighter jets eliminated in Gaza Fadi Al-Wadiya, who had developed and advanced the Islamic Jihad Wadiya's rocket array, and Wissam Abu Ashak, who was involved in smuggling weapons from Rafah for Hamas. While reconciliation talks between rival Palestinian factions Hamas and Fatah due to be held in China this month were delayed and no new date had been set according to *Reuters*, Hamas stood firm against global pressure that it accept Biden's proposed three-phase deal, stressing that any deal which did not guarantee a permanent ceasefire from the start "was not an agreement." Hamas leader Haniyeh released the statement after his sister was killed during an IDF airstrike in Gaza, accusing Israel of deliberately targeting her to pressure the group to take the deal. On other fronts, Israeli forces arrested twenty-four Palestinians during an operation overnight into Tuesday in several locations across the West Bank, and US officials warned Hezbollah that they might not be able to stop Israel from attacking Lebanon, whose overwhelmingly Arab population of over five million was currently grappling with severe political, economic and social crises. In New York City, more than 100 victims of the October 7 Hamas attacks sued seven current and former top UNRWA officials in the Southern District federal court, accusing them of knowing that Hamas siphoned off more than $1 billion from the agency to pay for, among other things, tunneling equipment and weapons that aided its attack on Israel on October 7.[56]

US Secretary of Defense Austin told his Israeli counterpart Gallant that war between Israel and Hezbollah "would be catastrophic for Lebanon, and it would be devastating for innocent Israeli and Lebanese civilians." According to the Pentagon, the two also discussed efforts to "surge more humanitarian aid into Gaza, and to stand together against Iranian and Iranian-supported attacks against Israel and destabilizing activities throughout the Middle East." The United States provided Israel with military aid worth approximately 6.5 billion dollars since the beginning of the war on October 7, the *Washington Post* reported. These understandings did not prevent US Ambassador to the United Nations Linda Thomas-Greenfield calling out the expansion of Jewish neighborhoods in Judea and Samaria as "an obstacle to the achievement of a two-state solution—the end state we all want to see." Speaking on June 25 at the monthly UN Security Council meeting on the Israeli-Palestinian file, she said the expansions were "inconsistent with international law," which "only serves to weaken Israeli security." The council also "cannot ignore" the record number of Palestinians killed in Judea and Samaria in 2023, or the "significant uptick in deadly" violence by "settlers," she added.[57]

In the larger Middle East context, Iran's intentions continued to be the US government's paramount concern. Washington sanctioned nearly fifty people and organizations that made up "multiple branches of a sprawling 'shadow banking' network" used by Iran's defense ministry and its Islamic Revolutionary Guard Corps "to gain illicit access to the international financial system and process the equivalent of billions of dollars since 2020," the US Treasury Department said on Tuesday. According to the US State Department, the "Iranian regime uses its profits to advance a wide range of destabilizing activities, including terrorism, lethal plotting and transnational repression; the development, procurement and proliferation of advanced weapons systems; extensive human rights abuses; and nuclear activities that lack any credible peaceful purpose." Israel and the United States also agreed to reschedule a high-level meeting on the Iranian threat that was canceled after Netanyahu had accused the Biden administration of withholding arms from Jerusalem, *Axios* reported. The decision reportedly came amid growing concern in Israel over Iran's efforts to weaponize components of its nuclear program.[58]

On Wednesday, Gallant warned that Israel was capable of taking Lebanon "back to the Stone Age" in any war with Hezbollah but stressed that his government preferred a diplomatic solution being pursued by the United States, *Reuters* reported. Gallant said he also discussed with US officials the need to resolve the "security situation in the north," insisting that Israel could not accept Hezbollah's "military formations" on the border with

Lebanon. "We do not want war, but we are preparing for every scenario," Gallant was quoted as having told reporters. In Khan Younis, IDF struck terrorists hiding on school campus after they used the school as a Hamas headquarters from which to direct activities against Israeli soldiers. The IDF started a re-invasion of the Shejaia neighborhood of Gaza City after finishing taking operational control there in January, killing dozens of terrorists who were hiding in UNRWA schools. Early Thursday morning, day 265 of the war, an Israeli soldier was killed and sixteen others were wounded, one in serious condition, by roadside bombs in the northern West Bank's Jenin refugee camp. That evening, about forty rockets were launched from Lebanon towards Safed (Tzfat) and the surrounding area. About half of the rockets were intercepted by the Iron Dome system; no casualties were reported, but damage was caused to property and fires broke out in several places.[59]

US officials warned Israel during meetings with Gallant that even a limited Israeli ground offensive in southern Lebanon could lead to a broad regional conflict involving Iran, regardless of whether Israel publicly declared it was not interested in one. The US Embassy in Beirut urged citizens to "strongly reconsider" travel to Lebanon, as "the security environment remains complex and can change quickly." This followed similar alerts from the governments of Germany and the Netherlands. Israel's State Comptroller Matan Engelman sent a letter to Netanyahu warning him that the country was not adequately prepared for evacuation of its northern residents if war with Hezbollah broke out. In the letter, Engelman stated "The unresolved reality, nine months into the war, at a time when tens of thousands of people from two areas of Israel are displaced from their homes, with the looming possibility of a war in the north, is unacceptable."[60]

On June 28, the IDF announced that its 98th Division launched an operation "above and below the ground" in Gaza City's Shejaiya neighborhood. *Haaretz* reported the same day Gallant saying at a security cabinet meeting that he told US officials Israel "isn't the one who wants war in the north," and that, if an agreement would be reached with Hezbollah including the withdrawal of the group's forces from the border, this "will be acceptable." The United States was moving its military assets closer to Israel and Lebanon in case it proved necessary to evacuate Americans from the region. The amphibious assault ship *USS Wasp* entered the eastern Mediterranean Sea that week as the United States positioned warships to try to keep fighting between Israel and Hezbollah in Lebanon from escalating into a wider war in the Middle East. In Jerusalem, the High Court of Justice ordered the state to respond within a month to a petition demanding the establishment of a state commission of inquiry into the events of October 7.[61]

Germany slammed the Israeli security cabinet's decision last night, announced by Finance Minister Smotrich on Thursday, to sanction the Palestinian Authority in response to Ramallah's support for steps against Jerusalem in international tribunals and for countries unilaterally recognizing a Palestinian state. "We condemn approval of new settlements and legalization of outposts," said a spokesperson for the German foreign ministry in Berlin. "Justifying this with the recognition of Palestine by some states is disturbing and cynical." "The conflict can only be solved with, not against a reformed PA; reject measures to weaken it," the spokesperson added. The European Union also condemned the decision, calling the move "another deliberate attempt at undermining peace efforts" and stressed that actions "weakening the Palestinian Authority must stop." Not surprisingly, a senior Palestinian Authority official concurred, rejecting the Israeli government's decision to legalize five West Bank outposts and impose sanctions on the PA, claiming the move was aimed at pursuing a "war of genocide" against Palestinians.[62]

The threat of Tehran's machinations remained on the surface. Iran's mission to the United Nations posted on X on Saturday that if Israel should "embark on full-scale military aggression, an obliterating war will ensue. All options, including the full involvement of all Resistance Fronts, are on the table." The Islamic Republic of Iran had so far installed four out of the eight clusters of advanced IR-6 centrifuges it said earlier this month it would quickly set up at its Fordow uranium-enrichment plant, the UN atomic watchdog said in a report, but had not yet brought them online. As for its Houthi proxy, the UN Security Council approved a resolution demanding that the terrorist rebel group halt all attacks on ships in the Red Sea and urged that the disruption to maritime security in a critical Middle East waterway be urgently addressed. In Israel's West Bank, a report citing senior officials in the Palestinian Authority security forces indicated that at the current rate of smuggling from Jordan with Iranian guidance, terrorist groups there would be able to launch rockets into Israel within a year, weapons far more sophisticated than the primitive projectiles launched from Jenin at the Afula and Bat Hefer areas on several occasions in the past year.[63]

The northern front gave Israel little respite. Three drones and dozens of missiles launched from Lebanon sparked fires in Israel's Western Galilee, while three anti-tank missiles struck the northern Israeli communities of Misgav Am and Tel-Hai. The Israeli army said it responded to these incidents with artillery fire on the launch sites. The IDF also said it struck Hezbollah sites Friday in the Jabal Safi area of south Lebanon, where surface-to-air missiles were launched at an Israel Air Force fighter, as well as other Hezbollah operational infrastructure in south Lebanon. "We aren't looking for a war [with Hezbollah], but we're ready for one," Gallant declared. An investigation by the *Financial Times* claimed that the IDF's operations in southern Lebanon were part of a plan to create a five-kilometer "dead zone" on the border. The report also stated that over 95,000 Lebanese had been displaced, as well as 60,000 Israelis, and that Israel had killed more Hezbollah commanders in this flare-up than died in the 2006 war. Denying that it was creating a buffer zone, the IDF claimed it was only pushing back Hezbollah in order to prevent persistent attacks on Israeli residents of the North.[64]

In Gaza, the Israeli army said dozens of terrorists were killed on Saturday in close-range combat and from the air in the Shejaiyeh neighborhood, and that its air force targeted tunnel shafts and other sites in southern Gaza's Rafah area. The pier built by the American military to bring aid to Gaza was removed ahead of a forecast of heavy seas, and the United States was considering not re-installing it unless aid began flowing to those who needed it, US officials said. The vast majority of the aid was still sitting in a storage yard due to the difficulty that agencies have had in moving it to where it is most needed in Gaza, and the storage area was almost full. As part of efforts to alleviate and strengthen the healthcare system and the medical response to the civilian population in Gaza, the passage of sixty-eight sick and injured children together with companions from the Gaza Strip was carried out on Thursday in coordination with officials of the US government, Egypt, and the international community. The facilitated passage was carried out via the Kerem Shalom Crossing of the Israeli Ministry of Defense's Land Crossing Authority for the children to travel for further medical treatment in Egypt and abroad, said the IDF Spokesperson's Unit.[65]

Netanyahu opened Sunday morning's Cabinet meeting by stating: "We are committed to fighting until we achieve all our objectives. We will not end the war until we achieve all our objectives." The IDF confirmed that Saeed al-Jaber, responsible for shooting and explosive attacks near Bat Hefer, had been eliminated in a drone attack in the Nur al-Shams refugee camp near the West Bank city of Tulkarm. A Palestinian Islamic Jihad commander who led terror cells and was involved in several attacks on Israeli civilians and soldiers in that area, he also had directed additional attacks and set up terrorist infrastructure. Among other things, al-Jaber was involved in the murder of Israeli Amnon Mukhtar on June 22 in Qalandia. Some relief for Gazans appeared with the news that humanitarian workers started moving tons of aid that piled up at the US-built pier off the Gaza coast, a day after it was shut down for the third time due to poor weather. At the same time, the Arab League's Assistant Secretary-General Hossam Zaki announced on Egyptian Al-Qahera News that the twenty-two member organization no longer classified Hezbollah as a terrorist group, viewed by experts as an attempt by Egypt to try a different approach and engage the Iran-backed militant group. Smotrich warned on Sunday of Iran's plan to "destroy" Israel, and he called to take immediate step to tackle it—including a "sharp, quick war" against Tehran's proxy in Leb+anon. The last day of the month ended then, as had all its eight predecessors, devoid of plausible settlement and final verdict.[66]

Endnotes

1 *Haaretz*, June 1, 2024.
2 Israel National News, June 1, 2024; *Haaretz*, June 1, 2024. The survey also examined what Israeli citizens thought of President Biden's policy towards the war. A majority (sixty) percent of Israelis said they disapproved of his handling of the war, while forty-one percent believed that Biden found the right balance between Israelis and Palestinians. When asked, "Do you trust Biden to correctly manage global affairs?," there was a ten-percent decline among Israelis who said yes, compared to last year.
3 Israel National News, June 2, 2024; *Jerusalem Post*, June 2, 2024; *Haaretz*, June 2, 2024; World Israel News, June 2, 2024; *Jerusalem Post*, June 5, 2024; JTA, June 3, 2024.
4 Israel National News. June 2, 2024; *Haaretz*, June 1, 2024; IDF News, June 2, 2024; *Jerusalem Post*, June 2, 2024.
5 *Haaretz*, June 3, 2024.
6 Israel National News, June 4, 2024; United with Israel, June 4, 2024; *Jerusalem Post*, June 4, 2024.
7 Alan Cullison, "Biden's Cease-Fire Plan Seeks to Push Hamas and Israel into a Deal Neither Wants," *Wall St. Journal*, June 4, 2024; *Haaretz*, June 4, 2024. Shortly after the *Time* interview was published, Biden walked back his comments about Netanyahu. "He's trying to work out a serious problem he has," the president said at the White House after a reporter asked him if he believed the Israeli prime minister was "playing politics with the war." Biden responded: "I don't think so." Ynet News, June 5, 2024.
8 *New York Times*, June 4, 2024; Israel National News, June 3, 2024; *Jerusalem Post*, June 3, 2024; *Haaretz*, June 4, 2024.
9 *Jerusalem Post*, June 4, 2024; *Haaretz*, June 3, 2024; Israel National News, June 4, 2024; JNS, June 3, 2024.
10 *Jerusalem Post*, June 5, 2024; *Haaretz*, June 4–5, 2024; *Wall St. Journal*, June 5, 2024.
11 Israel National News, June 5, 2024; *Reuters*, June 5, 2024; *Jerusalem Post*, June 5, 2024; AsiaOne, June 5, 2024.
12 Israel National News, June 5, 2024; IDF News, June 5, 2024; *Jerusalem Post*, June 5, 2024; *Haaretz*, June 5, 2024; Al Jazeera, June 5, 2024.
13 *Jerusalem Post*, June 6, 2024; *Wall St. Journal*, June 6, 2024.
14 *Wall St. Journal*, June 6, 2024; *Haaretz*, June 6, 2024; Israel National News, June 6, 2024; *Reuters*, June 6, 2024.
15 *Haaretz*, June 7, 2024; Yaakov Katz, "Can Hezbollah be Contained?," *Jerusalem Post*, June 7, 2024; *Times of Israel*, June 6, 2024.
16 *Wall St. Journal*, June 7, 2024; *Times of Israel*, June 7, 2024. This was the first time that Israel and Hamas were included on this list, joining the ranks of Russia, the Islamic State of Iraq and Syria (ISIS), Al-Qaeda, Boko Haram, Afghanistan, Iraq, Myanmar, Somalia, Syria, and

Yemen. Israel is believed to be the first democratic country included on the list. Last year, Russia was added to the list for the first time over its treatment of children in the war against Ukraine.

17 *Haaretz*, June 7, 2024; *Jerusalem Post*, June 7, 2024; AP, June 7, 2024; Israel National News, June 7, 2024. The Gaza Health Ministry stuck to the figure of 72–75 percent, but the AP study revealed that while women and children accounted for 64 percent of deaths in October in the immediate aftermath of the Hamas massacre of October 7, by April that figure had fallen to 34 percent. The total number of deaths also dropped.

18 *Times of Israel*, June 10, 2019; World Israel News, June 8, 2024. Another irony was the clandestine Israeli sale of military equipment to Tehran, which helped Iran from falling to the forces of Iraq's Saddam Hussein in a war, beginning in September 1980, that lasted eight years. Alex Winston, "Secret Deals and Shifting Alliances," *Jerusalem Post Magazine*, June 14, 2024. Ilan Ramon, who was added to the Operation Opera attack force at the last moment because of his familiarity with the task after having planned out the maps and fuel ranges, went on to become Israel's first astronaut. He perished in the February 1, 2003, Columbia Space Shuttle disaster which killed all seven crew members and destroyed the space shuttle. Returning to Israel from his training in the United States for the shuttle mission, Ramon had told a few IAF veterans of his thoughts before the 1981 attack: "My mother is an Auschwitz survivor who escaped with her shirt on her back. . . . I knew there was a chance that I would not make it back. . . . I remembered my origins and history and that of the Jewish people, and I thought, 'There's no way that I'm going to let that happen again, no matter what happens to me.' That's what helped me go on that mission." Ramon told the crowd that a discussion with a group of Holocaust survivors made him realize that "we are only a part of a bigger story. Even as Israelis, we are only a part of the Jewish people." *Jerusalem Post*, June 22, 2021.

19 Israel National News, June 8–9, 2024; *Washington Post*, June 14, 2024; *Haaretz*, June 8, 2024; *Al Jazeera*, June 8, 2024; *Jerusalem Post*, June 8, 2024; JNS, June 9–10, 2024; *Times of Israel*, June 8, 2024; *New York Times*, June 9, 2024; *Wall St. Journal*, 17, 2024. Al Jazeera and Palestinian Chronicle journalist June Abdallah Aljamal, a former spokesman for the Hamas-run labor ministry, was killed while reportedly attempting to prevent the rescue of the three male hostages, whom he had held captive in his apartment alongside family members.

20 Israel National News, June 9, 2024.

21 *Haaretz*, June 9, 2024; IDF News, June 9, 2024.

22 *Haaretz*, June 10, 2024; *Times of Israel*, June 10, 2024.

23 Israel National News, June 11, 2024; *Wall St. Journal*, June 11, 2024. In the Battle of Karbala on October 10, 680, or the 10th of Muḥarram (or ʿĀshūrāʾ), a small party led by al-Ḥusayn ibn ʿAlī, grandson of the Muslim Prophet Muhammad and son of ʿAlī, the fourth caliph, was defeated and massacred by an army sent by the Umayyad Caliph Yazīd I. The battle helped secure the position of the Umayyad dynasty, but among Shiite Muslims (followers of Ḥusayn) that date became an annual holy day of public mourning.

24 *Jerusalem Post*, June 11, 2024; *Wall St. Journal*, June 11, 2024; *Haaretz*, June 11, 2024.

25 *Wall St. Journal*, June 12, 2024; Israel National News, June 12, 2024; *Haaretz*, June 12, 2024.

26 *Haaretz*, June 12, 2024; *Reuters*, June 12, 2024; Israel National News, June 12–13, 2024; *Wall St. Journal*, June 12, 2024; *Jerusalem Post*, June 13, 2024.

27 *Haaretz*, June 11, 2024; *Jerusalem Post*, editorial, June 13, 2024.

28 Israel National News, June 13, 2024; *Wall St. Journal*, June 13, 2024. A more recent survey by the same organization found that 96 percent of Palestinians denied the Hamas October 7 massacre and 66 percent expressed support for the October 7 attack against Israel. Another 73 percent believed that Hamas made the right decision in launching the attack, and 79 percent of the respondents believed that Hamas would win the war—the highest rate since the beginning of the war. The data also showed that half of the residents of the Gaza Strip expected Hamas to win and return to power in the Strip after the war. Israel National News, June 14, 2024.

29 Israel National News, June 14, 2024; *Haaretz*, June 14, 2024.
30 Israel National News, June 15, 2024; *Haaretz*, June 15, 2024.
31 Israel National News, June 16, 2024; JNS, June 16, 2024; *Jerusalem Post*, June 16, 2024.
32 *Haaretz*, June 16, 2024.
33 *Washington Post*, June 17, 2024; *Times of Israel*, June 17, 2024.
34 *Jerusalem Post*, June 17, 2024; *Washington Post*, June 18, 2024.
35 UN Security Council Resolution 1701 was intended to resolve the 2006 Lebanon War. The resolution called for a full cessation of hostilities between Israel and Hezbollah, the withdrawal of Israeli forces from Lebanon to be replaced by Lebanese and UNIFIL forces deploying to southern Lebanon, and the disarmament of armed groups including Hezbollah. It emphasized Lebanon's need to fully exert government control and called for efforts to address the unconditional release of abducted Israeli soldiers. It also specified the creation of a demilitarized zone between Israel's northern border and the Litani River in Lebanon. Although it was unanimously approved by the United Nations Security Council on August 11, 2006, Hezbollah refused to accept the resolution and continued to maintain its forces south of the Litani River.
36 *Haaretz*, June 17–18, 2024; IDF News, June 17–18, 2024. One of the biggest Islamic holidays, this Feast of Sacrifice commemorates the Muslim Prophet Ibrahim's test of faith through slaughtering livestock and animals and distributing the meat to the poor. It draws upon the Quranic tale of Ibrahim's willingness to sacrifice his son Ismail as an act of obedience to God. Before he could carry out the sacrifice, God provided a ram as an offering. In the Jewish and Christian telling, the Prophet Abraham is ordered to kill his son Isaac, and a ram offering substitutes for the younger Isaac.
37 World Israel News, June 18, 2024; Israel National News, June 18, 2024; *New York Times*, June 18, 2024.
38 *Times of Israel*, June 18, 2024; Israel National News, June 18, 2024; JNS, June 18, 2024.
39 Israel National News, June 19, 2024; World Israel News, June 19, 2024; *Haaretz*, June 19, 2024.
40 *Haaretz*, June 19, 2024; IDF News, June 19, 2024; JNS, June 19, 2024; *Jerusalem Post*, June 18–19, 2024; *Times of Israel*, June 19, 2024. Hagari's remarks seemed to signal a rare, open dispute between the military and Netanyahu. Since the Hamas-led attack on October 7, Netanyahu repeatedly promised the Israeli public "absolute victory" over the Palestinian armed group, vowing that the war would not end until Israel destroyed Hamas's military and government. Netanyahu's office said on Wednesday following Hagari's remarks that the Israeli cabinet had set "the destruction of Hamas's military and governing capabilities" as one of the war's aims, and as such the Israeli military was "of course committed to this." Hagari indicated that it might take a long time to replace Hamas, saying that the group was "an idea" as well as a political movement that was "planted in people's hearts." But there was no path to weaken Hamas without an alternative, he repeated. "The political leadership must decide, and the Israel Defense Forces will execute," Hagari added. *New York Times*, June 19, 2024.
41 *Haaretz*, June 19, 2024; World Israel News, June 19, 2024.
42 Israel National News, June 20, 2024; *Wall St. Journal*, June 20, 2024; *New York Times*, June 20, 2024; World Israel News, June 19, 2024; *Haaretz*, June 20, 2024.
43 *Jerusalem Post*, June 20, 2024; World Israel News, June 19, 2024; Israel National News, June 21, 2024.
44 *Haaretz*, June 21, 2024.
45 Israel National News, June 22, 2024; *Jerusalem Post*, June 22, 2024; *Haaretz*, June 21–22, 2024.
46 Mosaic, June 22, 2024; JNS, June 24. 2024.
47 Israel National News, June 23. 2024; *Haaretz*, June 23, 2024; World Israel News, June 23, 2024; *Jerusalem Post*, June 23. 2024.

48 *Haaretz*, June 23, 2024; Israel National News, June 23, 2024; IDF News, June 23, 2024; *Times of Israel*, June 23, 2024
49 *New York Times*, June 24, 2024; *Wall St. Journal*, June 24, 2024; *Haaretz*, June 24, 2024.
50 Israel National News, June 24, 2024; *Haaretz*. June 24, 2024; *Jerusalem Post*, June 24, 2024. The Iran-backed terror group was said to respond by touting its ability to land heavy blows on Israel, while insisting that it, too, did not want all-out war. *Times of Israel*, June 25, 2024.
51 *Times of Israel*, June 24, 2024.
52 Israel National News, June 25, 2024; *Haaretz*, June 25, 2024.
53 World Israel News, June 20, 2024; *Jewish Chronicle*, June 18, 2024; JNS, June 24, 2024; *New York Times*, June 24, 2024; AP, June 25, 2024. In November 2023 Paul Kessler, a sixty-nine-year-old Jewish man, died when a young pro-Palestinian protester threw a megaphone at him during demonstrations between pro- and anti-Israeli stalwarts in Westlake Village, Ventura Country, in the greater Los Angeles area.
54 AP, June 13, 2024; *Jerusalem Post*, June 20, 2024.
55 *Jerusalem Post*, June 25, 2024; *Washington Post*, June 26, 2024.
56 Israel National News, June 25–26, 2024; *Jerusalem Post*, June 25, 2024; *Haaretz*, June 25, 2024; *New York Times*, June 25, 2024.
57 *Haaretz*, June 26, 2024; World Israel News, June 26, 2024.
58 JNS, June 26, 2024.
59 Israel National News, June 27, 2024; *Jerusalem Post*, June 27–28, 2024; *Times of Israel*, June 27, 2024.
60 *Haaretz*. June 27. 2024.
61 *Haaretz*, June 28, 2024.
62 *Times of Israel*, June 28, 2024; *Haaretz*, June 29, 2024.
63 *Reuters*, June 29, 2024; *Haaretz*, June 28, 2024; *Times of Israel*, June 27, 2024.
64 *Haaretz*, June 29, 2024; *Jerusalem Post*, June 28, 2024.
65 *Haaretz*, June 29, 2024; Israel National News, June 28, 2024.
66 Israel National News, June 30, 2024; *Haaretz*, June 30, 2024; Al-Monitor, July 1, 2024.

CHAPTER 4

... plus c'est la même chose

July opened with raids by the Commando Division brigade teams, Brigade 401, and the Yahalom Unit, under the command of Division 162, of a Palestinian Islamic Jihad outpost and, in the Tel-Sultan neighborhood of Rafah, the largest underground site in the Gaza Strip for the production of rocket parts and long-range rockets by the PIJ. While Israel released from detention fifty Palestinians including director Mohammad Abu Salmiya of Gaza's Al-Shifa Hospital (used by Hamas with his knowledge for storing weaponry), Netanyahu and Gallant saying they were not privy to a Shin Bet (Shabak, or ISA) senior director's decision, the IDF called on Palestinians to evacuate eastern Khan Younis neighborhoods. The Israeli army needed 10,000 soldiers immediately, declared Gantz. An editorial in *Haaretz* countered "Israel Must Avoid a Catastrophic Full-Scale War with Hezbollah." Spain asked to join South Africa's petition accusing Israel of genocide at the International Court of Justice. In turn, Smotrich remarked that he approved five new settlements in Judea and Samaria in response to countries unilaterally recognizing a Palestinian state.[1]

On July 2, day 270 of the war, the *New York Times* reported that top IDF generals were interested in a "cease-fire in Gaza even if it keeps Hamas in power for the time being." Six current and former security officials said they believed that a cease-fire with Hamas would be beneficial for several Israeli objectives: releasing the roughly 120 Israelis, both dead and alive, still held captive in Gaza; reaching a deal with Hezbollah to prevent a war on Israel's border with Lebanon; and giving the underequipped forces time to recuperate in case a war with Hezbollah did break out. A truce with Hamas could also make it easier to reach a deal with Hezbollah, according to the officials, most of whom spoke on the condition of anonymity. The military's attitude to a cease-fire reflected a major shift in its thinking over the past months as it became clearer that Netanyahu was refusing to articulate or commit to a postwar plan for Gaza. That decision had essentially created a power vacuum in the enclave which forced the military to go back and fight in parts of Gaza it had already cleared of Hamas fighters. In a statement after the article was published online, Netanyahu pushed back and said Israel would end the war "only after we have achieved all of its objectives, including the elimination of Hamas and the release of all of our hostages."[2]

In Gaza, the electric company started repairing electric wires that were damaged during the war, connecting them to Israel's grid to renew the operations of a water desalination and sewage plant west of Deir al-Balah. Israeli security officials said this was being done in conjunction with Jerusalem to prevent the outbreak of disease, adding that it was authorized and executed in line with the policy of expanding humanitarian measures in Gaza. Israel's government also pledged before the High Court of Justice that it would establish a system to allow the departure of very sick patients from Gaza via Egypt to receive medical treatment abroad. Parents of IDF female spotters killed and kidnapped on October 7 did not let up, vowing to fight until a state commission of inquiry into the events of the massacre was created. As for the northern front, Sheikh Naim Qassem, the deputy chief of Hezbollah, told the Associated Press that the only sure path to a cease-fire on the Lebanon-Israel border was a full cease-fire in Gaza.[3]

The next day, the IDF confirmed Lebanese reports that it had assassinated in a drone strike Muhammad Nimah Nasser, who commanded the Hezbollah unit in charge of the Beqaa Valley and the southeastern Syrian border. Hezbollah responded by launching 100 rockets at Israel's Upper Galilee. Gallant told soldiers near the Gaza border that the IDF "hits Hezbollah very hard every day," adding that Israel "will reach a state of full readiness to take whatever action is required in Lebanon or reach an agreement from a position of strength. We prefer the agreement, but if reality forces us, we will know how to fight." An Israeli soldier was killed in Gaza's Shujaiyeh neighborhood; an additional soldier was killed in a stabbing attack in Karmiel by an Arab Israeli citizen, who was shot dead. Biden would "likely" meet Netanyahu when the latter came to Washington to address Congress, the White House said.[4]

Hezbollah fired more than 200 rockets and 20 drones at northern Israel's Golan and Upper Galilee, responding to the assassination of senior commander Muhammad Nimah Nasser on Wednesday. An IDF officer was killed, and two reported wounded in that barrage; fires erupted as well from the rockets. The IDF retaliated with air strikes in southern Lebanon. It also hit two UNRWA schools in Gaza that it claimed were being used as Hamas headquarters. As for a possible cease-fire, Hamas's latest response, just received, to the current deal proposal was the "best yet," a senior source involved in negotiations told *Haaretz*. Netanyahu approved the departure of a negotiating team to continue talks for a hostage release agreement with Hamas. He also discussed Hamas's cease-fire proposal in a long telephone call with Biden. Encouraged by the rumored Hamas reply as reflecting a significant adjustment in the Jihadist group's stance, anti-government protesters blocked highways in central Israel calling for an immediate acceptance of the proposal.[5]

David Barnea, Israel's Mossad chief, departed for Qatar to continue truce negotiations. A senior US official said there had been a "breakthrough" in truce talks after Hamas made an important adjustment in its position in the matter. In northern Israel, firefighting and rescue teams gained control over most of the fires that erupted there following heavy rocket barrages from Lebanon on Wednesday. According to Israel's Nature and Parks Authority, nature reserves in the Galilee and the Golan Heights were severely damaged. At the same time, Hezbollah deputy leader Naim Qassam told the Russian news agency Sputnik that expanding the fighting with Israel "isn't a viable option at the moment," but added that the group "is prepared for any scenario."[6]

Israel's post-war plan for the Gaza Strip remained unclear as negotiations resumed in Doha, reported the Institute for the Study of War on July 5. Saudi Foreign Minister Faisal bin Farhan said that Saudi Arabia supported an international force under the auspices of the United Nations to support the Palestinian Authority in the Gaza Strip following the end of the war. Hamas, however, promised to prevent the deployment of foreign forces in the Strip. In Beirut, Hezbollah leader Hassan Nasrallah discussed the Israel-Hamas cease-fire talks and security developments in the Gaza Strip with a senior Hamas delegation, led by Political Bureau Deputy Chairman Khalil al Hayya. The Hamas delegation expressed appreciation for Hezbollah's support to Palestinian fighters in the Gaza Strip.[7]

All the while, violence in the West Bank against Israeli settlers escalated. About 1,100 Israeli attacks of all types on Palestinians occurred each year by a few extremists at the fringes of a half million-person strong and overwhelmingly peaceful community of Israelis who live over the so-called Green Line. This reality (dubbed "settler violence" by anti-Israel advocates) compared with more than 5,000 assaults in the same interval by Palestinians against Israeli civilians living in Judea and Samaria. Over the past year, Israel was forced to eliminate 450 terrorists in the West Bank in more than 60 brigade-level raids on Iranian-supplied terrorist groups in Nablus, Jenin, Tulkarm, Kalkilya, and elsewhere, and to arrest 3,600 other terrorists or those suspected of terrorism. Further, at least 90,000 Palestinian homes were illegally built in Israel-administered Area C in recent years, compared with some 500 structures by Jews which critics charged were "changing the footprint of Jewish presence in Judea and Samaria."

In addition, over the past few months, well over 1,000 fires had broken out in the area, many adjacent to Jewish communities and Israeli army bases, almost all caused by arson. This recalled the thousands of Hamas incendiary balloons sent over from Gaza in August 2020, firebombs that destroyed tens of thousands of acres of nature reserves and farmland in southern Israel, which experts claimed would take years to rehabilitate.[8]

Overnight Saturday, Meitham Mustafa Altaar was killed in a drone strike in eastern Lebanon, according to the IDF. A key operative in the Iranian terror proxy's aerial defense unit, he had led many of the unit's activities and took part in the planning and carrying out of numerous terrorist attacks against Israelis. Meitham also flew to Iran multiple times, where he gained knowledge and assisted in building up Hezbollah's force and arsenal of Iranian weapons. Alongside this announcement, *Yisrael Hayom* published the latest figures for IDF casualties in the war, separate from the 120 hostages still being held in Gaza. Of the 680 killed since the beginning of the war, 324 had been killed in battle since the ground operation began. Of the 4,091 wounded since the beginning of the war, 2,080 were wounded since the ground operation in Gaza began.[9]

The same day, a senior Hamas source revealed the group had dropped its demand that Israel first commit to a permanent cease-fire before signing the agreement and would allow negotiations to achieve that throughout the first phase. The source also said that the group had agreed to a revised proposal stipulating that talks to release hostages held in Gaza, including soldiers and male hostages, would start in a sixteen-day period after the deal's first phase. The source added that the proposal ensured mediators would guarantee a temporary cease-fire, aid delivery, and the withdrawal of IDF troops if indirect talks continued to implement the second phase of the deal. As thousands converged on Tel Aviv's "Hostage Square" for the weekly anti-government rally on Saturday night, a sense of cautious optimism filled the air. Relatives of Israeli hostages demonstrated outside IDF headquarters in Tel Aviv, calling on the government to accept a deal with Hamas that would see their family members released from captivity in Gaza. Two-thirds of the Israeli public believed returning the hostages was more important than continuing the war in Gaza, according to a poll published by Channel 12 News.[10]

As July 7 dawned, day 275 of the war marking nine months since Hamas's venomous assault on Israel's southern communities near the Gaza Strip, Israeli President Herzog asserted in a post on *X* that a majority of the public favored a deal to free hostages taken by Hamas terrorists during what he called the "barbaric attack" of October 7. Protests against the Netanyahu coalition government and calling for a deal to return the hostages, begun at 6:29 a.m.—the time the Hamas-led attack had erupted, were held across Israel in what was being called the "Day of Resistance." Thousands across the country blocked roads and demonstrated in front of the homes of coalition members. At the same time, a key stumbling block appeared to be Hamas's desire for "written guarantees" from mediators that Israel would continue to negotiate a permanent cease-fire deal once the first phase of a cease-fire went into effect. A Hamas representative told the Associated Press that the group's approval came after it received "verbal commitments and guarantees" from mediators that the war would not be resumed and that negotiations would continue until a permanent cease-fire was reached. According to a *Walla* report on Friday, however, Mossad chief Barnea had denied that Israel would give Hamas a written guarantee that the second phase of the agreement could be extended indefinitely.[11]

The nine months since the October 7 attack also led to an increase in Israeli Jews identifying with the right and a corresponding decrease in those affiliating with the left, a Hebrew University survey found. Agam Labs, a research institute led by the political psychologist Nimrod Nir, polled a representative sample of 4,000 adults in August and then from October 9 until May 2024 at the rate of around every ten days. Before the Hamas-led massacre and war in Gaza, around fifty-eight percent of respondents defined themselves as right-wing. By May, sixty percent were on the right. In contrast, in August of last year, seventeen percent were left-wing while in May of this year that figure was thirteen percent. Twenty-five percent of Israeli Jews identified as centrist in August compared to around twenty-seven percent in May. That represented more than 160,000 of Israel's some 7 million Jews leaving the left and more than 110,000 joining the right. "October 7 caused a complete collapse of the old Israeli left," Nir told the *Washington Free Beacon*.[12]

Critics of Netanyahu's coalition pointed out that, while the Israeli invasion was intended to destroy Hamas and free its hostages, it had accomplished neither to date. By the IDF's count, the military had killed at least 900 members of the Hamas brigade in Rafah and 15,000 Hamas fighters overall. Yet three months after Netanyahu declared that "total victory is within reach," the army acknowledged that the Rafah siege had eliminated only one-third of Hamas's brigade. Hamas's leadership remained intact, and roughly 120 hostages were believed to remain somewhere in Gaza, although about a third were thought to be dead. Tensions over the potential deal also surfaced within Netanyahu's own Likud party at the weekly cabinet meeting on Sunday. After the prime minister accused the defense minister, a rival, of playing politics, Gallant retorted by warning Netanyahu against any "politically driven attempt" to tie a hostage deal to other contentious issues dividing the government. "This is a delicate hour," Gallant said. "We must strike an agreement to secure the release of the hostages." Netanyahu repeated that he was not blocking an agreement.[13]

Two sources who were present at a meeting held at the Prime Minister's Office on Sunday told Kan Reshet Bet that the heads of the defense establishment "were stunned" by the office's statement regarding the conditions that Netanyahu laid out for the negotiations for a hostage deal. According to the sources, some of those at the meeting criticized the prime minister, who set the conditions before scheduling the meeting with them. Members of the defense establishment stated concerns that Netanyahu would prevent a deal because he feared the government would then be dissolved.[14]

That evening, the prime minister's office, emphasizing that Netanyahu's "strong stance against attempts to stop the IDF's operations in Rafah is what brought Hamas to the negotiating table," published his "red lines" in the negotiations with Hamas for a hostage deal ahead of a critical Doha summit on the matter Wednesday, which would be led by CIA Director William Burns. Its statement noted that "the Prime Minister continues to stand strongly for the principles that Israel already agreed on: 1. Any deal will allow Israel to return to fight until all the war's goals are met. 2. Weapons will not be allowed to be smuggled to Hamas from the Gaza-Egypt border. 3. Thousands of armed terrorists will not be allowed to return to the northern Gaza Strip. 4. Israel will maximize the number of living hostages that are freed from Hamas captivity." The statement concluded: "The outline that Israel agreed on and that received President Biden's blessing will allow Israel to bring back the hostages without harming the war's goals."[15]

Hezbollah fired some fifty rockets at northern Israel, claiming to have fired "dozens of Katyushas towards the Nimra base west of Tiberias," sparking fires in the area. The barrage, it announced, was in response to Israel's assassination of Hezbollah operative Meitam Mustafa Al-Atar on Saturday. A twenty-eight-year-old man was seriously wounded by shrapnel from the attack. In a separate incident. two people were wounded by a Hezbollah anti-tank missile fired towards the Western Galilee. Gallant responded that a hostage deal with Hamas did not limit Israel's ability to fight in the north, unless a separate agreement were reached with Hezbollah. That night, an IDF aircraft struck and eliminated Hezbollah terrorist Mustafa Hassan Salman in the area of Qlaileh in southern Lebanon. Hassan Salman was an operative in Hezbollah's Rockets and Missiles Unit, who took part in the planning and execution of numerous terror attacks against the State of Israel.[16]

Lt. Oriel Mashiach, commander of the Sabar Battalion in the Givati Brigade, provided some insight to *Ma'ariv* on Sunday into the combat operations in Rafah. "We are conducting very intense combat. Rafah is devoid of civilians, and what we see are the terrorists," he began. "We encounter a weary and demoralized enemy," he emphasized. "We have full control of the area and it seems the enemy struggles to fight. We face individuals who move independently. They operate on their own, tired and exhausted; some surrender upon seeing us, while others engage in suicidal actions." Mashiach and his soldiers had been fighting since October 7. However, he stressed that "Every soldier understands the mission and its significance. Our mission is to bring the hostages home. This burns in every soldier. We will continue the mission until we complete it, however long it takes."[17]

Concurrently, even as Hamas announced that the CEO of its Labor Ministry, Ehab al-Ghussein, was killed in an Israeli strike in Gaza City, its military wing spokesperson, Abu Obaida (Hudayfa Samir Abdallah al-Kahlout), said the organization had recruited thousands of new members to its ranks. Its "military capability is still strong," he stressed, and the war with Israel "will nurture new generations of Palestinian fighters." Realizing that the war appeared far from over, the Israeli government approved extending financial aid for evacuated residents of the Gaza border communities and the north until the end of August. It was also decided to extend the eligibility period for grants for residents of the towns still not safe to inhabit. IDF Spokesperson Rear Admiral Daniel Hagari stated once again that Hamas would not be destroyed, and that the terrorist organization would still exist in five years. During an interview with the American ABC network, Hagari was asked if in five years Hamas will still be a terrorist group that operated in Gaza, and he answered in the affirmative. "We are getting close to defeating the Rafah Brigade," he added.[18]

The extent of destruction caused by the war in the Gaza Strip may have led Hamas to lighten its demands in the hostage and cease-fire negotiations, the Associated Press reported on Monday citing several Middle Eastern and US officials. The AP report stated that messages from several senior Hamas officials in Gaza urged the group's exiled political leadership to accept the cease-fire proposal pitched by Biden despite the reluctance of Hamas leader in Gaza Yahya Sinwar. The messages, shared by a Middle East official familiar with the ongoing negotiations, described the heavy losses Hamas has suffered on the battlefield and the bad conditions in the Gaza Strip. (According to the Hamas-controlled Health Ministry in Gaza, at least 38,193 Palestinians had been killed and 87,903 wounded since the start of the war.) The report would back up Netanyahu's assertion on Sunday that "the Prime Minister's strong stance against attempts to stop the IDF's operations in Rafah is what brought Hamas to the negotiating table."[19]

Israel launched a new military offensive in Gaza City on Monday, with evacuation orders sowing confusion as tens of thousands of Palestinians fled the war-ravaged northern city amid what residents described as some of the worst bombardment since the start of the war. This followed intensified Israeli strikes and after an IDF spokesman published messages in Arabic calling on residents of specific city neighborhoods to evacuate, stating there would be safe passages for civilians. Around 200,000 to 300,000 people were estimated to have remained in Gaza City and in the north of the enclave, where the humanitarian situation had been most acute. Israeli forces raided and destroyed Hamas's combat compound and headquarters in Shujaiyeh. According to the army, the complex contained schools and a clinic, which had been converted from civilian use for terrorist purposes, and was occupied by the group's Shujaiyeh Battalion, who were staying there.[20]

Gallant told family members of the hostages being held in Gaza that Israel needed to translate the gains of its military pressure into a deal that would bring the captives home. The entire defense establishment saw the return of the hostages as "the main goal to be pursued, to do everything we can to take advantage of the situation that has been created," he said. "The military pressure has created conditions that allow us to move forward with a deal, the military will know how to halt and how to return to combat as needed," the defense minister added. "We need to take advantage of the military pressure to push forward with a deal and not to miss it."[21]

A controversy erupted in Jerusalem over what IDF Deputy Chief of Staff Maj. Gen. Amir Baram told a classified meeting of the Knesset Foreign Affairs and Defense Committee about how the military decided that the number of haredim (ultra-Orthodox) it could immediately integrate was 3,000, in addition to the around 1,800 it already had. The 3,000 was out of a class of around 10,000–12,000 per academic year, with over 60,000 haredim potentially in play from several academic years following the High Court of Justice's June 25 order for a universal draft and the freezing of funds to haredi institutions which did not comply. Yet, part of the idea was that haredim required special arrangements, including service environments with specific religious provisions and with fewer interactions with female soldiers. The haredi political parties, United Torah Judaism and Shas, were under pressure to regain their institutions' funding but had not shown clear signs of being willing to strike a compromise and push for an even larger partial draft. Netanyahu wished to postpone the issue to September, concerned that the haredim could bring the government down over their funds being frozen, but hoped that fear of a worse solution under a different government would hold them in line.[22]

Tehran presented the IDF with yet another great concern. Recent satellite imagery showed major expansions at two key Iranian ballistic missile facilities that two American researchers assessed were for boosting missile production, a conclusion confirmed by three senior Iranian officials. The enlargement of the sites followed an October 2022 deal in which Iran agreed to provide missiles to Russia, which had been seeking them for its war against Ukraine. Tehran also supplied missiles to Yemen's Houthi rebels and the Lebanese militia Hezbollah, both members of the Iran-backed Axis of Resistance against Israel, according to US officials. Images taken by commercial satellite firm Planet Labs of the Modarres military base in March and the Khojir missile production complex in April showed more than thirty new buildings at the two sites, both of which are located near Tehran. The grave threat of a nuclear attack by the Shia theocratic dictatorship committed to Israel's obliteration loomed far above the announcement by Jean-Luc Mélenchon, leader of France Unbowed (La France Insoumise) and a key member of the victorious left-wing New Popular Front (NPF) coalition in Sunday's National Assembly elections, that his government would recognize the "State of Palestine" as soon as possible. The NPF had condemned Israel's Gaza operation as "genocide" and Mélanchon, accused of antisemitism, refused to call Hamas a terrorist group.[23]

"Israel must prioritize hostages above all," editorialized the *Jerusalem Post* on July 9. "It's become increasingly clear that the twin objectives of freeing the hostages and ending Hamas's rule in Gaza cannot be both accomplished at the same time," the statement went on. "It could take years to achieve the latter, while if a deal is reached, it could take only a matter of weeks or months to get the remaining captives home." Yet Hamas's political leadership had just told the heads of Palestinian terrorist factions in Gaza that the chances of reaching a hostage release and cease-fire deal were slim because of Netanyahu's list of "red lines." "Netanyahu supports talks without a deadline in order to gain time," an official from one of the factions told *Haaretz*, adding that the prime minister's "goal is to address [the US] Congress while the war is still on and reach [the Knesset's] summer recess with a deal," and that "anyone expecting a breakthrough is living in an illusion." Hamas sources also told the Hezbollah-aligned Al Mayadeen channel that Israel had not expressed any will to retreat from the Philadelphi Corridor and was trying to enforce a new management regime at the Rafah border crossing. The Lebanese *Al-Akhbar* reported that Israel was conditioning every retreat from the Philadelphi route upon retaining complete surveillance of the area, as well as the freedom to operate there in cases of attempted arms smuggling.[24]

The majority of the Israeli public actually opposed the deal being negotiated with Hamas for the release of hostages, according to a poll published on Channel 14 on Monday evening. Respondents to the poll were presented with the details of the emerging deal: Israel will withdraw from the Philadelphi Corridor and the Netzarim Corridor, and Hamas operatives will be able to return and seize terrorist infrastructures that have not yet been destroyed. In return, Israel will receive eighteen living hostages, and about fifteen bodies. The recent data showed that a majority of fifty-three percent opposed the deal, thirty-six percent supported it, while eleven percent said they did not know. The poll was conducted by the Direct Polls institute among all sectors of Israeli society. It also demonstrated that an absolute majority (seventy-six percent) of the public did not think Egypt could be trusted to prevent smuggling on the Philadelphi Corridor, seventeen percent did trust Egypt, while seven percent had no opinion on the matter.[25]

Hagai Lober, whose son, twenty-four-year-old Staff Sergeant Elisha Yehonatan Lober from Yitzhar, of the 179th Reserve Armored Brigade's 8104th Battalion, fell in battle on December 25 in the southern Gaza Strip, echoed that sentiment when speaking at length in *Yisrael Hayom* to the hostage families who called to intensify the protests against the government. "Nobody will burn down my country. . . . Millions of people view you with mistrust, discord and honor," he began. "My son died while going to defend and free your children, leaving behind a pregnant wife, Aviya, and their ten-month-old son Elisha, he noted. You cannot block roads, clash with police, call for military recalcitrance, riot." Lober was prepared to send his three remaining children to risk their lives for those kidnapped by Hamas on October 7, but the protesters did not have "extra privilege" to disrupt the public peace. They had the right to express their opinions, but not to threaten the nation. "Don't hitch a ride on the pain of the families." In Lober's view, his son was killed because of the 1993 Oslo Accords and Israel's complete withdrawal in 2005 from Gaza. Now was the time to show love towards one another, he urged. If the protesters did not stop "for God's sake, for the country's sake, for victory's sake," he and other bereaved families, injured soldiers, and hostage families who thought differently "will stand together in the face of anarchy. And we won't let you. We just won't."[26]

Once the IDF subdued Khan Younis and Rafah, the *Jerusalem Post*'s senior military correspondent, Yonah Jeremy Bob, learned that Gallant stood with the majority of the IDF establishment, whose message was there was no large, organized Hamas force left to fight. Ending the war, consequently, was not much of a concession to make to get back hostages. According to this thinking, the five IDF re-invasions of parts of Gaza were large-scale "raids," similar to what the IDF routinely did in the West Bank and were not really invasions. Gallant and the IDF viewed the serious fighting stage of the war as already being over, regardless of what political slogans were "running around" about refusing to end the war. According to Gallant, this was then the moment to retrieve as many hostages as possible. Any delay, obfuscation, or attempt to stiffen the terms of the deal now, according to Gallant, was a political move which directly and unnecessarily endangered the hostages' lives. This was also the view of the IDF high command, who were stunned by Netanyahu's new conditions, which he made public on Sunday night and which contradicted significant aspects of the deal Israel had already nominally agreed to.[27]

In Gaza, the IDF said that it had located and destroyed six tunnels over the last week in the Shujaiya neighborhood, killed more than 150 terrorists, and located weapons and intelligence documents. Precisely a decade after Operation Protective Edge and six months after the battle in Swords of Iron, the IDF's name for the current war, army forces again entered the eastern neighborhood that had become a ruin. Reporters found it hard to find a single building completely intact there. The Palestinian Red Crescent said that all its facilities in Gaza City had been shut down due to IDF operations. "We are working intensely to destroy all Hamas's infrastructure to make sure that it will not be able to reestablish itself for years," declared Lt.-Col Gideon Eliyasam, the deputy commander of the Paratroopers Brigade. "We are clearing out the territory, both above and below the ground, to take away their capabilities. The objective is to create a completely different security situation to enable the Israeli residents of the border communities to return home."[28]

As to the northern front, Hezbollah published what it claimed were photographs of IDF bases and military infrastructure in that area of Israel. An Israeli drone killed Yasser Nemr Kranbish, Hezbollah leader Nasrallah's former bodyguard, on the Beirut-Damascus road, next to a Syrian army outpost. Hezbollah said that the barrage it fired at northern Israel later on Tuesday was a response to Kranbish's killing. Two people were killed in northern Israel following that rocket barrage from Lebanon. In turn, the IAF struck Hezbollah air defenses, as well as the location from which rockets had been fired on the Golan Heights. In the West Bank, the IDF arrested fifteen suspects and, in a fifteen-hour operation, destroyed terrorist infrastructure in the Nur Shams refugee camp near Tulkarm.[29]

Gallant told the Knesset on July 10 that sixty percent of Hamas terrorists in the Gaza Strip had been killed or wounded as a result of the IDF's ongoing operation, including the breakup of the majority of the twenty-four battalions that Hamas's military wing had at the start of the war. Kan reported that Israel sent a message by way of White House advisor for Middle East affairs, Brett McGurk, that it would agree to a deal in which an international force, not the PA, would rule the Gaza Strip after the war. Hardly mollified, hundreds of Israelis gathered outside the Defense Ministry's headquarters in Tel Aviv ahead of a march to Jerusalem led by hostages' family members. The Hostages and Missing Families Forum called on the public to join the march, which was expected to last three days and end on Saturday outside the prime minister's office in Jerusalem. Family members of hostages protested outside the Knesset in Jerusalem, locking themselves in cages and calling on Israeli lawmakers to join them. Earlier, pro-cease-fire, anti-government protesters partially blocked a main highway in central Israel. Police said that nine were detained for questioning on suspicion that they were violating public order.[30]

The IDF was still far from certain that it had or would find all of the cross-border tunnels between Gaza and Egypt, *the Jerusalem Post* learned during a visit embedded with IDF forces to the Philadelphi Corridor. In fact, the estimate for finding and destroying all of the cross-border tunnels was likely at minimum six months but could easily take longer. Of all the tunnel battles the IDF had taken on in Gaza, this was the most important by far because that route was "Hamas's oxygen" for receiving arms from the outside world, especially from Iran. October 7 could not have happened without the arms and intelligence training Hamas received through the Philadelphi Corridor.[31]

In addition, Tehran state media reported about a letter from Iran's President-elect Masoud Pezeshkian to Hezbollah leader Nasrallah promising continued support for his and other armed groups targeting Israel, declaring that "from Iran's perspective these are not terror groups but 'resistance.'" Iranian regime actors were also engaging influence campaigns to stoke and fund anti-Israel protests in the United States, Director of National Intelligence Avril Haines warned in a statement. Even as some thirty rockets were launched from Lebanon from Iran's proxy into Israel's north on Wednesday. Nasrallah said fighting along the Lebanon-Israel border would stop when a cease-fire in Gaza was secured, adding that his organization was "achieving the objectives of our campaign—to wear down the enemy [Israel] security-wise, morally, economically, and socially." That included husband and wife, Nir and Noa Baranes, residents of Kibbutz Ortal in the Golan Heights who were killed Tuesday while driving through the Nafah traffic junction near an IDF base when a Hezbollah rocket struck their car, survived by their three children, ages thirteen through eighteen.[32]

In Gaza, with leaflets distributed in Arabic, the IDF called on all residents of Gaza City to evacuate south to the Deir al-Balah area, indicating that Israel's high-intensity campaign against Hamas was not over. Residents were informed that they could leave the city safely towards the south through designated crossings. Jordanian Foreign Minister Ayman Safadi responded that the order was a "red line for Jordan and Egypt," emphasizing that both countries would strongly oppose the displacement of Palestinians in Gaza. France declared it was "gravely concerned" by reports that an Israeli strike hit a tent encampment in southern Gaza where displaced civilians had gathered to watch a soccer match. Palestinian health officials said that at least twenty-nine people—mostly women and children—were killed by the strike near the city of Khan Younis on Tuesday. The IDF announced it was investigating the incident, and that the strike targeted a member of Hamas who had taken part in the October 7 massacre and was executed by "a fighter jet [that] used precision munitions."[33]

Further, for the first time since the Hamas attack on October 7, an officer from the IAF admitted that the Israeli Air Force's competence and readiness for battle was significantly degraded as the result of the refusals to serve during the protests against the government's attempt to implement judicial reforms in 2023, Channel 12 News correspondent Amit Segal reported. According to the report, the commander of the Air Control and Flight School, Lt. Col. Yaniv Even, discovered that after the massacre there were many reservists in sensitive positions in the IAF who were no longer competent to fly on missions because they had refused to report for training prior to the war.[34]

As also reported in the *Wall Street Journal*, the spate of new political and legal initiatives against Israel was unprecedented, said Eran Shamir-Borer, former head of the international law department in the Israeli military. They included moves against Israel and its leaders at the United Nations' top court and the International Criminal Court. "I think there is definitely reason for concern for Israel," said Shamir-Borer, now a fellow at the Israel Democracy Institute. "Becoming a pariah state means that even if things don't happen formally, less companies feel that they want to invest in Israel in the first place, less universities want to collaborate with Israeli institutions. Things just happen when you get this symbolic status." Israelis were finding they are no longer welcome at many European universities, including participating in scientific collaborations. Their participation in cultural institutions and defense trade shows was increasingly becoming taboo as well. "Zionist-free Zone" signs also indicated that Israelis were increasingly unwanted at global tourism sites. From a hotel in Kyoto to a sandwich joint in Edinburgh, the world was becoming hostile toward Israelis who were learning that a vacation would not shield them from the Gaza war.[35]

A glimmer of hope was raised by the *Washington Post* reporting about Israel and Hamas agreeing that in the second phase of a potential deal neither of them would control Gaza, and it would be managed by an international force that involved the United States, moderate Arab countries, and likely also about 2,500 police and soldiers from the Palestinian Authority. An official noted that the breakthrough was made possible after Hamas abandoned its demand for a written guarantee for a complete end to the war, although US NSC Advisor Jake Sullivan cautioned "there's still miles to go before we close if we are able to close." The IDF was pleased to hear the *Wall Street Journal* reporting that the United States would soon ship weapons and arms that the Biden administration had suspended two months earlier. The weapons included 500-pound bombs that the administration had previously halted; heavier bombs, including 2,000-pound bombs were still on hold. The IDF announced that its forces eliminated Hassan Abu Kuik, operational security chief in Hamas's Internal Security Forces, and Naser Mehanna, team commander in Hamas's military intelligence.[36]

At the same time, G7 foreign ministers joined the UN and EU in condemning Israel's decision to legalize five outposts in the West Bank, labeling the plan "inconsistent with international law and counterproductive." US Treasury Secretary Janet Yellen urged Israel "to maintain economic stability in the West Bank" by consistently transferring the revenues it collected on behalf of the Palestinian Authority and ensuring "uninterrupted" banking relations between Israeli and Palestinian banks. USAID Administrator Samantha Power said that the United States would provide an additional $100 million in humanitarian aid for Palestinians in Gaza and the West Bank. The spokesman for the Palestinian Civil Defense, Mahmoud Basal, declared that eighty-five percent of the buildings in Gaza City's Shujaiya neighborhood were no longer suitable for living, and that thousands of bodies under the rubble contributed to the spread of diseases and infections among residents and displaced persons. In Israel's north, since the beginning of the Hezbollah attacks on Israel on October 8, nearly 5,000 acres of forest area had been destroyed due to enemy explosions. The Jewish National Fund estimated that once all areas designated as closed military zones were reached, the damage will be even greater.[37]

In Europe, a survey conducted by the European Union's Fundamental Rights Agency of 8,000 self-identified Jews from thirteen EU countries—Austria, Belgium, the Czech Republic, Denmark, France, Germany, Hungary, Italy, the Netherlands, Poland, Romania, Spain, and Sweden, as reported by the *Times of Israel*, found that ninety-six percent of respondents said they had encountered antisemitism in their daily lives before the ongoing war in Gaza.

Even a monument to Anne Frank, erected in Amsterdam's Merwede Square where she and her family had lived before going into hiding in 1942 until they were deported and Anne died from typhus in the Bergen-Belsen concentration camp in February 1945 at age fifteen, was vandalized with "GAZA" scrawled in red paint on the base. Some Holocaust memorials in other countries were defaced, showing that Jews everywhere, including Jews no longer alive, were being attacked in the name of antizionism. The reality since October 7, as in the United States, of attacks on Jews had gotten far worse and violent on numerous occasions. This did not deter fifty-four families of American citizens who were impacted by the October 7 massacre from filing a lawsuit against Iran for its support of Hamas on Friday. The suit, filed with the United States District Court for the District of Columbia, claimed 500 million dollars for mental and bodily harm caused by the Iranian regime through alleged financing, arming, and abetting of Gazan terrorist organizations.[38]

While an Israeli delegation led by Shin Bet chief Ronen Bar left for Cairo to continue truce talks, fifty-seven percent of Israelis opposed the US-mediated deal being negotiated with Hamas, according to a JNS/Direct Polls survey of public opinion carried out on July 9. The contours of the tentative agreement would require Israel to withdraw from the Netzarim Corridor that controlled north-south traffic in Gaza, and from the Philadelphi Corridor that controlled the Strip's border with Egypt. In exchange for the withdrawal and the release of hundreds of terrorists from Israeli prisons, Hamas would free eighteen living women and children and the bodies of fifteen deceased hostages. Thirty-three percent supported the prospective agreement. Even more telling, seventy percent of residents of the south, where Hamas carried out its October 7 massacre, said "no" to the Biden framework. Attending the IDF Officers' Course Graduation Ceremony, Netanyahu, who still took no responsibility for the numerous Israeli failures of October 7, reiterated his conviction that the government remained determined to achieve all goals of the war and return all remaining hostages, emphasizing that "only clarity and determination will get the hostages back."[39]

The same Thursday, Biden told reporters in Washington that gaps remained between Hamas and Israel on a cease-fire and hostage release deal, but "the trend is positive." "Six weeks ago, I laid out a detailed plan and that framework is now agreed on by both Israel and Hamas ... there's still gaps to close. We're making progress. The trend is positive," the president said, speaking at the NATO summit held in the US capital. Biden added that he would be sending a team to "hammer out the details." He was determined to bring about an end to the Hamas-Israel war, which he added "should end now." "I told Israel not to make the same mistake we did in Iraq and Afghanistan. I told them that we would help them find the bad guys—led by Yahya Sinwar. We have a chance now. The war can be ended. This does not mean that we will no longer pursue Sinwar and Hamas," said Biden. He also reiterated his past stance that "Israel should not occupy Gaza" once the war against Hamas ended.[40]

That evening, IDF Spokesperson Hagari apologized to residents of Kibbutz Be'eri, the hardest hit of Israel's southern communities near the Gaza Strip attacked by Hamas on October 7, saying that "the IDF was not in Be'eri, we failed to protect the kibbutz." Hagari was presenting the findings, just released to the public, in the military's first review of the slaughter. 101 of the kibbutz residents were murdered; 32 people were taken hostage, of whom 11 remained captives in Gaza. 150 houses were destroyed, and several complete security breakdowns took place. The IDF estimated that a total of 340 Hamas members had invaded the kibbutz, massively outnumbering the brave residents, who had only between 13–26 fighters at any given moment against 80–200 Hamas operatives. Israeli army units that achieved numerical superiority only arrived at 2:30 p.m., eight hours after the assault had begun. The report stated that "The army was not prepared for a scenario of a mass penetration into Israel like on October 7 that included multiple points of entry through which thousands of terrorists entered, and dozens of fronts where they attacked." For their part, Be'eri residents demanded in a statement the establishment of a state commission of inquiry "that will leave no stone unturned, examine the conduct of all parties involved, and provide us with definitive answers." Gallant called for the establishment of a commission examining the "conditions that led to the building of Hamas's power [in Gaza] over the past decade," adding that it should examine the conduct of Netanyahu himself and Israel's defense chiefs.[41]

On Friday, day 280 of the war, Biden said his cease-fire proposal "is now agreed to by both Israel and Hamas." Netanyahu denied reports that Israel and Egypt discussed using electronic surveillance along the Gaza/Egypt border that would facilitate the IDF's withdrawal from the area. In cease-fire negotiations, Mossad chief Barnea pushed Netanyahu's demand that the IDF retain the right to resume fighting after the first stage of any deal. Senior Hamas official Husam Badran said that the group proposed that a technocratic government agreed upon by all Palestinian factions and not affiliated politically with any organization run both Gaza and the West Bank. Israeli forces killed the deputy commander of Hamas's Shujaiyeh battalion, Aiman Shoidach, the IDF, and Shin Bet said in a joint statement. Israel's cabinet decided to extend mandatory military service for men from thirty-two to thirty-six months, with the legislation set to be advanced next week. The move came as the IDF faced a shortage of troops amid the war in Gaza and escalations on the Lebanese border.[42]

The next day, the co-architect with Sinwar of the October 7 massacre, Mohammed Deif, along with Rafa'a Salameh, commander of Hamas's Khan Younis Brigade, were targeted with large munitions above ground while in a low building between the al-Mawasi "safe zone" and Khan Younis in southern Gaza. According to the IDF's assessments, no hostages were held at the site when the strike was carried out. Deif's fate was unknown as of 8 p.m., although defense sources said there was a growing likelihood that the man credited with transforming Hamas from an insurgent militia into a fighting force had been killed. At least 70 people were reportedly killed and 280 wounded in the strike on Deif and Salameh, said the Gaza Health Ministry. Hamas spokesman Sami Abu Zuhri disputed that Deif had been injured, saying all casualties were civilians and that the attack showed Israel was not interested in reaching a cease-fire agreement. A Hamas statement added that Israeli claims about Deif's condition "are false and aimed at covering up its crimes." Egypt and Jordan condemned the strike on Khan Younis, with Egypt's Foreign Ministry declaring "the incident imposes dangerous obstacles on efforts to achieve calm."[43]

Following the IAF strike in Khan Younis targeting Deif, Hamas called on residents of "the West Bank, the Arab and Islamic nation, and free people of the world" to continue acts of identification with Gaza, until the end of "the aggression and mass destruction." PA President Mahmoud Abbas's office issued a statement condemning the attempted assassination of Deif, saying Israel and the United States bore full responsibility for the "horrific massacre," but then added that it also held Hamas partly responsible "for avoiding the effort toward Palestinian national unity." On the Israeli side, Gallant declared that "Hamas's capabilities are eroding every day, they are paying huge prices and their ability to rebuild is very limited. The pursuit of Hamas terrorists will continue for years to come—from the most senior ones to the terrorists in the field." At a press conference on Sunday, IDF Chief of Staff Halevi stated "We are determined to continue and pursue Hamas leaders, who planned the massacre and dedicated their lives to murdering innocents. Deif was afraid of dying and therefore hid in a way that harmed his ability to command. He hid and sacrificed his people and civilians who were around him, a few were harmed."[44]

The IDF pressed on with its Gaza operation. Nimer Hamida, a terrorist released in the 2011 Shalit deal, was killed in an attack in the Al-Shati refugee camp. The IAF struck and eliminated the terrorist Hossam Mansour, a platoon commander in Hamas's Internal Security Forces. He was also one of the directors of the Al-Khair Foundation, which transferred funds to terror organizations with the disguise of humanitarian activity. The IDF announced that it had wrapped up its two-week-long operation in Gaza City's Shejaiya neighborhood. During the operation combat engineers demolished eight major tunnels and killed more than 150 gunmen. At the same time, a ramming attack occurred at the Nir Zvi junction in Ramle on Sunday. The terrorist, who was killed, had been thwarted by the border police. Four soldiers were wounded by the East Jerusalem resident's attack. A group of hostage families, echoing the overwhelming sentiment heard from IDF soldiers on all fronts embracing the slogan "until the victory," demonstrated Sunday in Jerusalem together with bereaved families and evacuees in favor of continued military pressure on both Hamas and Hezbollah to ensure Israel's long-term security and gain the hostages' freedom.[45]

Israel officials made it clear on Sunday that negotiations for a hostage deal were continuing, despite the conflicting public statements by Hamas about possibly freezing the talks following Israel's assassination attempt on Hamas military chief Deif. Mossad Chief Barnea was due to leave for talks in Qatar in the coming days. Further, IDF Chief of Staff Halevi said on Sunday that a deal to secure the release of the hostages held in Gaza was an "urgent moral imperative" to save lives. Israel struck southern and central Gaza the next day to put more pressure on Hamas. The *Guardian* reported that, according to an assessment by the UN Environment Programme, it would take fifteen years to clear Gaza of almost 40 million tons of rubble with a fleet of over 100 trucks, and the operation would cost up to $600 million. In addition, the Biden administration would soon permanently shut down the star-crossed $230 million temporary pier that the US military had built to rush humanitarian aid to Gaza, US officials said recently. Facing a manpower shortage, the Israeli government raised mandatory military service to three years, leading the Attorney General's Office to question the measure's legality, calling on the government to "increase the equality of the burden."[46]

On Tuesday, the IDF Spokesperson's Unit stated that ground, air, and naval forces had been operating in the Gaza Strip for 263 days in order to achieve the objectives of the war. In this time, they eliminated and apprehended approximately 14,000 terrorists, including six brigade commanders, over 20 battalion commanders, approximately 150 company commanders, and half of the leadership of Hamas's military wing. To date, the IDF had struck approximately 37,000 targets from the air within the Gaza Strip, and more than 25,000 terrorist infrastructure and launch sites. Internal estimates showed that Hamas's Shejaia forces, for example, had dropped to 435 fighters from an initial

1,235, while rockets launched from Shejaia were down to 15 rockets from an original inventory of 63. The CIA believed that Hamas commanders were now pressuring Hamas leader Sinwar to end the war with Israel, CNN reported on Tuesday. According to its source, CIA chief Burns claimed that Sinwar was not "concerned with his mortality" but rather under pressure due to being blamed for the suffering of Gaza's residents. "Hamas suffered a serious blow" in the targeting of Deif and Salameh, said an Israeli government official; its response to the incident "has been very weak, bordering on a non-response" to the hostage release and cease-fire talks. As a result, Mossad's director had not yet departed on Tuesday for negotiations in Qatar.[47]

Israel's Finance Ministry Budget Department Chairman Yogev Gardos spoke that morning before the Foreign Affairs and Defense Committee, emphasizing the economic need to conscript all populations in Israel. He argued that enlisting 1,000 haredi soldiers would shorten reserve duty by fourteen days annually for all servicemen. According to the Treasury, conscripting 1,000 haredim into the IDF would save 1.3 billion shekels each year. Yet the IDF postponed the recruitment of female soldiers in the military's maneuver formation until November 2025 due to a lack of tanks in the brigade, Walla reported. An IDF spokesperson stated that "following the response submitted today to the High Court regarding a petition on the service of women in combat duty, we emphasize that weapons in the Maneuverable Armor Corps, including tanks and armaments, are currently assigned to the war as priority over the expansion of training soldiers, including training female personnel for combat duty."[48]

In a TV interview, Biden declared: "I transferred defensive weapons to Israel. I denied them offensive weapons and made it clear that they cannot use weapons in civilian areas." He answered in the affirmative to the question of whether he was a Zionist and added: "If there was no Israel, every Jew in the world would be in danger. That is why it is necessary for Israel to be strong, for there to be a safe place for Jews. And you don't have to be a Jew to be a Zionist." "By the way," he went on, "I'm the guy that did more for the Palestinian community than anybody. I'm the guy that opened up all the assets [who made sure that the border to Egypt was opened], that Arab countries help the Palestinians." "I have been very supportive of the Palestinians," he declared. "But Hamas, they're a bunch of thugs." In the opposing political camp, whose delegates at the Republican National Convention prayed for the release of the Israeli hostages in Gaza and chanted "Bring Them Home!," Donald Trump's running mate, Ohio Senator J. D. Vance, declared "We need to punch Iran hard. That's what Trump did with Qasem Soleimani. That action actually brought peace by checking the Iranians. If you want to check the Iranians, you need to withdraw their oil money, and enable Israel and the Sunni countries to work to counter Iran." The Abraham Accords, he claimed, were the key to such an approach. "You've got all the infrastructure to do it already sitting right there."[49]

Netanyahu stood his ground. IDF Chief of Staff Halevi bristled at him in a recent meeting and demanded an apology from the prime minister for saying there was no progress in hostage talks in recent months because the military was not applying enough pressure on Hamas in Gaza, Israeli television reported. No apology was forthcoming. Moreover, the prime minister pleaded total ignorance—despite widespread media coverage—when families of the fifteen slain female surveillance soldiers and the six taken hostage at the Nahal Oz outpost complained during a tense meeting in his Jerusalem office that these daughters were unarmed, and that their raising alarms before October 7 that Hamas was preparing an attack were ignored. Sharply criticized by them for not accepting responsibility for the devastating massacre, he once again rejected calls to form a state commission of inquiry to investigate the Israeli failures and government culpability surrounding the onslaught, stating that had to wait because "we're in an existential war" against Iran and Hamas had to be resoundingly defeated first. Mossad chief Barnea said Netanyahu's insistence that a mechanism be established for monitoring Gazans' movement from south to north Gaza might thwart a possible deal with Hamas, and that "the women hostages do not have time to wait."[50]

On Israel's northern border, Hezbollah Secretary-General Nasrallah declared that Israel increasing attacks on civilians in Lebanon would be answered with a widening of rocket fire that would target a bigger scope of Israeli towns. In the statement, aired for the ʿĀshūrāʾ, the holiest day for Shiite Muslims, he emphasized that Hamas's actions on October 7 were their full right, and that reports for a framework for an agreement with Lebanon were false. Residents of towns in northern Israel were furious at the measured response of the Israeli defense establishment to the incessant firing of heavy barrages of rockets from Lebanon at their homes every day. Over 60,000 residents remain evacuated; the economy is shattered. Rita Ben Yair, an evacuee from the north and a member of the leadership of the "Fighting for the North" organization, said, "It's time to change the equation, step away from the established patterns, and exact a price from the state of Lebanon. It is inconceivable that our house is burning and under such a threat and Lebanon is not burning. It's time to win this war and provide peace for decades to come, we must not return with an agreement of surrender."[51]

The price to pay would undoubtedly be heavy. Since October 7, Israel had killed seven Hezbollah lieutenant generals and some 360 fighters and commanders overall, at the cost of at least 19 soldiers and 12 civilians who died in rocket fire from Lebanon. Hezbollah's latest rocket and drone barrage—part of a total of some 7,000 rockets and missiles that it had fired into Israel since October 7—increased concern in many quarters about a possible escalation into full-scale conflict. With some 45,000 fighters and an arsenal of more than 150,000 rockets, drones, and missiles, many of them precision-guided, Hezbollah has always posed a much greater strategic threat to Israel than Hamas, which had been significantly degraded since Israel's offensive in Gaza. The IDF viewed the military pressure on Hamas in the Gaza Strip as having become more effective in recent weeks. According to the General Staff, a string of successes in battle during these weeks had increased the distress of senior members of Hamas's military wing and created better conditions for a deal to free the hostages. The far more serious threat from Hezbollah was an entirely different matter.[52]

The Knesset, by a vote of 68–9 (9 Arab MKs; the Labor Party members did not attend), passed a proposal late Wednesday night declaring its opposition to the establishment of a Palestinian state west of the Jordan River. It declared that the establishment of a Palestinian state in "the heart of the Land of Israel" would pose an "existential danger to the State of Israel and its citizens," perpetuate the Israeli-Palestinian conflict, and further destabilize the region. The proposal further asserted that a Palestinian state would quickly be taken over by Hamas, which would then use the sovereign territory to launch attacks on Israel. It called the establishment of a Palestinian state in the aftermath of October 7 "a reward for terrorism" and that such a reward would only encourage Hamas and other Jihadist groups, who would use it as a prelude to take over the Middle East. The measure was intended to apply pressure on Netanyahu, since he was likely to face opposite pressure from US officials on a hostage deal that could include future discussions of Palestinian sovereignty. Netanyahu himself was not present at the vote. The vote was also notable since Netanyahu had blocked a similar measure in February and chose instead to vote on a declaration that Israel opposed "unilateral" Palestinian statehood but did not oppose Palestinian statehood categorically.[53]

The killing did not let up. The IAF eliminated Anas Murad, the commander of the Islamic Jihad's Naval Forces in Gaza City. In another strike, an IAF aircraft eliminated the Islamic Jihad terrorist Ahmad Almasri, who took part in the October 7 massacre and was also responsible for the launches of numerous projectiles from Shejaiya toward Israel's southern communities. Deep in Lebanon's Beqaa region, Mohammed Jabarah, a senior terrorist in the Jemaah Islamiyah terror group, was killed Thursday morning in an Israeli airstrike. At the same time, as Hamas's power was collapsing, old feuds resurfaced. In May, Mahmoud Nashabat, a high-ranking military figure in the Fatah party (which controls the

West Bank-based Palestinian Authority), was gunned down in central Gaza. Nashabat was an officer in the Gaza wing of the Aqsa Martyrs' Brigade, a terrorist outfit that served as Fatah's vanguard during the second intifada, and now sometimes collaborated with Hamas. Yet his killers were Hamas members, and he was one of at least thirty-five Palestinians murdered in Gaza in the past two months as various terrorist and criminal groups went about settling old scores, some of which dated back to the 1980s.[54]

In addressing the Knesset on July 18, the prime minister compared himself to the Duke of Wellington before the Battle of Waterloo mocking the need to inspect the condition of a battalion's "jam jars," horse saddles, tent sheets, and tent poles during his fighting Napoleon's forces, implying that Netanyahu viewed a state inquiry of October 7 as what one newspaper termed "a bureaucratic nuisance" amid Israel's war on Hamas. Netanyahu also said he would not approve a decision by Gallant to establish a field hospital in Israel to treat children from Gaza, and, visiting Rafah, declared he was more convinced of the need to retain control over the border crossing with Egypt. The Knesset plenum ultimately voted 53–51 against a bill brought forth by Yesh Atid MK Meir Cohen that would have established a state committee of inquiry. Bereaved Israeli families responded that they were organizing to establish a civilian probe led by legal and security experts to that end. Despite the threats from ministers Ben-Gvir and Smotrich to topple the government, the coalition's ultra-Orthodox Shas party called on Netanyahu to finalize a hostage deal, saying: "We believe that the conditions created now . . . create an appropriate timing to reach a deal that preserves Israel's vital security interests and brings the hostages home." As the American humanitarian aid pier closed operations, USAID stated that it had enabled nineteen million pounds of aid to reach Gaza, adding that a cease-fire was urgently needed to enable the surge of assistance and the release of hostages.[55]

Two commanders of Hezbollah's Radwan Force were eliminated in Lebanon in IAF strikes, Ali Jaafar Maatuk and an additional commander responsible for the Force's operations in the Hajir region. Concurrently, a loud explosion from a an Iranian-made Samad-3 drone, apparently launched from Yemen 2,600 kilometers away, was heard on early Friday morning at the corner of Ben Yehuda Street and Shalom Aleichem Street in Tel Aviv, leaving one dead and ten injured. The military said the UAV, which traveled ten hours, was identified but not shot down by air defenses and sirens were not activated due to human error. The strike was clearly a wake-up call to Iran's multi-front threats; the Houthis, armed with increasingly sophisticated long-range weapons supplied by Iran, claimed responsibility. The Saudi channel Al-Arabiya reported that the

United States had intercepted a ballistic missile and three UAVs launched by the Houthis towards Israel, with the fourth UAV managing to reach Tel Aviv. Hagari added in his public report that "the signs indicating that the elimination of Mohammed Deif was successful were getting stronger. Rafa'a Salameh was certainly eliminated; Deif and Salameh sat next to each other at the time of the strike. Hamas is hiding what happened to Deif."[56]

Hamas's attack against Israel on October 7 would not have happened had he been president, Republican candidate Donald Trump said later that morning during his party's national convention in Milwaukee. The former president, who had survived an assassination attempt on July 13 at a rally in Butler, Pennsylvania, added, "We want our hostages back. And they better be back before I assume office, or you will be paying a very big price." It was unclear if Trump was speaking about the American-Israeli hostages or all of the Israeli hostages. Presumably, he was speaking of the American abductees since that was a repeating theme during the convention. Accepting the Republican presidential nomination, Trump promised "to end every single international crisis the current administration has created," and he blamed Biden for the Hamas attack against Israel on October 7.[57]

On Friday, the International Court of Justice in The Hague deemed Israel's occupation of the West Bank and East Jerusalem "de facto annexation" and that Israeli settlements were illegal under international law. The ICJ called for the evacuation of Israeli settlements, for the return of displaced Palestinians, and for the payment of reparations for damages. The Court also called out Israel's "systematic failure" to prevent settler violence against West Bank Palestinians and said that Gaza was effectively occupied by Israel—despite its 2005 disengagement from the Strip. Netanyahu lashed out at what he termed the ICJ's "lies," remarking "the Jewish people do not occupy their own land." On the other hand, Palestinian Authority head Mahmoud Abbas, encouraged by the European Commission's announcement that it would provide the PA with $435.5 million in emergency financial support in the coming two months, welcomed the court's decision. Calling it a "victory for justice," he added: "The Palestinian presidency urges the international community to demand that Israel, as an occupying power, end the occupation and withdraw unconditionally." Although the top UN court's advisory opinion was nonbinding, a ruling against Israel would likely lead to greater international sanctions against the settlement movement.[58]

In Operation Outstretched Arm, IDF fighter jets struck Houthi oil-refining targets and a power station in the area of the Hodeidah Port in Yemen on Saturday following the terrorist group's drone strike on Tel Aviv. The strike was the first time, despite 200 missiles and drones the Houthis had fired at the Jewish State since October 7, Israel had ever targeted Yemen, using eight squadrons consisting of F-35 aircraft with stealth striking capabilities and F-15 Eagles. This came one day after the *Wall Street Journal* reported that US intelligence agencies warned Russia might arm Houthi militants in Yemen with advanced anti-ship missiles in retaliation for the Biden administration's support for Ukrainian strikes inside Russia with US weapons. The new intelligence came as the top US Middle East commander recently advised in a classified letter to Defense Secretary Lloyd Austin that military operations in the region were "failing" to deter Houthi attacks on shipping in the Red Sea and that a broader approach was needed.[59]

Hezbollah launched heavy barrages on northern Israel the same day, this after the IDF announced that it had killed two commanders from Hezbollah's elite Radwan Force, as well as additional Radwan Force fighters. According to reports from Lebanon, eighteen people had been wounded in the earlier strikes. None were injured on Saturday after approximately forty-five rockets were fired from Lebanon, thirty of them towards the Golan Heights and fifteen towards the Galilee. As for Gaza, the IDF said an Israeli aircraft recently attacked and killed about twenty Hamas terrorists from the Shati Battalion, including Nukhba terrorists, spotters and snipers. Still, US Secretary of State Blinken declared that a cease-fire between Israel and Hamas was within sight, with negotiators "driving toward the goal line." UAE Special Envoy Lana Nusseibeh told the *Financial Times* that her country would send troops to Gaza if invited by the PA and if the United States would lead the mission. While Netanyahu prepared to leave for Washington to meet Biden and address a joint session of the US Congress, sources close to Biden told the *New York Times* that his advisers said he would not bow out of the presidential race before that visit so as not to give the Israeli prime minister "the satisfaction." The US chief executive had not offered Netanyahu a meeting in the White House since the latter was elected in December 2022.[60]

Following Israel's attack in Yemen's port city of Hodeidah on Saturday, which reportedly killed six people and wounded eighty, Houthi military spokesman Yahya Saree said several ballistic missiles were fired toward Israel's southernmost city of Eilat, and that a US ship in the Red Sea was also attacked. Saree claimed both assaults were "successful." The IDF said it intercepted a surface-to-surface ballistic missile fired from Yemen using the Arrow 3 missile defense system, while US Central Command said its forces shot down a Houthi drone over the Red Sea on Saturday. Three people were arrested in Spain and one more in Germany on suspicion of belonging to a network that supplied Hezbollah with parts to build kamikaze drones to be used in attacks in northern Israel. US Secretary of Defense Austin reaffirmed Israel's right to self-defense, noting that the Israeli strike on Saturday followed months of Houthi attacks. In addition, the US State Department said the International Court of Justice's advisory opinion, which declared Israel's West Bank settlements "unlawful" and added that Israel must end its presence there and in East Jerusalem, could "complicate efforts to resolve the conflict."[61]

The Israeli army and Shin Bet forces stated that the IDF killed twenty Hamas operatives including militant Nimer Hamida, who was involved in a West Bank attack that killed three IDF soldiers in October 2003. The military also confirmed the elimination of senior Al-Aqsa Martyrs Brigade member Az al-Din Akila last week. In a joint operation by the ISA, the IDF, and the Israel Police, a terrorist cell comprised of students who were members of the Hamas student organization at Bir Zeit University, known as "Kataeb Al-Islamiya," was recently arrested. The terrorists were suspected of acting on behalf of the Hamas headquarters in Turkey, aiming to provide an infrastructure for Hamas terrorist activities against Israelis. In a historic move, the IDF issued draft orders to 1,000 haredim aged 18–26 (85 percent single), 50 percent of a first wave of 3,000 conscription notices to be sent out. The same evening, most dramatic news came from cross the Atlantic when, after weeks of mounting pressure, Joe Biden announced in a stunning concession that he would step down as the Democratic nominee in the November presidential elections. In a statement published by the eighty-one-year-old president, he declared that he believed it to be "in the best interest of my party and the country for me to stand down and to focus solely on fulfilling my duties as president for the remainder of my term."[62]

Israeli politicians from across the spectrum responded by thanking Biden for his "unwavering support" for Israel over the years, Gallant's statement reflecting the general tone and adding "Your steadfast backing, especially during the war, has been invaluable. We are grateful for your leadership and friendship." President Herzog lauded his being the first US chief executive to visit Israel in wartime, a recipient of the Israeli Presidential Medal of Honor, and "as a true ally of the Jewish people, he is a symbol of the unbreakable bond between our two peoples." The Jewish Federations of North America recalled that Biden described himself as a "Zionist in my heart." Others pointed to his often recalling a meeting with then Prime Minister Golda Meir just before the Yom Kippur War, who told him "We have a secret weapon in our conflict with the Arabs. You see, we have no place else to go." The neophyte senator from Delaware retorted "We'll never stop working to ensure that Jews from around the world always have somewhere to go." "We'll never stop working to make sure Israel has a qualitative edge," he went on. "And whoever the next President is—Republican or Democrat—it will be the same because the American people, the American people are committed. The American people understand." In 2023, Biden made good on that promise, literally embracing Netanyahu in the wake of the October 7 attack by Hamas and pledging, "As long as the United States stands—and we will stand forever—we will not let you ever be alone."[63]

The IDF announced on Monday it was "about to forcefully operate against the terrorist organizations" in the eastern part of the humanitarian zone in the southern Gaza Strip due to intelligence information indicating Hamas terror infrastructure was located in the area. The IDF also said terror activities and rocket fire had been carried out towards Israel from there. As a result, the military stated it would adjust the humanitarian zone in Gaza in order to operate against the terror elements in the vicinity; its quick advance with tanks rolling into eastern Khan Younis killed scores of Hamas operatives. An IAF aircraft eliminated in the Gaza Strip Nukhba terrorist Muhammad Abu Seidu, who had participated in the October 7 massacre and led several attacks against IDF troops in Gaza. The military also noted that troops of the 162nd Division continued operations in the Rafah area. At the same time, in Tel al-Sultan, forces of the 401st Brigade killed dozens of terrorists in close-quarters combat and via an IAF aircraft.[64]

Meanwhile, Netanyahu headed for Washington, D.C., to, in his words, "anchor bipartisan support" for Israel, as well as to thank Biden for his help to Israel during the war and during "his distinguished career in public service." In addition, he would tell his friends on both sides of the Congressional political aisle that, regardless of whom the American people chose as their next president, "Israel remains America's indispensable and strong ally in the Middle East."[65]

The Shin Bet foiled an abduction plot by a terror cell from Aqabat Jabr, near Jericho. Mohammed Tariq, aged nineteen, and Amin Qatash, aged twenty, residents of that "refugee" camp, were arrested on suspicion of establishing a cell that aimed to carry out attacks on Israeli soldiers and civilians. A Canadian national who landed in Israel on Sunday and attempted to stab residents of the Israeli community of Netiv HaAsara near the border with Gaza was killed by local security. The number of IDF soldiers requesting mental health care had risen dramatically since the start of the Gaza war, data from the organization Natal (the Israel Trauma and Resiliency Center) showed. The same day, a group of prominent religious Zionist rabbis published a letter expressing opposition to a hostage deal, writing that "the price required for their release endangers the citizens of the country," and that the "public cannot accept" the conditions of withdrawing from Gaza and the end of the war before Hamas was subdued. The IDF said that seven drones were intercepted after crossing into Israel from Lebanon, and that it struck Hezbollah targets in southern Lebanon. French Foreign Minister Stéphane Séjourné criticized as "irresponsible and dangerous" comments by French lawmaker Thomas Portes of the far-left France Unbowed Party who said at a pro-Palestinian rally that "The Israeli delegation is not welcome in Paris. Israeli athletes are not welcome at the Olympic Games." Séjourné assured the Israeli delegation's safety during the competition.[66]

Senior Israeli army officials formulated a firm position according to which "the IDF could fully withdraw from the Gaza Strip for six weeks if a new hostage deal is signed," Kan News reported. According to the report, the defense officials predicted that the short period would not allow Hamas to critically regain new weapons or construct and rebuild tunnels. Their message sent to Netanyahu stated: "We are aware of the security consequences, but now is the time to prioritize the release of the hostage whose time is limited." This may have jarred the prime minister, who reportedly said the previous week at a security cabinet meeting that "the hostages are suffering but they are not dying"—even though of the 120 abductees still being held in Gaza more than half were believed to be no longer alive, with twenty having died to date in captivity. Following a prolonged discussion, Netanyahu instructed the negotiations team to travel to Doha, Qatar, after he met with Biden and addressed the US Congress.

Meeting on Monday night with representatives of the families of the hostages who accompanied the entourage to Washington, as well as with representatives of the families of the hostages who were in the United States, Netanyahu stressed "We are determined to bring them all back. The conditions to bring them back are ripe, for the simple reason that we are putting very, very strong pressure on Hamas. We are seeing a certain change, and I think this change will grow. We intend to do it—this is an objective of the war."[67]

On Tuesday, IDF aircraft attacked armed terrorists around the area of Tulkarm, operated in by the Menashe Territorial Brigade. *Al Jazeera* and local Palestinian reports claimed that Ashraf Nafi, commander in Tulkarm of the Izzadin al-Qassam Brigades, the military wing of Hamas, was killed together with Abu Abadhu, commander of the local Fatah Al-Aqsa Martyr Brigades group. The two terrorist groups acting in concert was also reflected in Chinese state media announcing that various Palestinian factions had agreed after three days of talks there to end their divisions and strengthen Palestinian unity by signing the Beijing Declaration on Tuesday morning. In Khan Younis, the troops of the 98th Division, led by the 7th Brigade, operated above and below ground over the past twenty-four hours, killing several terrorists in encounters with Hamas cells during the first hours of combat. The IDF also announced that several projectiles were launched the previous day by Hamas from the area of Al-Maghazi in western Khan Younis toward Israel. The projectiles fell inside the Strip, one hitting the UNRWA Al-Qarara school in Khan Younis. The World Health Organization (WHO) warned of a high risk of a polio outbreak in Gaza and beyond due to poor health and sanitation conditions; IDF soldiers began getting vaccination boosters against the disease.[68]

The US State Department rejected the idea of a Hamas-Fatah unity government in the Gaza Strip, following the announcement of a Palestinian Arab unity deal in Beijing. "Hamas has long been a terrorist organization. They have the blood of innocent civilians—both Israeli and Palestinian—on their hands," US State Department spokesman Matthew Miller said at a press briefing. Although Israeli public support for prioritizing a hostage deal over destroying Hamas climbed to seventy-two percent in July, after being at sixty-seven percent in June and forty-six percent in May, the Hostage and Missing Families Forum announced on Wednesday in citing a survey from Midgam Research and Consulting, the Israeli delegation set to depart for Qatar for hostage release talks on Thursday would only leave next week, an Israeli official said, after Netanyahu discussed the current cease-fire deal's framework with Biden. US Capitol Police said they arrested some 200 Jewish Voice for Peace activists protesting US military support for Israel inside a congressional building one day before Netanyahu was scheduled to deliver a speech to Congress. Trump posted: "Looking forward to seeing Bibi Netanyahu on Friday, and even more looking forward to achieving peace in the Middle East!"[69]

On the northern front, Hezbollah published drone footage allegedly taken on Tuesday of IAF planes, fuel storage facilities, command posts, underground facilities, control towers, and other military infrastructure at an airbase in northern Israel. The IDF said that the drone "only took footage" and did not affect the base's operations. A combat readiness exercise for a potential military operation in Lebanon was completed by the Reserve Brigade and the IDF's Northern Command led by the National Land Training Center, while IDF fighter jets struck Hezbollah targets in southern Lebanon twice on Wednesday. As for Gaza, Jerusalem announced that the IDF would evacuate sick and wounded Gazans to the UAE for medical treatment. An initial evacuation flight, carrying 250 patients, was expected to take off from Ramon airport near Eilat the following week. German Chancellor

Olaf Scholz said Berlin had made no decision so far to end its supply of weapons to Israel despite the International Court of Justice's opinion on the country's occupation of Palestinian territories.[70]

On July 24, Netanyahu turned his address to a joint meeting of Congress into a forceful, defiant defense of Israel's military campaign in Gaza. Citing the eulogy given by Yechiel Leiter at the funeral of his son Moshe, who fell in battle on November 10 of last year—"Because of the State of Israel, the Jewish people are no longer helpless in the face of our enemies," he cast it as a war for survival of the Jewish commonwealth and "a clash between barbarism and civilization." He called on four IDF soldiers and a few families of victims and hostages who were present to stand, eliciting long applause from the chamber, but made almost no mention of the tens of thousands of Palestinian civilians killed in Israel's drive to destroy Hamas. He condemned campus anti-Israel rallies and other critics of the war as "Tehran's useful idiots," aligning themselves with the world's most dangerous actors or apologists for terrorists. Netanyahu portrayed the conflict as a proxy fight with Iran that must be won at all costs to protect both Israel and the United States' "most radical and murderous enemy," advocating for a regional military alliance to counter Iran's influence and threats. Asserting that Israel "will not relent" until it defeated Hamas, he made a plea to God to bless the "great alliance between Israel and America forever" and praised both President Biden and former President Donald J. Trump while calling for more American weaponry to "finish the job." He placed the war in the context of the struggles of Jews throughout history, including the Holocaust. "After October 7, 'Never Again' is now," he declared, stressing the historical right of the Jewish people to the Land of Israel.

With this eloquent presentation, the Israeli prime minister surpassed British World War II Prime Minister Winston Churchill as the foreign leader who had addressed a joint session of Congress the greatest number of times—four. Yet the many standing ovations Netanyahu received (a record fifty-five) were clear evidence of how the longstanding US bipartisan consensus to back Israel had eroded since October 7, as Republicans clapped loudly and Democrats hung back, a few sitting silently and stone-faced. More than fifty Democratic lawmakers were absent, including Kamala Harris, their party's presidential nominee who was campaigning in the Midwest and declined to preside in her capacity as president of the Senate alongside Speaker Mike Johnson, a break with tradition. A *Jerusalem Post* editorial echoed the Israeli consensus: "By attending Netanyahu's speech in the vice president's role as president of the Senate, Harris would have sent one message. By not attending, she sent another. It's a bad start." Outside the Capitol, pepper spray filled the air as police officers tried to push back protesters who had gathered to jeer Netanyahu. More than 5,000 pro-Palestinian demonstrators held signs calling him a war criminal, burned an effigy of him and an American flag, as well as vandalized statues with anti-Israel slogans including "Free Palestine" and "Hamas is coming."[71]

During the anti-Israel protests, the Freedom Bell and a monument to Christopher Columbus were vandalized with graffiti endorsing Hamas, and the American flags that flew at Union Station were taken down and burned. Responding to these demonstrations in the nation's capital, Vice President Harris condemned "any individuals associating with the brutal terrorist organization Hamas, which has vowed to annihilate the State of Israel and kill Jews. Pro-Hamas graffiti and rhetoric is abhorrent, and we must not tolerate it in our nation," she said. Harris also condemned the burning of the American flag, "a symbol of our highest ideals as a nation and represents the promise of America." While supporting the right to peacefully protest, she emphasized (without offering a counterplan) that "antisemitism, hate and violence of any kind have no place in our nation." The same day, Biden stated, during an Oval Office semi-farewell address to explain his decision to depart from the 2024 presidential race, "I'm going to keep working to end the war in Gaza, bring home all the hostages, and bring peace and security to the Middle East and end this war," Trump also called for a quick end to Israel's war with Hamas and to secure the return of the hostages, adding that "Israel has to better manage its public relations."[72]

Hamas weighed in on Netanyahu's speech, saying he is "the one who thwarted all efforts aimed at ending the war and concluding a deal to release the prisoners" despite the continuous efforts of mediators in Egypt and Qatar. It also stated that Netanyahu's perception that the Gaza enclave should be led by Palestinians who do not seek to destroy Israel were "pure delusions and fantasies," noting that the "Palestinian people are the only ones who have the right to determine their fate and determine who will rule them." "Netanyahu's speech was full of lies, and it will not succeed in covering up for the failure and defeat in the face of the resistance to cover up for the crimes of the war of genocide his army is committing against the people of Gaza," Hamas senior official Sami Abu Zuhri said in an interview. He added that any alliance with Israel from any party would be a "treason to the blood of martyrs." Hamas also accused Washington of continuing to provide "all means of political and military support to Israel and giving the Israeli government the necessary cover to escape punishment." J Street, a progressive pro-Israel advocacy group, criticized the speech, echoing *Haaretz* and others for failing to offer "an actual plan for ending the war and bringing real security and peace to the region." In addition, Air Force General C. Q. Brown, chairman of the Joint Chiefs of Staff, said he still had not been able to see much from Israel about its "day after" planning once the war with Hamas ended.[73]

The bodies of hostages Maya Goren, Master Sergeant (res.) Oren Goldin, Staff Sergeant Tomer Ahimas, and Sergeant Kiril Brodski were recovered from Hamas captivity in Gaza, the IDF and the Shin Bet said in a joint statement on Thursday. The bodies were retrieved from a Khan Younis tunnel during an IDF operation led by ISA field analysts and coordinators. Not long thereafter, the IDF added: "It has been cleared for publication that during the joint IDF and ISA operation, the body of the fallen soldier held captive Sergeant Major (res.) Ravid Aryeh Katz, who fell in combat during the brutal October 7th attacks and whose body was abducted to the Gaza Strip, was also rescued." That left the count of 115 hostages, 41 of them no longer alive. Over the same day, more than sixty terror targets were struck by the IAF throughout the Gaza Strip, including military structures and terrorist infrastructure, while Division 98 destroyed some fifty terror infrastructures in the Khan Younis area.[74]

At the White House on Thursday, Netanyahu, speaking as "a proud Jewish Zionist to a proud Irish-American Zionist," thanked Biden for fifty years of public service and fifty years of support for the State of Israel. "President Biden," read the official US statement which followed, "expressed the need to close the remaining gaps, finalize the deal as soon as possible, bring the hostages home, and reach a durable end to the war in Gaza." The president also raised the need to remove any obstacles to the flow of aid to Gaza and "restoring basic services for those in need, and the critical importance of protecting civilian lives during military operations." Finally, it said, "President Biden reaffirmed the United States' ironclad commitment to Israel's security against all threats from Iran and its proxies, including Hamas, Hezbollah, and the Houthis."

Vice President Harris, meeting Netanyahu afterwards, also expressed strong support for Israel's right to defend itself from terrorism, but soon, echoing her party's left-wing base, declared in a tweet on X that "far too many innocent civilians" had died in Gaza and that "I will not be silent" about their suffering. Hamas, which she had not specifically condemned, reaffirmed that it insisted on adopting the latest proposal it submitted to hostage deal mediators and doubled down on its demand for a full Israeli withdrawal from the Gaza Strip, the Hezbollah-affiliated *Al-Mayadeen* reported on Saturday. According to its source, Hamas had demanded that Israel's withdrawal from the Strip would include the Netzarim Corridor and the Philadelphi Corridor. As for Biden's three-phase proposal, designed to let a hostage deal get underway while addressing the issue of a permanent cease-fire, Harris made it appear in her statement as if the deal would include a complete IDF withdrawal from Gaza in phase two, a step that had not been agreed upon. *De facto*, she gave Hamas a pledge of a permanent cease-fire before the deal got underway, which led a senior Israeli official to worry that this might harm the hostages' release. Other officials were also frustrated by the vice president's characterization of the food insecurity in Gaza, explaining that Netanyahu had also emphasized to Harris how many steps Israel was taking to provide humanitarian assistance to Palestinians in Gaza.[75]

After three years of mostly not speaking, Netanyahu and Trump had a warm reunion on Friday in what the latter likes to call the "Winter White House," his Mar-a-Lago Palm Beach Club. The Republican presidential candidate took the opportunity to accuse the Biden administration of bringing the world to the brink of war. "If we win, it will be very simple, it's all going to work out, and very quickly," Trump said as Netanyahu and his entourage looked on. "If we don't, you're going to end up with major wars in the Middle East and maybe a Third World War." Speaking after the meeting, Trump remarked that he had "always had a very good relationship" with the Israeli prime minister and called Vice President Harris's remarks on Israel after her meeting with Netanyahu "disrespectful."[76]

The next day, twelve Israelis were killed and twenty-nine injured, including eight seriously, in a rocket attack from Lebanon on the Druze town of Majdal Shams in the Golan Heights, the most serious incident caused by an attack from Lebanon since the start of the war. Most of the casualties were children and teens next to a soccer field and playground. EU foreign policy chief Josep Borrell condemned the attack on Majdal Shams as a "bloodbath" and called for an independent probe—with no mention of Hezbollah, which denied responsibility for the attack; the BBC, claiming that this occurred in "the Israeli-occupied Golan," joined CNN in initially headlining that the children "died" rather than were killed. Blinken said at a news conference on Sunday that there was "every indication" that the rocket was fired by Hezbollah. Gallant called the deadly attack a "terrible tragedy," pledging that Iran's Lebanese terror proxy "will pay the price." Iranian Foreign Minister Nasser Kanaani responded: "Any ignorant action of the Zionist regime can lead to the broadening of the scope of instability, insecurity and war in the region," adding that any "adventurism" in Lebanon could lead to "unforeseen consequences and reactions." In Gaza, Palestinians reported that Israeli strikes killed 23 people in the southern Gazan city of Khan Younis, and killed at least 30, wounding 100, at a school in central Gaza's Deir al-Balah. The IDF said Hamas was using the school as a command center.[77]

The Israeli military responded to the Majdal Shams attack with overnight IAF strikes, chiefly targeting places in Lebanon that it had often hit in the past, mostly close to the border with Israel or surrounding the southern port of Tyre. It reported one deep strike in the Beqaa Valley, roughly sixty miles north of the Israel-Lebanon border, where it had been striking less frequently since February. Israeli commanders were wary of opening up a second major war while the war in Gaza was still raging. After nine months of fighting with Hamas and Hezbollah, Israel's munitions stockpiles had dwindled, raising questions about how intense a battle it could fight in Lebanon. Israel's Foreign Ministry spokesman, Oren Marmorstein, said in a statement on Sunday that a full-scale war could still be averted through the enforcement of a never-implemented UN Security Council resolution 1701 from 2006 that would create a demilitarized zone in southern Lebanon. "Hezbollah will pay a heavy price, which it has not paid up to now," Netanyahu's office said in an overnight statement. In a joint statement by the UN special coordinator for Lebanon, Jeanine Hennis-Plasschaert, and the chief of UN peacekeeping forces in Lebanon, Lt. Gen. Aroldo Lázaro, the pair urged Israel and Hezbollah to "exercise maximum restraint," warning that "it could ignite a wider conflagration that would engulf the entire region in a catastrophe beyond belief." A Gaza cease-fire was the best way to diffuse Israeli-Hezbollah violence, Blinken said the next day.[78]

Thousands took part in the nighttime funerals of the twelve children and teens who were killed on Saturday. Druze spiritual leader in Israel Sheikh Mowafaq Tarif called the fatal incident the worst disaster in Druze history. "It's a Saturday that will be engraved in memory as a low point in humanity, the killing of children. The scenes of horror will never be erased," he said on behalf of Israel's 150,000 Druze citizens. IDF spokesperson Hagari noted that the rocket was manufactured in Iran and was only held by Hezbollah. He named local Hezbollah commander Ali Mohammed Yahya as responsible for the launch, which was made from the village of Chebaa in southern Lebanon. Lebanese Foreign Minister Abdallah Bou Habib said a significant Israeli attack would lead to "regional war," and that the United States had asked the Lebanese government to restrain Hezbollah. In turn, Lebanon asked Washington to urge restraint from Israel. In an interview with Al Hadath News, Bou Habib said that Hezbollah was ready to retreat behind the Litani River "on the condition that Israel stops its violations." Lebanon's caretaker Prime Minister Najib Mikati issued a statement "condemning acts of violence and attacks against civilians" and calling for an "immediate cessation of hostilities on all fronts." Netanyahu decided to postpone the transfer of sick and wounded Gazan children to receive medical treatment in the UAE, a source familiar with the matter told *Haaretz*, adding that the decision was made due to Hezbollah's rocket attack on Majdal Shams.[79]

On Sunday morning, senior Hezbollah official Mohammed Ra'ad warned Israel against "starting a widescale war against Lebanon," saying that doing so would be "[Israel's] end." Iran's new president told French President Emmanuel Macron that a possible Israeli attack on Lebanon would have "serious consequences." Hezbollah reportedly started transporting precision missiles ahead of a possible confrontation with Israel. While the Biden administration warned Israel against targeting Beirut in response to Hezbollah's rocket attack on Saturday, the US embassy in Lebanon urged American citizens there to be prepared to "shelter in a place for long periods of time" should commercial flights stop. About 200 residents of Majdal Shams protested against Netanyahu during his visit to the town, greeting him with chants of "Get out" and "Murderer." As locals called for him to leave, the prime minister pledged a "harsh response" against Hezbollah, saying that "the State of Israel cannot and will not normalize this." PA leader Abbas maintained silence regarding the attack, but Turkey's Islamist leader Recep Tayyip Erdoğan threatened to invade Israel if the Jewish State acted against Hezbollah.[80]

Protesters and far-right Knesset members broke into the Sde Teiman detention facility in the Negev after Military Police officers raided it and detained nine soldiers on suspicion of abusing a Palestinian detainee. IDF Chief of Staff Halevi reacted thus: "We are at war, and actions of this kind endanger the security of the country. I strongly condemn the incident, and we are working to restore order at the base." A statement from Netanyahu's office made the same point. Protesters then succeeded in breaking into the Military Police base in Beit Lid. attempting to reach the prison on-site where the soldiers were held for questioning. In response, New Hope-United Right Chairman Gideon Sa'ar posted on X, saying, "The anarchy must stop. Immediately." Separately, the IDF began investigating suspicions of a violation of international law by troops who blew up a main water reservoir in Rafah's northwestern Tel Sultan neighborhood, close to the Israeli-designated humanitarian zone. According to a report in *Haaretz*, the troops who carried out the demolition had received approval from their brigade commander but did not ask for permission from senior officers in the IDF Southern Command.[81]

US Secretary of Defense Austin said at a press conference he did not believe that a fight between Israel and Hezbollah was inevitable, and that Washington would like to see things resolved in a diplomatic fashion. Hezbollah, however, rejected calls from international envoys to avoid responding to an anticipated Israeli attack in retaliation for the rocket strike on the Druze town of Majdal

Shams. That IDF retaliation came on July 30, with a major explosion in southern Beirut that eliminated Fouad Shukr, considered the number two in Hezbollah and in charge of the organization's military activities. He had been leading the development of Hezbollah's missile arsenal and had helped command Hezbollah's forces in Syria, aiding the Assad regime in slaughtering its own people. Shukr also played the central role in the Majdal Shams attack and in the October 23, 1983, bombing of the US Marine Corps Barracks in Beirut which killed 241 US military personnel and wounded 128 others.

Defense Minister Gallant wrote on X that killing Shukr proved that no one could kill Israelis with impunity, and that "there is nowhere Israel will not strike in order to exact a heavy price from anyone for harming Israel." Halevi remarked that Israel "will not accept Hezbollah's presence on the border" and that "returning to October 6 is not the goal." The only way to prevent war with Hezbollah, Israeli Foreign Minister Katz insisted, was the immediate implementation of UN Resolution 1701 calling for Hezbollah to retreat beyond the Litani River. Ali Ammar, a Hezbollah representative in Lebanon's parliament, would have none of this, declaring Israel "demands war and we are up for it, God willing, we are up for it."[82]

Early Wednesday morning, a remote device detonated the explosive planted hours earlier in the Tehran apartment where Hamas political chief Ismail Haniyeh, present for the inauguration of Iran's new president, was staying. His killing would "take the battle to new dimensions" and have major repercussions, responded Hamas's military wing, while Senior Hamas official Khalil al-Haya said that "Hamas, Iran, and Lebanon will not let the assassination pass quietly." Iranian President Masou Pezeshkian announced that Iran would "defend its territorial integrity . . . and will make the terrorist occupiers regret their cowardly act." Iran's Islamic Revolutionary Guard Corps said in a statement that "the killing of Haniyeh will be met with a harsh and painful response," while announcing that avenging Haniyeh's assassination was "Tehran's duty" because it occurred in the Iranian capital. PA President Mahmoud Abbas condemned the "despicable" assassination and called on the Palestinian public to "stand tall and show unity, patience and stability in the face of Israeli occupation." Blinken said that Washington was not involved in, or made aware of, the intention to assassinate Haniyeh, but Iran's Foreign Ministry said it emphasized US "responsibility" for Haniyeh's assassination because of its support for Israel.

Other capitals reacted accordingly. The Iraqi militia Kataib Hezbollah said that Haniyeh's killing in Tehran "broke all rules of engagement." Qatar's Foreign Ministry minced no words in stating that "the assassination of Haniyeh is a heinous crime, a dangerous act and a clear violation of international and humanitarian laws and will destroy the possibility of achieving peace." Egypt said Haniyeh's killing indicated a lack of Israeli political will for de-escalating tensions in the region. The Jordanian Foreign Ministry condemned the killing and blamed Israel for breaking international law and harming regional stability. Germany's Foreign Minister Annalena Baerbock said that "Hamas is a terrorist organization that has carried out countless brutal terror attacks on Israel. The main issue right now is to prevent a regional flare-up, and not to cause the entire region to plunge into chaos." Russia's Foreign Ministry called on "all parties to refrain from steps that could trigger a large-scale conflict." China and Turkey condemned the assassination and warned it could plunge the region into chaos. "It has been revealed once again that the government of Netanyahu has no intention of achieving peace," Turkey's foreign ministry asserted.[83]

This last day of July ended with a question. Events of the last two months had appeared to corroborate the 1849 observation of Jean-Baptiste Alphonse Karr, French journalist, critic, and novelist, that "the more things change, the more they stay the same." Yet might the IDF's dramatic killings of Fouad Shukr and Ismail Haniyeh at July's end prove to be a game changer in the war that, come August 1, 2024, would be day 300? The same Thursday, Blinken and Qatari Prime Minister Al Thani spoke on the telephone about securing a cease-fire between Israel and Hamas in the Gaza Strip, while UK Foreign Secretary David Lammy and Defense Secretary John Healey were in Qatar to drive efforts to end that conflict. (A few days earlier, the *Daily Telegraph* had published a harsh column against Lammy for the Labour Party's "shameful betrayal of Israel" after he announced his decision to reinstate funding for UNRWA, "an organization so closely connected to Hamas.") In a conversation with Austin, Gallant said that Israel was working to achieve an outline that would allow the return of the hostages, and that Jerusalem did not intend to escalate the situation in the region any further.[84] The realization of this worthy prospect, as well as a peaceful Israel-Hezbollah resolution, remained in doubt—as elusive as ever.

Endnotes

1 Israel National News, July 1, 2024; *Haaretz*, July 1, 2024. The IDF Commando Brigade has special units. Egoz focuses on counterterrorism operations, Duvdevan on undercover counterterrorism operations, and Maglan on reconnaissance.
2 *New York Times*, July 2, 2024.
3 *Haaretz*, July 2, 2024.
4 *Haaretz*, July 3, 2024.
5 *Haaretz*, July 4, 2024; *Jerusalem Post*, July 5, 2024.
6 *Haaretz*, July 5, 2024.

7   Institute for the Study of War, July 5, 2024.
8   David M. Weinberg, "Judea and Samaria Are on Fire—Literally," *Jerusalem Post*, July 5, 2024. In the West Bank, Area A is exclusively administered by the Palestinian Authority; Area B is administered by both the Palestinian Authority and Israel.

    The Green Line refers to the line of demarcation that separated Israeli, Jordanian, Syrian, and Egyptian forces at the conclusion of Israel's 1948 War of Independence. It was delineated in the 1949 armistice agreements that formally ended the war, and served as Israel's *de facto* international border (the sovereign State of Israel constituting seventy-eight percent of Palestine under the British Mandate) until the 1967 Six Day War. Its name derives from the fact that the diplomats reportedly used a green marker in drawing up the agreement.

    The Jordanian parliament's annexation on April 24, 1950, of the West Bank, which it occupied during Israel's 1948 War of Independence, was recognized only by Great Britain, Iraq, and Pakistan. Jordan formally waived its claim over the territory in 1988, referencing the 1950 resolution.

    During the Six Day War in June 1967, with Israel attacked by Egypt, Syria, and Jordan, the Jewish State vastly increased the territory under its control, taking possession of East Jerusalem, the Golan, the West Bank, the Gaza Strip, and the Sinai peninsula. The Green Line thus came to mark the border between Israel and the territories it captured in that war. As the border between Israel and the West Bank remains the only boundary whose precise route remains in substantial dispute, the Green Line is most used today to refer to the dividing line between those territories.

    Israel has long maintained that the Green Line has no international legal significance, delineating merely the location where the armies that fought the 1948 war happened to be at the time a cease-fire was reached. Israel has also asserted that the 1949 borders are indefensible, sometimes referring to them, in Abba Eban's phrase, as "Auschwitz borders" because they would narrow Israel to just a few miles wide at their narrowest point. As a result, both Israeli right- and left-wing governments have insisted on maintaining a military presence east of the Green Line, even in the event of a peace agreement. Jerusalem continues to maintain that this territory is "disputed."

    Critics, maintaining that this territory is "occupied" (most Palestinian Arabs consider this for *all* of Israel), charge that Israel has been systematically undermining the significance of the Green Line (and by extension, the prospects for an Israeli-Palestinian peace deal) by continuing to build and expand settlements east of the line, and by routing its West Bank security barrier in ways that depart significantly from it, sometimes veering kilometers into territory that Palestinians hope one day will become the territory of a Palestinian state.
9   *Yisrael Hayom*, July 6, 2024.
10 *Haaretz*, July 6, 2024; *Times of Israel*, July 6, 2024.
11 *Haaretz*, July 7, 2024; *Times of Israel*, July 7, 2024; World Israel News, July 7, 2024.
12 JNS, July 7, 2024.
13 *New York Times*, July 7, 2024; *Wall St. Journal*, July 7, 2024.
14 Israel National News, July 7, 2024.
15 Israel National News, July 7, 2024. A security source involved in the talks said the document represented Netanyahu's personal opinion, and not that of other officials involved in the negotiations. Diplomatic sources expressed concern that Netanyahu's decision to issue a list of "red lines" was intended to scuttle the deal, with one telling *Haaretz* that "Netanyahu boxed himself in. Israel won't be able to compromise on any of these demands now and will find it difficult to show flexibility in places that could have helped to promote the deal." *Haaretz*, July 7, 2024.
16 *Haaretz*, July 7, 2024: AP, July 8, 2024.
17 *Jerusalem Post*, July 8, 2024.
18 *Jerusalem Post*, July 8, 2024; *Haaretz*, July 7, 2024; Israel National News, July 8, 2024.
19 AP, July 8, 2024.

20 *Washington Post*, July 8, 2024; *Haaretz*, July 8, 2024.
21 *Times of Israel*, July 8, 2024.
22 *Jerusalem Post*, July 8, 2024.
23 *Jerusalem Post*, July 8, 2024; *Haaretz*, July 8, 2024; JNS, July 8, 2024.
24 *Jerusalem Post*, July 9, 2024; *Haaretz*, July 9, 2024.
25 Israel National News, July 9, 2024.
26 *Yisrael Hayom*, July 8, 2024. Lober, rabbi and actor, had staged a one-man play hoping it would help him come to terms with his loss and bring comfort to others in wartime. *October 7* is an adaption of a one-man show that Lober wrote for his Aspaklaria theater company twenty years ago. It tells the story of Nadav, who is attempting to move on with his life and raise his three children alone after losing his wife, Orli, in a terror attack. Lober thought of putting on the play after the war broke out on October 7. He had planned to make some changes to the manuscript, telling the stories of those who lost their loved ones during that shocking, tragic day. On October 8, the sixth of his nine children, whom he called Yehonatan, was drafted for reserve duty. Lober was planning on staging the play on January 7, three months after October 7, then changed his mind. However, during the seven days of mourning (*shiv'a*) for his son, he saw how others needed comfort as well, and decided to put on the play. Lober performed *October 7* on January 25, marking thirty days since Yehonatan's death, and then on January 27 and 28, in the Gerard Behar Theater in Jerusalem. The hour-long play is a monologue delivered by a father who is grieving "but decides to live alongside his mourning," said Lober. *Times of Israel*, Jan. 27, 2024.
27 Yonah Jeremy Bob, "PM, Gallant Break over Hostages: Does Netanyahu Want Partial or No Deal?—Analysis," *Jerusalem Post*, July 9, 2024.
28 *Haaretz*, July 9–10, 2024; *Jerusalem Post*, July 9, 2024.
29 *Haaretz*, July 9, 2024; IDF News, July 9, 2024.
30 Israel National News, July 10, 2024; *Haaretz*, July 10, 2024.
31 *Jerusalem Post*, June 30, 2024.
32 *Jerusalem Post*, July 10, 2024; Israel National News, July 10, 2024; *Haaretz*, July 10, 2024; World Israel News, July 10, 2024.
33 *Haaretz*, July 10, 2024.
34 Israel National News, July 10, 2024.
35 *Wall St. Journal*, July 10, 2024; *Haaretz*, July 15, 2024.
36 Israel National News, July 11, 2024; *New York Times*, July 12, 2024; *Jerusalem Post*, Jan. 11, 2024.
37 *Haaretz*, July 11, 2024; *Jerusalem Post*, July 11, 2024. Israel National News, July 11, 2024.
38 *Times of Israel*, July 11, 2024; *Jerusalem Post*, July 11, 2024.
39 JNS, July 11, 2024; Israel National News, July 11, 2024.
40 Israel National News, July 12, 2024.
41 *Haaretz*, July 11, 2024; Israel National News, July 12, 2024.
42 *Haaretz*, July 12, 2024.
43 *Haaretz*, July 13, 2024; *Jerusalem Post*, July 13, 2024. On July 18, the IDF released multiple recordings obtained by military intelligence of Gazans praising Israel's assassination strike on Hamas military chief Deif. The Gazans on the recordings also expressed hope that the IDF would kill Gaza Hamas chief Sinwar in the near future, which would then hopefully bring an end to the war. They also reflected the common belief in Gaza that Deif was in fact dead, the primary view of IDF intelligence, although no Israeli official wanted to say that he was definitely dead since Hamas had not confirmed it and since no body was recovered. *Jerusalem Post*, July 18, 2024.
44 Israel National News, July 14, 2024; *Haaretz*, July 14, 2024.
45 Israel National News, July 14, 2024; IDF News, July 14, 2024; *Times of Israel*, July 10, 2024; *Jerusalem Post*, July 14, 2024; World Israel News, July 14, 2024. Sinwar was freed with more

than 1,000 Palestinian prisoners in a 2011 swap for the Israeli soldier Gilad Shalit, which Prime Minister Netanyahu had personally pushed for.
46 *Haaretz*, July 15, 2024; IDF News, July 15, 2024; *New York Times*, July 12, 2024; *Times of Israel*, July 15, 2024.
47 Israel National News, July 16, 2024; *Jerusalem Post*, July 16, 2024.
48 *Jerusalem Post*, July 16, 2024.
49 Israel National News, July 16, 2024. From 1998 until his assassination in a drone strike by the United States in 2020, Qasem Soleimani was the commander of the Quds Force, Iran's Islamic Revolutionary Guard Corps division primarily responsible for extraterritorial and clandestine military operations. The Abraham Accords were bilateral agreements on Arab–Israeli normalization signed between Israel and the United Arab Emirates and Bahrain on September 15, 2020. Mediated by the United States, the historic occasion was hosted by US President Donald Trump on the Truman Balcony of the White House. This was followed on August 11, 2021, with Morocco and Israel signing three accords on political consultations, aviation, and culture. In November 2021, Morocco and Israel signed a defense agreement. As a component of the deal, the United States agreed to recognize Moroccan sovereignty over the Western Sahara.
50 *Times of Israel*, July 17, 2024; *Haaretz*, July 17, 2024.
51 *Times of Israel*, July 17, 2024; *Haaretz*, July 17, 2024. For Shiite Muslims, ʿĀshūrāʾ is predominantly a day of mourning in memory of the martyrdom of Imam al-Ḥusayn ibn ʿAlī, the grandson of Prophet Muhammad, against the Umayyad forces loyal to the Caliph Yazīd I at the Battle of Karbala in 680 AD. They don black clothes, observe abstinence, fast, and schedule processions on the tenth day of the month of Muḥarram. They also refrain from attending and celebrating all joyous events in this period.
52 Judith Miller, "The Lebanon War Is Coming: Whose Side Will America Be on?," *Tablet*, July 17, 2024; *Haaretz*, July 17, 2024.
53 *Jerusalem Post*, July 18, 2024.
54 Israel National News, July 18, 2024; Einav Halabi. "As Hamas's Power Collapses, Old Feuds Are Resurfacing," Mosaic, July 18, 2024.
55 *Times of Israel*, July 18, 2024; *Haaretz*, July 18, 2024.
56 Israel National News, July 19, 2024.
57 Israel National News, July 19, 2024; *Haaretz*, July 19, 2024.
58 *Haaretz*, July 19, 2024; *Jerusalem Post*, July 19, 2024,
59 *Haaretz*, July 20, 2024; *New York Times*, July 20, 2024; *Wall St. Journal*, July 19, 2024.
60 *Haaretz*, July 18–20, 2024; Israel National News, July 19–20, 2024.
61 JNS, July 21, 2024; *Haaretz*, July 18, 21, 2024.
62 IDF News, July 21, 2024; Israel National News, July 21; *Times of Israel*, July 21, 2024; *New York Times*, July 21, 2024. The former editor-in-chief of the *Jerusalem Post* noted that the IDF currently was short fifteen battalions (around 10,000 soldiers), "and a blanket exemption for almost 1.5 million people has not been sustainable for a long time. Now, we all know that it is a national suicide." Yaakov Katz, "Time is Running Out for the Gaza Hostages," *Jerusalem Post*, July 19, 2024.
63 Israel National News, July 22, 2024; Ron Kampeas, "Biden Withdrawal is End of an Era of Democrat U.S. Presidents with Deep Israel Commitment," *Times of Israel*, July 21, 2024.
64 *Jerusalem Post*, July 22, 2024; IDF News, July 22, 2024.
65 JNS, July 22, 2024.
66 *Haaretz*, July 22, 2024. The Zionist rabbis included Ramat Gan Chief Rabbi Yaakov Ariel and leading hardliners, such as settler leaders Dov Lior and Elyakim Levanon and Safed Chief Rabbi Shmuel Eliyahu. *Times of Israel*, July 22, 2024.
67 Israel National News, July 22, 2024; *Jerusalem Post*, July 19, 2024; *Forward*, July 22, 2024.
68 *Jerusalem Post*, July 23, 2024; *Haaretz*, July 23, 2024; Israel National News, July 23, 2024. Both Hamas and Fatah said the accord signed in China, which provided no guarantees or

timeline, was only an initial step. German Foreign Minister Annalena Baerbock reacted with skepticism to the declaration, saying that "we now have to look at what this means," and that as a first step Hamas must release all the hostages it holds.

69 *Haaretz*, July 24, 2024; IDF News, July 24, 2024; *Jerusalem Post*, July 24, 2024.
70 *Haaretz*, July 24, 2024.
71 *New York Times*, July 25, 2024; *Wall St. Journal*, July 25, 2024; *Jerusalem Post*, July 25, 2024; Israel National News, July 25, 2024. The prime minister said nothing about the intelligence his country had collected ahead of the Hamas October 7 attack that warned a brutal terror strike was brewing. He called out the military heroes of that day but made no mention of the slow response of the Israeli defense forces nor of a possible hostage settlement. He did, however, hint at some flexibility in negotiations for a cease-fire and prisoner-release deal, just days after Secretary of State Blinken said those talks were at "the ten-yard line." He stopped short of saying Hamas had to be destroyed, a line he used in the past to slow talk of such an agreement. While almost everyone present stood and applauded after he pledged "I will not rest until all their loved ones are home," most of the roughly one dozen relatives of the eight American citizens being held in Gaza remained in their gallery seats directly across from Netanyahu. They stared stoically and uncomfortably, seeming utterly unconvinced by the prime minister's words.
72 Israel National News, July 25, 2024; *New York Times*, July 24, 2024; *Haaretz*, July 25, 2024.
73 *Haaretz*, July 25, 2024; Israel National News, July 25, 2024; *Jerusalem Post*, July 25, 2024.
74 Israel National News, July 25, 2024; IDF News, July 25, 2024.
75 JNS, July 26, 2024; *New York Times*, July 26, 2024; IDF News, July 26, 2024; *Jerusalem Post*, July 26, 2024. Harris's statement appeared ignorant of the facts that Hamas regularly used Palestinian civilians, including children, as human shields, built a vast tunnel system rather than better the living conditions of fellow Gazans, and stole water pipes to produce rockets against Israel, or that the pro-Hamas riots on US college campuses were coordinated by agents of the Iranian government, as charged by the Biden administration's Director of National Intelligence Avril Haines. Joel Leyden, "Vice President Kamala Harris Needs Cross-Cultural Middle East Training—Opinion," *Jerusalem Post*, July 29, 2024. On July 8, in an interview with the *Nation*, Harris remarked she could "understand" the sentiments of anti-Israel protesters. She said, "There are things some of the protesters are saying that I absolutely reject . . . but we have to navigate it. I understand the emotion behind it." World Israel News, July 30, 2024.
76 JTA, July 26, 2024; *Haaretz*, July 27, 2024.
77 *Haaretz*, July 27, 2024; Israel National News, July 28, 2024; *New York Times*, July 28, 2024; JNS, July 28, 2024.
78 *New York Times*, July 28, 2024; *Haaretz*, July 28, 2024.
79 Israel National News, July 28, 2024; *Haaretz*, July 28, 2024. The IDF released images of fragments recovered from the impact site which matched old photos of the Iranian Falaq-1 rocket. The rocket carried a 50-kilogram, or about 110-pound, warhead, an unusually heavy payload, Israel's military said. *Wall St. Journal*, July 28, 2024.
80 *Haaretz*, July 29, 2024; IDF News, July 29, 2024; JNS, July 29, 2024; United with Israel, July 29, 2024.
81 *Jerusalem Post*, July 29, 2024; *Times of Israel*, July 29, 2024. The Israeli government informed the High Court of Justice one month later that conditions at the Sde Teiman detention facility would improve starting in mid-September, when a new prison wing will be opened. The state added that inmates would be blindfolded and bound with steel handcuffs upon their arrival for ninety-six hours and then relieved from these constraints, and will not remain handcuffed and blindfolded for twenty-four hours a day as has been the custom to date. *Haaretz*, Aug. 30, 2024.
82 *Haaretz*, July 30–31, 2024. The United States had put a bounty of $5 million for the death of Shukr (also known as Al-Hajj Mohsen or Mohsen Shukr) after the deadly 1983 attack.

83 *Haaretz*, July 31, 2024. Two officials confirmed to Axios the earlier report from the *New York Times* that Haniyeh was killed by an explosive that had been planted in the room where he had been staying two months before the assassination. According to the London *Jewish Chronicle*, Israeli intelligence learned which room Haniyeh stayed in during each of his visits to Tehran and hired two Iranian Revolutionary Guard Corps members of the al-Mahdi security unit to plant an explosive that featured artificial intelligence technology similar in tactic to the remote-controlled AI robot weapon that Israel used to assassinate Iran's top nuclear scientist Mohsen Fakhrizadeh in 2020. The device was then detonated remotely nine hours later by Mossad agents in Iran after they received word that Haniyeh was in the room. The report also stated that the American government had not been informed of the assassination ahead of time. According to the source, Haniyeh was seen as a hardliner in the negotiations, and it was determined that removing him would remove an obstacle to a cease-fire deal, despite the "pragmatic" face Haniyeh attempted to present to the mainstream media. *New York Times*, Aug. 1, 2024; Israel National News, Aug. 1 and 6, 2024.

84 *Haaretz*, July 31, 2024; Israel National News, Aug. 2, 2024.

CHAPTER 5

The War Grinds On

Iran's Supreme Leader, Ayatollah Ali Khamenei, "issued an order for Iran to strike Israel directly, in retaliation for the killing in Tehran of Hamas's political leader, Ismail Haniyeh," two days earlier, the *New York Times* reported on August 1, citing three Iranian officials. Even as Netanyahu declared that Israel was at a high level of preparedness for any scenario, both defensively and offensively, Israel's National Security Council urged the public to take extra precautions while traveling, citing a possibility that Iran, Hamas, and Hezbollah might try to target embassies, synagogues, and other sites abroad. The South African government conveyed condolences to Haniyeh's family and demanded an investigation into his killing; Indonesia's President Joko Widodo termed the killing "intolerable." UN Security Council countries called for stepped-up diplomatic efforts to avert a wider Middle East conflict. Earlier on Thursday, the *Financial Times* reported that the United States and the European Union were pressuring Iran to avoid responding to Haniyeh's killing. Speaking at the funeral of senior Hezbollah commander Fouad Shukr, Hezbollah chief Hassan Nasrallah warned that a red line had been crossed and that "we have entered a new phase in all arenas." Nasrallah added that Shukr's assassination by Israel on July 30 would "definitely" prompt a response, and that those who want to end the war should focus on applying pressure to end the war in Gaza, and not on Hezbollah.[1]

US President Biden said on Thursday night that the elimination of Haniyeh in Tehran was not helpful for a cease-fire in Gaza. Referencing his telephone conversation with Netanyahu earlier that evening, the chief executive said he had urged the prime minister to quickly reach a deal for the release of the hostages and a cease-fire in Gaza, while discussing new US defensive military deployments to support Israel against threats such as missiles and drones. The White House had earlier released a statement summarizing the Biden-Netanyahu call in which it said, "The President reaffirmed his commitment to Israel's security against all threats from Iran, including its proxy terrorist groups Hamas, Hezbollah, and the Houthis." Not satisfied, the *Wall Street Journal* editorialized that the United States could help Israel prevent a larger war by putting pressure on Hezbollah and Iran with expediting weapons to Israel, including deep-penetrating bombs that would put Iran's nuclear facilities at risk, and enforcing oil sanctions again. Sending US warships to the eastern Mediterranean, as occurred after October 7, would also make Iran think twice about Hezbollah's next move, the newspaper added: "Israel has a right to defend itself, but more than that it has the right and ample cause to defeat the terrorists who won't let it live in peace."[2]

Reps. Brian Mast (R., Fla.) and Josh Gottheimer (D., N.J.) went further. The two congressmen unveiled the bi-partisan "Bunker Buster Act," which would allow the US president to provide Israel with the Massive Ordnance Penetrator bomb, a munition capable of destroying underground facilities developing nuclear weapons. The legislation would require the US Department of Defense to conduct a study with Israel to produce a report for Congress on whether transferring "bunker buster" bombs would serve America's national security interests. The weapon weighs 30,000 pounds, measures 20.5 feet in length, and, according to the Air Force, is intended to penetrate up to 200 feet underground before exploding. Biden did not possess the authority to give Israel this weapon. The legislation would provide congressional authorization for him—or the victor of the 2024 presidential contest—to do so following the completion of the study.[3]

In the meantime, during a targeted, intelligence-based operation, the IDF eliminated Mohammed al-Jabari, who was deputy head of weapons manufacturing for the Palestinian Islamic Jihad. Al-Jabari was responsible for financing weapons manufacturing infrastructure for Islamic Jihad in northern Gaza, distributing salaries and funds, and attempting to restore that terrorist organization's rocket manufacturing capabilities and infrastructure. It also confirmed "100 percent" that its July 13 airstrike targeting Hamas military leader Mohammed Deif had succeeded in killing him. The Imam of the Al-Aqsa Mosque on the Temple Mount, Sheikh Ekrima Sabri, eulogized Haniyeh during his Friday sermon at the mosque, saying that "the residents of al-Quds [Jerusalem] pray to Allah that he has mercy on the martyr. We ask for him mercy and heaven." While the Israeli police investigated if his words constituted incitement, Interior Minister Moshe Arbel announced his intention to revoke Israeli residency from Sabri, who lives in an illegal house on the Mount of Olives in Jerusalem. In Doha, the Emir of Qatar sat in the front row during prayers at Haniyeh's funeral, while thousands waved Palestinian flags and chanted "redeem his death."[4]

Thousands of protesters, including relatives of hostages held by Hamas in Gaza, demonstrated around the country Thursday evening to mark 300 days since the October 7 massacre, calling on the government to seal a hostage and cease-fire deal. Hundreds marched through Tel Aviv, holding yellow ribbons and photos of hostages, then blocked the Begin intersection near the IDF's Kirya headquarters before the main rally was held at Tel Aviv's Hostages Square. The families bound themselves in chains while walking along the route and unfurled a forty-meter-long flag counting the days since the war's outset. Similar protests were held around the country, including Jerusalem, Beersheba, and Herzliya.

In Jerusalem, hundreds of people marched from the First Station complex to the Great Synagogue, dressed in white and carrying yellow flags, Israeli flags, and yellow ribbons. After organizers played a recording of the emergency telephone call made by Supernova music festival participant Eden Yerushalmi before Hamas abducted her into the Gaza Strip, her sisters Shani and May spoke to the crowd. "[Eden's] last words to the police were: 'Find me, OK?' Eden is still waiting for us to find her," said Shani. The event was organized by the family of hostage Hersh Goldberg-Polin in support of the hostages, in memory of those killed, and in support of their families. Musician Aharon Razel led the crowd in singing songs of hope and sadness, of returning soldiers and hostages back to their borders, praying for the return of those held captive from sadness to happiness, from darkness to light.[5]

On Friday, a senior member of Israel's negotiating team described "a chasm" between Netanyahu and top defense officials over the hostage deal. One TV report quoted a heated exchange in which the prime minister accused them of being too "soft." According to Saudi reports, two members of Hamas's political bureau were killed last week by an Israeli strike in Gaza: Rawhi Mushtaha and Samah a-Srag. The Saudi news outlet Al Hadath reported that Hezbollah was transporting military equipment and command centers to central Beirut from the southern Shiite neighborhood Dahieh, fearing an Israeli air attack. US officials told CNN that Washington believed Iran could retaliate for the killing of Haniyeh in the coming days, and that Iran could also order its regional proxies to attack American forces in Iraq and Syria. Israeli ministers received satellite phones in case of damage to Israel's infrastructure during a possible Iranian retaliation over the Haniyeh assassination. The Rambam hospital in Haifa opened its underground parking lot turned emergency center as Israel and especially its northern communities braced for Iran's impending response. President Recep Tayyip Erdoğan, who had threatened that Turkey would invade Israel as it had in Libya and Nagorno-Karabakh, declared a day of national mourning over the murder of Haniyeh. The Turkish flag outside the country's embassy in Tel Aviv was lowered to half-mast to mourn Haniyeh, prompting Israel to summon Turkey's deputy ambassador.[6]

The IDF said fighter jets attacked Hezbollah targets in southern Lebanon overnight into Saturday. It confirmed that a drone killed Nazih Abed Ali, a key Hezbollah operative in southern Lebanon. The UK embassy in Lebanon urged British nationals in the country to leave now "as the situation could deteriorate rapidly," as did the US and Swedish embassies. US Defense Secretary Austin ordered navy cruisers and destroyers to the Middle East along with an additional fighter jet squadron, and to increase readiness to deploy more land-based missile defenses, the Pentagon said. Relatives of Israeli hostages held by Hamas protested outside Defense Ministry headquarters in Tel Aviv, saying that "Netanyahu chose to drag us to escalation instead of closing a deal." The IAF struck in Tulkarm, killing fourteen terrorists, including those who had murdered Amnon Muchtar on June 22 in Qalqilya.[7]

Inexorably, the killings went forward. Hamas's Ismail Nofal, who was responsible for rocket launches toward Israeli territory and participated in the October 7 massacre, was eliminated in the Nuseirat area, The IAF struck some fifty Hamas sites across the Gaza Strip, where over 100,000 cases of viral hepatitis B were recorded, the PA's health minister said. Two Israelis were murdered and two were wounded in a stabbing attack in the city of Holon on Sunday morning; the attacker, thirty-five-year-old Ammar Razek Kamel Odeh of the West Bank city of Salfit, was killed. Terrorists also threw Molotov cocktails at a bus terminal at the entrance to Beitar Illit in the West Bank, causing significant damage. Multiple rocket alerts sounded across northern Israel after approximately thirty projectiles were identified crossing from Lebanon, most of which were intercepted by the IDF Aerial Defense Array. Commanding officer of the Home Front Command, MG Rafi Milo, stated, "We are determined to continue fighting until we fundamentally change the security situation in the North and can bring the residents of the North back home from a place of safety and a sense of security. We are preparing and are prepared for any scenario and any response."[8]

Netanyahu's office on Saturday night responded to reports that Biden had expressed deep frustration at his management of the cease-fire and prisoner swap deal. "The Prime Minister does not discuss what was said in closed conversations with the President of the United States," the statement said. "He does not interfere in American politics and will work with whoever is elected president—just as he expects from the Americans not to interfere in Israeli politics." The next morning, Congressman Ritchie Torres (D., N.Y.) pushed back at criticism that Israel was causing an "escalation" with the recent assassinations of Hamas and Hezbollah leaders. "Since October 7th, Hezbollah has fired 7,000 drones, missiles, and rockets at Israel. Yet Israel is the one accused of 'escalation,'" Torres wrote on X. "The absurdity of the double standard has become too glaring to ignore. Yet ignored it continues to be." At the same time, he criticized Netanyahu for openly accusing the United States of withholding arms from Israel: "If you are looking to undermine the bipartisanship of the US-Israel relationship, then release a public video attacking the Biden Administration, which, despite hysterical opposition from the far left, has held firm in support of Israel for eight months and counting," Torres wrote. He continued: "Disagreements should be had in private. Hamas is emboldened by even the appearance of a ruptured relationship."[9]

The *Wall Street Journal* reported that Iran had rejected calls for restraint following the assassination of Haniyeh in Tehran last week, telling Arab diplomats on Saturday that they "did not care," as the report put it, if the Islamic Republic's response ignited a war. In the shadow of the looming full-scale war between Israel and Hezbollah, thousands of Lebanese citizens continued to make their way to Beirut's international airport in hopes of fleeing to safety. Satellite images of Hezbollah's "War of Fire" revealed that since the outbreak of hostilities—but mainly since May—some 210,000 dunams had been burned down in Israel and Lebanon. The total scorched area in Israel from Hezbollah rockets was three times greater than the area consumed by the two greatest fires in Israeli history. Residents of the Greater Tel Aviv area reported heavy GPS disruptions on Sunday, a move most likely initiated by Israel as it prepared for Hezbollah and Iranian strikes. Netanyahu spoke on Sunday at the state memorial ceremony for Revisionist leader Ze'ev Jabotinsky, held at Mt. Herzl in Jerusalem, and asserted that "Only increasing the military pressure on Hamas will lead to achieving all of the objectives of the war, including the return home of all of our hostages, the living and the deceased."[10]

A *Wall Street Journal* investigation explained that the strain on military manpower was one reason Israeli officials were hesitant to launch an all-out war against Hezbollah, which would require the same cohort of weary reservists to fight against a military power far superior to Hamas. It was also exposing longer-term vulnerabilities for Israel as the Jewish State confronted the possibility of conflicts with hard-to-conquer militias on its borders for years to come. In practice, less than half of draft-age Israelis serve, leaving the military heavily dependent on reservists, who outnumber full-time soldiers by more than two to one. Unlike conscripts, reservists are regular citizens who had jobs and were raising families. Many, having served multiple rounds and faced fierce fighting, had to shut businesses and delay investments. Nearly 150,000 had missed workdays, including many in Israel's crucial hi-tech sector. With so many disruptions, the Bank of Israel forecast that the country's economy would grow only 1.5 percent in 2024, after contracting 5.7 percent in the last quarter of 2023. It added that growth should rebound to 4.2 percent in 2025—but only if the war ended by early next year.[11]

On Sunday, the IAF eliminated Abed Al-Zeriei, who had served as Hamas's Minister of Economy in Gaza and was an operative in the Manufacturing Department of Hamas's military wing. During a strike in the area of the Hassan Salame school, Jaber Aziz, commander of Hamas's Al-Furqan Battalion, was eliminated along with additional terrorists. The United States was sending Israel the weapons shipment which it had previously delayed, *Yisrael Hayom* reported. The newspaper also reported that Washington recently transferred to Israel weapons which were held in US weapons storehouses in Israel, including air-to-air missiles used by the IAF to intercept UAVs. The United States also intended to send additional munitions to its storehouses, so that in case of need, it will be possible to transfer them quickly to the IDF.[12]

Iran issued a notice to pilots and aviation authorities to avoid its airspace amid ongoing threats by Iranian officials to attack Israel, and alerted pilots of GPS jamming in its airspace, similar to a warning it sent out before its attack on Israel on April 13. This notification on Monday came after Blinken told a Group of Seven foreign ministers that Tehran could attack Israel within twenty-four to forty-eight hours. The foreign ministers of Jordan and Saudi Arabia told Iran it must stay out of their airspace if it attacked Israel; the IDF declared it was prepared to defend against and respond to any Iranian attack. Washington had said it would help defend Israel, and the Biden administration was expected to assure Israel that it would be able to resume combat operations in Gaza after the first stage of a hostage release deal, a senior Israeli source told *Haaretz*. Israel's defense echelon estimated that Hezbollah had attempted on Sunday night to carry out a large-scale attack against IDF forces on the Israel-Lebanon border by launching three UAVs towards an IDF command center in the area. The Knesset building was illuminated in orange that evening, as a sign of solidarity with Ariel Bibas, who is being held captive in Gaza and whose fifth birthday was on Monday. At the request of the Bibas family, the Knesset was lit in orange, matching the color of Ariel's hair.[13]

As Mideast tensions ran high, Iran's initial steps in retaliating to Haniyeh's assassination began to unfold. Tehran was behind the rocket attack against American forces stationed at the Al-Asad airbase in western Iraq, both Austin and Gallant said on Monday, warning that this was a "dangerous escalation and demonstrated Iran's destabilizing role in the region." Seven US personnel were injured in the assault. Russia began transferring air defense systems to Iran, the *New York Times* reported. "We launched a stream of UAVs," Hezbollah announced hours after an Israeli airstrike in southern Lebanon killed five people; Israel said it had hit structures used by Hezbollah. The explosions left one critically injured and nineteen wounded in northern Israel and the Upper Galilee. The Golan regional council instructed residents of Israel's north to stay near shelters and safe spaces, to avoid crowds, and avoid non-essential travel. Senior IDF officers proposed to Gallant and Netanyahu to preempt Hezbollah and strike Lebanon, saying, "The chances of escalation on the northern front are increasing. It would be prudent to lead the initiative," according to a Channel 13 report. Gallant asserted that Israel's air force must make a "quick transition to offense." An IAF strike eliminated Ali Jamal Aldin Jawad, a commander in Hezbollah's elite Radwan force, the IDF reported. It also eliminated Mohammed Mahasneh, a Hamas commander responsible for smuggling operations, including the smuggling in and out of the Gaza Strip of military equipment used for terrorist activities.[14]

"We are engaged in intense diplomacy, pretty much around the clock, with a very simple message—all parties must refrain from escalation," Blinken said during a press conference on Tuesday. "It's also critical that we break this cycle by reaching a cease-fire in Gaza," he added, as the United States asked top officials in Cairo, Baghdad, and other Arab capitals to urge that any response from Tehran and, potentially, its militant allies be restrained to avert an explosion of violence across the Middle East. A defense official told the *Washington Post* that the destroyers *USS Laboon* and the *USS Cole* had moved into the Red Sea along with a squadron of F-22 jet fighters to the region as part of a repositioning of US military assets ahead of the expected assault. The source said the *USS Theodore Roosevelt* aircraft carrier was also apparently moving toward Israel. Iran, for its part, had insisted on Monday that it was not looking to escalate regional tensions, but believed it must "punish" Israel to prevent further instability. "Iran seeks to establish stability in the region, but this will only come with punishing the aggressor and creating deterrence against the adventurism of the Zionist regime," Foreign Ministry spokesman Nasser Kanaani said, adding that action from Tehran was "inevitable."[15]

The tit-for-tat attacks were further ratcheting up anxiety in a region bracing for retaliation for the twin strikes that killed Haniyeh and Shukr. Iran started mobilizing missile launchers and conducting military drills in recent days, the *Wall Street Journal* reported. The Saudi Al-Hadath news agency reported that an IDF drone killed five Hezbollah fighters in the southern Lebanese village of

Maifadoun, including Amin Badr al-Din, nephew of Hezbollah senior member Mustafa Badr al-Din, who was assassinated in 2016 and was accused of murdering former Lebanese Prime Minister Rafic Hariri in 2005. Ibrahim al-Amin, the editor-in-chief of the pro-Hezbollah daily *Al-Akhbar*, wrote in its editorial that Hezbollah's target "could be Tel Aviv itself," and that the group might aim to attack the very "body that killed Fouad Shukr," potentially harming civilians. In a televised speech, Nasrallah said that "Israel used to down our drones when they were still above Lebanese land, now they reach Acre. . . . Residents of Haifa should be prepared." He also declared that "Iran and Syria shouldn't be part of an open war, but provide logistical, diplomatic and financial assistance to the axis of resistance," adding that "the nerve-racking anticipation" ahead of Iran and Hezbollah's attack "is part of the response. The goal is that the waiting will exhaust Israel and all its resources."[16]

Tuesday morning, Hamas operatives fired anti-tank missiles at IDF troops who were operating around eastern Rafah, adjacent to the Humanitarian Route. Multiple IDF soldiers were injured and evacuated to a hospital to receive medical treatment. Consequently, movement along that route was temporarily halted as the area was now constituted an active combat zone. The IAF struck a Hamas and Palestinian Islamic Jihad weapons production facility embedded inside the humanitarian area in Deir al Balah. Eight Palestinians were killed, including four teenagers, and another seven were wounded during IDF raids in the West Bank, Palestinian officials said. Four were killed in two airstrikes in the city of Jenin, where the IDF said it struck two squads of armed terrorists. The IDF announced it had confirmed the death of seventy-six-year-old Bilha Yinon, the last Israeli unaccounted for after the October 7 massacre, nearly ten months to the day after she went missing in her hometown of Netiv HaAsara. Admitting that nine UNRWA employees may have been involved in the October 7 massacre, the UN fired them. Haredim broke into the Tel HaShomer military base in the neighborhood of Ramat Gan, amid the IDF's first call-up order for 500 to be recruited, chanting "we will die and not enlist." The IDF responded by calling it a "serious offense against the law," and the police made twenty-six arrests. The first day of the draft of haredim ended in reported failure, as only eight percent of all ultra-Orthodox youths who were summoned showed up at recruitment offices.[17]

That evening, Hamas officially announced that Yahya Sinwar would be the terror group's new politburo chief, its highest-ranking figure, following the assassination of Haniyeh last week. Sinwar was selected by Hamas's fifty-strong Shura Council, a consultative body composed of officials elected by Hamas members in four chapters: Gaza, the West Bank, the diaspora, and security prisoners in Israeli jails. Sinwar "is now the most powerful figure in Hamas, formally too," noted Palestinian affairs analyst Ohad Hemo on Israeli TVs Channel 12. "That was already essentially the case, now it's official." "It's a show of faith" by the terror group, "whose leadership is rapidly shrinking," added Hemo, "and it returns the formal center of Hamas power to Gaza," whereas in recent years much of the official leadership was overseas, including Haniyeh and Khaled Mashaal. "This is happening precisely when Hamas is in its worst shape ever in Gaza," he said: "It's a highly significant move" by Hamas, "an expression of faith in the man who has been leading it in Gaza and, if I may so, into the abyss." It also made a cease-fire less likely, noted the *Economist*, and, as the *Wall Street Journal* put it, "cements" the militant group's strategic ties to Iran. A senior Hamas official told Agence France-Presse on condition of anonymity that Sinwar's selection sent "a strong message to the occupation [Israel] that Hamas continues its path of resistance."[18]

The drums of war were increasingly heard on Israel's northern front. On Wednesday, the IDF said it killed Hassan Fares Jeshi, a commander in Hezbollah's anti-tank unit, in the town of Jouaiya, while the Air Force attacked Hezbollah targets in southern Lebanon. Gallant told a reserve paratrooper brigade that Israel would expand its operations against Lebanon if necessary, which "could also deteriorate into a state of war," adding that Nasrallah "may drag Lebanon into paying a very heavy price." Families of the UN Interim Force in Lebanon tasked with patrolling the border with Israel were evacuated from Lebanon, and any officials already outside the country were told to return without their families. The United States communicated to Iran and Israel that there was a consensus in the Middle East that the conflict must not escalate. French President Macron stressed to his Iranian counterpart Pezeshkian that Tehran had to call on the "destabilizing players it supports" to exercise the utmost restraint to avoid a conflagration. Halevi declared that the IDF was "at peak readiness" and would know how to attack quickly "anywhere in Lebanon, anywhere in Gaza, anywhere in the Middle East—above ground and below ground." "The Zionist regime will soon receive a strong and definite response, and there is no doubt about it," to the killing of Haniyeh, Chief Commander of the Iranian Army Abdolrahim Mousavi said the same day, adding "they definitely cannot save themselves from annihilation."[19]

Outgoing Israeli ambassador to the UN Gilad Erdan, bidding farewell to his colleagues, stressed the importance of the hostages' release, and warned that the UN's silence on Iranian threats only emboldened Iran and was akin to the free world's silence on Hitler's "Final Solution of the Jewish Question"—the Holocaust. (Thinking otherwise, Turkey filed a request with the International Court of Justice at The Hague to join South Africa's lawsuit accusing Israel of genocide in Gaza.) Some fifty-nine percent of Israelis recently polled said they favored Jerusalem making an immediate hostage deal that included ending the war. White House National Security Communications Adviser John Kirby declared "we are as close as we think we have ever been" to securing a hostage release and cease-fire deal, adding that Sinwar "has always been the chief decision-maker when it comes to negotiations over the course of these nine months . . . And as the chief decision-maker, he needs to decide . . . He needs to accept the deal."[20]

Rahm Emanuel, the US ambassador to Japan, and his UK counterpart would not participate in Japan's annual Nagasaki Peace Memorial Ceremony on Friday as Israeli Ambassador Gilad Cohen was not invited to the event due to "security concerns," the *Japan Times* reported. Nagasaki mayor Shiro Suzuki explained that this decision was to ensure that the ceremony remained peaceful and focused on remembering the victims. However, some critics believed excluding Israel was a political move that sent the wrong message about standing up against terrorism and supporting global unity. The decision to exclude Cohen from Nagasaki's atomic bomb commemoration ceremony while inviting representatives from countries with serious human rights violations "raised concerns," the newspaper added. The list of invited nations included Syria, Yemen, Venezuela, China, Myanmar, and Afghanistan, all of which had notable records of human rights abuses. Most controversially, the Iranian ambassador received an invitation despite Tehran's designation as a primary sponsor of terrorism by the United States and its allies.[21]

Iran's Masoud Pezeshkian asked the Islamic Republic's Supreme Leader to refrain from attacking Israel, according to a report by Iran International on Wednesday. The new Iranian president cautioned that an Israeli retaliatory attack could cripple Iran's economy and infrastructure, and even lead to the country's collapse. Khamenei remained "noncommittal," it was reported, "neither supporting nor opposing Pezeshkian's concerns." Concurrently, two senior US officials told Politico that Iran had decided against conducting a direct attack on Israel in retaliation for the killing of Haniyeh. According to the report, Tehran was now convinced that Haniyeh was not killed in a direct military operation. Washington stressed to Tehran that such an action, so long as no Iranian citizens were killed, did not justify a direct military operation against Israel. France's Macron urged Netanyahu to "avoid a cycle of reprisals that would put the populations and stability of the region at risk," after making a similar plea to his Iranian counterpart. Hezbollah looked increasingly like it might strike Israel independent of whatever Iran might intend to do, two sources familiar with intelligence told CNN. According to them, Hezbollah was moving faster than Iran in its planning and was looking to strike Israel in the coming days.[22]

In a front-page interview in the week's *Time* magazine, Netanyahu expressed remorse for the October 7 massacre, but again without explicitly taking any responsibility for the heavy failure on his part as prime minister. "Of course, of course. I am sorry, deeply, that something like this happened. And you always look back and you say, 'Could we have done things that would have prevented it?,'" adding that "there'll be enough time to deal with it. But I think that dealing with it now is a mistake. We're in the midst of a war, a seven-front war. I think we have to concentrate on one thing: winning." Netanyahu blamed those protesting his coalition's press for judicial reform, specifically the thousands who declared they would not serve in the IDF: "The refusal to serve because of an internal political debate—I think that, if anything, that had an effect." As for his approval of money transfers by Qatar to Hamas, "we wanted to make sure that Gaza has a functioning civilian administration to avoid humanitarian collapse." Hamas's threat to Israel was not based on the funds from Qatar, but rather "the main issue was the transfer of weapons and ammunition from the Sinai into Gaza." He called claims that he was dragging out the war a "canard," and emphasized the victory in the war must be so decisive that, when it ended, Hamas could not claim control of Palestinian territories or pose a threat to Israel. Regarding the threat to Israel's image, especially if the war turned into a wider regional conflict, Netanyahu replied that he was aware of the risk, but "being destroyed has bigger implications about Israel's security, I'd rather have bad press than a good obituary."

Not interested in overseeing the creation of a Palestinian state, Netanyahu offered another option of having limited pockets of autonomy in Palestinian areas, similar to the way the West Bank is run today. Doing so would be "a detraction of sovereign powers, there's no question about it," he admitted, but also noted that he was aware of the dilemma Israel faced. "I agree we should maintain a Jewish majority, but I think we should do it in democratic means." "That's why I don't want to incorporate the Palestinians in Judea and Samaria as citizens of Israel. They should run their own lives. They should vote for their own institutions. They should have their own self-governance. But they should not have the power to threaten us," he added. When Netanyahu was asked if he intended to remain prime minister of Israel, he responded "I will stay in office as long as I believe I can help lead Israel to a future of security, enduring security and prosperity." "In any case," he concluded, "that's the decision of the people."[23]

Gallant posted an unusual Arabic-language warning to the Lebanese people on his *X* account, saying Israel will "fight with all its might" if attacked, and "Those who play with fire should expect destruction." US National Security Advisor Jake Sullivan told PBS that Biden "is determined to hold both sides' feet to the fire to get to a conclusion where we have a cease-fire and a hostage deal" between Israel and Hamas. The IDF called on residents of areas in southeast Gaza to evacuate to a humanitarian zone. Gaza rescue services reported that fifteen people were killed in strikes on schools in Shujeiyah, which the IDF said were Hamas headquarters. The IDF announced that an air strike in the Gaza Strip on July 24 killed senior Hamas official Nael Sakhl, who had operated in Hamas's "West Bank Headquarters" responsible for directing terror activities in Judea and Samaria. Israel informed Norway that it was revoking the diplomatic status of eight Norwegian diplomats who worked at the country's mission to the PA in response to Oslo's decision to formally recognize a Palestinian state. The leader of the Iran-backed Houthis, Abdul-Malik al-Houthi, said that there would be a response to the Israeli attack at the port of Hodeidah last month, and that all parties in the Iranian-led "axis of resistance" made a joint decision to attack Israel.[24]

After announcing it would operate in Khan Younis for a third time and telling some residents to evacuate the city, the IDF attacked over thirty sites and several Hamas terrorists were killed. The same day, the IDF struck thirty more terror targets in Gaza. An IAF strike in Lebanon eliminated Samer Mahmoud al-Haj, the commander of Hamas's military forces in the Ein el-Hilweh Palestinian refugee camp near Sidon, and responsible for recruiting and training terrorists; Hezbollah responded with the launch of several explosive-laden drones at northern Israel. Austin told Gallant that the arrival of US F-22 fighter jets in the Middle East "symbolizes the extensive efforts to curb Iranian aggression." A US official told the *Wall Street Journal* that Washington warned Iran of a "serious risk of consequences" to its economy and new government if it launched a major attack on Israel. According to the *Telegraph*, Iran President Pezeshkian was attempting to dissuade generals in Iran's Islamic Revolutionary Guard Corps (IRGC) who wanted to strike Tel Aviv, and instead supported targeting Israeli assets in Iran's neighboring countries. White House National Security Council spokesperson Kirby blasted Finance Minister Bezalel Smotrich, who had said the hostage release and cease-fire deal proposed by the United States would be an agreement of surrender to terrorism: "He's dead wrong."[25]

According to rescue services in the Strip, over ninety people were killed in an Israeli strike on a school sheltering displaced people in Gaza City on August 10. In response, the IDF said it used targeted munition to strike a Hamas command center embedded in the Al-Taba'een school and adjacent to a mosque, killing thirty-one Hamas terrorists, and that the number of casualties reported "do not align with the information held by the IDF, the precise munitions used, and the accuracy of the strike." UK Foreign Minister David Lammy said that he was "appalled by the Israeli military strike on that school and the tragic loss of life," adding that "Hamas must stop endangering civilians. Israel must comply with International Humanitarian Law. We need an immediate cease-fire to protect civilians, free all hostages, and end restrictions on aid." Condemnation also came from EU foreign policy head Josep Borrell, Egypt, Jordan, Saudi Arabia, and Qatar as a "deliberate killing," a "horrific massacre," and "a flagrant violation of international law and of all humanitarian values." US Vice President Kamala Harris commented to reporters about the IAF strike: "Yet again far too many civilians have been killed. Israel has the right to pursue Hamas terrorists, but it has the responsibility to avoid harming civilians. President Biden and I are working around the clock on a deal that will free the hostages and bring about a cease-fire." The IDF also said it killed Walid al-Sousi, the head of Hamas's general security and operative in the group's military wing, in southern Gaza.[26]

The United States was releasing $3.5 billion in military funding to Israel, part of a larger $14.1 billion package passed by Congress in April, CNN reported, citing several sources. Concomitantly, Blinken told Gallant in a telephone call that the escalation of tensions in the Middle East was "in no party's interest" while also stressing the need for a cease-fire in Gaza, the State Department said. Senior Hamas official Mousa Abu Marzouk told the Qatari Al Araby television channel that "Israel is seeking to thwart the negotiations" for a cease-fire and hostage release deal. For its part, Jerusalem announced it would send a negotiating team to Doha or Cairo on August 15 to finalize an agreement. At this point, the Hamas-controlled Health Ministry in Gaza declared that at least 39,790 Palestinians were killed (not differentiating between combatants and civilians) and 91,722 wounded since the start of the war. The IDF announced that, since October 7, 689 soldiers had been killed and 4,303 wounded. It did not report on those who had been hospitalized due to psychological impairments. At that same moment, the horrific injuries inflicted by the Hamas terrorists on twenty-six Israeli women and children freed hostages were now documented for the first time in medical literature by researchers at the Schneider Children's Medical Center in Petah Tikva, published in the international scientific journal *Acta Paediatrica*.[27]

Seventy-one out of more than 200 soldiers who completed their officer's training course sent a pointed letter on August 11 to Chief of Staff Herzi Halevi, warning that the IDF was still far from victory over Hamas. They cautioned against moving to the stage of only pinpoint raids: "It is important to us that the public knows that this is not how wars are won, wars are won on foot. You conquer territory, cleanse it, hold it, and move on to the next target. We did not come to revolt, we will be here every time and everywhere they call us, we came to push forward from the bottom up, there is a whole movement of people here who want to win, who want to defeat the enemy after years of endless rounds of fighting." Their letter came on the heels of the assertion by Ahmad Bakhshayesh Ardestani, a member of the Iranian Parliament's National Security Commission, that "Iran's aerial operations against Israel could last three to four days." He added that Iran "is certainly prepared for the consequences of such an attack and will be ready for any subsequent developments." Ardestani's comments were made as Biden was asked on Saturday night what his message was to Iran, who had threatened to attack Israel in retaliation for the elimination of Haniyeh in Tehran. "Don't," Biden replied with one word to reporters who asked him the question as he was exiting a church near his home in Rehoboth Beach, Delaware.[28]

"The plan I put together, endorsed by the G7, endorsed by the UN Security Council, et cetera, is still viable," Biden told CBS. "And I'm working literally every single day—and my whole team—to see to it that it doesn't escalate into a regional war. But it easily can." Diplomatic sources told *Haaretz* that it had been clarified to Netanyahu that the Biden administration—which until now had solely blamed Hamas for the deadlock in talks for a cease-fire deal—was reaching the point where the prime minister's behavior would result in the White House publicly accusing him of harming the talks and preventing the release of the hostages. On the other hand, Qatar and Egypt, which had primarily criticized Israel in recent weeks, also made it clear that if Hamas torpedoed the cease-fire/hostage talks, they would say so clearly.[29]

Responding to threats by Iran and Hezbollah to retaliate against Israel for assassinations in Beirut and Tehran, Gallant said on day 310 of the war that "anyone who hurts us in a way they haven't operated before, is expected to be hurt by us in a way we haven't operated before, and the IDF has significant abilities." Arab officials asked Hezbollah to postpone its response to Shukr's assassination until after the start of the summit for negotiations on a hostage release deal set to begin Thursday, according to reports in Lebanon; the officials declared an attack against Israel before then could harm negotiations and the group would bear responsibility for doing so. Across the Atlantic, Mahdy Akil Helbawi was arrested in Colombia on suspicion, among other things, of "illicit use of natural resources," the funds of which were reportedly used to finance Hezbollah. In addition, documents seen by the German news website Der Spiegel revealed that the Islamic Centre Hamburg (IZH), which was recently shut down by Germany's Interior and Homeland Affairs Federal Ministry, had taken direct orders from the Islamic Republic of Iran and aided Hezbollah. A report also circulated that the IDF was preparing for a potential preemptive strike against Hezbollah, pending orders from the security cabinet. Haifa Mayor Yona Yahav noted the significant advancements in Hezbollah's arsenal since the Second Lebanon War of 2006, warning that the terror group could fire 4,000 missiles at Israel each day. He urged citizens to prepare enough food and water to stay in shelters for four to six days.[30]

The Middle East entered what the *New York Times* called a "high-wire week of risk and opportunity" on Monday, suspended between the prospect of a broadening conflict and intensive diplomatic efforts to prevent one. Austin ordered the deployment of the ballistic-missile submarine *Georgia* and the USS *Abraham Lincoln* carrier strike group to the Middle East, the Pentagon announced. Amid fear of an Iranian attack, Commander of the IAF Maj. Gen. Tomer Bar ordered the suspension of overseas leave for career service members. The IDF prohibited its soldiers from staying in Azerbaijan and Georgia considering threats of an attack from Iran, announced Israeli public broadcasting site Kan. Israel offered to evacuate tens of thousands of Palestinians to Egypt until the cessation of the Hamas-Israel war, it also reported, but the Egyptians refused the offer. The IDF announced new closures starting from 12 p.m. in portions of the South. The United Kingdom, France, and Germany called on Iran and its allies to refrain from attacks that jeopardized cease-fire and hostage release talks. Approximately thirty rockets crossed from Lebanon, following the sirens sounded in northern Israel overnight. Several of them fell in open areas; no injuries, wounded, or damage were reported. A Lebanese media outlet said Hezbollah moved people, computers, and other equipment from its headquarters in Beirut's Dahieh southern suburb to "prepare for the worst" as it threatened to attack Israel.[31]

In a closed-door briefing of the Knesset's Foreign Affairs and Defense Committee, Gallant said that the threats from Iran and Lebanon might actualize, and that the IDF was in a state of high alertness, adding that decision-makers were obliged to "create the necessary conditions" to release the hostages—including by military pressure. When asked why Israel was not initiating a war with Lebanon, he replied: "I hear the heroes with the drums [of war], [talking about] 'total victory' and other nonsense." Following these leaked comments, Netanyahu's office blamed the defense minister for adopting an "anti-Israel narrative" that harmed the chances of reaching a hostage deal, asserting that "Israel has only one option: to achieve a decisive victory, which means eliminating Hamas's military and governmental capabilities and freeing our hostages—and this victory will be achieved."[32]

Unpublished documents reviewed by the *New York Times* implied that Netanyahu had added new conditions to Israel's demands for a cease-fire/hostage deal, additions that his own negotiators feared raised extra obstacles to a deal. It charged that Israel relayed a list of new stipulations in late July to American, Egyptian, and Qatari mediators which added less flexible conditions to a set of principles it had made in late May. Among other conditions, the latest document, presented to mediators shortly before a summit in Rome on July 28, suggested that Israeli forces should remain in control of Gaza's southern border, a detail that was not included in Israel's proposal in May. It also showed less flexibility about allowing displaced Palestinians to return to their homes in northern Gaza once fighting was halted. Netanyahu's office, which did not dispute the authenticity of the documents, denied that he had added new conditions and declared "The July 27 letter does not introduce new terms, To the contrary, it includes essential clarifications to help implement the May 27 proposal."[33]

Only a cease-fire deal in Gaza would hold Iran back from directly retaliating against Israel for the assassination on its soil of Hamas's Haniyeh, three senior Iranian officials told *Reuters*. The *Washington Post* reported that Iran had expressed concern that Israel and the United States might target its nuclear program, using the broader conflict as a pretext, citing a Lebanese source with close ties to Hezbollah who added that "the Iranians and their allies are treading cautiously." An Iraqi parliament member with links to Iran-backed militias in the country told the American newspaper that Tehran "does not want to expand the war." At a security assessment meeting at an intelligence base in northern Israel, Gallant said that residents must be "returned safely to their homes after we make Hezbollah withdraw north of the Litani River," adding that Israel was "engaged in preparing all the options to be able to attack wherever we decide." It was also reported that Israel would soon begin to manufacture heavy bombs for the air force to overcome supply delays and establish independence in weapons development. According to *Yisrael Hayom*, one of the most significant lessons Israel had drawn from the war was that it must manufacture and develop critical munitions for the IDF by itself. At the same time, the credit ratings agency Fitch downgraded Israel's credit rating from A+ to A, stating "In our view, the conflict in Gaza could last well into 2025 and there are risks of it broadening to other fronts."[34]

The UN Security Council convened for an urgent session, at the request of Algeria (which does not recognize Israel), regarding the IDF's strike on the Al-Taba'een school in Gaza. Coming one day after *Tish'a B'Av*, world Jewry's mourning the destruction of the Holy Temple in Jerusalem by the Babylonians (585 BCE) and the Romans (70 CE), Israel's outgoing ambassador to the UN, Gilad Erdan, presented the Council with images of the Hamas terrorists who were eliminated in the school, then remarked: "You convened for these terrorists who used a school as their terror base, but for the children of Majdal Shams, murdered by Hezbollah's rocket fire, you couldn't find the time for an urgent session! Shame on you!" He could have added the IDF report on Wednesday that Hamas operatives, dressed in civilian clothes, launched rockets from a site near the Humanitarian Aid Route in Khan Younis toward central Israel. In the meanwhile, soldiers from the Givati Brigade operated in the Shabura area in Rafah under the command of the 162nd Division, where they eliminated approximately 100 terrorists during recent days; numerous weapons and terror infrastructure sites were also destroyed.

Across the Atlantic, the Biden administration approved about $20 billion in new weapons sales to Israel over the next several years, amid fading hopes that a negotiating session scheduled for Thursday would lead to a Gaza cease-fire and hostage release. Notification of the pending sale was sent to Congress on Tuesday. It included fifty upgraded F-15 fighter jets, 120mm tank ammunition, tactical vehicles, all-weather AIM-120 AMRAAM antiaircraft missiles, and high-explosive mortars.[35]

Growing rifts surfaced in both rival camps. A source close to the IRGC's Quds Force revealed to the Kuwaiti news outlet that a heated meeting took place on Sunday in Tehran between representatives of Iran's regional allies and the IRGC leadership. This meeting exposed a significant break which escalated into a verbal clash and ended with some allies storming out in anger. The source told Kuwait's *Al-Jarida* that representatives from Hezbollah, Hamas, the Palestinian Islamic Jihad, various Iraqi factions, and the Houthis attended the meeting to coordinate a response to Israel. According to the source, Islamic Revolutionary Guard Corps representatives urged the allies to hold off on retaliation, at least until after the conclusion of hostage negotiations in Gaza, set to end on Thursday. In Israel, dozens of ultra-Orthodox young men blocked the entrance to the Upper Galilee Michveh Alon military base to protest the planned recruitment of male members of their community to the IDF. The protesters lit a fire on the road leading up to the base and blocked it with stones, leading the police to forcefully evict them and arrest twelve demonstrators. A decision four days earlier by Deputy Attorney-General Gil Limon, announcing that the state may no longer subsidize daycare for children of full-time yeshiva students whose exemption from IDF service had expired, further fueled tensions. The ruling would likely lead to a financial blow to thousands of haredi families. just weeks before a new school year was set to begin.[36]

After meeting Nabih Berri, Lebanon's parliament speaker, in Beirut, Biden top Mideast envoy Amos Hochstein remarked "we continue to believe that no one truly wants a full-scale war between Lebanon and Israel." A senior Israeli security official told the *Wall Street Journal* that a disproportionate response from Hezbollah could "lead to an Israeli attack that will lead to a new reality on the northern border." As for Israel's southern front, where the IAF attacked over forty targets throughout Gaza in the past twenty-four hours, the ambassadors of the United States, the United Kingdom, and Germany to Israel issued a public call to immediately accept a Gaza cease-fire/hostage release deal one day ahead of a summit to negotiate an agreement in Qatar. However, Hamas's representative in Lebanon, Ahmad Abdul Hadi, told the *New York Times* that the group would not send a delegation to Doha on Thursday because "Netanyahu is not interested in reaching an agreement that ends the aggression completely, but rather he is deceiving and evading and wants to prolong the war, and even expand it at the regional level." The US-based news website Politico raised speculation that Saudi Arabian Crown Prince Mohammed bin Salman was at risk of assassination over his push for normalization ties with Israel. The desert ruler referenced this threat in talks with US congressmen to explain why it was important that the deal also include an immediate pathway to Palestinian statehood.[37]

An Israeli delegation led by Mossad director David Barnea and Shin Bet head Ronen Bar landed in Doha on Thursday, where talks over a Gaza cease-fire and hostage release deal restarted. Protesters, among them family members of hostages in Gaza, gathered outside the Likud Party headquarters in Tel Aviv to call for a hostage deal, while hundreds of Israelis assembled in front of the Tel Aviv building where Israel's Declaration of Independence was signed before marching to the city's Hostage Square to demand a deal. IDF chief Halevi said the military would be prepared to secure and monitor the Philadelphi Corridor if the government chose to withdraw forces from there and would retain the possibility of attacking there if need be; the IDF destroyed about fifty sections of Hamas tunnel routes in a week along the Philadelphi Corridor and killed more than 17,000 Hamas terrorists since the war began. According to the Hamas-controlled Health Ministry in Gaza, at least 40,000 Palestinians, out of which nearly seventy percent were women and children, had been killed in the Gaza Strip since the war between Israel and Hamas had started. Up North, twenty rockets were fired by Hezbollah; seven fire and rescue teams battled a fire that broke out near Kibbutz Shamir in the Upper Galilee due to rockets. The municipality of Kiryat Shmona asked its residents to stay near bomb shelters until further notice and to avoid crowds, in accordance with the IDF's orders. A similar request was made by the Upper Galilee's regional council to the residents of the kibbutzim near the border.

White House spokesperson Kirby informed CNN that "information tells us that Iran has not moved off its threat to attack Israel, hopefully it doesn't come to that." Israel's Foreign Ministry urged Israeli citizens visiting countries bordering with Iran—Turkmenistan, Azerbaijan, Armenia, and Turkey—to be on high alert and take precaution. Civilian aircraft operated by the Iran-based Caspian Airlines had been smuggling weapons and fighters to both Syria and Lebanon, *Yisrael Hayom* reported, quoting the second generation of Iranians-in-exile website Wikiran. Iran was also resuming tests to produce nuclear bomb detonators, reported the Persian-language news television channel headquartered in London Iran International, citing three independent sources in Iran.[38]

Dozens of Israeli civilians, some of whom were masked, entered the village of Jit near Nablus in the West Bank on Thursday night, hurling stones and Molotov cocktails and setting vehicles and buildings on fire, the IDF said. Forces were transferred to the area and removed the rioters from the village. The head of the Samaria Regional Council, Yossi Dagan, and the head of the Kedumim Council, Ozel Vatik, issued a joint statement criticizing the riot by far rightists in that Palestinian Arab town: "Violent rioters are not welcome here." Rabbi Yaakov Medan, Rosh Yeshiva of Har Etzion, warned that recent anti-Arab attacks by extremists might bring economic sanctions on all Jews living in Judea and Samaria, and the silence of rabbis and leaders in the face of this violence would harm Jewish residents there. Netanyahu also condemned the incident in a statement saying that "those responsible will be caught and sentenced according to the law." President Herzog wrote on X that "a small, radical minority . . . is harming the law-abiding settler public and Israel's status during this hard and sensitive time." "Attacks by Israeli settlers against Palestinian civilians in the West Bank are unacceptable and must stop," the White House declared.[39]

Hezbollah's Nasrallah refused to meet with Head of the Syrian General Intelligence Directorate General Hussam Louka, who was sent to Beirut under direct orders from President Bashar al-Assad. Reports suggested the decision was taken to not expose his location amid tensions with Israel, and also reflected tensions of late between Hezbollah and the Syrian government since Syria had reduced attacks on Israel after being pushed to do so by Russian President Vladimir Putin. At the same time, a source close to Hezbollah told the *Washington Post* on Thursday that the organization would not "launch its retaliation operation" against Israel so long as the talks in Qatar on a ceasefire and hostage release deal were ongoing because" it did not want to be held accountable for obstructing the talks or a potential deal." The *New York Times* would report the next day that Israeli, American, and Iranian officials said that Iran was expected to delay an attack on Israel in retaliation for Haniyeh's assassination in order to allow mediators time to "make a high-stakes push" for a cease-fire to end the war in Gaza.⁴⁰

Israel's foreign minister told his British and French counterparts on Friday, day 315 of the war, that "If Iran attacks, we expect the coalition to join Israel not only in defense but also in striking significant targets in Iran." Austin informed Gallant the same day that the United States "continues to monitor attack planning from Iran and its proxies and is well postured across the region to defend Israel and protect US personnel and facilities," the Pentagon announced. Lebanon's Health Ministry said ten people were killed in an Israeli strike in the country's south; the IDF responded that it struck a Hezbollah weapons storage facility there. The Israeli army declared that it killed Hassin Ibraheem Kasseb, a commander in Hezbollah's elite Radwan Force, in a strike near the Lebanese city of Tyre. After a heavy barrage of some fifty-five rockets was launched from Lebanon, firefighting crews battled flames in over ten sites in Israel's north. In Gaza, the IDF told residents of the northern neighborhoods of Khan Younis, as well those around Deir al-Balah, that they must evacuate, saying that, "due to the exploitation of the area for terrorist activities and firing at Israel, remaining in these areas has become dangerous," not only in defense but also in "striking significant targets in Iran." Palestinians reported that seventeen people were killed and dozens wounded in an Israeli strike in central Gaza on Saturday. As for the latest round of talks held in Qatar, Hamas senior official Ghazi Hamad said no major issue was agreed upon, and he blamed Israel for sabotaging the negotiations, reported *Haaretz*.⁴¹

Forces from the 98th Division expanded their operations in Gaza during Sunday accompanied by air support, destroying dozens of terror infrastructure sites and eliminating terror cells. The 7th Brigade combat team reached the outskirts of Dir El-Balah after eliminating dozens of terrorists and destroying a tunnel complex in Khan Younis, while the Paratroopers Brigade combat team did the same when expanding its activities into western Khan Younis and the Hamid neighborhood. As for the Doha talks, the US proposal presented to the negotiating teams did not include the IDF's withdrawal from Gaza and a commitment to a permanent cease-fire after the first phase of the deal, the Saudi news outlet Al Sharq reported, citing a Hamas source familiar with the talks, who said the proposal "completely contradicts the document they agreed to on July 2." The proposal included a reduction of the IDF presence in the Philadelphi Corridor running along the Gaza-Egypt border without a complete withdrawal of forces and stated that Israel would be able to resume fighting if the parties did not reach an agreement on the second phase of the deal. Energy Minister Eli Cohen told Israel's Army Radio that Jerusalem would insist on maintaining security control in Gaza, including a "physical presence on the Philadelphi route," a provision Netanyahu consistently insisted on and Hamas does not accept.[42]

Biden said on Sunday that a Gaza cease-fire and hostage release deal remained a possibility. and that "we're not giving up." His comments came after Hamas officially announced it was rejecting the proposal for an agreement as presented at the summit in Doha. "The proposal completely meets Netanyahu's conditions and especially his refusal to a permanent cease-fire and a complete withdrawal from the Gaza Strip, and his insistence on continuing to occupy the Netzarim axis, the Rafah crossing and the Philadelphi Corridor. It also adds new conditions regarding the exchange of prisoners, and a withdrawal of the Israeli position in other sections, which prevents the success of the deal," Hamas said. It ended with this: "Hamas places full responsibility on Netanyahu . . . , as well as the full responsibility for the lives of the hostages, who face the same dangers that the Palestinians face due to the war." It demanded a complete withdrawal of the IDF from the Philadelphi Corridor and a minimal release of living hostages.

Egyptian authorities agreed to Israel's demand not to set a timetable for the IDF's withdrawal from the Philadelphi Corridor as a precondition for a cease-fire and prisoner swap deal between Hamas and Israel, Lebanon's *Al-Akhbar* newspaper reported. The agreement represented a change in Egyptian policy and showed that the negotiations bore fruit in the form of an Israeli agreement to reduce the number of soldiers stationed along the route "in preparation for Israeli withdrawal from the route at a later time." An Egyptian source said that Cairo was refusing to discuss the option of sending its forces to Gaza and was demanding that there first be a cease-fire agreement, alongside an Israeli commitment to solve what it called the "Palestinian issue." Secretary of State Blinken met with officials in Israel on Monday at what he called "a decisive moment" for diplomatic negotiations aimed at reaching a cease-fire in Gaza and securing the release of all hostages. After months without progress, talks that ended in Qatar on Friday and were expected to resume this week in Egypt represented "probably the best, maybe the last, opportunity to get the hostages home, to get a cease-fire, and to put everyone on a better path to enduring peace and security," Blinken said as he met with Herzog in Tel Aviv.[43]

Events on the ground continued, however, to challenge the US secretary of state's hopes. IDF officials said that the explosion in southern Tel Aviv on Sunday night was an attempted attack aimed at a synagogue. The terrorist was killed while carrying the bomb in the first such attack in Tel Aviv in years, for which Hamas and Palestinian Islamic Jihad both took responsibility. In their statement, the groups announced that suicide attacks inside Israel would return to the forefront as long as the "occupation's massacres and assassination policy continue." A soldier was killed and another was in critical condition from a Hezbollah drone attack on Monday in the Western Galilee's Moshav Ya'ara; three others were lightly wounded. The 603rd Battalion and the Yahalom Unit located and destroyed an underground tunnel route approximately a kilometer and a half long in Khan Younis. The Israeli military called up reserve soldiers previously released from service due to a personnel shortage; an estimated 15,000 would be involved.

IDF surveillance post operators who served in Judea and Samaria told Israel's Channel 13 News that the IDF had not learned lessons from October 7 and warned of another horrific scenario in the near future. "Thousands of Palestinians approach the fence and the IDF does nothing," they warned. "We have been seeing 60,000 people—and that is just one hole in the fence. There are many breaches in the fence, thousands could cross in one night. Maybe some go to work, beyond that we have no idea what they are doing here."[44]

A two-state solution for two peoples seemed further away than ever. Khalil Shikaki, in his Ramallah office at the independent Palestinian Center for Policy and Research (PCPSR), declared "Right now, Israelis and Palestinians do not believe that the other side are human beings."

In fact, support for side-by-side states had been dwindling for well over a decade. While surveys from the late 1990s until around 2010 showed solid majorities of Israelis and Palestinians backing that resolution, it had been downhill ever since. Now, only thirty-two percent of Palestinians believed in the formula, according to a PCPSR survey released in June. Among Israeli Jews, belief in peace based on two states had collapsed to nineteen percent, according to a survey by the Pew Research Center published in May, from thirty-two percent shortly before October 7. Most Israelis and Palestinians knew they needed to find a way to share the land between the Jordan River and the Mediterranean Sea, concluded a *Wall Street Journal* analysis, "but they can no longer see a partner on the other side."[45]

"Only total victory will bring home all 115 of our hostages and allow the traumatized evacuees of the Southern border communities to return home safely. We plead with you—don't put your weight behind Hamas; support our Prime Minister so that we can win this war and bring them all home." These words were written by the Tikva Forum of Hostages' Families to Blinken "to make it clear that it's imperative the U.S. does not support an irresponsible and irrational deal," the Forum's letter concluded. Choosing to maintain balance, however, Biden stressed in his speech to the Democratic National Convention in Chicago on August 19 that his administration would continue to work to bring about the release of those held hostages by Gaza terror groups, "end the civilian suffering of the Palestinian people and finally, finally deliver a cease-fire and end this war." Justifying the anti-Israel protesters, he added, "They have a point. A lot of innocent people are being killed on both sides." For its part, Israel stood firm in insisting, after Netanyahu met with Blinken in Jerusalem to discuss how to advance the hostage negotiations, that the IDF must retain a military presence in the Philadelphi Corridor. The same evening, six bodies, some riddled with bullets, were retrieved Monday night from a tunnel in Khan Younis in an IDF operation. All three had been kidnapped to Gaza by terrorists during the October 7 massacre and were murdered in captivity.[46]

More than 100 Hezbollah projectiles entered Israeli territory after alarms were triggered on Tuesday in the Upper Galilee and Golan Heights, the IDF reported. Netanyahu told grieving hostage families of the Heroes Forum that his focus lay in guarding Israel's strategic assets rather than returning their loved ones. The mother of a hostage held in Gaza said she was told by Israel's Mossad chief that a hostage deal was impossible "in the current political constellation." The Prime Minister's Office, on behalf of the Mossad, stated that the comments "were never said. . . . The Mossad chief continues to work towards securing an agreement for the release of all hostages as soon as possible." "There could be a long wait for Iranian retaliation against Israel," Iran's Revolutionary Guard Corps spokesperson declared. Egyptian President Abdel Fattah El-Sisi warned of the risk of the Gaza war expanding regionally in a way "difficult to imagine" during a meeting with Blinken, and he called to end the war in Gaza.[47]

Senior Hamas official Osama Hamdan told *Reuters* that Hamas had already confirmed to mediators that "we don't need new Gaza cease-fire negotiations, we need to agree on an implementation mechanism" for the agreement. Speaking to the terror group's Al-Aqsa channel, he blamed Washington for failing to convince Netanyahu to accept the deal proposed by Biden, and claimed that the United States was trying to gain time in order to allow the continuation of the "destruction" of the "Palestinians." Hamdan emphasized that a potential agreement would include an end to the "aggression," the withdrawal of Israeli forces from Gaza, and the reconstruction of the area. Kibbutz Be'eri representatives said that the government should be busy closing a hostage deal, not producing a memorial ceremony to mark one year since October 7, 2023. The IDF announced that about seventy-five rockets were fired from Lebanon at northern Israel. Fires broke out in two sites in Israel's north after the volleys, Israeli rescue services said. There could be a long wait for Iran's retaliation against Israel for the killing of Hamas's Haniyeh in Tehran, IRGC spokesperson Alimohammadi Naini said, according to Iranian state media.[48]

Israeli and US officials believed that current cease-fire and hostage deal negotiations between Israel and Hamas were "on the brink of collapsing," Politico reported, adding that the current proposal, "tailored to the demands of both Hamas and Israel" by the United States, Egypt, Qatar, and Israel, was accepted by Israel, while Hamas said it will not accept the proposal. An Egyptian official with direct knowledge of the negotiations said that it did not clearly say Israel would withdraw its forces from two strategic corridors in Gaza, the Philadelphi route and the Netzarim Corridor, and that Israel offered to downsize its forces in Philadelphi, with "promises" to withdraw from the area. "This is not acceptable for us and of course for Hamas," he concluded. That same evening, chants of "Bring Them Home" echoed throughout the Democratic National Convention on Wednesday night as Rachel Goldberg-Polin and Jon Polin took the stage with strips of masking tape over their hearts bearing the number 320, the number of days their twenty-three-year-old son Hersh, his dominant left forearm blown off by a Hamas grenade, was been held captive in Gaza. Photos of Hersh and the seven other American abductees shone overhead on the main screens. Their plea for the release of remaining hostages and a cease-fire that "will stop the despair in Gaza," charging that "in a competition of pain there no winners," drew tears and enthusiastic applause.[49]

On the northern front, Hezbollah launched more than fifty rockets toward the Golan on Wednesday. The attack led to destruction in Katzrin, a large town in central Golan, the largest of its kind there since that terror organization started attacking Israel in October 2023. The IDF said it killed Al-Aqsa Brigade militant Halil al-Maqdah near Sidon in southern Lebanon, adding that he was in the service of Iran's Islamic Revolutionary Guard Corps and involved in directing terror attacks and transferring finances and weapons to the West Bank. The person killed was the brother of the Fatah official in Lebanon, Munir al-Maqdah, and a former senior member of Fatah himself and currently active in the Iranian Quds Force. As for Gaza, Gallant said during a tour there that Hamas's Rafah Brigade and its four battalions had been dismantled by IDF Division 162 under the command of Brig. Genl. Itzik Cohen, and that the remaining tunnels would be easy to find and destroy, adding that "the most important thing in my view is to remember what the war's goals are, both regarding Hamas and the hostages, and looking north now."[50]

Biden stressed the urgent need to secure a Gaza cease-fire and hostage deal and pointed to upcoming talks in Cairo as crucial in a telephone call with

Netanyahu, the White House said. A potential cease-fire and hostage release agreement "is now within reach," US Ambassador to the United Nations Linda Thomas-Greenfield informed the Security Council on Thursday. She urged members of the Council to push Hamas to agree to a compromise proposal that Israel had already accepted. Yet while the United States assented to two Israeli observation towers on the Philadelphi Corridor, Egyptian officials rejected any towers at all, as they would give Israel a military presence in the area. The IDF said its forces had intensified their activity in Deir Al-Balah in central Gaza and Khan Younis in the south, dismantling military structures, locating rockets, and killing dozens of Hamas militants over the past twenty-four hours. Later on Thursday, the IDF called on residents of north and east Khan Younis to evacuate to the west of the city. The Israel Police arrested three adults and a minor suspected of carrying out "terrorist acts against Palestinians," including the violent attacks in the village of Jit last Thursday, a police statement said.[51]

In an inspiring moment, 200 North Americans made *aliya* on Thursday, on five different group flights, breaking records and setting the stage for an extraordinary week in this regard. Over the course of the week (August 20–28), 600 newcomers would make Israel their new home, on fourteen flights facilitated by the Nefesh B'Nefesh organization. This latest wave of immigrants was part of a larger movement that witnessed 2,000 *olim*, ranging in age from just two months to ninety seven years, embark on their journey to Israel this summer. Concurrently, a wave of grief descended on Israel as the six bodies retrieved by the IDF from Khan Younis tunnels returned for the final time to the villages that, in life, they had called home. Months of anguished waiting at an end, mourners embraced, wept, read tributes, and lowered into the soil the remains of Israeli hostages recovered that week from the Gaza Strip. Grief had to share space with fury at Israel's leaders, including Netanyahu, for not agreeing to a cease-fire with Hamas that might have saved the captives' lives. In an open letter to Netanyahu, Herzog asked that the production and holding of the ceremony marking the first anniversary of the October 7 massacre be coordinated by the President's Residence instead of by the premier's political ally, Transportation Minister Miri Regev, whose appointment had led many kibbutzim to announce they would not attend, "so that we will be able to lower the flames of dispute and prevent unnecessary quarrels and conflicts."[52]

Shin Bet Chief Bar warned Netanyahu, ministers, and the attorney general that Jewish terrorism in the West Bank was endangering Israel's existence, according to a letter published by Israel's Channel 12 News on Thursday. He wrote that Jewish terrorist leaders "want to cause the system to lose control, causing indescribable damage to Israel," adding that police incompetence in the face of these acts and "perhaps a sense of hidden support" for them were increasing considerably, reflected in "the significant expansion" of those taking part. The letter also mentioned far-right National Security Minister Ben-Gvir's recent visit to the Temple Mount, when hundreds of Jews prayed with him in violation of the status quo, adding that such acts could drag Israel "to profuse bloodshed and change the state's face unrecognizably." In response, Ben-Gvir's Otzma Yehudit (Jewish might) party took out a paid advertisement accusing Bar of compromising Israeli security. "Ronen Bar failed on October 7 and is leading Israel to another disaster. Say no to a reckless deal," the ad read, next to a photograph of the senior official. Opposition Leader Yair Lapid soon declared that "only an unstable clown like Ben-Gvir is capable—in the middle of a war, while the residents of the north are in shelters and soldiers are being killed—of publishing a paid ad against the head of the Shin Bet, a patriot and a real fighter the likes of which Ben-Gvir was not and never will be."[53]

"I will always stand up for Israel's right to defend itself," US Vice President Kamala Harris said on Thursday night when accepting the Democratic Party's nomination for President of the United States, adding "because the people of Israel must never again face the horror that a terrorist organization called Hamas caused on October 7." She went on to describe the massacre at a music festival that Saturday morning ten months ago, specifically noting the "unspeakable sexual violence" that morning—an accusation Hamas continued to deny. She then went on to talk anew about the "devastating" damage and "innocent lives lost" as the Israelis retaliated: "The scale of the suffering is heartbreaking." When Harris said that she was also working so that "the Palestinian people can realize their right to dignity, security, freedom and self-determination," the crowd offered among the loudest roars of approval for any of her remarks. Her and President Biden's goal, she said, was an end to the war that ensured Israel's security, the release of the hostages and a stop to "the suffering in Gaza." But, like Biden, she gave no indication that, if elected, she would use the leverage of America's military support for Israel to pressure it to change tactics. She offered no hint of the tension in the relationship with Netanyahu, which she had witnessed firsthand, as a listener-in, and sometimes participant, in the tense phone calls with the Israeli leader.[54]

On Friday, over 100 rockets were fired on Israel from Lebanon, causing fires in several locations. The IDF attacked several targets in Lebanon, killing at least seven Hezbollah operatives. The IAF eliminated terrorist Saeed Mahmoud Daeb, a member of Hezbollah's Rocket and Missile Unit, in the Tyre area. Earlier that morning, the IAF eliminated Muhammad Mahmoud Negm, a significant terrorist in Hezbollah's Rocket and Missile Unit in southern Lebanon. The IDF also eliminated Taha Abu Nada, a member of Hamas's weapons manufacturing headquarters and began targeted operations against terror infrastructure in Gaza City.

A man wielding a knife killed two men along with a fifty-six-year-old woman and wounded eight others in Germany's Fronhof Central Square in Solingen; a twenty-six-year-old Syrian man was taken into custody. The ISIS (Islamic State of Iraq and Syria) terrorist organization claimed responsibility for the attack, and claimed it was "revenge for the Muslims in Palestine." A man was arrested in France after a synagogue there was set ablaze early Saturday morning, in at least the second French synagogue arson in recent months. As for foreign dignitaries engaged in negotiations for a hostage and cease-fire deal, the British and French foreign ministers decided to remove the yellow pins supporting the kidnapped in Gaza before meeting a Palestinian Authority leader. UK Foreign Secretary Lammy and French foreign minister Stéphane Séjourné wore the yellow pins when they met with Israel's foreign minister last Friday but removed the pins before meeting with PA Prime Minister Mohammed Mustafa later that same day. During a three-hour meeting on Friday with families of hostages, Netanyahu said "To overcome an ideology, you have to use a lot of force, or eliminate it," he said of Hamas, which he noted still insists on victory by demanding Israel leave the Strip and the Philadelphi Corridor. He called Sinwar a "crazy man." In Sinwar, "We actually have a psychopath," he said. "Whoever told you that there was a deal ready and that we didn't take it for this reason or that reason, for personal reasons, it's just a lie," the prime minister said.[55]

On Saturday, Biden spoke with Egypt's President El-Sisi and Qatari Emir Sheikh Tamim Al Thani on the need to finalize a deal and overcome remaining barriers, according to a White House statement. Following Netanyahu's meeting on Friday with hostages released from Gaza and their families, one of the participants said to *Haaretz* that she had told the prime minister to "take responsibility" for the October 7 massacre. She added that Netanyahu's wife, Sara, then responded that the Israeli army was also responsible. In the West Bank, a resident said eight settlers wearing face coverings entered the village of Susya near Hebron with a few teenagers, went into homes, beat a woman, and also wounded a man. The resident also reported acts of vandalism, into which the police said they opened an investigation. Israeli police also said there were "mutual assaults" in the village and that all those involved had dispersed. In Lebanon's twelve Palestinian refugee communities and their descendants, a *New York Times* survey disclosed, the mood was "nothing but exuberant." Recruitment for Hamas and its armed wing, the Qassam Brigades, was way up in Ein al-Hilweh, the largest of these communities, and elsewhere. Hamas and Lebanese officials said that hundreds of new recruits had joined the militants' ranks in recent months, "exhilarated" by Hamas's ongoing war with Israel.[56]

August 25, day 321 of the war. Claiming that Hezbollah was preparing to fire at 5 a.m. some 6,000 rockets and missiles at Israel, the IDF launched a preemptive strike in a daring raid before dawn that Sunday. About 100 fighter jets destroyed more than forty launch areas in Lebanon whose thousands of rocket launcher barrels had been aimed for immediate fire toward northern and central Israel, as well as 270 military objectives. Gallant noted that Israel's "self-defense act to remove these threats" had come after the "more than 6,700 rockets, missiles, and explosive UAVs fired by Hezbollah at Israeli families, homes, and communities since October 8th." Red alert sirens were sounded in a number of towns in the Upper Galilee; several explosions were detected, there were no injuries. Israel said it had largely thwarted the strikes, and an Israeli military spokesman said there had been "very little damage." Following the IDF's announcement, residents of the conflict line and towns in the Golan were asked to stay close to shelters.[57]

Hezbollah published a statement in which it claimed that 320 rockets had been launched at nearly a dozen "military targets" in Israeli territory. (The IDF claimed that ninety percent were fired from civilian centers.) As part of what it called "the first phase" of the retaliation to the Israeli attack that resulted in the death of Fouad Shukr and others, including women and children, Hezbollah initiated an air strike using a large number of drones deep inside Israel, "targeting a military site that will be disclosed later," the terrorist organization stated. "At the same time, rockets were fired at a number of Iron Dome outposts and batteries. The operations will take time. Later on, a detailed announcement will be issued about the move and the goals," it added. Earlier, it had been reported that Hezbollah planned to launch a number of precision-guided missiles at the Glilot area where the Mossad headquarters and 8200 Intelligence Unit base are located.[58]

Yet, within hours of the attacks, both sides signaled they were easing, stopping short of all-out war, with Hezbollah saying its military operation had "finished for the day." Israel reopened Ben-Gurion International Airport near Tel Aviv after a brief closure, in a sign that officials believed the strikes would be contained, although the Israeli military said it was still carrying out airstrikes against Hezbollah targets. For now, at least, the exchange of attacks fell short of the major escalation that many had feared after the IAF killed Shukr in July. Still, the attacks underscored the threat of a wider war in the Middle East and added urgency to the Biden administration's push to close a cease-fire deal between Israel and Hamas in Gaza, an effort to lower temperatures in the region. Gallant briefed Austin by telephone on the IDF strikes and they discussed "the importance of avoiding regional escalation," the Israeli Ministry of Defense said. In a joint statement, the UN peacekeeping mission and the UN special coordinator for Lebanon urged "a return to the cessation of hostilities" between Israel and Hezbollah and called on all sides to "refrain from further escalatory action." An Israeli delegation was still expected to head to Egypt later that day to advance talks on a cease-fire and hostage release deal in Gaza, according to two Israeli officials who spoke on the condition of anonymity. Hamas representatives had arrived in the city on Saturday night, but it was not clear whether they would participate in the negotiations.[59]

Israel and Hezbollah traded barbs and warned that their war was not over in the hours that followed the IDF's preemptive strike. "What happened today is not the end of the story," Netanyahu told his weekly government meeting. In a televised speech on Sunday evening, Nasrallah said that the group's military operation had ended and "we'll see what will happen in the future." That same evening, senior Hamas official Hamdan told his organization's Al-Aqsa Channel in the Gaza Strip that "Israel has set new conditions for accepting the agreement and reverted from what it had previously agreed to. Today the delegation informed the mediators of our position. We will not accept any withdrawals from what we agreed to on July 2 or any new demands." He added that "the U.S. administration is sowing false hopes by talking about an agreement that is close, while this is only for election purposes." Bassem Naim, a spokesman for the terror group, told *Newsweek* that the United States was "buying time" with the negotiations, explaining that the Americans were pushing hard for discussions in order "to cool the regional front," and adding that the Democratic party needed "a cease-fire deal for internal reasons related to the elections."[60]

The heads of three regional councils in northern Israel reacted sharply to the preemptive strike. They issued a joint statement saying that they were "ceasing communication with all government officials until a complete and comprehensive solution is reached for the residents and children of the northern border," adding that "we have not been of interest to you for ten and a half months, from now on you don't interest us." Slamming the strike against Hezbollah on early Sunday morning, which in their view was aimed at preventing attacks on central Israel, they charged that the operation did nothing to bring security for residents living in the north and still targeted by the enemy. They demanded "a solution that includes full security for the return of the displaced from their homes, ensuring the well-being of all residents and approval of an economic plan for the rehabilitation of the north."[61]

In cease-fire negotiations in Cairo on Monday, Egypt denied Israel's claim that any tunnels running under its border with Gaza could be used for smuggling and reiterated that it would not accept an Israeli military presence in the Philadelphi Corridor or the Rafah border crossing. The source added that all the weapons found in Gaza in recent months appeared to have been manufactured inside Gaza or smuggled through the Rafah crossing with Egypt or by other means, and that "this may indicate that Israel underestimated Hamas's ability to manufacture its own ammunition prior to October 7." Iran's Ayatollah Ali Khamenei did not address the Hezbollah operation directly but said "war has many forms," adding: "It doesn't always mean holding a gun. It means thinking correctly, speaking correctly, identifying correctly, aiming accurately"; Iran's foreign ministry claimed that "the Israeli terrorist army has lost its effective offensive and deterrent power." Austin informed Gallant that he had ordered the presence of two aircraft carrier strike groups in the Middle East, the Pentagon announced. Kibbutz Holit declared it would not participate in the government's ceremony to mark the October 7 massacre. Last week, the Hostages and Missing Families Forum and a number of Gaza border kibbutzim—including Nirim, Be'eri, Kfar Azza, Nir Oz, Yad Mordechai, and Nahal Oz—announced they would boycott the ceremony.[62]

The latest round of hostage negotiations ended without results as the Israeli delegation led by Mossad chief David Barnea returned home from Cairo on Sunday. Mediators tried unsuccessfully to convince the sides to agree to a four-to-seven-day humanitarian cease-fire to deliver polio vaccines and other medical equipment, Qatari newspaper *Al-Araby Al-Jadeed* reported. More than 1.2 million doses of the polio vaccine arrived in Gaza on Monday, in preparation for an expansive effort to inoculate more than 640,000 Palestinian children and curb a potential outbreak. At the same time, medical professionals and volunteers trained for administering these vaccines warned that if a cease-fire were not secured it would be difficult to carry out the entire vaccination campaign, as Israeli bombings could endanger the medical staff. Another fear was the evacuation of residents, they said. Reasonable conditions for the vaccination campaign did not exist in Gaza, because the medical infrastructure there had already been destroyed, a Palestinian Health Ministry official told *Haaretz*.[63]

The IDF conducted airstrikes on Hamas headquarters in central and southern Gaza, and eliminated over ten terrorists, the military announced on Tuesday morning. At least five people, including two children, were killed in an Israeli drone strike on the Nur Shams refugee camp near Tulkarm in the West Bank, the Palestinian Health Ministry said. The IDF confirmed the strike, saying it had targeted what it called the command room of a "terror cell," including Jibril

Ghasan Jibril, a terrorist involved in activity in the areas of Tulkarm and Qalqilya who was released as part of the hostage/prisoner agreement in November 2023. Also eliminated were Mohanad Kamal Qarawi and Muhammad Sheikh Yussef, who were involved in terrorist activity in Nur Shams, and Muhammad Allan and Adnan Ayser Jaber, who manufactured explosives intended to harm IDF forces. Separately, the health ministry said one person had been shot dead and three injured during an attack by Israeli settlers near Bethlehem. The IDF said it was investigating the reports.[64]

The same day, Shayetet 13 troops, the Yahalom unit, and the Shin Bet rescued the hostage Qaid Farhan al-Qadi, found alone in a booby-trapped Rafah underground tunnel. In "stable medical condition," the fifty-two-year-old father of eleven—the youngest only six months old, a Muslim resident of the Bedouin city Rahat in the Negev, had been kidnapped by Hamas on October 7 from where he worked in Kibbutz Magen as a security guard at the packing house. One of the eight Bedouin hostages taken by Hamas, he had taken a bullet rather than lead terrorists to Jews who lived near the packing plant.

"Our brother has returned," an emotional President Herzog told him, calling it "a moment of joy for the State of Israel and Israeli society as a whole." "This operation joins a series of actions taken by the IDF that bring us closer to achieving the goals of this war. I would like to reiterate and emphasize: Israel is committed to taking advantage of every opportunity to return the hostages home to Israel," Gallant declared. "His family had been waiting 326 days to receive the news they did today. But there are still 108 hostages, whose families are still waiting to hear news that their loved ones are home. And they should know that we will not rest until we fulfill our mission to bring all our hostages back home. We will pursue the return of our hostages through all means possible I repeat through all means possible," he concluded. "We hope there will be a celebration not just by us, but all the families of hostages will experience this joy," the free man said. Al-Qadi was the eighth kidnapped Israeli to be rescued by the IDF from Gaza, the first live hostage to be freed from a tunnel. Two other abductees from Rahat, a father and a son, remained in captivity.[65]

On August 28, the Israeli military launched a major counterterror air-and-ground assault across the West Bank, a move it said was aimed at preventing terrorist attacks originating from the Palestinian-operated territory (Area A), which was rapidly developing into a third front for Israel on top of Gaza and its northern border. The Palestinian Health Ministry reported at least eleven deaths so far in the IDF operation—six in Jenin and five in Tubas, a city northeast of Nablus (Shechem). "We need to operate to remove immediate terror threats in real time," said Israeli military spokesman Nadav Shoshani, who stated that some 150 shooting and explosive attacks had originated from the West Bank in the past year. The Palestinian Health Ministry said a total of 660 Palestinians had been killed in the West Bank and East Jerusalem since the war in Gaza began in October, numbers that did not distinguish between civilians and combatants.

UN Secretary-General António Guterres called on the IDF "to use lethal force only when it is strictly unavoidable to protect life" and urged Jerusalem to bring the operation to a halt immediately. Israeli UN Ambassador Danny Danon responded: "The State of Israel will not sit idly by and wait for scenes of buses and cafes exploding in city centers." That afternoon, Israel confirmed that an airstrike had killed Faris Qasim, a senior Palestinian Islamic Jihad terrorist, near the Syria-Lebanon border, along with other Islamic Jihad members. It also announced that Mohamed Jaber, known as Abu Shuja'a, the commander of the Palestinian Islamic Jihad-led Tulkarm Battalion, was one of five militants Israeli forces killed inside a mosque in Tulkarm. In the evening, the IDF returned for burial at home the body of a soldier, his remains abducted to Gaza, who had died defending the southern communities in Hamas's assault on October 7.[66]

The IDF published the findings of its investigation into the settler attack earlier this month on the Palestinian village of Jit, in which settlers burned vehicles, attacked residents, and killed a twenty-three-year-old. According to the findings, the Shin Bet had provided the IDF and police with intelligence that settlers were planning "nationalistic violence" ahead of the incident, and the IDF should have "operated with more determination." The United States imposed sanctions on Yitzhar settlement security chief Yitzhak Levi Filant and on HaShomer Yosh, an Israeli NGO whose volunteers, according to the State Department, fenced off a Palestinian village to prevent residents from returning after they were forced to leave in January.

As for the kidnapped, *Haaretz* reported 147 hostages had been returned to Israel and 108 were still in Gaza—38 of them declared dead. CIA Deputy Director David Cohen emphasized that Hamas's leader Sinwar held the key to resolving the Gaza hostage crisis and cease-fire. About 100 who had returned from Hamas captivity and the families of hostages who returned or remained in captivity wrote to Transportation Minister Miri Regev that they would not agree to "the cynical use of the names of the hostages that the state has abandoned for nearly a year" as part of the national memorial ceremony marking October 7, asking that the ceremony be reconsidered and calling for it to focus on returning the hostages. Ultimately, a compromise was achieved whereby hostage families would hold a ceremony open to the public in Tel Aviv's Yarkon Park at 7:10 p.m., starting with a moment of silence and the traditional *Yizkor* memorial prayer, while the official government ceremony would be broadcast at 9:15 p.m.[67]

During a video address to a conference in Istanbul, Hamas leader abroad Khaled Mashaal announced, "Resistance operations in the West Bank are escalating despite the harsh conditions," according to CNN Arabic. "We want to return to martyrdom operations. This is a situation that can only be addressed by open conflict. They are fighting us with open conflict, and we are confronting them with open conflict," he continued. "The enemy has opened the conflict on all fronts, seeking us all, whether we fight or not. The enemy says, 'I am crazy,' and it is up to the [Arab] nation to assume its responsibilities. I reiterate my call for everyone to participate on multiple fronts in the actual resistance against the Zionist entity."[68]

A convoy of families of hostages arrived on Thursday at the Israel-Gaza border near Kibbutz Nirim to send messages to their loved ones, projected through speakers facing Gaza. French President Macron and UK Prime Minister Keir Starmer discussed "the need to de-escalate the situation in the Middle East" during a meeting in Paris, afterward reiterating their call for an immediate cease-fire. The Palestinian Health Ministry said that sixteen Palestinians had been killed in IDF activity over the past day in the cities of Jenin, Tubas, and Tulkarm. Israeli forces eliminated Osama Gadallah, a senior commander in the military intelligence of Palestinian Islamic Jihad, during ongoing operations in the Gaza Strip. Gadallah, who played a significant role in the Hamas October 7 invasion, was targeted and killed in Rafah by the IAF along with dozens of other terrorists in fierce fighting. Muhammad Katrouy, commander of the Palestinian Islamic Jihad's Central Camps Brigade, was eliminated in a separate airstrike. Outgoing EU foreign policy chief Josep Borrell announced he had asked other member states if they were willing to impose sanctions on "some Israeli ministers" for inciting against Palestinians; his effort failed as many refused. Gallant said the IDF would bolster its forces and add security measures to schools in northern and southern Israel so the school year could begin as scheduled on September 1, adding that the war's goals must be expanded to include the repatriation of residents of northern Israel to their homes.[69]

That morning, the IDF discovered a laboratory for the manufacture of explosive devices and a terrorist operations room while searching inside the Abu Bakr al-Siddiq Mosque in the Jordan Valley. In Gaza, despite military sources previously stating it could take six months, IDF sources claimed that eighty percent of the Philadelphi Corridor tunnel network had been destroyed, while also confirming Gallant's announcement on August 21 that Hamas's last battalion there had been taken apart. Yet, even in the northern part of the Strip, which the

IDF entered six months earlier than it had entered Rafah, there was no indication that the IDF had reached anywhere near destroying eighty percent of the tunnels, with estimates ranging from just under fifty percent to just over fifty percent. UN officials declared that, starting this weekend, Israel would pause military operations in a staggered schedule across Gaza to allow health workers to give polio vaccinations to about 640,000 children under the age of ten. Israel emphasized the move was not the first step to a cease-fire. Iran, meanwhile, increased its enrichment of uranium to sixty percent, and was not cooperating with the International Atomic Energy Agency, the world's center for promoting the safe, secure, and peaceful use of nuclear technology. US assessments at this point were that Iran was just one or two weeks away from having enough fissionable material for a nuclear weapon.[70]

On Thursday, the Israeli government's Political-Security Cabinet approved maps determining that the IDF would remain in the Philadelphi Corridor. The move was approved by a majority of eight, with Gallant strongly objecting in what degenerated into a shouting match, arguing that Philadelphi was not important enough to Israel's security to scuttle the talks. On Saturday night, some argued this would endanger a hostage deal; Ben-Gvir abstained. The maps were drawn by the IDF, and adopted by the United States as part of a hostage deal proposal. Cabinet ministers said during the meeting that the decision rendered the possibility of a hostage and cease-fire deal more feasible, clarifying to Hamas that it will have to compromise on the Corridor like its compromise in its demand to end the war. Netanyahu clarified that the October 7 massacre was made possible because Israel was not in control of the Corridor. According to him, a huge amount of weapons was transferred through the Corridor, used by terrorist organizations in Gaza. That evening, US Vice President Harris said once again that the war in Gaza "must end" and "we must get a deal that is about getting the hostages out." Asked in a CNN interview whether she would withhold some weapon shipments to Israel as many Democratic Party progressives had requested, Harris replied, "Let me be very clear: I'm unequivocal and unwavering in my commitment to Israel's defense and its ability to defend itself, and that's not going to change."[71]

As much as Israel's—and the world's—focus has been on the war in Gaza, a *Jerusalem Post* editorial pointed out on Friday, it became apparent in recent months that the conflict was inseparable from what had been taking place in the West Bank. The Mujahideen Brigades threw IEDs (improvised explosive devices) toward the settlement of Karmei Tzur in Gush Etzion on Wednesday. Two days earlier, armed Palestinian terrorists opened fire toward Israeli civilians in Mitzpeh Yosef, near Nablus. Palestinian areas had become breeding grounds for terror cells. That is why the IDF and Shin Bet had been conducting a huge, complex counterterrorism operation during the past week, specifically around localities like Jenin and Tulkarm, the most extensive operation in the area in several months. We should be proud of the IDF, the editorial concluded, "for not only cracking down on Palestinian terrorism but also fighting the extremists from the Israeli side. As a democratic country, we cannot tolerate violence of any kind. But make no mistake, the fringe of the settler movement isn't the main problem—it's the thousands of Palestinian terrorists who would kill any Jew if they only had a chance."[72]

That morning, the IDF and Shin Bet identified a terrorist cell led by Wassem Hazem, head of the Hamas terrorist organization in Jenin, in a vehicle there. Shortly after eliminating him in gunfire, an IDF aircraft killed Misra Masharqa and Arafat Amer, two additional Hamas operatives while they attempted to flee from the vehicle. The troops of the 98th Division completed their divisional operation in the Khan Younis and Deir al-Balah area after about a month of operational activity, having eliminated over 250 terrorists and destroyed dozens of terrorist infrastructure. The Yahalom Unit, along with the 7th Brigade and the Paratroopers Brigade, destroyed six underground tunnel routes spanning approximately six kilometers, where they located terrorist hideouts and weapons and killed Hamas operatives. The IDF said that it had killed twenty terrorists and detained seventeen suspects in an operation in the northern West Bank. About forty rockets were launched toward the Western Galilee in a barrage fired from Lebanon. At the same time, the Israeli negotiating team for a cease-fire deal with Hamas returned to Israel after a summit in Qatar, with sources telling *Haaretz* there had been no breakthroughs on the current sticking points in talks.[73]

On Saturday, day 330 of the war, four Israelis were wounded overnight in two West Bank car bomb attacks at the Karmei Tzur settlement near Hebron and the Gush Etzion junction; both assailants were killed, and six suspects arrested. Israeli security officials said the explosives came from the same lab in Hebron. Two Hamas-affiliated militants were killed in Jenin as the IDF's West Bank counterterrorism operation entered its fourth day. Palestinian health officials in Gaza said Israeli airstrikes on the Strip killed at least forty-eight people that day; the Israeli army declared that fourteen terrorists had been killed so far, and that dozens of explosive devices were destroyed.[74]

As August drew to a close, the IDF Central Command's 877th "Judea and Samaria" Division, responsible for Israeli military activity in the Judea and Samaria area, announced that since October 7, 2023, more than 5,000 suspects had been arrested there, among them 2,000 Hamas terrorists. In

11,000 military operations, about 6,000 terrorists were eliminated, and in IAF airstrikes another 100 killed. The Gaza front reflected a never-ending Sisyphean war, while the region continued to teeter on the brink of wider war. The nation with the most to lose could be Lebanon, with its economy in crisis, a reality that leaders of Hezbollah recognized. "They know if they were to strike Israel with the capacity they have, Israel will hit back and hit back with everything they have," said Nader Hashemi, a professor of Middle East politics at Georgetown University who concluded "Lebanon is currently a fragile state." As for the hostages still in Gaza, the IDF announced that troops had just found several bodies underground in Gaza, likely of Israelis kidnapped on October 7. The fate of others? Unknown.[75]

Endnotes

1 *New York Times*, Aug. 1, 2024; Israel National News, Aug. 1, 2024; *Washington Post*, Aug. 1, 2024.
2 AP News, Aug. 2, 2024; *Haaretz*, Aug. 1, 2024; *Wall St. Journal*, Aug. 1, 2024.
3 JNS, Aug. 1, 2024.
4 Israel National News, Aug. 2, 2024; *Jerusalem Post*, Aug. 1–2, 2024. Former Palestinian Authority Grand Mufti of Jerusalem Sabri was barred from the Temple Mount for six months after lauding Haniyeh in his sermon on August 2, Israeli police said on Thursday. JNS, Aug. 8, 2024.
5 *Times of Israel*, Aug. 1, 2024.
6 *Haaretz*, Aug. 2, 2024; World Israel News, Aug. 2, 2024; Voice of America, July 28, 2024.
7 *Haaretz*, Aug. 3, 2024; IDF News, Aug. 3, 2024.
8 *Haaretz*, Aug. 4, 2024; Israel National News, Aug. 4, 2024; IDF News, Aug. 4, 2024; JNS, Aug. 4, 2024; Ynet News, Aug. 4, 2024; *Jerusalem Post*, Aug. 4, 2024.
9 Israel National News, Aug. 4, 2024.
10 Israel National News, Aug. 4, 2024; *Haaretz*, Aug. 4, 2024.
11 *Wall St. Journal*, Aug. 4, 2024. Typically, these reservists are former conscripts who continue to train and serve about one month annually until they are forty, or forty-five for officers. At the height of the war in Gaza, about two-thirds of Israel's fighting power was drawn from reservists—some 300,000 drafted reserve personnel, compared with a standing army of around 150,000.
12 *Haaretz*, Aug. 5, 2024; *Yisrael Hayom*, Aug. 5, 2024. At the same time, a report by the American Enterprise Institute's Critical Threats Project, the Institute for the Study of War, and CNN stated that only three out of the twenty-four Hamas battalions were considered combat ineffective. The report added that thirteen battalions had been "degraded", and were able to conduct sporadic, and largely unsuccessful guerrilla-style attacks. Eight of them were still fully capable to carry out missions against Israeli soldiers on the ground in Gaza.

Yet, as the *Jerusalem Post*'s senior military correspondent pointed out, most of the recent IDF re-invasions into areas of Gaza since March involved one brigade of around 1,000 soldiers, and full re-penetration and achieving control occurred within hours. The fact that the IDF could retake these areas so much faster and with so few troops was not "just a mathematical tactical issue"; it meant that most reservists who were called up for the first few months of the war are at home, working, or back in university.

In addition, Hamas's fighting numbers as organized groups were smaller. Instead of 10,000 usually, Hamas fights in groups of 5–10, with some situations reaching groups of 50. Calling 50 Hamas forces with no experienced commander (most experienced commanders were now dead or hiding in tunnels cut off from their forces) just "degraded" missed the point. A more accurate definition would be "existing but on life support."

Further, since January—for seven months—Hamas's rocket threat had been reduced from a strategic threat that could hold most of Israel hostage to "an annoyance that most Israelis barely notice." Likewise, Hamas's tunnel network, while it could take the IDF years to destroy all of it, was no longer in any position to come close to facilitating a surprise attack on Israel and had been reduced very much in its effectiveness. Yonah Jeremy Bob, "Why CNN's View of Hamas' Readiness is Crucial but Misses Some Huge Issues," *Jerusalem Post*, Aug. 6, 2024. Also see Andrew Fox, "The IDF's Boot Is on Hamas' Throat," Tablet, Aug. 13, 2024; Yaakov Amidror, "CNN's Optical Illusion," *Jerusalem Post*, Aug. 13, 2024.

13 *Haaretz*, Aug. 5, 2024; *Wall St. Journal*, Aug. 5, 2024; Israel National News, Aug. 5, 2024; *Jerusalem Post*, Aug. 5, 2024. Pnina Bibas, Ariel's maternal grandmother, wrote this in an open letter to Ariel that was published in the *Daily Mail*: "My dear Luli, Nine months have passed since you were taken from us by bad people. Nine months of tears, prayers, and unwavering hope. The world around us continues to turn, but time seems to have frozen without you. You've grown a year older, but there's no celebration." Israel National News, Aug. 6, 2024.

14 *Jerusalem Post*, Aug. 5–6, 2024; *Haaretz*, Aug. 6, 2024; Israel National News, Aug. 6, 2024; World Israel News, Aug. 5, 2024.

15 *Times of Israel*, Aug. 6, 2024; *Washington Post*, Aug. 6, 2024.

16 *Haaretz*, Aug. 6, 2024.

17 Israel National News, Aug. 6, 2024; *Haaretz*, Aug. 6, 2024; JNS, Aug. 6, 2024; AP, Aug. 6, 2024; *Jerusalem Post*, Aug. 6, 2024.

18 *Times of Israel*, Aug. 6, 2024; *New York Times*, Aug. 6, 2024; *Economist*, Aug. 6, 2024; *Wall St. Journal*, Aug. 7, 2024. Hamas's decision to appoint October 7 mastermind Sinwar as its paramount leader proved that Israel should "retain full security control west of the Jordan River," reacted Foreign Minister Israel Katz. "Israel must maintain control over security and foreign affairs to prevent the establishment of another Iranian-Islamist extremist stronghold and enable Palestinians to manage their internal affairs," he tweeted. JNS, Aug. 7, 2024.

19 *Haaretz*, Aug. 7. 2024.

20 *Jerusalem Post*, Aug. 7, 2024; *Haaretz*, Aug. 7, 2024. The poll, released Wednesday by the Hostage Family Forum, was conducted by the Midgam polling institute led by Mano Geva. The fifty-nine percent in favor compared to thirty-three percent of all respondents who opposed such a deal, with the rest undecided. Among coalition voters, this support stood at forty-one percent in favor, with forty-nine percent against, and the rest undecided.

21 *Jerusalem Post*, Aug. 7, 2024.

22 *Jerusalem Post*, Aug. 8, 2024; Israel National News, Aug. 8, 2024.

23 Israel National News, Aug. 8, 2024; *Jerusalem Post*, Aug. 8, 2024. A *Jerusalem Post* editorial on August 9 reflected the Israeli majority: "A recent Channel 12 poll showing over 70 percent of Israelis want Netanyahu to resign is a damning indictment of how betrayed the public feels. . . . Netanyahu's *Time* interview is a false apology and a sign that he won't face up to his public. It's time he addresses the public in their language and finally answers his constituents' questions."

24 Israel National News, Aug. 8, 2024; *Jerusalem Post*, Aug. 8, 2024; *Haaretz*, Aug. 8, 2024. In 2011, Sakhl, like Sinwar, was among 1,027 convicted terrorists freed in exchange for kidnapped IDF soldier Gilad Shalit. Others included Warchi Mushtaha, Ahmed Andor, Abdulah Barghouti, Izzadin Sheikh Khalil, Musa Dudin, Jihad Yamour, and Hassan Salameh—among today's Hamas leaders. Other Palestinian terrorists released in that deal went on murder Israelis: Baruch Mizrachi by Ziad Awad; Malkachi Rosenfeld by Ahmas Najar; Rabbi Miki Mark by Mohamed Fakih, and many more. Mahmoud Qawasameh, also freed in the Shalit

deal, planned the killing of teenagers Naftali Frankel, Eyal Yiftach, and Gilad Shaer in Gush Etzion in 2014, while Jasser Barghouti directed from Gaza the murders of Yosef Cohen, Yuval Mor Yosef, and the child Amiad Israel Ish-Ran. David M. Weinberg, "Terrorists for Hostages: The Agonizing Dilemma," *Jerusalem Post*, Aug. 16, 2024.

25 Israel National News, Aug. 9, 2024; *Times of Israel*, Aug. 10, 2024; *Jerusalem Post*, Aug. 9, 2024; *Haaretz*, Aug. 9, 2024.

26 *Haaretz*, Aug. 10, 2024. At the same time, should an Iranian attack take place, Amman will allow Israel to use its airspace to fend off any aerial threats, a Jordanian official told Channel 12 on Saturday. "We will allow Israel to repel the Iranian attack in our airspace," the official said, adding that "it stems from a security interest, and this is the policy, just as in April Jordan helped Israel stop the Iranian attack. It is ultimately an ally of the United States." JNS, Aug. 11, 2024.

27 *Haaretz*, Aug. 10, 2024; *Jerusalem Post*, Aug. 10, 2024. Of these hostages, prolonged constipation was reported in ten patients, one of them a toddler, as a result of prolonged hunger, thirst, and insufficient food that was not rich in the fats and dietary fibers that are important for the digestive process. Two women and nine children suffered from prolonged diarrhea. The stool tests showed the growth of multiple fecal bacteria, a result of the severely unhygienic conditions in which they lived.

All the hostages suffered from starvation, and their nutritional status was poor: fifteen of them showed a significant weight loss of up to fifteen percent of their body mass. According to a report from the hostages, the diet was based on a little rice and white bread, without vegetables, protein, or fats. Upon arrival at the hospital, all patients received a specific nutritional regimen graded to avoid the risk of a severe syndrome known as "over-feeding." All patients were also treated with multivitamins during hospitalization.

All twenty-six patients reported poor sanitation and poor hygiene conditions. Two women and six children were underground for most of their captivity. Some of them also suffered as a result of a lack of vitamin D, which is important for normal bodily function.

Most hostages reported limited access to running water throughout their captivity. In six of the patients, head lice were found, which required hair shaving and the start of drug treatment. One woman and five children suffered from multiple insect bites and intense skin irritation.

Three of the children had a history of asthma and experienced attacks during captivity that required the use of inhalers, but it is not clear whether they were treated. One woman and two children suffered from generalized muscle pain shortly after hospitalization. Their lab tests showed high levels of the CPK enzyme, indicating significant muscle damage, likely from the prolonged immobility of sitting in captivity.

Blood tests showed that about half of them had suffered from tick-borne fever, Q fever transmitted by inhaling dust or contact with sick animals, and murine fever caused by bacteria. These infections can cause neurological problems, breathing difficulties, damage to muscles and joints, and are sometimes life-threatening.

Of these hostages, fourteen were wounded during the attack and kidnapping, including nine with shrapnel wounds that remained in their bodies in the chest, limbs, and pelvis. One of them had a fractured rib and a lung injury with bleeding. Another patient suffered a gunshot wound to the lower abdominal wall.

Everyone underwent a mental evaluation and received social and psychological support during their stay in the hospital. All reported psychological terrorism, with various psychological warfare strategies, including isolation, intimidation, food and water restriction, and psychological abuse.

Upon admission to the hospital, all children less than seven years of age exhibited a submissive behavior pattern. Some of them suffered from repeated nightmares. The kidnapped children spoke in a whisper, accustomed to being threatened by terrorists. Three toddlers took the food served to them and saved it for a later time. Some of the hostages

suffered immediate anxiety disorders and began psychiatric medication. *Jerusalem Post*, Aug. 11, 2024.
28 Israel National News, Aug. 11, 2024. Biden had previously said "don't" for the first time to deter Israel's enemies in the days after the October 7, 2023, Hamas-led massacre in Israel's northwestern Negev. The U.S. president used the single word a second time to warn Iran against an attack on Israel in mid-April 2024.
29 *Jerusalem Post*, Aug. 11, 2024; *Haaretz*, Aug. 11, 2024.
30 *Haaretz*, Aug. 11, 2024; *Jerusalem Post*, Aug. 11, 2024; Zaka Tel Aviv, Aug. 11, 2024.
31 *New York Times*, Aug. 12, 2024; Israel National News, Aug. 12, 2024; *Times of Israel*, Aug. 12, 2024; *Jerusalem Post*, Aug. 12, 2024; *Haaretz*, Aug. 12, 2024.
32 *Haaretz*, Aug. 12, 2024; *New York Times*, Aug. 12, 2024.
33 *New York Times*, Aug. 13, 2024. Seth Mandel pointed out that, for months, Israel said it would agree to a cease-fire only if its soldiers could screen the returning Palestinians for weapons as they moved from southern to northern Gaza. Then, in its May proposal, Israel softened that demand. While its position paper still stated that the returnees should not be "carrying arms while returning," it removed the explicit requirement that Israeli forces screen them for weapons. That made the policy seem more symbolic than enforceable, prompting Hamas to agree to it. Israel's July letter revived the question of enforcement, stating that the screening of people returning to the north would need to be "implemented in an agreed upon manner." Seth Mandel, "Leaked Documents Vindicate Netanyahu on Ceasefire Deal," *Commentary*, Aug. 14, 2024.
34 *Jerusalem Post*, Aug. 13, 2024; Israel National News, Aug. 13, 2024; *Times of Israel*, Aug. 13, 2024.
35 Israel National News, Aug. 14, 2024; *Jerusalem Post*, Aug. 14, 2024; i24 News, Aug. 14, 2024; *Washington Post*, Aug. 14, 2024. It was reported the same day that the eleven-year-old girl declared the most seriously wounded victim of the Majdal Shams soccer field massacre regained consciousness as her condition improved. A number of *kinot* (verses of lamentation), joining those traditionally said on *Tish'a B'Av*, were written to commemorate the October 7 massacre. For one recalling the bloodbath at Kibbutz Be'eri, see the Appendices.
36 *Jerusalem Post*, Aug. 14, 2024; *Haaretz*, Aug. 14, 2024; *Jerusalem Post*, Aug. 11, 2024. Another Israeli fissure emerged when five senior rabbis, including Israel's former Sephardi Chief Rabbi Yitzhak Yosef and Rabbi of the Old City of Jerusalem Avigdor Nebenzahl, echoed the Shas Party and the secular party opposition in condemning visits by Jews to the Al-Aqsa/ Temple Mount complex in a video published one day after far-right National Security Minister Itamar Ben-Gvir's visit to the holy site on *Tish'a B'Av*, August 13. "I call on the nations of the world, do not see those government ministers as representing the people of Israel.... Please act to calm the spirits, we all believe in one God and want peace between the nations, and we must not let extreme fringes lead us," Yosef said in the video. UK Foreign Secretary David Lammy also condemned Ben-Gvir's Temple Mount visit, writing on X that "such actions undermine the Hashemite Kingdom of Jordan's role as custodian of the sites and the longstanding Status Quo arrangements." *Haaretz*, Aug. 14, 2024.
37 *Haaretz*, Aug. 14, 2024; *Jerusalem Post*, Aug. 14, 2024.
38 *Haaretz*, Aug. 14–15, 2024; Israel National News, Aug. 14–15, 2024; IDF News, Aug. 15, 2024.
39 Israel National News, Aug. 16 and 18, 2024; *Haaretz*, Aug. 16, 2024.
40 Israel National News, Aug. 15–16, 2024; *Haaretz*, Aug. 16–17, 2024; *Washington Post*, Aug. 16, 2024.
41 *Times of Israel*, Aug. 16, 2024; *Haaretz*, Aug. 17, 2024; Israel National News, Aug. 17, 2024.
42 *Haaretz*, Aug. 18, 2024; IDF News, Aug. 18, 2024.
43 Israel National News, Aug. 19, 2024; *New York Times*, Aug. 19, 2024. According to reports, Israel agreed to compromise on its ability to veto the release of certain highly dangerous convicted terrorists in exchange for an increase in the number of hostages released each

week during the first stage of the proposed deal. The US mediators also proposed to support Israel's demand that weapons not be smuggled from southern Gaza to northern Gaza, and that, if such smuggling were detected, it would constitute a violation of the deal and allow Israel to resume military operations in Gaza. Netanyahu responded: "Once again, I would like to emphasize: Up until now, Hamas has been completely obstinate. It did not even send a representative to the talks in Doha. Therefore, the pressure needs to be directed at Hamas and Sinwar, not the Government of Israel. Strong military and diplomatic pressure are the way to secure the release of our hostages."

44 *Haaretz*, Aug. 19, 2024; *Jerusalem Post*, Aug. 19, 2024; IDF News, Aug. 19, 2024; Israel National News, Aug. 16 and 19, 2024.
45 *Wall St. Journal*, Aug. 19, 2024.
46 Israel National News, Aug. 19–20, 2024; *Jerusalem Post*, Aug. 19, 2024. Outside the convention arena on the first day of the Democratic National Convention, pro-Palestinian protesters clashed with police. Inside, pro-Palestinian Democrats celebrated what they called a significant breakthrough: a panel discussion, sponsored by the Harris campaign, that highlighted the toll of Israel's military campaign against Hamas in Gaza. The event was the first time in decades that the Democratic Party gave a platform to pro-Palestinian activists. The "uncommitted" delegates, a group of about thirty or so representing Democratic primary voters who had declined to support Biden because of his staunch support for Israel, had pressed unsuccessfully for a speaking slot on the main convention stage. But this official concession was nonetheless met with gratitude, even as they insisted that Vice President Harris would have to go further than her position backing a cease-fire to fully earn their support.

Keith Ellison, the Minnesota attorney general, led the panel, which included two Palestinian American Democrats, as well as James Zogby, a longtime member of the Democratic National Committee; former Representative Andy Levin of Michigan, a progressive Democrat; and Dr. Tanya Haj-Hassan, a pediatric physician who has treated patients with aid groups in Gaza. Hala Hijazi, a Democratic organizer and fund-raiser on the panel, said that over 100 members of her family had been killed in the war in Gaza. Dr. Haj-Hassan also shared stories of treating young children in Gaza. Members of the audience openly wept listening to her testimony. Leaders of the uncommitted movement called on Harris to commit to halting the flow of American weapons to Israel if elected. The Democratic platform, released on Sunday, featured the party's traditional message of supporting Israel and did not include support for an arms embargo. Hours later, Representative Alexandria Ocasio-Cortez, a high-profile progressive from New York accorded a prime speaking spot, lauded Harris from the main stage for "working tirelessly to secure a cease-fire in Gaza." Members of the audience cheered and applauded, with some standing and raising their fists. *New York Times*, Aug. 20, 2024.
47 *Jerusalem Post*, Aug. 20, 2024; *Haaretz*, Aug. 20, 2024.
48 *Haaretz*, Aug. 20, 2024; Israel National News, Aug. 21, 2024.
49 *Haaretz*, Aug. 21, 2024; *Jerusalem Post*, Aug. 22, 2024.
50 *Jerusalem Post*, Aug. 21, 2024; *Haaretz*, Aug. 21, 2024.
51 *Haaretz*, Aug. 22, 2024; Israel National News, Aug. 23, 2024. Also see Yonah Jeremy Bob, "Why Isn't the IDF Catching More Jewish Terrorists?," *Jerusalem Post*, Aug. 30, 2024.
52 Israel National News, Aug. 22, 2024; *New York Times*, Aug. 23, 2024. *Aliya* (meaning "ascent" in Hebrew) signifies the move from abroad to live in Israel; *olim* are those who choose the path of *aliya*.
53 *Times of Israel*, Aug. 23, 2024; *Haaretz*, Aug. 23, 2024; *Times of Israel*, Aug. 25, 2024. Ben-Gvir soon claimed there was a new policy at the Temple Mount/Al-Aqsa Mosque compound allowing Jewish prayer, prompting a denial from Netanyahu. *Haaretz*, Aug. 26, 2024. Hamas issued a statement calling the desire of Ben-Gvir "the terrorist" to build a synagogue on the Temple Mount a "dangerous announcement" that reflected the Israeli government's quest to

Judaize the site and take over it. It called on Palestinian Arabs to come to Al-Aqsa Mosque, stay there, and stop Israel's plans and on the "resistance organizations" in Judea and Samaria to escalate the confrontations with the "criminal enemy and his hordes of settlers." Israel National News, Aug. 27, 2024. *Yated Ne'eman*, affiliated with the Ashkenazic haredi party Degel HaTorah (Torah Banner), published a headline in Hebrew and Arabic on its front page criticizing the new policy of Ben-Gvir, writing that "It is the opinion of all the Jewish halakhic decision-makers for generations, that it is prohibited for Jews to ascend to Temple Mount and this has not changed. The political pyromaniac is burning the area for the second time." *Haaretz*, Aug. 27, 2024.

54 *Washington Post*, Aug. 23, 2024; *New York Times*, Aug. 23, 2024.
55 Israel National News, Aug. 24, 2024; Israel War Room, Aug. 23, 2024; NPR, Aug. 25, 2024; JTA, Aug. 25, 2024; *Haaretz*, Aug. 24, 2024; World Israel News, Aug. 26, 2024.
56 *Haaretz*, Aug. 24, 2024; Middle East Eye, Aug. 24, 2024; *New York Times*, Aug. 24, 2024.
57 *Haaretz*, Aug. 25, 2024; IDF News, Aug. 25, 2024; Israel National News, Aug. 25, 2024. By omitting the word "preemptive" in an early headline on August 25—"Israel strikes Hezbollah in Lebanon, which fires rockets at Israel," the *New York Times* presented a skewed image of an aggressive Israel, seemingly provoking a broader regional conflict by needlessly attacking Hezbollah.
   One Israeli civilian was moderately injured by the Hezbollah response. In addition, an Israeli sailor on a naval vessel was killed and two others wounded in an incident involving the interception of a drone—the details of which remained unclear. Among the civilian structures hit by the Hezbollah barrage was a chicken coop, a fact that led to much mockery on Arab social media, where the Iran-backed terrorist group's tough talk was contrasted to its "chicken massacre." World Israel News, Aug. 26, 2024.
58 Israel National News, Aug. 25, 2024; IDF News, Aug. 27, 2024; *New York Times*, Aug. 25, 2024. A second Hezbollah statement mentioned that it was the "40th day after the martyrdom anniversary of the third Shiite imam, Imam Ḥusayn." This period is important for Shi'ite Muslims and is called *Arba'iniyat Al-Ḥusayn*. (The Arabic word for the number 40 is *arba'in* (similar to the Hebrew *arba'im*) and signifies the end of a forty-day mourning period for Husayn and others killed at Karbala.) Many Shiites take part in pilgrimages in places such as Iraq. *Jerusalem Post*, Aug. 25, 2024.
59 *Wall St. Journal*, Aug. 25, 2024; Axios, Aug. 25, 2024. Hamas lauded the Hezbollah attack on Israel's north, while the Houthi political office congratulated Hezbollah and Nasrallah on what it called a "large and courageous attack" and a "strong and effective response" against Israel. *Haaretz*, Aug. 25, 2024.
60 *Haaretz*, Aug. 25, 2024; Israel National News, Aug. 25, 2024; World Israel News, Aug. 26, 2024.
61 *Jerusalem Post*, Aug. 25, 2024; i24News, Aug. 25, 2024. In like vein, the right-wing journalist Assaf Sagiv penned a poem on his Facebook page, an ironic update of Natan Alterman's iconic 1947 poem for *Davar Magash HaKesef* (The Silver Platter). Daniel Gordis, "Israel from the Inside," Aug. 26, 2024.
62 *Haaretz*, Aug. 26, 2024; *Wall St. Journal*, Aug. 26, 2024; Israel National News, Aug. 26–27, 2024. The 500th aircraft in the joint airlift of weapons and equipment operation from the United States to Israel to assist with the ongoing war effort recently landed, the Defense Ministry announced on Monday. Since October 7, the Biden administration had sent Israel over 50,000 tons of military equipment, both offensive and defensive. In addition to the airlift, Washington had sent Jerusalem 107 shipments of military supplies by sea. *Jerusalem Post*, Aug. 26, 2024. Washington was delivering the final six million pounds of aid from the Joint Logistics Over-the-Shore project—the pier anchored to the Gazan shore which was beset by problems until it was retired—the Pentagon said last week. JNS, Aug. 26, 2024.
63 World Israel News, Aug. 26, 2024; *New York Times*, Aug. 26, 2024; Israel National News, Aug. 27, 2024; *Haaretz*, Aug. 27, 2024.

64 *Jerusalem Post*, Aug. 27, 2024; BBC, Aug. 27, 2024; *World Israel News*, Aug. 27, 2024; *Haaretz*, Aug. 27, 2024.

65 Israel National News, Aug. 27, 2024; *Haaretz*, Aug. 27, 2024; *New York Times*, Aug. 27, 2024. The freed Bedouin later testified that "his friend," eighty-five-year-old Aryeh Zalmanovich, one of the founders of Kibbutz Nir Oz, was held hostage alongside him until his death; he "did not get the medicines and care he needed." Israel National News, Aug. 29, 2024; *Times of Israel*, Aug. 29, 2024. Netanyahu, regularly criticized by hostage families and his own security establishment for holding up a cease-fire deal, said he called Al-Qadi after the rescue and that he remains committed to freeing the remaining hostages. "We do this in two main ways: through negotiations and rescue operations," he said. "Both ways together require our military presence in the field and unceasing military pressure on Hamas." *Wall St. Journal*, Aug. 27, 2024.

66 *Wall St. Journal*, Aug. 28, 2024; Israel National News, Aug. 29, 2024; *New York Times*, Aug. 28, 2024; JNS, Aug. 28, 2024.

67 *Haaretz*, Aug. 28, 2024; *Jerusalem Post*, Aug. 28, 2024; IDF News, Aug. 29, 2024. For a mordant critique of Transport Minister Miri Regev's initial plan for the government ceremony, see Amotz Asa-El, "Miri Regev's Ministry of Truth," *Jerusalem Post*, Aug. 30, 2024. Hamas was losing control of Gaza's smaller terror groups, the London-based *Jewish Chronicle* reported Wednesday, citing Israeli military sources. The report noted that some of the smallest organizations, such as the Popular Front for the Liberation of Palestine (PFLP), the Mujahideen Brigades, the Al-Nasser Salah al-Deen Brigades, and the Al-Aqsa Martyrs' Brigades, no longer heeded Hamas leader Sinwar's instructions. Only about twenty living hostages were held by Hamas, while the other terror groups held the remaining hostages.

According to the newspaper, twenty-two handcuffed hostages were still believed to be alive—out of 108 still in Gaza—and those hostages were being forced into service as Sinwar's human shields. Israel had multiple opportunities to eliminate Sinwar, but the orders to do so were not given due to the risk to the hostages who surround him. Last week, reports said that Sinwar was demanding that his life and safety be assured as part of any cease-fire and hostage swap deal. *Jewish Chronicle*, Aug. 28, 2024,

68 JNS, Aug. 29, 2024;

69 *Haaretz*, Aug. 29, 2024; Israfan, Aug. 29, 20224; IDF News, Aug. 30, 2024.

70 JNS, Aug. 29, 2024; *Jerusalem Post*, Aug. 29, 2024; IDF News, Aug. 29, 2024; *New York Times*, Aug. 29, 2024; Yaakov Katz, "Iran Toys with the West as It Continues to Edge Closer to Nuclear Capability," *Jerusalem Post*, Aug. 30, 2024.

71 *Jerusalem Post*, Aug. 30, 2024; Israel National News, Aug. 30, 2024.

72 Editorial, "West Bank Unrest: The Overlooked Battle amid Gaza War," *Jerusalem Post*, Aug. 30, 2024. The editorial observed that according to data by the NGO Foundation for Defense of Democracies (FDD) and the Shin Bet, 3,425 violent terrorist incidents occurred in Judea, Samaria, and eastern Jerusalem during the first seven months of 2024. During August, an additional 145 terrorist incidents were reported, bringing the total to 3,570. In addition, since the war broke out on October 7, 2023, approximately 4,600 terrorist actions in Judea, Samaria, and eastern Jerusalem accounted for 92 percent of all terror incidents in Israel during this period. In 2020, the lowest number of attacks was reported compared to recent years, with 1,320 incidents. In 2023, 414 significant attacks occurred in Judea, Samaria, and eastern Jerusalem, with 43 Israelis killed and 224 injured. In the first seven months of 2024, 685 significant attacks were thwarted, Also see Khaled Abu Toameh, "Iran and Hamas are Trying to Bring the War to the West Bank," Mosaic, Aug. 30, 2024.

73 *Haaretz*, Aug. 30, 2024; Israel National News, Aug. 30, 2024.

74 *Haaretz*, Aug. 31, 2024.

75 IDF News, Aug. 31, 2024; *New York Times*, Aug. 29, 2024; *Jerusalem Post*, Aug. 31, 2024.

CHAPTER 6

No End in Sight

September 1 brought the tragic news that the IDF had identified the bodies of four men and two women—all shot in the head multiple times and elsewhere at point-blank range—retrieved the night before from a tunnel some sixty-five feet under Rafah, including that of the American citizen Hersh Goldberg-Polin whose mother had become a tireless, eloquent voice for the ongoing agony of families over their loved ones kidnapped into Gaza on October 7. Praising Hersh's parents, Rachel and Jon, as "relentless and irrepressible champions of their son and of all the hostages," US President Joe Biden declared, "I admire them and grieve with them more deeply than words can express. I know all Americans tonight will have them in their prayers, just as Jill and I will. I have worked tirelessly to bring their beloved Hersh safely to them and am heartbroken by the news of his death." Israeli President Isaac Herzog said the "heart of an entire nation is shattered to pieces" and apologized to the families for failing to bring them back safely. Minutes after the military's announcement that the six had likely been executed by Hamas a day or two before Israeli troops got to them, the Hostages and Missing Families Forum charged: "Netanyahu abandoned the hostages! This is now a fact." Its statement also called on the public to prepare for new demonstrations starting as soon as Sunday. Roughly 100 other abductees were still held in Gaza, about two-thirds of whom were believed to be alive, reported the *New York Times*.[1]

Defense Minister Gallant said the security cabinet must immediately convene and reverse the decision it made to keep an Israeli military presence along the Philadelphi Corridor, adding that "it is too late for the hostages who were murdered in cold blood," but hostages who remained alive in captivity must be returned. Former war cabinet member and opposition lawmaker Benny Gantz went further: "The prime minister should protect the hostages and the citizens of Israel, not his coalition controlled by extremists . . . the public has to go out into the street. The time has come to replace the government of complete failure." As the school year began, mass protests calling to secure a hostage deal were held across Israel, with hundreds of thousands rallying in city centers and blocking intersections across the country. On the other hand, Finance Minister Bezalel Smotrich declared "the cabinet will not allow a deal of surrender that compromises Israel's security, but will instruct the defense establishment to extract heavier prices from Hamas," adding that "Gaza must be reduced in size. IDF troops need to advance two kilometers from the current border and clear everything in their path. This is territory that will never return to the Gazans." Minister of Justice Yariv Levin, spearhead of the coalition's earlier judicial reform initiative, declared "we cannot create a situation where 'murdered hostages equals concessions.' Where will this lead? What will it do to the negotiations?"

US National Security Advisor Jake Sullivan held a virtual meeting with the families of the US hostages still in Gaza; four of the eight American citizens kidnapped were now confirmed dead. For many Israelis, grief turned to rage upon hearing that three of the six hostages, including Goldberg-Polin, were reportedly scheduled to be released in the first phase of a cease-fire proposal discussed in July. Dozens of diplomatic ambassadors attended a vigil in memory of the six hostages whose lifeless forms were recovered on Saturday. US ambassador to Israel Jack Lew said a hostage release must be reached because "there simply is no time . . . we lost six precious lives, we have to get this done." Following a meeting with hostage families, Arnon Bar-David, chairman of the Histadrut, the country's largest labor union with an 800,000 membership, announced a twenty-four-hour general strike across Israel on Monday, saying "it is impossible to stand by anymore when our children are murdered in the tunnels of Gaza." The head of the Israel Bar Association, Amit Bachar, called on all lawyers to join the protest demanding the return of the hostages, adding that "this is a necessary and moral step." In the wake of the IDF's discovery of the six bodies, UN Secretary-General Guterres called for the unconditional release of all hostages and an end to "the nightmare of war" in Gaza.[2]

US Defense Secretary Austin told Gallant that Hamas leaders must be held accountable for "vicious, illegal, and immoral executions." Canadian Prime Minister Justin Trudeau and opposition leader Pierre Poilievre, harshly condemning the hostages' murder, called for Hamas to surrender and for its removal from Gaza. Netanyahu's apology "that the State of Israel did not succeed in returning Alexander and the other five hostages alive," delivered Sunday to the parents of one of the six, Alex Lubnov, was a first for the prime minister who until now had said that accountability should come after Hamas was defeated in the war it launched on October 7. "Too little, too late from Israel's leadership, as the nation mourns the six hostages" editorialized the *Jerusalem*

Post. Thousands gathered in New York and across the United States to honor the six killed in Hamas captivity and call for an immediate cease-fire and hostage release deal. *Per contra*, bereaved families from the Heroes Forum and their supporters marched outside the Israeli cabinet meeting on Monday morning to push back on pressure to stop the war and give in to Hamas's demands. During the march, demonstrators called on Netanyahu and his ministers not to provide Hamas leader Sinwar with victory. Far-right National Security Minister Ben-Gvir told members of the Forum that he was "not ashamed to say" that he was using his power in the government "to prevent a reckless deal and to stop any negotiations altogether."[3]

The Biden administration was discussing with Egypt and Qatar a final "take it or leave it" proposal for a cease-fire between Israel and Hamas, which it planned to present to the negotiating parties in the coming weeks, the *Washington Post* reported. As he exited Marine One on the White House lawn, the US president was asked a series of questions by waiting reporters about whether Netanyahu was doing enough to achieve a deal to get the hostages back. He responded simply and tersely: "No." In a press conference on Monday evening, Netanyahu expressed his regret to hostage families that their loved ones were not yet home but still maintained that Israel's controlling Philadelphi Corridor was "the road to achieving the goals" of this war. In an impassioned if defiant voice, he raised this question: what kind of message would Israel be sending to Hamas by leaving the Corridor "after they killed six of our hostages in cold blood?" Hamas, in a statement, blamed Israeli bombings for the deaths of the six hostages, adding that "if President Biden is concerned about their lives, he must stop supporting this enemy with money and weapons and pressure the occupation to end its aggression immediately."

While tens of thousands attended the funeral in Jerusalem of Hersh Goldman-Polin, tears shed freely as his mother said in a heartbreaking farewell to her only son "finally, finally, finally—my sweet boy, you're free," there were 101 remaining hostages in Gaza, of which 66 were presumed to be alive. The general strike announced by Israel's labor federation to press for an immediate hostage and cease-fire deal, in which large number of municipalities, regional councils, and institutions declined to take part, ended at 2:30 p.m. after a Tel Aviv court ruling in response to a petition that claimed the strike was "clearly political." In a cruel, final taunt, Hamas posted messages from the six hostages before they were murdered. A car bomb, intended by Hamas to attack a crowded school bus, was disarmed at the entrance to the Atarot settlement in the West Bank, with no casualties reported. Israel Police said that the car contained nearly 110 pounds of explosive material in two gas tanks. Fourteen terrorists were killed and twenty-five arrested to date in the IDF Menasheh Brigade's on-going operation in Jenin. As for the Hezbollah front, the IDF reported that about thirty-five rockets were fired from Lebanon at northern Israel, causing no casualties.[4]

On Tuesday, the IAF struck a compound where Hamas terrorists were operating in Gaza City. Eight Hamas terrorists from the Daraj Tuffah Battalion were eliminated during the strike, including Ahmed Fozi Nazer Muhammad Wadia, commander of the Nukhba Company in the Battalion. On October 7, he had invaded the community of Netiv HaAsara using a paraglider and taken command of the massacre of civilians carried out by Hamas terrorists, where Wadia killed Gil Taasa in front of his two young sons—the atrocity recorded on camera. An initial IDF investigation showed that Hamas, observing the forces approaching the area near the six abductees, decided to murder them. The fact that Hamas appeared to have ordered fighters to kill hostages if they believed the IDF was closing in meant it was losing the capacity to easily and stealthily move around in the tunnels those who had been kidnapped. At the same time, Channel 12 cited a security source saying that Hamas had enlisted some 3,000 new operatives into its ranks in that area of Gaza. Additionally, the terror group had provided them with weapons, ammunition, and payment for carrying out terrorist activities.[5]

Israel National News reported that the Global Imams' Council, created in 2014 and representing 860 communities worldwide, issued a statement two days earlier "condemning in the strongest possible terms the barbaric actions of Hamas in the brutal execution of six innocent hostages in a tunnel in the Gaza city of Rafah." Further, it held Hamas "directly responsible for the deaths and suffering of all innocent lives lost since October 7, as their actions have also led to immense suffering for the Palestinian people through Hamas's reckless and inhumane tactics, using civilians as shields and exploiting their plight." "We also recognize," the Council added, that "the regime in Iran shares equal responsibility for these tragedies, as its continued support and endorsement of Hamas's actions perpetuate violence and instability in the region." It called on all religious leaders "to unite against acts of terror and work towards a future of peace and respect for human life."[6]

In Israel, rifts widened over the war, a growing schism about the country's immediate priorities. Early that morning, to the sound of a shofar, three activists stood in front of the Jerusalem home of Netanyahu confidante and Minister of Strategic Affairs of Israel Ron Dermer, one shouting in a bullhorn "how did you sleep last night?" and other accusations against the government. Three heavily armed policemen came to stand guard; the protesters left. On the other side of the divide, activists from the Im Tirtzu organization demonstrated outside the Kiryat Ono home of the head of the Histadrut labor union. Chairman Shai Rosengarten said, "We came to cry the cry of the nation and to tell Bar-David: 'You failed! Go home! We will not allow you to cause any more harm to civilians whose only sin is that they think differently than you.'" Speaking at the Israeli Bar Association's conference, Herzog demanded that the judicial reform not be resumed. "I smell the dangerous fumes of gasoline in the air, and there are some in Israeli society who would strike the match. I warn you against them." He added: "Is this what the Israeli society needs now? Is this what thousands of bereaved families need? I warn you now, cease and desist. Don't you dare. We need to recover from that terrible divide."[7]

Across the Atlantic, Israeli Ambassador to the UN Danon appealed to the UN after Hamas's barbaric murder of six hostages to convene an emergency discussion to condemn the terrorist organization for a crime that "should shock the world" and to discuss the situation of the hostages still held captive in Gaza. Danon added: "It is a shame that eleven months have passed since the massacre in which 1,200 Israelis were murdered and the Council still has not condemned Hamas or expressed concern for the fate of the hostages." For the first time, the Security Council consented to a request from the United States, United Kingdom, and France to hold a meeting on the remaining abductees. New York City Congressional Representative Richie Torres condemned CNN and *New York Times* for neglecting to mention that six Israeli hostages were murdered by Hamas and were not just "found dead." His posting on X continued: "Hostages like Noa Argamani were not just 'released.' They were rescued by Israel." "The rockets did not just 'land' on Druze children and civilians. They were fired by Hezbollah." "Words matter because the truth matters," he concluded.[8]

The US Justice Department announced on Tuesday criminal charges on seven counts against Hamas leader Sinwar and five other leading members in connection with the October 7, 2023, attack and earlier ones dating back to the 1990s. Seth J. Frantzman, the *Jerusalem Post*'s senior Middle East correspondent, responded "this is an important step because it marks a turning point in the public effort to bring Hamas to justice." Since October 7, Hamas had hoped that Qatar and Egypt might help it broker a deal and had been using hostages to get this deal. However, Hamas recently murdered six hostages, including an American citizen. The United States had now openly said that Hamas was responsible for planning, supporting, and perpetrating the October 7 massacre and that Hamas had killed at least forty-three American citizens. Hamas may now be learning, Frantzman went on, what Osama Bin Laden and Abu Baqr al-Baghdadi, the leaders of Al-Qaeda and ISIS, learned in the past: They were both hunted down by US forces and killed. The IDF did likewise for Hamas leaders

Mohammed Deif, Marwan Issa, and Ismail Haniyeh, named now in the criminal charges. The charges the United States unsealed on Tuesday also included Yahya Sinwar in Gaza, Khaled Mashaal in Qatar, and Ali Baraka in London. In accusing Hamas leaders of a plethora of crimes, the Justice Department detailed the group's rise and also its backing by Iran. Frantzman concluded: "This is a historic document. It is a major shot in the war on terror and the war to hold Hamas accountable for October 7."[9]

"In a world increasingly defined by the struggle between democratic ideals and the forces of tyranny," editorialized the *Jerusalem Post*, the United Kingdom's recent decision to freeze weapon sales to Israel "is both perplexing and deeply troubling." By suspending some arms contracts with Israel, the UK chose, in effect, to side with those who would see the only democracy in the Middle East weakened just when Israel "is currently engaged in a fierce and morally justified battle against Hamas." It also ignored the reality on the ground, the editorial noted, where Israel had gone to extraordinary lengths to minimize civilian casualties and adhere to international law, even as Hamas cynically used Gaza's civilian population as human shields. Calling the UK decision "disgraceful," Netanyahu insisted that Israel's effort to destroy Hamas was akin to "Britain's heroic stance against the Nazis." Taking the same position, the United States privately warned the United Kingdom against suspending arms sales to Israel, amid concerns it could damage efforts to broker a cease-fire, a senior US official told the *New York Times*.[10]

In even sharper criticism, Colonel Richard Kemp, former commander of the British military forces in Afghanistan who declared that "anything Hamas does is a war crime," charged that this move aligned the Labour government with Hamas and against Israel. "It plays right into the hands of Hamas who are desperate for Israel to end the war, which is their only chance to survive and rebuild their terrorist base. They hope to achieve this through the kind of international pressure by their supporters which resulted in the arms embargo," he said. Kemp observed that the British government's decision, which affected just thirty out of 150 licenses for arms exports to Israel, "will have relatively little if any practical effect on the IDF," which would continue meanwhile to fight this war. "But it gives ammunition to the pro-Hamas camp in Britain and elsewhere and will incite even greater antisemitic attacks for which the government will be culpable."[11]

Hamas faced several major challenges at this point in the war. A *Wall Street Journal* analysis pointed out that having fewer living Israeli "prisoners" (the newspaper's use of this noun accepted Hamas's equating Israeli hostages with terrorists) made it harder to win the release of thousands of Palestinian prisoners held in Israeli jails, many with blood on their hands—the release Sinwar used as a justification for the group's October 7 attack. Freeing Palestinian prisoners was also important to sustaining the group's legitimacy after eleven months of war had destroyed most of Gaza and, according to the local Health Ministry, which did not distinguish between civilians and combatants, resulted in the deaths to date of more than 40,000 Palestinians. Of the remaining ninety-seven hostages kidnapped to Gaza, thirty-three of them had been declared dead by Israel. In talks with Arab mediators, Hamas said it might have no more than thirty living hostages in total, including twelve women, elderly, or injured people. In addition, Hamas declared it could no longer communicate within the Gaza Strip, and its leaders in Qatar had largely lost touch with those in the area. Hamas claimed it was able to quickly recruit new fighters, but they would not have the same level of training as the ones who were killed. The Israeli military was also taking greater control inside the strip, damaging the influence of Hamas as a civilian administrator.[12]

Netanyahu had said at his press conference on Monday that "if you want to release hostages, you've got to control the Philadelphi Corridor." Yet Mossad Chief Barnea told truce mediators that Israel was willing to withdraw from Philadelphi in the second stage of a hostage release deal, mere hours before Netanyahu's public declaration. Qatar's Foreign Ministry responded to Netanyahu's remarks, saying that he "tried to use Egypt's name to distract Israeli public opinion and obstruct joint mediation efforts," warning that this would "lead to the demise of peace efforts and the expansion of violence in the region." IDF Chief of Staff Halevi declared that none of the war's goals should be abandoned, adding that the army was doing "everything to bring the hostages back alive." This appeared to lend credence to a Russian state media report that Israel was conducting talks with Moscow on how to release the remaining hostages in Gaza. Still, seventy-three percent of Israelis did not believe that the government would successfully reach a deal that will bring home the hostages, according to an Israel Democracy Institute survey. Opposition leader Yair Lapid went much further, declaring that although "ending the war is in Israel's interest—a security, economic, and political interest," "as long as this government exists, the war will continue. . . . This government prefers war because it frees it from having to deal with the challenges. It's time to change the government and end the war."[13]

Focusing on the Philadelphi Corridor, however, overlooked Hamas's primary demand, expressed regularly in the negotiations by Sinwar deputy Khalil al-Hayya, whose achievement could enable it to claim victory—that the IDF end the war and depart the entire Gaza area permanently. With both the Israeli government and military unprepared to do so, the prospect of a hostage and cease-fire deal appeared chimerical.

Meanwhile, the war continued taking its heavy toll on three fronts. In Gaza, the IDF said that forces operating in the Tel al-Sultan neighborhood killed over 200 militants in recent weeks, uncovered a significant cache of weapons, and discovered an underground bunker where Hamas militants were hiding. Seventy rockets were fired from Lebanon over Wednesday, multiple ones exploding in Kiryat Shmona, setting a home on fire and igniting several brush fires. Mariam Majdouline Lahham, a reporter for Lebanon's MTV News, asserted that Hezbollah was no different than ISIS, but the terror group reigned supreme in that very troubled country. As for the West Bank, Gallant warned that the "resurgence of [Palestinian] terrorism" there was an issue the government must "remain focused on at all times," adding that "the time will come" to "pull it out by the roots." The Israeli defense minister also said that IAF strikes in the area were being carried out "to prevent endangering soldiers where it is not necessary."[14]

On the same day, Hamas released two videos of four of the six murdered hostages, recorded before their deaths. Rights groups and international law experts said that such videos were, by definition, made under duress, and that making them can constitute a war crime. Israeli officials characterized the videos as a form of "psychological warfare." The Hostages and Missing Families Forum called the second video "horrific" and "yet another testament to Hamas's ruthless cruelty." At the special Security Council meeting that morning devoted to the Israeli hostages, Israeli UN Ambassador Danon, calling on that international body to condemn Hamas unequivocally, spoke of the events of October 7 and of those who remained captive, "their cries for mercy ignored by international indifference." Dr. Efrat Bron-Harlev, a physician at the Schneider Children's Medical Center of Israel, addressed the Council about the trauma of those child hostages who had returned to Israel. (Over thirty children were taken captive on October 7, with two still in Gaza.) He said that in captivity the children were not allowed to cry or laugh, hardly ate, and were moved frequently. At the hospital, the released children were scared to look out the window or get out of bed.

The meeting's focus did not remain on just the Israelis kidnapped. Many diplomats and senior UN officials also criticized Israel for excessive force in Gaza, for the suffering of Palestinians, and for recent Israeli military operations in the West Bank. They called for an immediate cease-fire deal and for Hamas to release the hostages. Amar Bendjama, the UN ambassador of Algeria and the only Arab member of the Council, said the lack of a deal was costing the lives of Israeli hostages and Palestinians in Gaza. Russia's Deputy Representative

Dmitry Polyanskiy said "We note the very alarming reports of... the mass graves of dead Palestinians with traces of torture and the removal of internal organs." Nobody objected to this blood libel reminiscent of the fraudulent *Protocols of the Elders of Zion*. After a three-hour discussion, the Security Council failed to adopt any condemnation of Hamas or to designate Hamas as a terrorist organization.[15]

Also on Wednesday, the Israeli military announced that the shaft leading to the tunnel in which the bodies of the six hostages were found, extensively booby-trapped, was located inside a children's playground. The shaft, its images showed, "was located next to stuffed animals and wall art of cartoon characters." The walls were painted with figures, including one of Mickey Mouse, and a large red heart with the word "LOVE" in English written over it. A stuffed brown bear lay amid the rubble. In a separate post on social media, the Hostages and Missing Families Forum recalled the six slain hostages as "young, beautiful, and happy." It added, "Six that will never dance again, nor will they ever hug, travel, or love. Six who will forever live in our memory, and may their memory be a blessing." Not placated, the American families of hostages held in Gaza urged Biden to consider a deal with Hamas that did not include Israel, NBC News reported.[16]

That night, IAF aircraft conducted a targeted strike on terrorists in the West Bank's Tubas area. For nine days, Israeli forces had been raiding this region as part of what they said was a major counter-terrorism operation. So far, at least thirty-six Palestinians had been killed, including twenty-one from the Jenin governorate and eight from Tubas, according to the Palestine Health Ministry. Among the five eliminated in the drone strike was Muhammad Zakaria Zubeidi, a significant terrorist from the Jenin area who took part in a shooting attack around the security fence and in terrorist activity against IDF soldiers throughout Judea and Samaria. His father, Fatah leader Zakaria Zubeidi, had been admittedly responsible for the 2002 Beit She'an attack and the mastermind behind the 2021 Gilboa prison break.[17]

A US official admitted during a press briefing on Wednesday night that Hamas had toughened its positions over the course of the negotiations, calling for the release of a larger number of terrorists with blood on their hands, as well as additional demands. US National Security Council spokesperson John Kirby told reporters that "the biggest obstacle to a deal is Hamas, no question about it." Over the course of the last couple of weeks, Jerusalem had produced a proposal by which the IDF would "significantly" reduce its presence on the Philadelphi Corridor. (Two former IDF chiefs of staff, Benny Gantz and Gadi Eisenkot, now Netanyahu rivals, joined other security officials who said that Israel could afford to withdraw temporarily from the Corridor to allow for the fulfillment of the first phase of the hostage deal.) Hamas insisted that Netanyahu's refusal to withdraw from the Corridor aimed to thwart an agreement to end the war and secure the release of the hostages.[18]

On Thursday, US Ambassador Lew declared it "absolutely essential to get into phase one" of a hostage release deal. "That's how you save lives—after this weekend we must understand that time is of the essence, that these lives won't be left to be saved if we wait too long." He refuted Netanyahu's claim that a full IDF withdrawal from Gaza and the Philadelphi Corridor were part of the current proposal's initial phase, adding that "there is no mention of the Philadelphi Corridor in the document itself. It wasn't even an issue when the framework was drafted."[19]

In the West Bank, the IDF reported that thirty-six terrorists were killed and forty-six arrested over the past week. Several sites for terrorist infrastructure were destroyed in Jenin, including a weaponry storehouse and a lab used for manufacturing explosives located under a mosque. Jordanian Foreign Minister Ayman Safadi declared that Israel had begun a new war in that area and called on his visiting German counterpart to impose sanctions on the Jewish State. Up north, Hezbollah targeted Kibbutz Neot Mordechai, the pro-Iranian *Al-Mayadeen* media said. Hezbollah had been claiming over the last month that it was expanding the number of places it targets, which included Kibbutzim Shamir and Ayelet HaShachar in the Hula valley, as well as additional attacks in the Golan over the last several months. The terror organization carried out more than 8,600 rocket attacks on Israel since October 7 and launched around 200 UAVs, according to a Ynet report the previous month.[20]

A Palestinian terror squad based in Jenin planned to infiltrate Israeli communities in Samaria and carry out an October 7-style massacre, according to an indictment published by Channel 14. It reported that the charges filed against Osama Bani Fadl, who stood accused of murdering Israelis Shai Silas Nigrekar and his son Aviad Nir on August 19, 2023, in Huwara, revealed that he fled to Jenin after the shooting and joined a terror cell there. It accused Fadl and other members of the terrorist squad of making preparations for a mass slaughter targeting Jewish residents of Samaria, infiltrating Israeli towns using vehicles. The terror cell reportedly also planned attacks inside the town of Ma'aleh Efraim in the Jordan Valley, and a drive-by shooting and car bombing at the gas station outside the Eli community in the Binyamin region of Samaria. In Gaza, Israeli forces recently paved a road along the Philadelphi Corridor, the BBC reported, this move seen as a show of determination regarding Israel's stance on not leaving the Corridor.[21]

The situation in Gaza is "beyond catastrophic," and more than one million people did not receive any food rations in August in southern and central Gaza through humanitarian means, UN spokesman Stéphane Dujarric declared. Responding to Hamas's video of their son, recorded shortly before he was murdered, Rachel and Jon Goldberg-Polin issued a statement asserting that it "must serve as an immediate wake-up call to the world to take action today to secure the release of the remaining 101 hostages before it is too late." In the West Bank, Aysenur Ezgi Eygi, a twenty-six-year-old human rights activist with US and Turkish citizenships, was shot and killed by Israeli soldiers while participating in a demonstration in Beita, near Nablus, according to Palestinian reports. The IDF said it "responded with fire toward a main instigator of violent activity who hurled rocks at the forces and posed a threat to them," and that it was looking into claims that a foreign citizen was killed by gunfire. The same day, Democratic vice-presidential nominee Tim Walz said on the Michigan NPR radio station WCMU that anti-Israel protesters were "speaking out for all the right reasons," and that more pressure should be applied to Netanyahu to accept a Palestinian state. (Michigan, a major swing state in the 2024 presidential contest, has the United States's largest Arab population.) He added that Hamas's October 7 attack was a "horrific act of violence against the people of Israel," that the Jewish State has the right to defend itself, and the United States "will always stand by that."[22]

On Friday, IAF aircraft struck a command-and-control center used by Hamas and Palestinian Islamic Jihad terrorists, which was embedded inside the designated humanitarian area of Deir al-Balah, and killed two prominent terrorists. One was Abdallah Khatib, commander of the Palestinian Islamic Jihad's Southern Deir al-Balah Battalion who led the terrorist activity of the battalion during the October 7 massacre; the other was Hatem Abu Aljidian, commander of the Palestinian Islamic Jihad's Eastern Deir al-Balah Battalion who carried out attacks against IDF troops throughout the war. Local medics in Gaza told *Reuters* that Israeli army strikes across the Strip killed at least sixty-one people over a period of forty-eight hours. The IDF responded that shelters for displaced Palestinians in the Jabaliya refugee camp and a school compound in Gaza City both housed Hamas command centers. CIA chief William Burns and MI6 head Richard Moore urged in an unprecedented joint plea that "hard political compromises" be made by both sides for a cease-fire to end Gaza civilians' "appalling loss of life" and hostages' "hellish confinement." Unfortunately, reported the *Washington Post*, the latest obstacle—the abrupt introduction by Hamas of a new demand surrounding which prisoners Israel would release—underscored the frustrating, often excruciating process that had preoccupied top US officials, and Biden himself, for nine months.[23]

Sirens were sounded in Kiryat Shmona and other communities in northern Israel during the night leading to Saturday. The IDF said that at least fifty rockets were fired from Lebanon by Hezbollah towards the area. The IAF in turn struck Hezbollah military structures in the areas of Aitaroun, Maroun El Ras, and Yaroun in southern Lebanon, and eliminated terrorists from the Amal terrorist organization that operated within a Hezbollah military structure. The IDF announced that in the last week it had destroyed more than forty terrorist infrastructures and killed more than 100 terrorists in the Gaza Strip and thirty-five terrorists in the West Bank, including the elimination of dozens of Hamas operatives on Saturday. The IDF also declared that last week Israeli forces assassinated the commander of the rocket unit of Hamas's Khan Younis brigade, Ra'af Omar Salman Abu Sha'ab. For his part, Turkish President Erdoğan declared that Islamic countries should form an alliance against what he called "the growing threat of expansionism" from Israel.[24]

Three Israeli men were murdered in a shooting attack at the Israel-Jordan border's Allenby Bridge, about three miles east of Jericho, on Sunday morning, the deadliest on record at that border crossing. The terrorist, who arrived in a truck from the Jordanian side, was killed. The government quickly decided to close all three border crossings to Jordan. Sending condolences on behalf of the government and himself to the families of those who were murdered, Netanyahu said. "We are surrounded by a murderous ideology led by Iran's axis of evil. In recent days, abhorrent terrorists murdered six of our hostages and three Israel police officers in cold blood. The murderers do not differentiate between us. They want to murder us all, right and left, secular and religious, Jews and non-Jews, until the last one." He concluded: "When we stand together, our enemies cannot overcome us; therefore, their main objective is to divide us and to sow discord among us." Not surprisingly, Palestinian Islamic Jihad applauded the "heroic" shooting, "which represents the mindset in Jordan and the Arab world." Jordan's Foreign Ministry, however, condemned the shooting attack at the Allenby crossing, stressing its "firm stance rejecting and condemning violence and harm to civilians for any reason." The statement also highlighted Jordan's efforts to secure a permanent cease-fire in Gaza, curb escalating West Bank violence, and lead a "genuine political effort."[25]

President Biden was expected to convene his national security team on Monday to discuss the current state of cease-fire talks after US officials told Qatari and Egyptian officials over the past several days that Hamas's new demands concerning the hostage-prisoner exchange went beyond previous agreements. *Per contra*, Hamas official Izzat Al-Risheq said that "if pressure is not put on Netanyahu to implement what was agreed on Biden's proposal, the hostages won't see the light of day." Meanwhile, soldiers of the 16th Reserve Brigade, under the command of the 252nd Division, operating in the Zeitoun area in the central Gaza Strip, raided terror targets where Hamas operatives had embedded themselves, eliminated dozens of terrorists, and dismantled numerous terrorist infrastructure. The IDF called on residents of northwestern Gaza to evacuate their homes following rockets from the area into Israel, warning them that the area is a "dangerous combat zone." Thirteen suspects were arrested on Israel's Route 6, believed to be planning a terror attack. IAF missile strikes on Syria, which Damascus claimed killed twenty-five, also targeted military sites in the eastern city of Masyaf. Israel accused Iran of using a scientific research center there to develop weapons and missiles intended for its aligned regional militias, including Hezbollah. As for the latter threat, officials from the IDF's Northern Command told *Haaretz* that they had detected the group's preparations for prolonged fighting with Israel in the event of a collapse of negotiations over a ceasefire and hostage deal with Hamas.[26]

Israel's foreign minister threatened to "dissolve" the Palestinian Authority should Ramallah move forward with its plans to pursue a United Nations resolution ordering Israel to ethnically cleanse Judea and Samaria of its Jewish population. The General Assembly was scheduled to vote on a draft resolution proposed by the Authority's mission to the UN, demanding that Israel's presence in Judea and Samaria—both military and civilian—be withdrawn within six months. Almost simultaneously, UN High Commissioner for Human Rights Volker Türk, during his address at the fifty-seventh session of the Human Rights Council on Monday, asked countries to act on what he called Israel's "blatant disregard" for international law in the West Bank and Gaza.

Türk devoted the largest section of his speech to the war between Israel and Hamas, spending most of that time criticizing Israel rather than the terrorist organization. He compared the plight of the Israeli hostages who were kidnapped on October 7 to the imprisonment of terrorists by Israel and criticized Israel's efforts to combat terrorism in Judea and Samaria. He did not speak at such length about any other country or conflict, mentioning the plight of women in Afghanistan and the human rights situation in Iran in just one sentence each. The war between Russia and Ukraine merited one paragraph, as did the human rights situation in Sudan, still a fraction of the time given to criticizing Israel.[27]

President Herzog and his wife Michal met that day with the family members of Karina, Liri, Daniela, Naama, and Agam—the female observers who were kidnapped from their base at the Nahal Oz outpost on October 7 and held captive by Hamas in Gaza ever since. "This is a decisive moment," Herzog claimed, "if we want to bring the hostages back home, we need to be united with all our strength. And that also means answering the call that was made here right now—the political echelon must come together with all its strength, bear communal responsibility to ensure the release and return of the hostages back home as soon as possible. Together, we have to all take responsibility, we have to take every possible step to push the decision-makers to bring the hostages home." In like vein, the angry father of Paratrooper Brigade soldier Ori Danino pleaded with Netanyahu "on behalf of the hostages still in Gaza" when the prime minister came to express his condolences over the murder of Rabbi Elhanan Danino's son and five others by Hamas two weeks ago, to "strengthen love of Israel." The anguished man, accusing the prime minister of engaging in "petty and cheap politics" and of emboldening Hamas during his many years in power and of sowing division in the nation, went on: "You people on high have to stop—stop!—dealing with nonsense and stirring up fights and disagreement." "Think about where your Jewish values are." "This disaster happened," he ended, "because of the division and schism we had here. It's as clear as the sun that that's what happened."[28]

On day 340 of the war, the Israeli military launched an airstrike early on Tuesday night targeting Hamas members in the Al-Mawasi area near Khan Younis, which it had designated a humanitarian zone, an attack Gaza officials said destroyed twenty tents sheltering Palestinians and killed dozens. Among those targeted, the IDF said, were Samer Ismail Khadr Abu Daqqa, head of Hamas's aerial unit in Gaza; Osama Tabesh, head of the observation and targets department in Hamas's military intelligence; and Ayman Mabhouh, another senior Hamas official, all of whom had taken part in executing the October 7 assault. Hamas condemned the attack, calling it "a horrifying new massacre"; the terrorist organization did not address the Israeli military's claim that it had killed three senior Hamas members. The IDF, saying that it used precise munitions, accused Hamas, in turn, of continuing to endanger noncombatants by conducting attacks from within safe zones. In that connection, the *New York Times* reported that Gaza residents in a school compound, already forced to evacuate their homes because of Israel's intense bombardment and wanting to avoid becoming a target for Israeli forces hunting down Hamas militants, recently did not allow armed men to enter. The residents' testimonies also suggested that "Hamas's grip on the enclave may be weakened by the war and that ad hoc community groups were starting to operate outside the organization's control, at least on a small scale."²⁹

An IDF statement revealed, in expressing its "deepest regret," that soldiers "likely" killed Turkish-American activist Aysenur Eygi on Friday "unintentionally" during an altercation in the West Bank which included dozens of Palestinians throwing rocks and burning tires at soldiers at the Beita Junction near Nablus. Blinken responded to what he termed an "unprovoked" action: "Israeli security forces need to make some fundamental changes in the way that they operate in the West Bank, including changes to their rules of engagement." In addition, the IDF confirmed it mistakenly killed three hostages in a Gaza city strike in December—Elia Toledano, Nik Beizer, and Ron Sherman—that eliminated Gaza City Brigade Chief Admed An-Dur.³⁰

The fighting in Gaza continued without pause, the IDF striking Hamas control and command complexes inside and nearby a building previously used as a mosque in the Bureij area. The IDF and Shin Bet said they killed the commander of Hamas's Tel al-Sultan Battalion. Mahmoud Hamdan, who played a significant role in the October 7 massacre, and three additional company commanders from the battalion. Hamas's military capabilities in Gaza had been considerably diminished to the extent that the group's military formation no longer exists there, Gallant said, according to a report in the *Guardian*. Israel's defense establishment did not find any signs that Hamas was preparing to move Israeli hostages from Gaza into Egypt via tunnels passing beneath the Philadelphi Corridor, despite Netanyahu's claims that this was a possibility, defense officials told *Haaretz*.³¹

UN Secretary-General Guterres told the Associated Press that the UN had offered to monitor any cease-fire in Gaza but added that it was "unrealistic" to think the organization could play a part in Gaza's future because Israel was unlikely to accept a UN role. The same day, at the end of an IDF exercise simulating ground combat inside Lebanon, Gallant told journalists that "the [war's focus] is being moved to the north ahead of the completion of the tasks in the south [in Gaza]. . . . We have an unfulfilled mission here, and this mission is to change the security situation and return the residents [of northern Israel] to their homes." The IDF said it killed Muhammad Kassem Al-Shaer, a commander in Hezbollah's elite Radwan Force in southern Lebanon. A volley of dozens of rockets was launched at northern Israel from Lebanon later in the day.³²

Gal Hirsch, Israel's chief negotiator for hostages and missing persons, in an interview with Bloomberg News, offered safe passage to Sinwar, his family, and "whoever wants to join him" in exchange for the remaining 101 hostages. "We want demilitarization," he added, "de-radicalization of course—a new system that will manage Gaza." In a Telegram post, the spokesperson for Hamas's armed wing, the al-Qassam Brigades, Abu Obaida, wrote, "Netanyahu's insistence on liberating the prisoners through military pressure instead of concluding a deal will mean that they will return to their families inside coffins and their families will have to choose whether they are dead or alive." A source familiar with the Israel-Hamas negotiations told *Haaretz* that "all parties are waiting for the US administration to decide whether and when to present the final mediation proposal," adding that "at the moment, the gaps between the sides are great and there is no breakthrough on the horizon. It must be remembered that the fate of the hostages is our main focus. If the deal collapses, the chances of rescuing them in the near future will be very low and the danger to their lives will increase." Qatari PM al-Thani met with hostages' family members in Paris and told them Doha would continue to promote cease-fire talks.[33]

New evidence, appearing on Israeli media, showed that the six hostages were likely murdered hours before the IDF found them in the tunnel ten days ago, and there was also some indication that the four male hostages had fought their captors to defend the two females. The tunnel was so narrow they could barely stand up, and no more than two could lie down at a time. There was also very little air, and the ventilation was so poor that many of the hostages likely had trouble breathing. The tunnel had no toilets or showers, and the hostages had to use bottles of water to bathe themselves. The tunnel's entrance was in a children's play area, the IDF pointed out, underscoring Hamas's extensive use of civilian infrastructure as protection for its military activity. The IDF's stark footage of this reality, shown first to the hostage families and the security cabinet, drew a strident reaction from leading politicians: Liberman: Stop all the aid to Gaza; Ben-Gvir: The response to this should be clear. Bennett: "This is an abominable Nazi enemy." Each side found support for its position after viewing this shocking video, those pressing for a hostage deal saying why such an agreement was needed immediately to save the remainder. Those opposed to letting Hamas dictate the terms of a deal and believing that only more military pressure would ultimately free the hostages asked how could a deal be made with such heartless terrorists? What surely qualified as a devil's dilemma remained.[34]

The same Tuesday, a General Assembly resolution overwhelmingly granted the Palestine delegation for the first time certain new rights as an "observer state," which still excluded it from being able to vote or be a member of the Security Council. Starting with the 79th General Assembly session, which began that day, the Palestinians could submit proposals and amendments, as well as sit among member states. The Palestinian Authority's envoy to the United Nations, Riyad Mansour, took his place that afternoon at a table marked "State of Palestine" between Sri Lanka and Sudan. "This is not merely a procedural matter. This is a historic moment for us," said Egyptian Ambassador Osama Mahmoud Abdelkhalek Mahmoud. During the resolution's adoption Jerusalem denounced the move, Jonathan Miller, deputy Israel ambassador to the United Nations, stating "Any decision and or action that improves the status of the Palestinians, either in the UN General Assembly or bilaterally, is currently a reward ... for terrorism in general and the Hamas terrorists in particular."[35]

That evening, Gallant revealed a letter written to the Sinwar brothers by Rafe Salama, who had commanded Hamas's Khan Younis Brigade and served as the deputy of Hamas military chief Mohammed Deif before both of them were eliminated by an IAF strike in July. Salama stated that seventy percent of Hamas's weapons had been destroyed, half of its operatives killed or wounded and a great many fled, leaving them with twenty percent according, to him, and ninety-five percent of their rockets destroyed—"a real loss that hurts Hamas and is felt by its most senior commanders," Gallant noted. The IDF announced that last week an airstrike had eliminated Abdallah abu Reala from the Hamas Shati Battalion, who took part in the October 7 massacre, was involved in carrying out attacks on IDF troops throughout the war, and was one of the terrorists responsible for holding captive CPL Noa Marciano, who was abducted on October 7 and killed in the Shifa Hospital in Gaza City. The IAF also eliminated Ayman Khaled Ahmed Abu Allahyani, a Nukhba terrorist, who took part in the attack on the Erez Humanitarian Crossing on October 7.[36]

The war continued. Two Israeli soldiers were killed and four seriously wounded in a helicopter crash in Gaza's Rafah area during an effort to evacuate a wounded soldier. Sgt. Geri Gideon Hanghal from Nof HaGalil was killed in a ramming attack near Givat Asaf in the West Bank by fifty-eight-year-old Hayil Dhaifallah from the Palestinian town of Rafat near Ramallah, who was neutralized by an armed civilian. Six terrorists were killed and much infrastructure destroyed during an on-going IDF action in northern Samaria. Over sixty rockets and drones were fired at northern Israel from Lebanon. During a visit to Israel's border with Jordan, Netanyahu said that Israel will work with its neighbors to "establish a stronger barrier against [arms] smuggling" and terrorist infiltrations.

Meanwhile, the Biden administration announced new sanctions on Iran's national airline in response to its role in shipping ballistic missiles to Russia to use against Ukraine, as well as on a network which smuggled gas and oil that provided millions of dollars to Hezbollah. The US chief executive called American-Turkish activist Aysenur Ezgi Eygi's death in an IDF operation near

Nablus "totally unacceptable," adding that "the violence in the West Bank has been going on for too long.... I will continue to support policies that hold all extremists—Israelis and Palestinians alike—accountable for stoking violence and serving as obstacles to peace." Vice-President Harris declared that it raised "legitimate concerns" about the conduct of IDF personnel in the West Bank, and that "Israel must do more to ensure that incidents like this never happen again."[37]

On Thursday, Muhammad Abu Atiya, who had murdered US Navy Seal Master Sergeant Maxim Rizkov in October, was eliminated in Tulkarm along with Imad Shahadeh and Salah Albado, all three members of the Palestinian Islamic Jihad. Responding to UNRWA's statement that six of its staffers were killed in Nuseirat in the central Gaza Strip on Wednesday, the highest death toll among its staff in a single incident, the IDF said it was able to verify the identities of some of those killed and published the names of nine Hamas operatives, including two which it said were employees of UNRWA: Yasser Ibrahim Abu Sharar and Iyad Matar. A *Washington Post* investigation charged that Aysenur Ezgi Eygi, the American-Turkish activist who Israel claimed was accidentally killed by the IDF last Friday in the West Bank, was shot "more than a half-hour after the height of confrontations." As for the kidnapped Israelis still in Gaza, Netanyahu's office said that Hamas was "trying to conceal the fact that it continues to oppose a deal to release the hostages, and is foiling it," adding that while Israel "accepted the final bridging proposal the United States made on August 16, Hamas refused the proposal, and even murdered six of our hostages in cold blood." That same week, Israeli commandos rappelled from helicopters to boldly attack an Iranian missile production facility in Syria, remove equipment, and then destroy the site, a sign that the war's epicenter was moving north.[38]

Declaring "I failed, I am deeply sorry," Brig. Gen. Yossi Sariel, the commanding officer of Unit 8200 for the past three years, notified his commanders that he would step down in light of his part in the October 7 disaster. Sariel was the second senior IDF intelligence official to step down given the failures, following former Intelligence Directorate Chief Maj. Gen. Aharon Haliva. Israeli Justice Minister Levin, acting on behalf of Netanyahu, asked Attorney General Gali Baharav-Miara to open a criminal investigation into Netanyahu and Gallant in order to nullify a request to issue arrest warrants against the two at the International Criminal Court, Israel's Channel 12 News stated. Netanyahu reportedly wanted the probe to be opened and then closed, informing the ICC that the charges had been investigated. The Pentagon announced the withdrawal of the *USS Theodore Roosevelt* aircraft carrier from the Middle East after it had been stationed there alongside the *USS Abraham Lincoln* for several weeks following Israel's killing of senior Hezbollah commander Fuad Shukr and the assassination of Haniyeh in Tehran.[39]

Lebanese media reported on a letter sent by Sinwar to Nasrallah, thanking him for continuously attacking northern Israel since the massacre Hamas committed in southern Israel on October 7. Sinwar thanked Nasrallah for the condolences he had expressed on the death of Haniyeh and claimed that the current war would be remembered as "one of the most honorable historical battles of our people." He also thanked Nasrallah for Hezbollah's solidarity with Gaza "expressed in blessed actions on the front lines of the resistance axis. Hamas will continue to stand firm against Israel and will remain loyal to the blood of the martyrs." Sinwar further asserted that Hamas would continue to adhere to the principle of resistance until the "expulsion of the occupation from our land and the establishment of a Palestinian state."[40]

Come Friday, the IDF claimed that its forces had defeated Hamas's Rafah Brigade after four months of targeted raids there, killing more than 2,000 terrorists and destroying some eight miles of tunnels. In Khan Younis, the former commander of Division 98 and as of May Maj. Gen. Dan Goldfus had succeeded in breaking up Hamas's single giant web network of tunnels. Concomitantly, Netanyahu's demand for an Israeli presence in the Philadelphi Corridor remained the main obstacle to reaching a hostage and cease-fire deal, officials familiar with the talks Hamas held with mediators said to *Haaretz*. IDF Chief of Staff Halevi told parents of hostages held in Gaza that the longer the war went on, the more difficult it would be to bring them home. "I said this to decision-makers in the government as well," added Halevi, according to Channel 12. Halevi also admitted that he did not know when exactly the war would end, just that "we're not close yet. If we don't fight and put pressure on Hamas, it will take even more time." Hezbollah fired some twenty rockets toward the northern city of Safed early that morning, saying it had targeted a military installation in revenge for a deadly strike in southern Lebanon one day earlier. No injuries were reported in the early morning barrage, the IDF said, but the rocket fire sparked a blaze in the Birya Forest, north of Safed.[41]

The next day, the IDF declared that its fighter jets had attacked operatives in a Hamas command and control center operating out of a building previously used as the Shadi al-Zaytun school in Gaza City. The IDF said two rockets were fired from northern Gaza at the southern Israeli city of Ashkelon. After the launches, the IDF's Arabic-language spokesman, Avichai Adraee, called on residents in some northern Gaza neighborhoods to evacuate their homes, warning that "the specified area is considered a dangerous combat zone." UAE Foreign Minister Sheikh Abdullah bin Zayed Al Nahyan wrote on *X* that the UAE would not take part in a plan for "the day after" in Gaza without the establishment of a Palestinian state. On the northern front, the Israeli army noted that around fifty-five rockets were fired from Lebanon into Israel in the morning, sparking fires in the north and triggering sirens in the Galilee. The IDF responded by attacking tens of rocket launch sites in southern Lebanon with jets and artillery fire.[42]

After meeting in London, US Secretary of State Blinken and British Foreign Secretary Lammy issued a joint statement expressing support for Israel and the ongoing mediation efforts to conclude the agreement for a cease-fire in Gaza and the release of hostages. "It's important to avoid escalatory action," they advised. The two governments were especially concerned that Russia was sharing nuclear secrets with Iran, as well as classified information which might aid Iran in achieving its nuclear goals, Bloomberg News and the *Guardian* reported. According to the report, the information was provided in exchange for Tehran's provision of ballistic missiles to Moscow, to be used in Russia's war against Ukraine.[43]

Yemen's Houthis fired at least one ballistic missile, possibly more, on the Tel Aviv and central Israel areas, IDF sources said. Nine people were lightly wounded while running to safe rooms following the sirens. Hamas and the Palestinian Islamic Jihad hailed the launch, Sinwar publishing on the Hamas website his congratulations for the "success in reaching the depth of the enemy entity." The IDF stated that the Arrow air defense system shot the missile down. Still, pieces of shrapnel fell near Gezer and possibly in three other areas, including the Pa'atei Modi'in train station near Modi'in and Rehovot, signaling that Israel's systems failed to shoot down the missile outside of Israeli airspace. The IDF noted that the missile apparently fell apart midair and was not hypersonic, as claimed by the Houthis. Later that afternoon, the Iran-backed militia published an announcement warning residents of Tel Aviv that the area was an active war zone and urging them to evacuate to the "humanitarian zone" in the Negev desert. Netanyahu's response: Israel would exact a heavy price from the Houthis for his attack: "We are in a multi-front campaign against Iran's evil axis that strives to destroy us. Anyone who attacks us will not escape."[44]

IDF Major General Ori Gordin, commander of the IDF's Northern Command, recommended in closed discussions that the IDF be allowed to create a buffer zone in southern Lebanon, *Yisrael Hayom* reported Monday morning. According to the report, the proposed new security zone would be under Israeli control. Gordin explained that only recently did the situation allow for the IDF to execute such a process: For many years, terrorists from Hezbollah's elite Radwan Force were positioned along the border fence. Now, many had been killed by the IDF or escaped northwards. In addition, much of the civilian population in southern Lebanon had evacuated the area; it was estimated that only about twenty percent of the residents who lived there before the October 7 massacre in Israel were still in their homes. This significant reduction in civilians in the area would allow the IDF to carry out such a move much more easily and quickly. In this connection, ninety-seven community security squads in northern Israel received new weapons along with medical and shielding equipment, the Defense Ministry announced.[45]

Gallant told Austin that the possibility for a deal with Hezbollah "is running out." He reiterated Israel's commitment to the removal of Hezbollah presence in southern Lebanon, and to enabling the safe return of Israel's northern communities to their homes. Stressing the urgency of war against Hamas and Hezbollah, he said "Hezbollah continues to tie itself to Hamas—the trajectory is clear." He also asserted that Israel would operate "by any means" necessary to return the hostages held in Gaza captivity and to destroy Hamas. Addressing the crisis in the north on Sunday, Netanyahu vowed that "We will do everything necessary to return our residents safely to their homes ... The status quo will not continue. This requires a change in the balance of power on our northern border." For Hezbollah's part, deputy chief Naim Qassem declared the previous day that his group had "no intention of going to war," but if Israel did "unleash" one "there will be large losses on both sides." Hezbollah official Nawaf Mousawi went far further, claiming that Israel had never had the upper hand in a ground war and that Hezbollah fighters "crave a ground war so they can smash [the Israelis'] heads and break their backs."[46]

Negotiations for a cease-fire and hostage release deal between Israel and Hamas were currently on hold, awaiting a decision from the United States on whether and when to present the mediators' final proposal. In the north, six crews combatted fires that broke out in northern Israel near Kibbutz HaGoshrim from Hezbollah rockets and a drone attack; IAF jets responded by strikes against weapon storages in southern Lebanon. In the West Bank, Israeli settlers attacked Palestinians and left-wing activists at a school in the village of Mu'arrajat, claiming that they were looking for a village resident who struck their friend. A young Israeli shepherd sustained a head injury after he was attacked by a number of Palestinians, claiming that shortly after "a group of Israelis" arrived at the location where the alleged Palestinian assailants were hiding, which led to "friction" during which several Palestinians were wounded. The IDF claimed that, along with police forces, it defused the clashes and arrested several suspects. Speaking at *Haaretz*'s National Security Conference in Tel Aviv, German Ambassador to Israel Steffen Seibert said he was "the Ambassador to Israel in accordance with its '67 borders. I'm not the ambassador outside the Green Line ... We see certain actors looking to turn the occupation into annexation and we are not going to stand on the sidelines and allow that to happen." Berlin had not approved any requests for arms exports to Israel since March.[47]

Tuesday morning, Israel's security cabinet approved adding the return of 60,000 residents of the north to their homes to the goals of the war, the first official mention of the military campaign in the north as part of Israel's stated military objectives. The Shin Bet foiled a recent attempt by Hezbollah to assassinate a former senior Israeli security official (unnamed) using a remotely detonated explosive device, the security agency announced. Hours after this revelation, explosions took place simultaneously in the Hezbollah-controlled Dahieh region of Beirut and the Seyedah Zeinab neighborhood, a Shiite stronghold, in Damascus. Subsequent investigation revealed that lithium batteries in beepers, each with some explosive, were detonated remotely. According to the Lebanese health minister, the pager explosions wounded close to 28–30 thousand people critically, the majority Hezbollah fighters, and killed twelve. According to a report by the Saudi-based Al-Hadath outlet on Wednesday, the first pager bombings also killed nineteen members of Iran's Islamic Revolutionary Guard Corps stationed in the Deir Ez-Zur province of eastern Syria and wounded 150. While Jerusalem kept silence, Hezbollah said Israel was responsible and would get "its fair punishment." Lebanon's information minister condemned the explosions as "Israeli aggression."[48]

The IAF announced it had eliminated Ahmed Aish Salame al-Hashash, who served as the head of the Palestinian Islamic Jihad's Rocket and Missile Unit in the Rafah area. UN Secretary-General Guterres once again criticized Israel over its operation in Gaza, accusing it of "collective punishment" of the people living there. Maj. Gen. Gadi Shamni, former commander of the IDF's Gaza Division, told the *Times* that while Israel was tactically stronger than Hamas, "Hamas is winning this war," adding that Hamas had retaken cities the IDF withdrew from within "fifteen minutes." Shamni noted that "there's no one that can challenge Hamas there after Israeli forces leave," and that the greatest failure of the war was that Netanyahu did not create an alternative governing model for Gaza earlier. Hamas senior official Khaled Meshaal, too, maintained that the group "has the upper hand," telling the *New York Times* that "it has remained steadfast" and brought the Israeli military into "a state of attrition." During the interview in his Doha living room, Meshaal made clear that Hamas officials were not in a rush to conclude a cease-fire with Israel at any price and would not give up on their main demands for an end to the war and an Israeli withdrawal. Thousands of Hamas fighters and government officials continued to wield control over large parts of Gaza, he noted.[49]

The reporter noted that many Palestinians in Gaza have lashed out at Hamas for launching the October 7 attack, accusing the group of giving Israel a pretext to wage a massive bombing campaign that reduced cities to rubble. Meshaal dismissed criticism of Hamas's decision, however. Palestinian critics of Hamas represented a minority, he averred. "As a Palestinian, my responsibility is to fight and resist until liberation," He acknowledged that the assault had caused enormous destruction but said it was a "price" Palestinians must pay for freedom. Asked how the Hamas-led attack helped improve the situation given the devastation in Gaza, he insisted it was less about achieving a military victory over Israel than making it realize its policies were not sustainable. "Before October 7, Gaza was dying a slow death," Meshal said. "We were in a big prison and we wanted to get rid of this situation."[50]

On Wednesday, the UN General Assembly voted 124–14, with 43 abstentions, to strip Israel of the right to self-defense against Palestinian terrorism in the West Bank, Gaza, and East Jerusalem. The text of the resolution was based on the International Court of Justice's advisory opinion in July that Israel's occupation of Palestinian territory was illegal. Prior to the vote, UN Secretary-General Guterres said he supported the ICJ option and would abide by the vote, which called on the IDF to withdraw to the pre-1967 lines within twelve months. The resolution also called on member states not to sell arms or military equipment to Israel that would be used in Gaza, the West Bank, and East Jerusalem, as well as to boycott of all Israeli products produced over the pre-1967 lines. The United States, Israel, Argentina, Hungary and a handful of smaller states voted against the resolution.

Israeli ambassador to the UN Danon urged member nations to reject the resolution, describing it as "an attempt to destroy Israel through diplomatic terrorism" that never mentions Hamas's atrocities and "ignores the truth, twists the facts, and replaces reality with fiction." US Ambassador to the UN Linda Thomas-Greenfield told reporters that the resolution had "a significant number of flaws," saying it went beyond the ICJ ruling, did not recognize that "Hamas is a terrorist organization" in control of Gaza, and that Israel had a right to defend itself. Riyad Mansour, the Palestinian UN ambassador, called it a turning point "in our struggle for freedom and justice."[51]

The IDF moved the 98th Division, whose forces had been fighting until recently in Gaza, to Israel's north following a security cabinet decision to shift more of the military's capabilities to the region. In addition, the IDF decided on a limited recruitment of reserve personnel to be deployed in the north in case of a security escalation, including air defense, Home Front Command, and Medical Corps personnel. Defense Minister Gallant said Israel was "entering a new phase in the war." Perhaps to confirm this, in a second wave of Hezbollah-targeted explosions on hand-held walkie-talkies the next day, the Lebanese Health Ministry said that 608 were wounded and at least 25 killed, including the son of Hezbollah MP Ali Ammar. Iranian Foreign Minister Abbas Araghchi said he told his Lebanese counterpart that he "strongly condemned Israeli terrorism." Moscow's reaction to the explosions: "Thousands of innocents were wounded in the attack, whose purpose was to stimulate a big war in the Middle East." The United States, Israel's closest ally, denied any involvement, while Blinken said at a news conference in Cairo it was "imperative that all parties refrain from any actions that could escalate the conflict."[52]

The collective high that Israel felt on Tuesday when it heard of the "exploding pager" operation carried out in Lebanon that left some 4,000 Hezbollah operatives wounded was short-lived, tempered by news of the death of four IDF soldiers and four wounded in Rafah. Editorialized the *Jerusalem Post*: "This is emblematic of the roller-coaster nature of this war: some days bring victories, others deliver setbacks. Often, setbacks and victories come on the same day. It is best not to let the victories go to one's head, or the setbacks to cause abject demoralization." The very next day, five IDF soldiers were injured after an anti-tank missile landed in northern Israel. US Secretary of Defense Austin had a telephone conversation with Gallant, the Pentagon reported, "to review regional security developments and reiterate unwavering US support for Israel in the face of threats from Iran, Lebanese Hezbollah, and Iran's other regional partners." The Biden administration announced that it imposed new sanctions on Iranian officials responsible for the regime's crackdown on the "woman, life, freedom" protests in the wake of the killing of Mahsa Amini in 2022. As for the two-day explosions against Hezbollah, further accounts indicated that rather than the reported twelve killed yesterday and fourteen today, there were many dozens of dead, if not more. In addition, the operation caused massive damage to Hezbollah's elite Radwan unit, which lost much of its leadership.[53]

A new poll reflected dramatic change in Palestinian circles regarding Hamas's October 7 invasion of Israel. The latest Palestinian poll showed that for the first time in nearly a year of fighting, only a minority of Gazans still supported the attack which sparked the war. The Palestinian Center for Policy and Survey Research (PCPSR) survey showed that only thirty-nine percent still backed the invasion, a massive drop of eighteen percentage points from the last survey taken three months ago. Among Palestinian Authority Arabs, the decision to attack still enjoyed sixty-four percent support, although this number reflected a drop of thirteen points since the last poll, conducted in June. Taken together, a slight majority of fifty-three percent still said that Hamas was correct to invade.[54]

Airstrikes in Lebanon followed strikes on Metula: the IAF struck approximately 30 Hezbollah launchers and terrorist infrastructure sites, containing approximately 150 launcher barrels that were ready to fire projectiles toward Israeli territory. Reports in Lebanon said that at least seventy targets were struck simultaneously. In an unusual statement, the IDF announced that over the weekend it would carry out activities in all training areas in the north. Hezbollah leader Nasrallah called the two days of deadly blasts linked to electronic devices in Lebanon this week an "act of war" by Israel, admitting that his enemy had dealt an "unprecedented blow" to Hezbollah and Lebanon. But he also struck a note of defiance, saying the group's operations would not stop until Israel ended its war in Gaza. "They will face a severe reckoning and just retribution, whether they expect it or not," Nasrallah said of Israel. The nature, size, and location of any retaliatory attack would be kept secret, he said. "We tell Netanyahu, Gallant, and the Israeli military—you won't succeed in returning the residents of the north to the north, do what you want, you won't succeed." Israel will face "a crushing response from the axis of resistance," Iran's Commander Hossein Salami told Nasrallah, according to state media.[55]

On Friday, day 350 of the war, the IDF and ISA eliminated Shadi Zakarana, the head of a terror group in Qabatiya, alongside six additional terrorists, in a northern Samaria counterterror operation. The previous night, the IDF reported that fighter jets had struck hundreds of rockets that were ready for immediate launch into Israeli territory. Starting on Thursday afternoon, a total of about 100 rocket launchers and other military infrastructure were attacked, including about 1,000 rockets that were ready for immediate launch, the IDF said. Most significantly, Israel said it killed Hezbollah's head of operations and acting head of the elite Radwan Force, Ibrahim Aqil, in an airstrike on a building in the Dahiyeh neighborhood of Beirut. IDF Spokesperson Hagari said that more than a dozen senior commanders of Hezbollah's Radwan Force were also killed in the strike, describing them as "commanders who conceived and led Hezbollah's plan to launch an attack in Israeli territory in the north, which they called "the plan to conquer the Galilee." They planned to invade Israel, enter communities, abduct, and murder civilians. Aqil was also wanted by the United States, and there was a $7 million reward for information about him due to his role in the 1983 bombings at the US embassy in Beirut and the US Marine barracks, as well as involvement in taking US and German hostages in Lebanon.[56]

Halevi approved battle plans for Israel's northern front with Hezbollah, adding that the IAF was conducting strikes in southern Lebanon. The IDF declared it had now prioritized its front with Hezbollah, but was awaiting clear government policy about sustaining military action to achieve other declared goals of the war, including the return of the hostages held in Gaza. Some 200 rockets were fired at northern Israel from Lebanon. Hezbollah said that Ahmed Wahbi, a top commander who oversaw the Radwan Force's military operations during the Gaza war until early 2024, was also killed by Friday's Israeli strike on Beirut. The IDF said at least sixteen Hezbollah members, including senior Radwan Force members, were killed in the strike.[57]

Lebanese Foreign Minister Abdallah Bou Habib warned the UN Security Council that if it did not compel "Israel to stop its aggression . . . we will be silent witnesses to the great explosion that is looming on the horizon today." UN High Commissioner for Human Rights Volker Türk said that the orchestrators of the pager explosions in Lebanon violated international law. He called for a thorough investigation into the attack. The IDF said that its fighter jets attacked 180 targets in southern Lebanon on Saturday, striking thousands of Hezbollah rocket launchers. The IDF said sixty-five rockets were fired at northern Israel in multiple barrages during the day, adding that it killed Muhammad Mansour, a Hamas operative who held a key role in the group's military intelligence. Hezbollah fired its deepest barrage into Israel since the beginning of the current war, with four rounds of over 150 rockets, cruise missiles, and drones fired into the in the early hours of Sunday morning, the IDF confirmed, wounding seven. The Health Ministry ordered hospitals in northern Israel to move patients to protected areas amid increased Hezbollah rocket fire from Lebanon.[58]

The IDF said it hit 1,600 Hezbollah terror targets in several waves on Monday; 210 rockets were launched from Lebanon at northern and central Israel. The Israeli army urged residents in south Lebanon to distance themselves from weapons storage sites. The IDF confirmed that it had killed Hezbollah missile unit commander Ibrahim Qubaisi in a Beirut strike. The next day, over 300 rockets were fired from Lebanon, the most in single day since the beginning of war. In a UN General Assembly address, Biden called for an end to the Gaza war, together with de-escalation between Hezbollah and Israel. Hardly open to compromise, on Wednesday Hezbollah targeted Tel Aviv for the first time with a surface-to-surface missile that was intercepted by the David's Sling air defense system. National Security Council spokesperson John Kirby called Hezbollah's missile launch at central Israel "deeply concerning," adding that it is evidence "that Israel is facing a legitimate threat from a terrorist group backed by Iran . . . No nation should have to live with these threats right across their border, right next door." In total disagreement, the foreign ministers of Iraq, Jordan, and Egypt, meeting at the sidelines of the UN General Assembly in New York, accused Israel of "pushing the region toward an all-out war" and "emphasized that stopping this escalation begins with halting the Israeli aggression on Gaza."[59]

The IDF mobilized two brigades of reservists for operational missions in Israel's north against Hezbollah, to protect Israeli citizens and to create "the conditions for the safe return of the residents of the north to their homes." It struck about 280 Hezbollah targets in Lebanon the same day, including launch sites from which northern Israeli communities were fired at, and some sixty Hezbollah intelligence targets. Blinken told CBS that closing a hostage/cease-fire deal between Israel and Hamas "is a question of political will . . . In the first instance, that political will needs to be demonstrated by Hamas. We haven't seen it the last couple of weeks. Israel would have some hard decisions to make to bring this to a close, but we've got to see if Hamas is actually serious."[60]

Biden and Macron, supported by a number of Western countries, Saudi Arabia, the UAE and Qatar, jointly called on Wednesday for an immediate twenty-one-day cease-fire to allow for negotiations in the escalating conflict between Israel and Hezbollah that had killed more than 600 people in Lebanon in recent days. The joint statement—not mentioning Hezbollah, negotiated on the sidelines of the UN General Assembly in New York, said the recent fighting was "intolerable and presents an unacceptable risk of a broader regional escalation. We call on all parties, including the governments of Israel and Lebanon, to endorse the temporary cease-fire immediately." The United States hoped the new deal could lead to longer-term stability along the border between Israel and Lebanon. While the deal applied only to the Israel-Lebanon border, the US officials said they were looking to use a three-week pause in fighting to restart stalled negotiations for a cease-fire and hostage release deal between Israel and Hamas. The US officials said Hezbollah would not be a signatory to the new cease-fire proposal but believed the Lebanese government would coordinate its acceptance with the group. They expected Israel to "welcome" the proposal and perhaps formally accept it when Netanyahu addressed the General Assembly on Friday.

Najib Mikati, the Lebanese caretaker prime minister, publicly threw his support behind the French-US plan that "enjoys international support and which would put an end to this dirty war." He called on the Security Council "to guarantee the withdrawal of Israel from all the occupied Lebanese territories and the violations that are repeated on a daily basis." Israel's UN Ambassador,

Danny Danon, told journalists that Israel would like to see a cease-fire and the return of people to their homes near the border: "It will happen, either after a war or before a war. We hope it will be before." Addressing the Security Council later, he made no mention of a temporary cease-fire but said Israel "does not seek a full-scale war." Both Danon and Mikati reaffirmed their governments' commitment to Security Council resolution 1701 that ended the 2006 Israeli-Hezbollah war. Never fully implemented, it had called for a cessation of hostilities between Israel and Hezbollah, the withdrawal of Israeli forces from Lebanon to be replaced by Lebanese forces and UN peacekeepers, and the disarmament of all armed groups including Hezbollah.[61]

Netanyahu's office said that he had not yet responded to the cease-fire proposal, and that he had not issued any directive "to moderate the fighting in the north," rather, he had "instructed the IDF to continue fighting with full force." Netanyahu reversed his stance on a cease-fire with Hezbollah in Lebanon, retracting verbal commitments he had made to the US administration, in response to mounting political pressure from within Israel, diplomatic sources involved in the US-French truce proposal told *Haaretz*. National Security Minister Itamar Ben-Gvir said that his party would not support a government vote backing a temporary cease-fire with Hezbollah and would leave the government if the cease-fire was permanent. Israeli opposition leader Yair Lapid called on Israel to accept the proposal "but only for seven days, in order to not allow Hezbollah to rehabilitate its command-and-control systems," rejecting any proposal allowing Hezbollah to remain on Israel's northern border.[62]

The IDF said it attacked infrastructure on the Syria-Lebanon border used by Hezbollah to transfer weapons and struck around seventy-five Hezbollah targets in Lebanon overnight into Thursday. Israeli troops completed a training drill simulating ground combat scenarios inside Lebanese territory, the IDF remarked, adding that the exercise took place several kilometers from the Lebanese border. Blinken told MSNBC's Morning Joe that a cease-fire between Israel and Hezbollah "may create some space and maybe even some momentum to try to get the Gaza cease-fire and hostage deal over the finish line," adding that "the challenge we have right now is it's unclear whether Hamas is serious about concluding an agreement." Hamas reached an agreement with Fatah on managing civilian affairs in Gaza, the Saudi outlet Al-Hadath reported, citing a Hamas official.

Saudi Arabia had formed a global alliance to push for a two-state solution to the Israeli-Palestinian conflict, foreign minister Prince Faisal bin Farhan Al Saud said on Thursday on the sidelines of the UN General Assembly.

The alliance included a number of Arab and Muslim countries and European partners, Saudi state news reported. EU foreign policy chief Josep Borrell said on X that the first meetings would take place in Riyadh and Brussels. Speaking at the UN General Assembly, Palestinian Authority President Mahmoud Abbas said that Palestinians "will not allow a single centimeter of Gaza to be taken by Israel." Abbas also called to "Stop the killing. Stop the genocide. Stop sending weapons to Israel." Israeli ambassador to the UN Danon said in response that "Abbas spoke for twenty-six minutes and did not say the word 'Hamas' once."[63]

The IDF announced that the strike that killed Hezbollah's missile unit head on Tuesday also killed his deputy, Abbas Ibrahim Sharaf Al-Din, as well as another senior operative in the group's missile unit, Hussein Hani. The head of Hezbollah's air defense system, Mohammed Surur—allegedly killed in an Israeli strike on Beirut on Thursday—returned to Lebanon from Yemen three days ago and was responsible for the launching of missiles and drones by Houthi forces, Al-Arabiya reported. Hamas stopped responding to cease-fire proposals relayed by countries mediating truce talks in recent weeks, a diplomatic source told *Haaretz*, adding that "we have no information suggesting that Yahya Sinwar is dead, but he has been out of contact for at least a few weeks. In fact, we are not receiving any communication from Hamas, but we cannot determine if this is related to Sinwar." Hamas's military wing has been defeated and is currently operating as a guerrilla organization in the Gaza Strip, IDF sources told *Haaretz*. The Hamas-controlled Health Ministry in Gaza said at least 41,534 Palestinians were killed and 96,092 wounded since the start of the war.[64]

In his speech before the seventy-ninth session of the UN General Assembly on Friday morning, which prompted some delegations to walk out, Netanyahu declared that "Israel's war on Hamas and Hezbollah will continue unabated," adding that Israel did not "seek to resettle Gaza, we seek a demilitarized and deradicalized Gaza. All Hamas needs to do is surrender, lay down its arms, and release the hostages." He said Israel was "ready to work with regional and other partners to support a local civilian administration in Gaza committed to peaceful coexistence," while insisting Hamas could have no role in post-war Gaza. He averred that Israel had "no choice and every right" to strike Lebanon, and warned that Israel "will continue degrading Hezbollah until all objectives are met. We won't rest until our citizens can return safely to their homes. We will not accept a terror army perched on our northern border."

Speaking of the UN, the Israeli prime minister minced no words in asserting that "until this antisemitic swamp is drained, the UN will be viewed by fair-minded people everywhere as nothing more than a contemptuous farce," adding that the possibility that an ICC arrest warrant will be issued against him is "hard to explain as anything other than pure antisemitism." He told the world to choose peace and to battle the "Iranian curse." Promising his audience (with a reference to the poet Dylan Thomas) that Israel "won't go gently into that good night," he exclaimed "We will never need to rage against the dying of the light because the torch of Israel will forever shine bright." Citing the Hebrew phrase "*Am Yisrael chai!*," he ended thus: "The people of Israel live now, tomorrow, forever."[65]

That afternoon, shortly before the Sabbath, IDF Chief of Staff Herzi Halevi confirmed that the IAF had conducted a precise strike eliminating Hezbollah's leader, Secretary-General Hassan Nasrallah. The strike, named "A New Order" by the IDF, took place on Hezbollah's headquarters under a residential building located in the predominantly Shiite Muslim suburb of Dahieh in the south of Beirut. Ali Karki, the commander of Hezbollah's Southern Front, and nineteen other commanders were also killed in the same attack. "The strike was conducted while Hezbollah's senior chain of command was operating from the headquarters and advancing terrorist activities against the citizens of the State of Israel," the IDF report stated, stressing that it will "continue operating against anyone who promotes and engages in terrorism against the State of Israel and its people."

Eighty-three tons of 2,000-pound bunker buster bombs were dropped on the headquarters, embedded four stories below ground. The attack used a series of timed, chained explosions to penetrate the subterranean bunker, a senior Israeli military official said. Nasrallah and numerous other Hezbollah leaders were meeting there to hear Netanyahu's speech at the UN. Netanyahu's decision to go ahead with his trip to the General Assembly despite the escalating fighting with Hezbollah "was part of a diversion" to lull Nasrallah into believing Israel would not target him while the premier was in New York, a senior Israeli official told the *Telegraph*. Some present in the bunker, the *Wall Street Journal* reported, planned to use the meeting to express frustration that Iran was restraining them from responding more forcefully to the Israeli attacks.

Israeli intelligence learned of the meeting in which Nasrallah was killed only hours before it took place, Israeli officials told the *Wall Street Journal*. Jerusalem was notified by an Iranian source on Friday afternoon about Nasrallah's expected arrival at the organization's headquarters, the French daily *Le Parisien* reported, citing a Lebanese security source. According to *Reuters*, it was the biggest strike on Beirut since Hezbollah opened hostilities on October 8. Amid reports that a series of powerful explosions rattled the Lebanese capital, Hezbollah's Al-Manar channel said that four buildings in the city had been destroyed. Israeli defense officials estimated that about 300 people were killed in Friday's Beirut strike, including those in nearby buildings.[66]

In his first statement after the elimination of Nasrallah, Iran's Supreme Leader Khamenei accused that "the Zionists have learned nothing from their war in Gaza." He clarified that Iran stood alongside Hezbollah, and that "the fate of the region will be determined by the force of resistance." According to him, "the Zionists are too small to significantly harm the strong structure of Hezbollah. Lebanon will make the enemy regret." According to an earlier report by the *Reuters* news agency, sources familiar with the matter said that Khamenei, "was moved to a safe place with enhanced security measures" shortly after the IDF confirmed that Nasrallah was killed. Hamas's Sinwar relocated within the Gaza Strip after learning about the Israeli airstrike that eliminated Nasrallah, according to a Saturday report by Saudi state-owned television channel Al-Arabiya. The report also claimed that Sinwar's security circles had changed in the past few days and that Hamas leaders also had decided to stop communicating with high officials abroad and canceled all their meetings in Lebanon "until further notice." According to KAN, their communication was now only limited to written messages, Other senior Hamas officials in Gaza also decided to halt their movement in the Strip after Nasrallah's death, the Al-Arabiya report claimed. Additionally, Islamic Jihad terrorists in Lebanon also decided to stop meeting and moving from place to place.[67]

On Saturday, Hezbollah confirmed the killing of Nasrallah, declaring that he had "joined his great and immortal martyred companions, and it pledged to continue with his "commitment to resistance." Iran's Khamenei said the "massacre of the defenseless people in Lebanon" had "exposed the brutal nature" of Israel and underscored the "shortsightedness and foolish policy" of its leaders. Hamas offered its condolences, stating that Nasrallah was "martyred along with a group of his fellow leaders" and that Israel should bear "full responsibility for this ugly crime" together with the United States. It said Nasrallah's life had been "full of sacrifices" for Palestinians, commending his "brave resistance." The deputy head of Hamas's political wing, Khalil al-Hayya, condemned Nasrallah's assassination, calling it "a criminal act of terrorism," adding that it "will not break the axis of resistance to Israel, but will lead to a new stage in the process of revenge." Iraq would set three days of mourning for Nasrallah, the prime minister's office said in a statement that lambasted Israel's "aggression," adding that Nasrallah and others had "devoted their lives to the cause of resisting the oppressive occupation." Iraq said Israel's attacks in Lebanon on Friday showed a "reckless desire to escalate the conflict," and it urged the United Nations and others to deter the violence.[68]

Israeli officials gave their American counterparts, who were already peeved that Netanyahu had brushed off the US-French twenty-one-day cease-fire proposal, no advance warning of the strike that eliminated Nasrallah. Biden said the killing was "a measure of justice" for victims of Hezbollah terrorism, expressing no regret over the killing and noting that Hezbollah was responsible for killing hundreds of Americans over the decades. At the same time, he called on the combatants in the region "to de-escalate the ongoing conflicts" and agree to diplomatic deals to end the fighting. Biden also announced that he had ordered US forces in the region to enhance their "defense posture" to deter aggression and to reduce the risk of a broader regional war.[69]

The same day, the IDF said its fighter jets killed the "head of Hamas infrastructure in southern Syria, Ahmed Muhammad Fahd, and attacked Hezbollah production sites and smuggling routes on the Syrian border." This was part of a larger effort to prevent Iran from resupplying the stocks of weapons that the IDF had been systematically destroying, beginning that day when Israel prevented Iranian cargo planes from landing in Beirut. UN Secretary General António Guterres warned during a UN Security Council meeting on the Middle East that "war in Lebanon could lead to further escalation involving outside powers" and that "we must avoid a regional war at all costs." Ahead of a UN Security Council meeting on Gaza, Jordan's Foreign Minister Ayman Safadi said that "the truth is, unless Netanyahu is stopped, unless this government is stopped, war will encompass all of us." After Netanyahu had castigated the UN as "antisemitic" for its perceived anti-Israel bias in his General Assembly speech, US Ambassador to the UN Thomas-Greenfield told MSNBC that while she "will not comment on antisemitism," she believed "the prime minister is right in the sense that there is an unfair focus on Israel."[70]

The IDF Spokesperson's Unit announced Sunday morning that Nabil Qaouk, the commander of Hezbollah's preventative security unit who was considered close to the organization's senior leadership, was eliminated in an airstrike in Beirut overnight. Israel continued heavy strikes on Lebanon, claiming to attack dozens of Hezbollah targets. More than 1,000 people, including at least eighty-seven children, had been killed in Israeli attacks on Lebanon in the past two weeks, Beirut health officials said. When asked if an Israeli ground invasion of Lebanon was now inevitable, Biden replied: "It's time for a cease-fire." Iranian Foreign Minister Abbas Araghchi declared that while Nasrallah's assassination was "a great loss," he believed it would "increase the strength and motivation of Hezbollah." Citing Israeli forces' conflicts in Gaza and Lebanon, he remarked "there is certainly no future for them in the region" and accused the United States, a staunch ally of Israel, of being complicit in Israel's "crime."

Au contraire, IDF officials believed that a ground offensive in Lebanon was the only way for residents of northern Israel to return to their homes, adding that there was a short window of opportunity for such a maneuver that would be lost if Hezbollah managed to recover and regroup. Lebanon's Mikati said that his country had "no option but the diplomatic option" to the escalating conflict between Israel and Hezbollah.[71]

The next morning, the IAF hit Houthi sites with its most powerful strikes of war, attacking Yemen's Hodeidah and Ras Issa ports, oil reserves, and military supplies, sources told the *Jerusalem Post*. Dozens of Israeli aircraft, including Boeing "Ra'am" F-151 fighter planes, participated in the operation, striking 1,800 kilometers from Israeli territory after the Houthis fired three ballistic missiles on the Tel Aviv and central Israel areas in recent weeks, including one on Saturday. The Houthi Health Ministry said the Israeli attack resulted in the deaths of four fighters and the wounding of twenty-nine, without the ministry distinguishing between Houthi members and civilians. Hamas announced that its leader in Lebanon, Fatah Sherif al-Amin, was killed with his wife, son, and daughter in a refugee camp for Palestinians during an airstrike in the southern part of the country. The attack appeared to be the latest in a series of moves by Israel targeting the leadership of militias backed by Iran across the Middle East.[72]

Israeli forces had been conducting small-scale incursions into southern Lebanon, including into Hezbollah's tunnels, ahead of a possible Israeli ground operation in the area, the *Wall Street Journal* reported on Monday, citing anonymous sources. The purpose of these operations was to gain information in preparation for a possible invasion, the sources informed the newspaper, which could begin as soon as this week. According to the report, such operations had been carried out in the past few months as well as more recently, as part of Israel's attempt at striking the terror group embedded on its border with Lebanon.[73]

Hezbollah was prepared for a possible Israeli ground invasion of Lebanon even though "the battle might be long," the militant group's deputy leader, Naim Qassem, said in a video address. An Israeli airstrike hit an apartment in western Beirut's largely Sunni Muslim Cola neighborhood, the first within the capital's city limits since the war with Hezbollah in 2006. The Popular Front for the Liberation of Palestine announced that three of its senior leaders were killed in the bombing. IAF fighter jets struck and eliminated Eid Hassan, the commander of Hezbollah's medium-range rocket array, the military said. It also killed the commander of Hezbollah's long-range rocket unit, Hassan Nazer, in a strike in Beirut, as well as the leader of the Popular Front for the Liberation of Palestine, Nadal Abdel Alal. As fears mounted of further Israeli attacks, people were trying to leave Lebanon. UN High Commissioner for Refugees Filippo Grandi said in an X post; the number of people crossing into Syria had reached 100,000. On Sunday, the European Commission announced it was providing an additional $11.2 million in humanitarian aid to assist people in Lebanon.[74]

According to a Western official, the Biden administration relayed to Tehran via a third country that it would find it "difficult to restrain Israel," and that a direct attack would provoke a harsher Israeli response than in April, when Iran had launched hundreds of missiles and drones against Israel. The United States was also trying to revive cease-fire discussions in Lebanon and Gaza, despite low prospects for success. Iranian Foreign Ministry spokesperson Nasser Kanaani said that Iran will not send forces to Lebanon, AFP reported, adding that Lebanon and the Palestinians "have the capability and strength to defend themselves against the aggression."[75]

Netanyahu opened Monday's cabinet meeting saying Israel "is in a war for our very existence," adding that these are "days of historic achievements, but also great challenges still ahead of us." Responding to Netanyahu's UN speech which contended that Israel is surrounded by those who want to destroy it, Jordanian Foreign Minister Safadi said: "We're here—members of the Muslim-Arab committee, mandated by fifty-seven Arab and Muslim countries—and I can tell you very unequivocally, all of us are willing to guarantee the security of Israel in the context of Israel ending the occupation and allowing for the emergence of a Palestinian state." He added that "All of us in the Arab world here, we want a peace in which Israel lives in peace and security, accepted, normalized, with all Arab countries," and that Netanyahu was escalating the war "because he simply does not want the two-state solution. If he does not want the two-state solution, can you ask Israeli officials what is their end-game—other than just wars and wars and wars?"[76]

The IDF said that at least seventy rockets were fired at northern Israel from Lebanon on Monday. Fires broke out in several locations in the Western Galilee after a barrage from Lebanon. Gallant told armored corps soldiers at Israel's northern border that, in order to return Israeli citizens to their homes in the north, "We will deploy whatever is needed—you, other forces, from the air, from the sea, and from the land." The United States was sending an additional "few thousand" troops to the Middle East to bolster security and to be prepared to defend Israel if necessary, the Pentagon said. Lebanon's Prime Minister Mikati declared his government was ready to implement UN Resolution 1701 and send the Lebanese army to the south of the country, to ensure that the region remains demilitarized up to the Litani River.[77]

Addressing the Iranian people in a social media video, Netanyahu said that Israel stood with them against "a regime that subjugates you, makes fiery speeches about defending Lebanon, defending Gaza. Yet every day, that regime plunges our region deeper into darkness and deeper into war," adding that "when Iran is finally free—and that moment will come a lot sooner than people think—everything will be different." In Gaza, the Hamas-controlled Health Ministry stated that at least 41,615 Palestinians were killed and 96,359 wounded since the start of the war. In Jerusalem, the families of abductees and other protesters demonstrated outside Netanyahu's residence, calling for a hostage release deal. In Vatican City, while not mentioning Israel specifically, Pope Francis replied to a question about the IDF's campaign in Lebanon that all countries must beware the tendency to go "beyond morality" when conducting wars. In Istanbul, a Turkish paper considered close to the regime of President Erdoğan plastered a headline across its front page that asserted "The world will not be safe until Israel is destroyed." The article in *Yeni Safak* came as a direct response to the IDF's assassination of Nasrallah. In Washington, Israel informed the United States that it was "currently conducting limited operations targeting Hezbollah infrastructure near the border," the State Department said. As night fell on September 30, day 360 of the war, there was no end in sight.[78]

Endnotes

1 *JTA*, Aug. 31, 2024; *Washington Post*, Sept. 1, 2024; *New York Times*, Sept. 1, 2024. Responding to Hamas's killing of the six Israelis, Netanyahu observed that a terrorist (who was later killed) had murdered three police officers near the Tarqumiya Checkpoint in the Hebron area that very morning, one of whom had a daughter who was killed while defending the Sderot police station on October 7. He then declared that three months ago, on May 27, Israel had agreed to a hostage release deal with full backing from the United States but Hamas refused. "Even after the United States updated the deal framework on August 16— we agreed, and Hamas again refused. Whoever murders hostages does not want a deal," he concluded. "For our part, we will not relent. The Government of Israel is committed, and I am personally committed, to continue striving toward a deal that will return all of our hostages and ensure our security and our existence." Israel National News, Sept. 1, 2024.

2 *Haaretz*, Sept.1, 2024; Israel National News, Sept. 1, 2024; *Jerusalem Post*, Sept. 1, 2024.

3 *Haaretz*, Sept. 2, 2024; Israel National News, Sept. 2, 2024; *JTA*, Sept. 1, 2024; *Jerusalem Post*, Sept. 2, 2024.

4 *Haaretz*, Sept. 2, 2024; *New York Times*, Sept. 2, 2024; *Washington Post*, Sept. 1, 2024; World Israel News, Sept. 2, 2024; IDF News, Sept. 2, 2024; Israel National News, Sept. 2, 2024. For Rachel Goldberg-Polin's full remarks, see the Appendices.

   Two new polls, one released on Tuesday by the Jewish People Policy Institute (JPPI) and a July survey by the Direct Polls revealed that a plurality to a majority of Israelis supported maintaining control of the Philadelphi Corridor, even at the expense of a hostage deal with Hamas. In the first, a majority (58.5 percent) of Jewish respondents agreed that Netanyahu's reasons stem from military considerations, while the majority of Arabs (66.5 percent) said he was trying to prevent an agreement. The results were also highly dependent on political orientation: among Jewish Israelis, 77.5 percent of left-wing respondents said

Netanyahu's motivations were political while 78 percent of right-wing respondents said they were strategic. JNS, Sept. 3, 2024; *Times of Israel*, Sept. 4, 2024. However, a *Ma'ariv* poll, published on September 6, showed that a majority of the Israeli public preferred giving up control of the Philadelphi Corridor in exchange for a prisoner-hostage deal (48 percent), over maintaining control of the corridor at the cost of forgoing the deal (37 percent). Among Jewish-Israeli respondents, there was a much smaller margin between those who preferred to relinquish control of the corridor to make a deal (44 percent) and those who wished to maintain control of the corridor even at the cost of not reaching an agreement (42 percent). Among opposition party voters, 75 percent supported giving up control of the Corridor for the deal, whereas 74 percent of coalition party voters opposed it, even if it meant no hostage-prisoner exchange deal. A fourth poll, of English-language respondents, the only one to present Hamas's conditions as relayed the previous day by Sinwar's representative for a final hostage/cease-fire deal, found that 81 percent opposed. Abu Ali Express, Sept. 1, 2024, https://t.me/englishgabuali/33570.

5 World Israel News, Sept. 3, 2024; IDF News, Sept. 3, 2024; *Jerusalem Post*, Sept. 3, 2024. Earlier in the week, a Hamas spokesperson admitted that the terror group had killed the six hostages. According to him, "The instructions for dealing with hostages will be updated when the IDF approaches the scene." Previously, Hamas had claimed that the hostages were killed in an Israeli airstrike or by IDF gunfire. Israel National News, Sept. 4, 2024.
6 Israel National News, Sept. 3, 2024. See the Appendices for the Council statement.
7 Israel National News, Sept. 3, 2024; *Jerusalem Post*, Sept. 3, 2024. And see note 4. The author, witness to the Jerusalem scene, wished the policemen, who expressed their appreciation, "a quiet day." A recent Pew Research Center poll found that political divisions further shaped opinions on censorship. Among Israelis on the right, seventy-six percent wanted to block posts supporting Gaza's civilians, compared to only twenty-five percent on the left. *Haaretz*, Sept. 5, 2024.
8 Israel National News, Sept. 3, 2024; *Jerusalem Post*, Sept. 3, 2024.
9 *New York Times*, Sept. 4, 2024; Seth J. Frantzman, "U.S. Charges are Important Step to Bring Hamas to Justice—Analysis," *Jerusalem Post*, Sept. 4, 2024. The Justice Department cited the breadth of Hamas's attacks in the complaint: "Hamas and its leaders have continued to espouse the destruction of Israel as Hamas's core purpose, and the use of murder and other acts of violent terrorism against Israelis and those who support Israel, including Americans, as its principal means of accomplishing that objective. As a central component of that mission, Hamas leaders have specifically called for retaliation against the United States in response to U.S. support of Israel's existence."

Perhaps, however, as one observer pointed out, this was a case of "too little, too late," especially as Hamas had been designated a terror organization by US law for almost thirty years yet the current administration "took no meaningful action" against Hamas. Reading his critique, Mosaic editor Andrew Koss suggested that the Biden administration could take some economic or military action against Iran, for instance, which might then pressure the terrorists in Gaza. It could also demand that Qatar, an officially designated US "major non-NATO ally," extradite senior Hamas officials and turn over their bank account. Andrew C. McCarthy, "Justice Department's Prosecution of Dead Hamas Leaders Is Just for Show," Mosaic, Sept. 5, 2024.
10 *Jerusalem Post*, Sept. 4, 2024; Ynet news.com, Sept. 3, 2024; *Haaretz*, Sept. 4, 2024.
11 Israel National News, Sept. 3, 2024.
12 *Wall St. Journal*, Sept. 4, 2024.
13 *Haaretz*, Sept. 4, 2024.
14 *Haaretz*, Sept. 4, 2024; Israel National News, Sept. 4, 2024. The other Hamas demands, from March onwards, included a permanent cease-fire; Gaza's reconstruction; and the release of Palestinian prisoners. The last-named would, in the first stage, have fifty in exchange for each female IDF soldier and thirty prisoners for each Israeli civilian. In the second stage, 500 prisoners for each male IDF soldier.

15 *New York Times*, Sept. 5, 2024. The *Protocols of the Elders of Zion*, a fraudulent document attributed to the secret police of Tsarist Russia that was first disseminated in the early twentieth century, purporting to detail a Jewish plot for global domination. is the most widely distributed antisemitic publication of modern times.

The blood libel, where Jews were falsely accused of killing a Christian child and using the victim's blood for the baking of *matza* (unleavened bread) for the Passover holiday, first appeared in Norwich, England, in 1144. Subsequent cases of this ritual murder charge appeared during the Middle Ages in France, Spain, Germany, and elsewhere in England. The Medieval poet Geoffrey Chaucer's "The Prioress's Tale" (in the *Canterbury Tales*) also invokes this motif. By the seventeenth century it became increasingly common in Poland and Lithuania. The antisemitic canard surfaced in the Arab world with the Damascus Affair (1840) and in Shiraz, Iran (1910). The Nazi Julius Streicher highlighted this myth in his *Der Stürmer* newspaper. It sparked the Kielce pogrom (1946), which sparked a mass Jewish exodus from Poland. The Roman Catholic Church repudiated the blood libel charge in 1965. Yet it was resorted to in the 2003 TV series broadcast in Syria and Lebanon, and, after the Hamas-Israel war began, in false accusations of Israel harvesting organs of Palestinians, with cartoons depicting "the occupation" consuming Palestinian babies' blood.

16 *New York Times*, Sept. 5, 2024; *Jerusalem Post*, Sept. 5, 2024.
17 Israel National News, Sept. 5, 2024; BBC, Sept. 5, 2024. The Gilboa Prison break occurred on September 6. 2021, when six Palestinian prisoners escaped through a tunnel from that maximum security prison in northern Israel. Among the escapees was Zakaria Zubeidi, former leader of al-Aqsa Martyrs' Brigade in Jenin. In an interview in 2005. he assumed responsibility for the 2002 Beit She'an attack. During the Second Intifada, in the 2002 Beit She'an attack, six Israelis were killed and over thirty were injured by two Palestinian militants, who opened fire and threw grenades at a polling station in the center of Beit She'an where party members were voting in the Likud primary. He is currently in solitary confinement in Ashkelon Prison.
18 *Haaretz*, Sept. 5, 2024. Strategic Affairs Minister Ron Dermer had stressed on Wednesday that, while Israel was not going to withdraw from the Philadelphi Corridor in the first phase of any cease-fire/hostage deal with Hamas, it would be prepared to leave the door open for a full withdrawal in a negotiated second phase down the line. "In phase one, Israel is going to stay on that line until we have a practical solution on the ground that can convince the people of Israel . . . that what happened on October 7 will not happen again, that Hamas will not rearm," Dermer told the Bloomberg TV network. *Times of Israel*, Sept. 4, 2024.
19 Israel National News, Sept. 5, 2024.
20 IDF News, Sept. 5, 2024; *Jerusalem Post*, Sept. 5–6, 2024.
21 Janglo News, Sept. 5, 2024; World Israel News, Sept. 5, 2024; *Jerusalem Post*, Sept. 7, 2024.
22 *Haaretz*, Sept. 6, 2024; JNS, Sept. 6, 2024.
23 Israel National News, Sept. 7, 2024; *Times of Israel*, Sept. 7, 2024; *Washington Post*, Sept. 7, 2024.
24 Israel National News, Sept. 8, 2024; IDF News, Sept. 7, 2024; i24News, Sept. 8, 2024; *Haaretz*, Sept. 7, 2024.
25 *Haaretz*, Sept. 8, 2024; Israel National News, Sept. 9, 2024.
26 *Haaretz*, Sept. 9, 2024; JNS, Sept. 9, 2024; Israel National News, Sept. 9, 2024; *Wall St. Journal*, Sept. 9, 2024; IDF News, Sept. 9, 2024.
27 World Israel News, Sept. 9, 2024; *Haaretz*, Sept. 9, 2024; Israel National News, Sept. 9, 2024.
28 Israel National News, Sept. 9, 2024; *Times of Israel*, Sept. 9, 2024.
29 *Wall St. Journal*, Sept. 10, 2024; IDF News, Sept. 10, 2024; JNS, Sept. 10, 2024; *New York Times*, Sept. 10, 2024.
30 *Jerusalem Post*, Sept. 10, 2024; Israel National News, Sept. 10, 2024.
31 *Haaretz*, Sept. 10, 2024.
32 *Haaretz*, Sept. 10, 2024.

33 *Times of Israel*, Sept. 10, 2024; *Haaretz*, Sept. 11, 2024.
34 World Israel News, Sept. 10, 2024; *Times of Israel*, Sept. 11, 2024. The four male hostages were Hersh Goldberg-Polin, Ori Danino, Almog Sarusi, and Alexander Lobanov, the female hostages Carmel Gat and Eden Yerushalmi.
35 *Times of Israel*, Sept. 11, 2024. The Assembly adopted the resolution by a recorded vote of 143 in favor to 9 against (Argentina, Czech Republic, Hungary, Israel, Federated States of Micronesia, Nauru, Palau, Papua New Guinea, United States), with 25 abstentions. Full membership would not only need a vote by the General Assembly but would also require a Security Council recommendation. The United States had vetoed a Security Council recommendation on the matter on April 18.

The observer for the State of Palestine said "I stand before you as more than 35,000 Palestinians have been killed, 80,000 have been maimed, 2 million have been displaced. and everything has been destroyed. Palestinians in Gaza are hunted by bombs and bullets in an ever-narrowing space, famine is setting in and, instead of opening crossings, Israel has closed them." "At the time where the world was calling to flood Gaza with humanitarian aid and calling for a cease-fire, Israel imposed a drought," he emphasized, adding: "Its plan has not changed—destroy and displace." Recalling that he "has stood hundreds of times before at this podium"—often in tragic circumstances—he underscored that he has never done so "ahead of a more significant vote than the one about to take place—"a historic one". He stressed that, while Palestinians did not write the Charter of the United Nations—nor enact international law—"we just demanded to see them applied to us—and have been, until now, denied their protection."

Stating that occupation, colonialism, death, and destruction "are not Palestinians' fate—they are imposed," he underscored: "But freedom is our sole destiny." "Israel has made clear that it wants to destroy Palestinian Statehood," and he questioned what it means to support a two-state solution if one allows for the destruction of the Palestinian State. Palestine has been—for generations—"the ultimate test for humanity's ability to live up to its promises," he stressed, calling on those who invoked the Charter during negotiations to abide by Palestinians' right to self-determination, which is guaranteed by that document. "Voting 'yes' today is a vote for Palestinian existence—it is not against any State, but it is against attempts to deprive Palestinians of a State." He added: "In simple words, voting 'yes' is the right thing to do."

The representative of Israel said that, while Holocaust Remembrance Day was commemorated that week, "this shameless body has chosen to reward the modern-day Nazis with rights and privileges." "Today's destructive vote will only open the doors of the United Nations to the terrorists-supporting Palestinian Authority, which does not even have control of its own territory. Hamas controls Gaza and has also taken over Palestinian neighborhoods in the West Bank. The group was predicted to win a Palestinian election." "You are about to grant privileges and rights to the future terror State of Hamas," he said. "In the years to come, the Assembly will have to explain how—in opposition to all morality and the Charter of the United Nations—it supported mass murderers—"the Hitler of our time." "If Hamas rises to power, the Palestinian representative who just spoke here will be recalled, and the UN will have a representative of Hamas sit in this Hall." "Today another travesty is being committed by the Assembly," he said.

According to the Charter of the United Nations, its membership can be granted to all "peace-loving States," he recalled, adding: The admission of any such State to membership is decided by the Assembly on the recommendation of the Security Council. "With today's vote, you're totally bypassing the Security Council in violation of the Charter," he declared. "The Palestinians are the exact opposite of peace-loving. They have only tried to destroy Israel. The Palestinians indoctrinate their children to murder Israelis and commit terrorism. When Israel defends itself, the Palestinian representative comes here shedding his crocodile tears." "When it comes to the lives of Israelis and Jews, the Charter "means nothing to you," he deplored. "I will hold up a mirror—this is your mirror so you can see exactly what you are inflicting upon the UN Charter with this destructive vote," he said, and shredded a few pages of a UN Charter booklet before leaving the podium. UN Meetings Coverage and Press Releases, May 10, 2024, press.un.org/en/2024/ga12599.doc.htm.

36 Israel National News, Sept. 11, 2024.
37 JNS, Sept. 10, 2024; *Haaretz*, Sept. 11, 2024; IDF News, Sept. 11, 2024; *Jerusalem Post*, Sept. 11, 2024; Israel National News, Sept. 11, 2024; *Guardian*, Sept. 11, 2024.
38 Israel National News, Sept. 12, 2024; *Haaretz*, Sept. 12, 2024; *Jerusalem Post*, Sept. 12, 2024.
39 Israel National News, Sept. 12, 2024; *Jerusalem Post*, Sept. 12, 2024; *Haaretz*, Sept. 12, 2024.
40 Israel National News, Sept. 13, 2024.
41 Janglo News, Sept. 13, 2024; Yonah Jeremy Bob, "Hero of Khan Younis, Destroyer of Hamas Tunnels," *Jerusalem Post* Magazine, Sept. 13, 2024; *Haaretz*, Sept. 13, 2024; *Jerusalem Post*, Sept. 14, 2024; *Times of Israel*, Sept. 13, 2024.
42 *Jerusalem Post*, Sept. 14, 2024; *Haaretz*, Sept. 14, 2024.
43 Israel National News, Sept. 15, 2024.
44 *Jerusalem Post*, Sept. 15, 2024; Israel National News, Sept. 16, 2024; IDF News, Sept. 15, 2024.
45 Israel National News, Sept. 16, 2024.
46 *Haaretz*, Sept. 16, 2024; AFP, Sept. 16, 2024; World Israel News, Sept. 16, 2024.
47 *Haaretz*, Sept. 16, 2024. For the Green Line, see Chapter 4, note 8.
48 *Jerusalem Post*, Sept. 17–18, 2024; *Times of Israel*, Sept. 17, 2024; *New York Times*, Sept. 17–18, 2024; IDF News, Sept. 18, 2024. On Tuesday night, the *New York Times*, citing American and other officials, reported that Israel had hidden explosive material within a new batch of Taiwanese-made pagers imported into Lebanon. *Al Monitor* reported on Wednesday that Israel only intended on detonating the Hezbollah terrorists' pagers if war were to break out, but decided to execute the plan early due to suspicions by some of the terrorists. According to the report, two Hezbollah terrorists suspected that something was wrong with the devices, leading Israel to quickly decide not to wait for a war. Israel National News, Sept. 18, 2024. A Lebanese security source said that the Mossad planted explosives in 5,000 pagers ordered by Hezbollah from Taiwan several months ago. *Haaretz*, Sept. 18, 2024. The Taiwanese company Gold Apollo issued a statement that the reportedly retrofitted AR-924 pagers were made and sold by a Hungary-based company using Gold Apollo's trademark. *New Yorker*, Sept. 18, 2024.
49 Israel National News, Sept. 17, 2024; *Haaretz*, Sept. 17, 2024; *New York Times*, Sept. 17, 2024.
50 *New York Times*, Sept. 17, 2024.
51 *Jerusalem Post*, Sept. 18, 2024; *New York Times*, Sept. 18, 2024; *Washington Post*, Sept. 18, 2024.
52 *Haaretz*, Sept. 18, 2024; IDF News, Sept. 18, 2024; BBC, Sept. 18, 2024; *Wall St. Journal*, Sept. 19, 2024.
53 Israel National News, Sept. 19, 2024; Editorial, *Jerusalem Post*, Sept. 19, 2024; JNS, Sept. 18, 2024; World Israel News, Sept. 19, 2024.
54 World Israel News, Sept. 18, 2024.
55 Israel National News, Sept. 19, 2024; *Washington Post*, Sept. 19, 2024; *Haaretz*, Sept. 19, 2024.
56 Israel National News, Sept. 20, 2024; *Jerusalem Post*, Sept. 20, 2024; *Times of Israel*, Sept. 20, 2024.
57 World Israel News, Sept. 19, 2024; Janglo News, Sept. 20, 2024; *Haaretz*, Sept. 20, 2024.
58 *Haaretz*, Sept. 21–22, 2024; *Jerusalem Post*, Sept. 22, 2024; *Times of Israel*, Sept. 22, 2024.
59 *Haaretz*, Sept. 23–25, 2024.
60 *Haaretz*, Sept. 25, 2024,
61 AP, Sept. 26, 2024.
62 *Haaretz*, Sept. 26, 2024.

63 *Haaretz*, Sept. 26–27, 2024.
64 *Haaretz*, Sept. 27, 2024.
65 *Haaretz*, Sept. 27, 2024; *New York Times*, Sept. 27, 2024. For the full text, see the Appendices.
66 *Times of Israel*, Sept. 27, 2024; *New York Times*, Sept. 27, 2024; *Israel National News*, Sept. 27, 2024; *Wall St. Journal*, Sept. 29, 2024. Among the terrorists eliminated alongside Nasrallah: Ibrahim Hussein Jazini—Head of Nasrallah's Security Unit; Samir Tawfiq Dib—Nasrallah's long-time confidant and advisor on terrorist activities; Abed al-Amir Muhammad Sablini—Head of Hezbollah's Force-Build Up; Ali Naaf Ayoub—responsible for coordinating Hezbollah's firepower. Ibrahim Hussein Jazini and Samir Tawfiq Dib were among Nasrallah's closest associates. Due to their proximity to him, they served a significant role in the day-to-day operations of Hezbollah and of Nasrallah in particular. *Israel National News*, Sept. 29, 2024. Abbas Nilforoushan, a top leader in Iran's Islamic Revolutionary Guard Corps, was also killed in Israel's Friday strike in Beirut, Iranian state media reported. Nilforoushan, a brigadier general, was the IRGC's deputy chief of operations and the IRGC Quds Force commander for Syria and Lebanon. *Axios*, Sept. 28, 2024. The same day, former Prime Minister Ehud Olmert confirmed Israel's role in the assassination in 2008 of Imad Mughniyeh, Hezbollah's military chief, stating, "what detonated then was the bumper of the car we arranged to place there." *Haaretz*, Sept. 28, 2024.
67 *Times of Israel*, Sept. 28, 2024; *Israel National News*, Sept. 28, 2024; *Jerusalem Post*, Sept. 28, 2024.
68 *Washington Post*, Sept. 28, 2024.
69 *New York Times*, Sept. 28, 2024.
70 *Haaretz*, Sept. 28, 2024; *L'Orient Today*, Sept. 28, 2024; *Jerusalem Post*, Sept. 29, 2024. The evidence that has emerged is "quite convincing," two investigators observed, that Iran continues to exploit maritime routes to conceal weapons shipments to Hezbollah, and the [Syrian] port of Latakia has become a critical part of this strategy. Hezbollah has also been using Latakia as a logistics hub for fenethylline (the drug also known as Captagon) shipments. Emanuele Ottolenghi and Joe Truzman, "Israel's War to Cut Off Hizballah's Supply Chain," *Mosaic*, Nov. 18, 2024.
71 *Israel National News*, Sept. 29, 2024; *Washington Post*, Sept. 29, 2024; *Haaretz*, Sept. 29, 2024.
72 *New York Times*, Sept. 30, 2024; *Jerusalem Post*, Sept. 30, 2024; *Israel National News*, Sept. 30, 2024.
73 *Jerusalem Post*, Sept. 30, 2024.
74 *Washington Post*, Sept. 30, 2024; *Jerusalem Post*, Sept. 30, 2024; *New York Times*, Sept. 30, 2024; *Haaretz*, Sept. 30, 2024.
75 *Haaretz*, Sept. 30, 2024.
76 *Haaretz*, Sept. 30, 2024.
77 *Haaretz*, Sept. 30, 2024.
78 *Haaretz*, Sept. 30, 2024; *JNS*, Sept. 30, 2024; *World Israel News*, Sept. 29, 2024; *Washington Post*, Sept. 30, 2024.

Conclusion

In the six months of war between April and October 2024, foisted upon the State of Israel by Hamas's savage, genocidal assault on its southern communities near the Gaza Strip, Israel dramatically improved its security situation vis-à-vis that radical Islamist organization. Surveying at length this reality already in May 2024, Yonah Jeremy Bob, the *Jerusalem Post*'s senior military correspondent, noted that eighty percent of Hamas's organized military had been eliminated by the Israel Defense Forces (IDF). It had killed around 14,000 terrorists, wounded potentially close to a similar number, and arrested thousands more. Facing a unified and organized combat group, the IDF had demolished the vast majority of Hamas's military force and put a halt to the majority of rockets in the terrorist organization's arsenal. "Hamas is no longer a threat, invasion-wise," he deduced. The IDF established a new security zone running along the entire Gaza border. True, many Israeli southern residents might not return for months or even longer to their homes, especially in towns that were physically destroyed on October 7, and would need longer to recuperate, yet most residents had returned or were in the process of returning.

The IDF had destroyed dozens of kilometers of attack, defense, and strategic tunnels throughout Gaza in both the north and south. Israel had recovered, mostly in the hostage deal back in November 2023 and in operations, over 80 of the original 253 hostages who were kidnapped by Hamas. To the Israeli public, this registered mostly as a failure because it was only around one-third of the original number; but it was "still far greater than zero." Along with the 80 hostages returned, approximately 100 hostages were presumed dead, and around 70 were still held by Hamas. The government ignored the day-after issue, which would have included a proper replacement for Hamas. Without such a plan, Hamas continued to rally for three more months after it was defeated in early February in Khan Younis.

The sheer length of the war, Bob argued, was not properly calculated by the government in terms of the toll it would take on Israel's relationship with the United States, its global legitimacy, and specifically threats from the International Criminal Court (ICC). This was all without getting into questions about a new front in the North with Hezbollah, he added. But after these shortcomings, other than "the Day After mess" and maybe that a few dozen more hostages could have been freed somehow (probably there would have been legitimacy problems even with a shorter war), the largest problem for understanding the war as a success or failure was that the government "overpromised."[1]

For its part, Hamas claimed considerable success. In June, its Al-Aqsa TV had published a video on the Telegram channel detailing the "consequences of the Al-Aqsa Flood on the Zionist entity." At the top of Hamas's achievements in the October 7 attack, the Al-Aqsa channel listed the killing of over 2,500 Israelis, the kidnapping of more than 250, including senior officers, the evacuation of over a million residents (*sic!*) from their homes in the south and the north, and the complete collapse of the perception of the IDF as an undefeated army. The channel also noted that the October 7 attack thwarted the normalization plan of Israel with Arab countries, harmed thereby the "Deal of the Century," shattered the internal unity among the "enemy," and created a deep rift between Israel's political parties. Additionally, the issue of "Palestine" had returned to the central status among the Arab and Islamic nations; all arenas of confrontation were activated in the "historic campaign"; the hope for release among security prisoners was revived; there was a decrease in Israeli tourism; investments shrank; the economy contracted; and Israel became an accused party in the ICC and the United Nations.[2]

Focusing on the battlefield, international warfare experts disagreed. According to a published report authored by US military legal experts and former commanders, the IDF had conducted its war against Hamas in Gaza "effectively and legally." The authors of the report, published in May by the Jewish Institute for National Security of America, included Gen. (ret.) David Rodriguez, former head of US Africa Command; Adm. (ret.) Michael Rogers, former commander of the US Navy; and Gen. (ret.) Charles Wald, former deputy commander of US European Command. Hamas was described in the report as a "terror army" with the structure, training, and advanced weaponry of a conventional force. Its tactics included not wearing uniforms, attacking civilians, and using civilian infrastructure for military purposes. Hamas, the authors wrote, "has intentionally and systemically" been violating the laws of war "by dragging civilians into the fight, using them to shield their personnel and assets in an attempt to compel the IDF to inflict civilian casualties so as to trigger opposition to Israel by the United States, European countries, the United Nations, and international courts as well as in public opinion." By contrast, "We . . . observed that the IDF took steps to mitigate the risk of civilian casualties in the conduct of hostilities and, on many occasions, we believe, prioritized mitigating civilian risk over anticipated tactical advantage or striking legitimate military targets." "The IDF's performance on Gaza's complicated battlefield demonstrates operational and tactical excellence," the authors concluded.[3]

As for the ICC, Maj. (ret) John W. Spencer, Chair of Urban Warfare Studies at West Point's Modern War Institute, posted on X in July that "What I saw in Gaza convinced me that Israel took the necessary steps to avoid civilian casualties." Israel went above and beyond what was expected of a state in an attempt to prevent harm to non-combatants. Spencer asserted that Israel had implemented almost all "civilian over harm reduction methods" required in urban warfare and the legal norms detailed in international humanitarian law, and had also created some new ones that no military has ever attempted. These included giving the civilian population an extended period of time to evacuate by ensuring safe routes for civilians to use, a humanitarian area to which they could flee during the fighting itself, and personal text messages and announcements flown in drones in order to inform the civilian population that they must evacuate. Spencer also observed that "no one knows how many civilians died in Gaza, especially not Hamas." According to this expert, it was impossible for organizations to track civilian deaths on a daily basis, down to the single-digit level. This was because "the fog of urban warfare is thicker than any other battlefield." Hamas was an adversary, Spencer concluded, that "hardly cares to protect its own people. In fact, it employs a strategy of human sacrifice in an attempt to cause the death of as much of its population as possible."[4]

Nor did all Palestinians embrace the Hamas narrative. While those in Area A (not living in Gaza) under the Palestine Authority's control strongly did so, its Advisor on Religious Affairs and Islamic Relations, Mahmoud Al-Habbash, asserted that Iran, by funding Hamas, had done nothing to help Palestinians. During an interview with the Fatah-affiliated network Awda TV on June 26, Fatah's spokesman in Europe and a member of its Revolutionary Council, Jamal Nazzal, accused Hamas of sacrificing Palestinian civilians against their will. In the interview, Nazzal argued that Palestinians killed as a result of Israel's war with Gaza *"did not chose to* become martyrs but were instead sacrificed by Hamas." "We consider them to be martyrs, but they did not sacrifice themselves—they were sacrificed," Nazzal said, adding "The people who applaud this—especially from abroad—did not try to live in Gaza." Gazans themselves increasingly, but most often anonymously to avoid Hamas retribution, echoed these sentiments as the humanitarian aid meant for them was stolen by Hamas, their homes, in which Hamas had embedded weapons, were reduced to rubble in Israeli airstrikes, and their casualties mounted.[5]

As for Arab Israelis, a study released on June 19 by the Moshe Dayan Center for Middle Eastern and African Studies at Tel Aviv University, representing approximately 308,700 Israeli citizens out of an Arab Israeli population of around 2.1 million, found that some 14.7 percent of Arab Israelis believed the Hamas terrorist group should govern Gaza after the war. The majority of respondents, 58.5 percent, felt that other Palestinian groups should govern Gaza. Some 34.4 percent of respondents said that an external, non-Palestinian body should govern Gaza after the war. (An international force was the preferred option with 19.4 percent support.) Other key findings included that while nearly three-quarters of Arab Israelis reported a low sense of personal safety during the war, more than half the Arab Israeli public (51.6 percent) said there was a shared sense of destiny that has been created by the Hamas-Israel war. The sense of a shared destiny showed a majority among members of all religions: 51.4 percent of Muslims, 62.5 percent of Druze and 61.2 percent of Christians. A large majority (68.6 percent) supported an Arab political party joining a governing coalition established after the next Knesset election.[6]

At September's end, the IDF Spokesperson's Unit published updated data on its operational activity during the past twelve months. Since the start of the war, eight terrorist brigade commanders had been eliminated in Gaza. Approximately thirty terrorist battalion commanders had been killed, and approximately 165 terrorist company commanders. In the northern arena, more than 800 Hezbollah terrorists had been eliminated, and approximately ninety commanders. In the central arena, approximately 690 terrorists had been killed. Approximately 40,300 targets had been struck from the air in Gaza. In addition, over 1,000 rocket launcher sites had been dismantled and about 4,700 tunnel shafts had been located. In the northern arena, approximately 4,900 targets had been struck from the air. About 6,000 ground targets were struck since the beginning of the war. More than 10,000 counterterrorism operations had been conducted and more than 5,000 wanted suspects arrested in Judea and Samaria and the Jordan Valley since the start of the war. In addition, there were more than 150 brigade-scale operations, approximately thirty terrorists' residences had been demolished, and approximately 1,000 munitions confiscated.[7]

A few remarkable achievements stood out from all the rest. First, the killing on July 31 of Hamas political leader Ismail Haniyeh in a military-run guesthouse after he had attended the inauguration ceremony in Tehran for Iranian president Masoud Pezeshkian. Hours before his death, Haniyeh had declared in an interview from the comfort of his office that Israel would not last because "it's a civilization based on occupying of other people's land"; Islamic Republican Guard Corps (IRGC) commander Maj. Genl. Hossein Salami now vowed the "Israeli occupation" entity "will receive a crushing response" and that Israel "is digging its own grave." Yet Iran's earlier massive barrage of more than 180 ballistic missiles at Israel in April (to be repeated in October) was intercepted by Israel's air defenses—the Iron Dome, David's Sling, and the Arrow system—with help from a few allied nations. Those not intercepted landed in sand, water, and empty spaces. Not one Israeli casualty was reported.

Far more impressive was the Israeli Mossad security organization's spectacular attack on Hezbollah towards the end of those six months. The simultaneous pager-explosion and walkie-talkie attacks of September 17–18 in Lebanon and Syria, maiming more than 3,000 of that terror organization's fighters, represented an extraordinary and unprecedented espionage triumph for the IDF. Hezbollah's longtime chief Hassan Nasrallah called this "a declaration of war that crosses all red lines," and declared that Israel would receive "a just punishment" for its actions. On September 27, the man long on Israel's kill list for decades met his end, along with key Hezbollah commanders, in an Israel Air Force strike on his headquarters four stories below a street in the Dahieh southern suburb of Beirut. Iran's Supreme Leader Ayatollah Ali Khamenei, announcing five days of public mourning, called Nasrallah "the flag-bearer of resistance" in the region. Nasrallah's death sent shockwaves in Lebanon and throughout the Middle East and might prove a game changer in Jerusalem's war with Hezbollah. A terrorist army, more powerful than al-Qaida and ISIS combined, had been permanently diminished and, for now, decapitated.[8]

At the close of September, the *New York Times* concluded "Facing a Big Test, Iran's 'Axis of Resistance' Flails." Iran had united militias to take on Israel, but as the Israelis pummeled one, Hezbollah, the rest had so far largely failed to come to its aid. "The so-called axis of resistance from its very beginning was more or less a propaganda fiction created to enhance the prestige of the Islamic Republic," said Ali Alfoneh, a senior fellow at the Arab Gulf States Institute in Washington. In recent years, he observed, the network's members had chalked up some small military victories, "but when it comes to more serious adversaries, or a state actor like Israel, it is a different game."

In Syria, the only state member of the axis besides Iran, the government of President Bashar al-Assad had maintained an official state of war with Israel but kept their disputed border quiet. It appears there was a deep-seated belief in Damascus that Hezbollah could hold its own against Israel. And Iran's reticence about directing an immediate response—at least so far—left Syrian officialdom unclear about the next military steps. al-Assad waited two days after Nasrallah's death to issue a statement mourning him, even though Hezbollah had sent thousands of fighters to beat back rebels threatening his government just a few years earlier. Hamas was "too degraded from nearly a year of war with Israel in Gaza to do much." The Houthis in Yemen and militias in Syria and Iraq launched attacks aimed at Israel or American military bases in the Middle East, but these had largely been repelled. Tehran appeared to be torn between a desire to retaliate against Israel and fear that doing so might lead Israel to attack Iran directly. "They are in a strategic bind, because if they do nothing it will further weaken them and weaken their credibility and their deterrence," said Kawa Hassan, a nonresident fellow at the Stimson Center's Middle East and North Africa Program in Washington, D.C. Yet, if the Iranians respond, he said, that would risk provoking Israel at a time when the IDF appeared "really ready to go after them."

The alliance was always loose, with Iran largely leaving axis members free to make their own decisions, even when that meant starting battles "that gave Iran headaches." The Houthis went against Iran's advice and tried to take over all of Yemen, and Hamas ultimately did not coordinate with Iran before launching the October 7 assault on Israel that started the Gaza war. Since Nasrallah's death, the commanders of two armed groups in Iraq told the *New York Times* that they had received no instructions from Iran on how to respond. Speaking on the condition of anonymity so as not to anger their patron, one said that everyone was still in shock at Nasrallah's killing. Thomas Juneau, instructor of public and international affairs at the University of Ottawa, explained that as long as the violence between Israel and its foes was low-level, Iran could maintain the "perception that the axis of resistance was, if not winning, at least scoring important points." But once Israel brought the full weight of its military and technological superiority to bear, it overwhelmed Hezbollah. "We are in conventional warfare, and Israel's significant and clear domination now is manifest," Juneau said. Experts warned, however, that the network's members remained important regional players. Even if its members had struggled in recent months to inflict grave harm on Israel, Iranian patronage had significantly enhanced their military know-how, increasing their ability to exercise power in Israel's violent neighborhood.[9]

At the same time, for all of Israel's significant military achievements once engaged in the longest war in the history of the Jewish State, October 7, 2023, marked a rupture in time, in the phrase of a Tablet collection of responses by a new generation of Israeli writers "a moment that made the before and after feel irreconcilable." Israel and the Jewish people continue to live in the fallout of that day. For many, the trauma remains great, wounds cut deep that may never fully heal. One small example may suffice: Joining the more than 700 IDF soldiers killed since the war began, Egoz, an elite commando unit specializing in guerrilla warfare, special reconnaissance, and fighting in complex terrains. had suffered more than twenty killed and 235 wounded by early July. What of the widows, the orphans, the 80,000 forced evacuees still not returning to their homes near Gaza and Lebanon—more than ten percent of the state's territory abandoned and lost for the very first time, the combatants needing physical and mental rehabilitation?[10] Further, 101 hostages taken on October 7 are unaccounted for or continue to be held captive by Palestinian terrorists. A serious reckoning of those culpable for the intelligence failures leading to Hamas's brutal onslaught one year earlier has yet to emerge, several current—and past—leaders in the political and military echelons still not taking responsibility for the consequences that followed.

The sordid responses of world leaders, organizations, and the media to what on October 7 was without question a crime against humanity cannot be overlooked. The UN, UNRWA, the Red Cross, Amnesty International, and the International Court of Justice are all in the dock. So, too, women's organizations who did not condemn the rape and mutilation of Israeli females during the Hamas slaughter and the Black Lives Matter movement's embrace of antisemitism and the pernicious slogan "From Ferguson to Palestine." So, too, universities which sanction under the banner of free speech the calls of students for a *Judenrein* Israel and "Back to Auschwitz." The Hamas-Israel war has made political allies out of some unusual bedfellows, yet the strangest pairing on display is probably "Queers for Palestine," most notably because those stateside protesters would risk summary execution should they take their demonstrations to the Gaza Strip.[11]

The BBC's "deeply worrying pattern of bias against Israel," to quote the findings of a team of researchers headed by British lawyer Trevor Asserson, was matched by several newspapers accepting without hesitation the Hamas and Hezbollah narrative. Mark Memmott, CBS News's senior director of standards, even sent an email to all employees in late August not to report that Jerusalem is part of Israel because of its "disputed" status—"The status of Jerusalem goes to the heart of the Israeli-Palestinian conflict." The Wikipedia site seems to be intentionally trafficking in disinformation related to Jews, Israel, and Zionism.[12]

By October, the *Washington Post* could report that Israel had already received more US military aid worth several billions of dollars than any other country since World War II. Yet the same administration also held back the IDF's entry into Rafah for months, delayed the supply of munitions vital for Israel's defense, and Joe Biden declared in this presidential election year that anti-Israel protesters "have a point." Harris recently lectured Americans on the dangers of "Islamophobia," but no one was going to the streets to beat up Muslims, burn Palestinian flags, or celebrate the slaughter of Arab infants. "Islamophobia" is a made-up concept, writes journalist Lee Smith, "designed to give cover to the terror adjuncts laying waste to American cities and college campuses."[13]

Nor could the sharp rise in antisemitism across the globe, sparked by the war, be dismissed. In the United States alone, almost half (forty-four percent) of Jewish students and recent graduates said they never or rarely felt safe identifying as Jews on their campus, a survey in August by Alums for Campus Fairness (ACF) revealed as the new school year began. Fully eight in ten remarked that they or someone they knew had experienced antisemitic remarks from another student. Sixty percent of the respondents said that either they or someone they know had even received offensive or threatening antisemitic comments from faculty or staff at their educational institutions. Condemning the virulent anti-Israel protests in Washington, D.C., during Netanyahu's last visit, New York Democratic Congressman Ritchie Torres shared a photo of an anti-Israel protester holding up a sign showing a mushroom cloud that said, "Allah is gathering all of the Zionists for a Final Solution." He posted this on X: "The Free Palestine movement is not about freeing Palestinians. It is about pursuing a 'final solution' against the world's only Jewish State, which is home to half of the world's Jewish population." He then added, "When antisemites reveal their antisemitism by calling for a genocide against Jews, believe them."[14]

Holocaust memorials were desecrated. The Block of Women monument in central Berlin, commemorating the non-Jewish women who in 1943 publicly protested against the Nazis when their Jewish husbands and fathers were set to be deported, was sprayed across with pro-Palestinian and antisemitic graffiti, including "Jews are committing genocide" in English. The words "Free Palestine," accompanied by the image of a Palestinian flag, were sprayed on the ground below. Earlier in the summer, a Seattle Holocaust museum was tagged with pro-Palestinian graffiti, and US synagogues defaced with anti-Israel messages. In the Netherlands, a statue of Anne Frank was vandalized with spray paint in July, and in the autumn a mural in Italy honoring Frank was also damaged.[15]

Terrorist plots against Jews living outside of Israel continued to surface. A Paris court in May detained and charged a couple on accusations that they were involved in Iranian plots to kill Israelis and Jews in Germany and France, police sources told Agence France-Presse. Since 2015, "the Iranian [secret] services have resumed a targeted killing policy," the French security agency wrote, adding that "the threat has worsened again in the context of the Israel-Hamas war." Shots were fired near the Israeli consulate in Munich on September 5. No casualties ensued; the attacker was killed by German police. The incident occurred on the anniversary of the summer 1972 Munich Olympics attack, in which eleven Israeli athletes were murdered by Black September Palestinian terrorists. Four days later, the United States and Canada busted a planned terrorist attack on New York's Jewish community that was intended to mark the one-year anniversary of the October 7 attack. Muhammad Shahzeb Khan, a twenty-year-old Pakistani citizen residing in Canada who was charged with acting on behalf of ISIS, was arrested.[16]

The threat of Iran, whose apocalyptic foreign policy aim of world power embodies Jew hatred, did not disappear either. UN atomic watchdog chief Rafael Grossi on May 7 decried "completely unsatisfactory" cooperation from Tehran after returning from a visit to the Islamic Republic, where he urged leaders to adopt "concrete" measures to address concerns over its nuclear program, Agence France-Presse reported. Grossi's visit came at a time of heightened regional tensions and with his International Atomic Energy Agency (IAEA) criticizing Iran for lack of cooperation on inspections and other outstanding issues. One week later, US deputy ambassador to the UN Robert Wood called on Iran to halt its transfer of an "unprecedented" amount of weaponry to Yemen's Houthi rebels, and told the UN Security Council that it should collectively "call Iran out for its destabilizing role and insist that it cannot hide behind the Houthis."[17]

In one of the many homes torched by Hamas on October 7 in the ravaged Kibbutz Be'eri, a singed page with the last seven lines of a poem was found— "*Im yesh et nafshecha la'da'at*" ("If your soul wants to know," 1898). Thinking about Jewry's martyrs over the millennia, Chaim Nahman Bialik, Zionism's first national poet, wrote a phrase that would be repeated years later at the State of Israel's *Yom HaZikaron* (Memorial Day) ceremony: "*u'v'motam tzivu lanu et ha'chayim*" (In their deaths they commanded us to live). Would the grieving nation be worthy of its dead and wounded in this war, of its widows and orphans, a new land sprouting out from what the Israeli journalist Igal Sarna more than twenty years earlier had called "a charred ground zero"?[18]

Israel will not return to the reality of October 6, 2023. An embattled country about half the size of America's Lake Michigan is facing difficult years of a prolonged existential struggle, burdened with memories that are profound, painful, and long-lasting. It is imperative for Israel to be led by a leadership that enjoys the broad trust of the public. Confronting a world where unequivocal moral clarity is often wanting, it cannot say, with Franz Kafka's Hunter Gracchus "My ship has no rudder and no compass and no steering wheel."

Threading the needle, finding harmony, or striking a balance between conflicting domestic forces and interests, will be a formidable challenge for the one Jewish State. At the same time, Golda Meir, who resigned as Israel's prime minister in the wake of the Yom Kippur War, told the *Observer* one year later "Pessimism is a luxury that a Jew can never allow himself."[19] Bloodied but unbowed, the citizenry's resolve strengthened by the remarkable unity which quickly came to the fore within its ranks and those of world Jewry, Israel's resilience, often tested ever since the Zionist enterprise took root, had proven itself once again. Not surprisingly, a refrain commonly heard during the war was "*Am ha-netzach lo mefached mi-derech aruka*" (The eternal people is not afraid of a long way).[20]

Well did Meirav Eilon Shahar, Israel's permanent representative to the UN and International Organizations in Geneva for the last four years, remind her UN listeners about *Kintsugi*. Most people do not purposefully shatter their cherished pieces of pottery, she noted, but that is not always the case in Japanese culture. Adorning broken ceramics with a lacquer mixed with powdered gold is part of a more than 500-year-old Japanese tradition which highlights imperfections rather than hiding them. This not only teaches calm when a cherished piece of pottery breaks; it is a reminder of the beauty of human fragility as well. The fifteenth-century practice of *Kintsugi*, meaning "to join with gold," is a reminder to stay optimistic when things fall apart and to celebrate the flaws and missteps of life. This art not only teaches calm when a cherished piece of pottery breaks; it is a reminder of the beauty of human fragility as well. In this fashion will the State of Israel respond now and in the years to come, she concluded, joining grief and resolve to move forward.[21] Indeed, rabbinic tradition had acknowledged this approach millennia ago, Rav Huna stating in the Babylonian Talmud (*Bava Batra* 14b) that both the tablets which Moses shattered and the second tablets of the Covenant were placed in the Holy Ark.

Resilience rose to the fore. *K'sheh ha-lev bocheh* (When the heart cries), a now classic Israeli song by Sarit Hadad, took on new meaning in post-October 7 Israel with its plea "Make me strong, my God, so I will not be afraid. / The pain is great and there is nowhere to run. / Make it end, I don't have any strength left." Concomitantly, another popular ballad was *ani nish'ar* (I am staying) by the Ma Kashur trio of Assi Israeloff, Tzvika Baruch, and Shalom Michaelshvili, whose opening stanza is this: "It's correct that the situation here isn't brilliant, / There are wall-to-wall problems and mistakes, / And something inside us is slightly broken, / But precisely because of this I'm staying."

Solidarity surfaced quickly. A letter dated June 10, 1939, by Albert Einstein to Miss Sayde Klein of the Veteran Relief, who worked at the Department of

Welfare in New York of behalf of refugees escaping Nazism, was recently auctioned in Los Angeles. Written shortly before the outbreak of World War II, it read: "The power of resistance which has enabled the Jewish people to survive for thousands of years has been based to a large extent on traditions of mutual helpfulness. In these years of affliction our readiness to help one another is being put to an especially severe test. May we stand this test as well as did our fathers before us." "We have no other means of self-defense than our solidarity and our knowledge that the cause for which we are suffering is a momentous and sacred cause," the letter continues. "It must be a source of deep gratification to you to be making so important a contribution toward rescuing our persecuted fellow-Jews from their calamitous peril and leading them toward a better future," Einstein concluded. In like vein, 300,000 young Israelis scrambled on planes eighty-five years later to get home and join in their country's battle for survival, while Jews across the globe sent badly needed military supplies in the critical, first weeks of the war.[22]

Responsibility was manifest. One example among many: Twenty-two-year-old Captain Eitan Yitzhak Oster of Modi'in, the first IDF soldier to be killed in the ongoing ground operation in Lebanon, sent a last recorded message before his death fighting Hezbollah operatives on October 2, 2024: "To my dear family. GK Chesterton once said that 'The true soldier fights not because he hates what is in front of him, but because he loves what is behind him.'" Calling his military mission a "historic opportunity" that he is proud to carry out so that his young nieces and nephews aren't forced to deal with this burden when they grow up, Oster continued: "I embrace and recognize the weight of the responsibility on my shoulders and the responsibility I have for all of the soldiers under my command." In the spirit of Judaism's High Holy Days, the former student at Yeshivat Ohr Torah Stone's Neveh Shmuel High School in Efrat apologized to anyone he might have harmed over the past year and wished his family a good New Year. "Until victory! I love you all," he declared at the end of the video, Editorialized the *Jerusalem Post*: this "now serves as his powerful ethical will and lasting legacy."[23]

Stickers that preserve memories of the IDF fallen and the civilians murdered in this war, posted across the country and the world, became another significant vehicle for passing on their legacy. Some examples: "Sagi Idan, 1999–2024. I have no other land, especially when my land is burning, and if I'm going to die, let it be for our homeland." "As long as someone remembers me, I'm still alive. Hero of Israel, Yogev Aharon, z'l," along with the emblem of the Golani Brigade. Also calls for solidarity: "I did not sacrifice my hand in vain. Let's extend our hands to each other. Eden Bach'ri, a fighter in Combat

Engineering," and at the bottom "Unity now." Another: "It's permissible to disagree. It's forbidden to stop loving. Sergeant Major Shai Biton Hiyun." The last lines tragically read: "In their deaths, they commanded us to unite. Unity now."[24]

"Ein lanu eretz acheret" (We have no other country) became a widespread mantra. Lt. Col. Alim Abdallah, forty years old, the deputy commander of the 300th "Baram" Regional Brigade, was killed in a gun battle along the Lebanon border on October 9, 2023, while he was responding to an infiltration alert. Abdallah, a married father of three, hailed from the northern Druze village of Yanuh-Jat and served in the military for close to twenty-three years. Netanyahu paid a condolence visit at the home of Sheikh Mowafaq Tarif, the Druze community house in the northern Israeli village of Julis. Mona, Alim Abdallah's widow, told the prime minister that she had recently opened her husband's things and found gifts that he had prepared for his soldiers ahead of his discharge, including a Land of Israel medallion upon which the words "I have no other country" were written. "We have no other country," Mona added. "We sacrificed what is most dear to us and it must be made certain that the blood of our soldiers is not in vain." Netanyahu replied, "I came to talk as the prime minister and as a brother, and I will refer to the two foundations of the longstanding partnership between us: A covenant of blood and a covenant of life."[25]

Inclusivity brought change in the Israeli military as well. Recently, the Personnel Directorate of the IDF announced for the first time that the army will recognize soldiers who died of "personal circumstances," such as suicides or non-combat related accidents, as war casualties. According to an article in *Haaretz*, between October 7, 2023, and May 11, 2024, ten soldiers died by suicide. Reports of suicide among the Nova music festival survivors and their families are widespread, although numbers are hard to come by. Listeners of a podcast on Daniel Gordis's "Israel from the Inside" met a woman far from the headlines who took a classically Israeli step, turning her grief at the loss of her own brother from suicide, years ago, into a drive to create a new organization designed to help those contemplating suicide. Gal Nissim-Emanuel is not backed by the government, or any large organization. "Her drive," Gordis added, "is fueled by grief and grit, nothing more."[26]

The Israel Defense Ministry also approved a request by bereaved families to include religious phrases on the headstones of fallen soldiers. The decision followed a complaint by a bereaved family member and a public outcry over the ministry's initial refusal to include "*hy'd*" (*HaShem yikom damo/dama*), the three-letter Hebrew acronym for "may God avenge his/her blood," on the stones. A committee established by Defense Minister Yoav Gallant recommended allowing the acronym, which had heretofore not been allowed on military graves, as well as the commonly used abbreviation for "z'l" (of blessed memory). The issue was first raised by the Chabad Hassidic family of Cpt. Yisrael Yudkin, who was killed in Gaza on May 22, 2024. Yudkin had served in the ultra-Orthodox Netzach Yehuda Battalion, but his family said this was not a religious issue. "This is not a haredi custom, it's one that has been an idea in Judaism for thousands of years. It can't be that, in the State of Israel, we're not allowed to include this on a grave," his mother, Tzipi, said. After the IDF decision to let family members decide, she declared "It's one less burden in our grief for our son."[27]

Different ways have been found to contend with the October 7 tsunami of radical jihadist evil. Michal Zemora, widow of thirty-six Yamam (National Counter-Terrorism Unit) commander Arnon, who died during the successful mission to rescue four hostages from central Gaza on June 8, 2024, expanded her tailor-made books for families helping young children through challenging transitions to books with such titles as "My Father/Mother Is in the Reserves" and "A Story for Children Who Lost a Parent in Battle," Recently, she posted this on her page: "Dear Customers: Due to the load, we cannot accept additional orders at the moment." Memoirs and books of poetry and prayer continue to appear. Tablet offers a collection "Hamas's War on Israel," while the National Library of Israel has created "Bearing Witness," gathering and recording for posterity Jewry's collective voice on the war. The research project "Jewish Responses to October 7," led by Dr. Adi Sherzer, is a joint project of the Melton Centre for Jewish Education, the "Ideas and Cultural Codes" research group led by Ben-Gurion University Professor Arieh Saposnik, and the Israel Movement for Reform and Progressive Judaism. A letter from 500 Jews at Columbia University in praise of Israel, wrote legendary Soviet refusenik Natan Sharansky, "may be a landmark in the struggle to escape a stifling regime of doublethink and ensure the American Jewish future through proud and open dissent."[28]

Remarkably, even though the Hamas-Israel war had not loosened its death choke on the country, 31,000 new immigrants arrived to live in Israel (*aliya* in Hebrew) from more than 100 countries during the past Jewish calendar year, most from the West, the Ministry of Immigration and Absorption announced at the end of September 2024. The number of *olim* from Russia and Ukraine remained high, following the war between these countries and the strengthening of Russia's authoritarian government. There was an increase of close to 355 percent in the opening of *aliya* cases from France, with more than 5,500 new cases opened since the outbreak of the war, compared to about 1,200 in the corresponding period last year.

More than 6,000 people from the United States opened *aliya* files in that timespan, a 62 percent increase compared to the same period last year. Canada also recorded an 87 percent spike in the number of people opening *aliya* cases, with more than 800 Jews expressing their desire to immigrate to Israel. In the United Kingdom, a similar number of immigration cases were opened in recent months, with an increase of 63 percent. Close to one-third (31 percent) of this year's *olim* were young people aged 18–35.[29]

Moreover, despite its ongoing war with Hamas and escalating tensions with Lebanese Hezbollah, Israel has been ranked as the second-best country in the world for retirement, according to a new study by Confidence Club. The company based in the United Kingdom, dedicated to helping retirees, released its "Aging Gracefully Index," which examined thirty-nine countries for this study. Information was drawn from economic data of the Organization for Economic Development and Cooperation and the cost-of-living database known as Numbeo, among other sources, to assign scores to and rank each country. Israel came in second place, receiving a score of 85, which was only bested by Iceland's total score of 87. Finland, the Netherlands, and Switzerland rounded out the top five. South Africa ranked last with a score of 43, slightly edging out Greece, Latvia, Slovakia, and Italy for the other bottom-five countries in descending order.[30]

Still, numerous questions remain to be answered for a country always beset by enemies committed to its extinction. The Chinese term for crisis, or *weiji*, is made up of the characters for danger (*wei*) and for opportunity (*ji*). Israel faces a period of great danger but also one pregnant with opportunity for a new, dynamic path. Can the moment be seized? Will the traumas of war endure? Can the "start-up nation" fully restore its deterrence power, the IDF realizing soon after the Hamas slaughter erupted that surveillance technology cannot become a substitute for strategy, initiative, and foresight, and regain regional preeminence? One recalls Golda Meir's comment to the young Senator Joe Biden of Delaware some five weeks before what would be the near calamitous 1973 Yom Kippur War, words President Biden quoted when he visited Israel soon after October 7, 2023: "Our secret weapon is that we have nowhere else to go." The indomitable spirit of personal sacrifice and professional ability exhibited throughout the war by young IDF soldiers and reservists strongly reflects Meir's belief. Can these continue to contend ably and triumph in a world where, to cite W. B. Yeats's pessimistic lines in the aftermath of World War I, "The blood-dimmed tide is loosed, and everywhere / The ceremony of innocence is drowned; / The best lack all conviction, while the worst / Are full of passionate intensity"?[31]

Can the extraordinary unity of Israel's 7.3 million Jews in the face of grave danger be maintained, or will polarization and division resurface within their ranks after the guns are silent? What of the 8.5 million Jews living outside of Israel, including 6.3 million in the United States, hitherto embracing a liberal, universalist conviction that runs counter to the Jewish State's insistence on a particularist reality?[32] What of the strident antisemitism that quickly swept across the planet once the IDF went on a successful counterattack against Hamas, Hezbollah, and Iran, followed by increasing numbers of Palestinian dead and wounded?

Numerous other questions arise. When and how will this bloody conflict end? Is meaningful peace between Israel and all of its neighbors a pipe dream? Is any two-state solution viable that might satisfy both Israelis and Palestinians? Are there prominent Muslim voices who could endorse the affirmation in June 2024 of the Ontario-based Council of Muslims Against Antisemitism (CMAA), expressing solidarity with the Jewish community and condemning both Hamas and the Iranian IRGC in an advertisement taken out in the *National Post* under the headline "Not in the Name of Islam"? Can long-standing Arab adversaries concede that Jews are the only people for whom Eretz Israel was their ancestral homeland and their national kingdom, acknowledging, too, the archeological discovery one month later of a massive moat that was used to fortify and protect the Temple Mount and the king's palace in biblical-era Jerusalem?[33] What of a devastated Gaza's future and that of Lebanon, where the atmosphere is understandably heavy with loss and disappointment, like overcast skies on a cold and bitter day? Will Iran, now partnered in its Axis of Resistance with fellow-dictatorships China, Russia, and North Korea, remain a serious threat to Israel's existence? Might the imminent election of a new US president alter the tormented face of the Middle East?

At this fraught moment but one also laden with promise, the author must resort to the same concluding observation of this book's predecessor, a study of the first six months of the war:[34] **The final narrative has yet to be told.**

Endnotes

1 Yonah Jeremy Bob, "Israel is Winning the War if You Ignore Original Unrealistic Goals Set by the Gov't—Analysis," *Jerusalem Post*, May 6, 2024.
2 Israel National News, June 15, 2024.
3 JNS, May 31, 2024. In September, a high-ranking delegation of former NATO military officers was in Israel on a fact-finding mission to assess the conduct of the IDF in the war against Hamas in the Gaza Strip. Gen. Sir John McColl, the British former Deputy Supreme Allied Commander of NATO, spoke for group when saying "I came away from the trip satisfied that

the IDF's operations and rules of engagement were rigorous compared to the British Army and our Western allies . . . Israeli soldiers are fighting in conditions of extraordinary complexity and risk." This was a sharp if tacit rebuke to Britain's Starmer administration, which had recently announced a partial arms embargo on Israel. Melanie Phillips, "The Media War Against Israel," Israelunwired, Sept. 15, 2024.

4 *Jerusalem Post*, July 15, 2024. The Hamas-run Gaza Ministry of Health cannot provide names of more than 10,000 of the 34,000 it says have died during the war with Israel, the Foundation for the Defense of Democracies reported. "While the Health Ministry conceded earlier this month that it has 'incomplete data' for nearly one-third of the deceased, this is the first admission that it lacks an essential data point necessary to establish these deaths have even taken place," the Washington-based think tank noted. JNS, May 5, 2024.

5 World Israel News, July 6, 2024; Sept. 15, 2024; *Jerusalem Post*, July 12, 2024.

6 JNS, June 21, 2024.

7 Israel National News, Oct. 7, 2024.

8 World Israel News, Aug. 2, 2024; Anadolu Ajansi, Aug. 5, 2024; CTV News, Sept. 28, 2024; *Times of Israel*, Sept. 19, 2024. Also see Hussein Aboubakr, "Hamas's Messianic Violence," Mosaic, Oct. 10, 2023; Diana Bletter, "For the Southern Lebanese Generation, Nasrallah's death is a 'Breakthrough,'" *Times of Israel*, Oct. 10, 2024; Robin Wright. "What Israel's Assassination of Hezbollah's Leader Means for the Middle East," *New Yorker*, Sept. 28, 2024.

9 *New York Times*, Sept. 30, 2024.

10 "Reflections on October 7," *Tablet*, Oct. 7, 2023; *Tablet*, July 11, 2024. The number of patients at medical rehabilitation centers across Israel had risen dramatically since October 7, according to data presented at a Knesset panel. According to the data, 17,825 people were treated at centers in the first three months after the Hamas massacre—more than three times the total number of patients treated in 2022. *Haaretz*, May 29, 2024. Also see Shlomo Fischer, "Religious Zionists against the Land of Israel—Opinion," *Jerusalem Post*, July 18, 2024.

11 *Jerusalem Post*, Sept. 8, 2024; When it comes to "Queers for Palestine," what is richly ironic is that many LGBT Palestinians seek asylum in Israel—the same country these protesters are rallying against. Billy Binion, "The Contradictions of 'Queers for Palestine,'" *Reason*, Oct. 27, 2023. Just before departing the UN as Israel's permanent representative for the last four years, Gilad Erdan posted a video of the exhibit. at the UN visitors' entrance, on terrorism across the globe including 9/11, Boston, Indonesia, Kenya, and others. Past terrorist attacks by Palestinians against Israelis were not given; Hamas's genocidal attack on October 7, 2023, against Israel's southern communities near the Gaza Strip went unmentioned. A terrorist act on a Palestinian woman was featured, the event taking place in 2019—in New Zealand. "There is no place more corrupt and morally twisted than the UN," Erdan concluded. AIJAC, Aug. 21, 2024, https://youtu.be/JkM32r29-DU?feature=shared.

12 *New York Post*, Oct. 10, 2024; Izabella Tabarovsky, "Wikipedia's Jewish Problem," *Tablet*, July 25, 2024. Also see Ohad Merlin, "Wikipedia in Arabic: A Hotbed for Bigotry, Misinformation, and Bias—Investigative Report," *Jerusalem Post*, Nov. 3, 2024. The BBC sparked controversy once again with its recent airing of an acclaimed documentary chronicling Hamas's devastating October 7 attack on the Israeli Nova music festival. In the original *Surviving October 7: We will Dance Again* aired in America and around the world, the opening title states "The IDF says that 3,000 terrorists breached the forty-mile-long border. . . ." However, the word "terrorists" does not appear in the BBC program. World Israel News, Sept. 2, 2024.

13 *Washington Post*, Oct. 15, 2024; David M. Weinberg, "Do 'They' Have a Point?," *Jerusalem Post*, Aug. 23, 2024; Lee Smith, "He the People," *Tablet*, July 30, 2024. Critics have observed that US President Barack Obama fundamentally reshaped the Democratic Party when he struck the 2015 deal legalizing the nuclear weapons program of Hamas's sponsor, Iran. By legitimizing Tehran, Obama "sidelined" the Jews and other centrists and made the progressive, anti-Israel faction the party's new center of gravity. The Obama White House also allowed UN Security Council resolution 2334, declaring that the Israeli settlements in "Palestinian

territories occupied since 1967, including East Jerusalem," constituted a flagrant violation of international law, to pass by abstaining in the vote on December 23, 2016, which passed 14–0. And see Caroline Glick, "Trump's Rhetoric vs. Harris's Policies," JNS, Aug. 11, 2024. Israel changed its plans for a Rafah offensive, thus avoiding Biden's "red line," because of pressure applied by the United States as far back as March 2024, the *Wall Street Journal* reported. Two IDF divisions were meant to sweep through the city, but after an intensive discussion with US officials, the offensive's focus shifted to establishing a military presence along the Egypt-Gaza border together with smaller raids on the southern Gazan city. *Wall St. Journal*, June 2, 2024. Also see Michael Oren, "Israel is Losing the North," *Times of Israel*, July 11, 2024.

14 United with Israel, Aug. 28, 2024; World Israel News, July 26, 2024.
15 JTA, Aug. 30, 2024.
16 *Times of Israel*, Sept. 9, 2024; Israel National News, Sept. 5, 2024; "Pakistani National Charged for Plotting Terrorist Attack in New York City in Support of ISIS," US Department of Justice, Sept. 9, 2024, https://www.justice.gov/opa/pr/pakistani-national-charged-plotting-terrorist-attack-new-york-city-support-isis.
17 Israel National News, May 8, 2024; *Haaretz*, May 14, 2024.
18 National Library of Israel website, July 17, 2024; Igal Sarna, *The Man Who Fell into a Puddle* (New York: Random House, 2002), Preface, x.
19 *Observer*, Dec. 29, 1974.
20 Another popular song in this vein is Eyal Golan's *Am Yisrael chai!* (The Jewish people lives!), which is commonly referred to by the words that repeat, "*Am ha-netzach l'olam lo mefached*"—"the eternal nation is never afraid."
21 AIJAC, Oct. 9, 2024, https://youtu.be/KG2uTe5gs3g?si=UuBfrSxtJ2iUgSW6.
22 JNS, July 22, 2024. In this regard, the Israel Bonds organization said it sold more than $3 billion in bonds since October 7, nearly three times its normal annual total. *Forward*, May 15, 2024.
23 *Jerusalem Post* editorial, Oct. 6, 2024.
24 Daniel Gordis, "Israel from Inside," June 17–18, 2024; Hodaya Karish-Hazoni, "Mabat chadash al ha-merchav ha-tziburi," *Makor Rishon, D'yokan*, Oct. 23, 2024.
25 *Times of Israel*, Oct. 22, 2023; Israel National News, July 15, 2024.
26 Daniel Gordis, "Israel from the Inside," Sept. 16, 2024. In this connection, an Israeli medical study found a correlation between so-called "broken heart syndrome" and national trauma, showing a 100 percent increase of cases since October 7, 2023. The research, the first of its kind, was presented earlier this month at Israel's Cardiology Association Conference. *Jerusalem Post*, June 16, 2024.
27 JNS, July 8, 2024.
28 Daniel Gordis, "Israel from the Inside," July 18, 2024; Jenna Romano, "Inscribing the Oct. 7 Collective Memory," *Jerusalem Post, In Jerusalem*, Oct. 25, 2024; Natan Sharansky, "The 500," *Tablet*, May 26, 2024, and see the Appendices; Lee Yaron, *10/7: 100 Human Stories* (New York: St. Martin's Press, 2024); Amir Tibon, *The Gates of Gaza: A Story of Betrayal, Survival, and Hope in Israel's Borderlands* (New York: Little, Brown and Co., 2024); R. Korazim, M. Bohnen, and H. Silverman, eds. and trans., *Shiva, Poems of October 7* (New York: Institute for Jewish Research and Publications, 2024); S. L. Sheps, R. S. Danziger, and A. Gordon, eds., *Az Nashir, We will Sing Again* (Jerusalem: The Layers Press, 2024). Tamar Biale of Jerusalem has a podcast featuring *midrashim* by women responding to the war. The *Times of Israel* website offers "Picture This," an English-subtitled video series of powerful interviews with October 7 survivors, produced by Israel's national broadcaster, Kan, in partnership with ChaiFlicks, the leading Jewish streaming platform.
29 *Jerusalem Post*, Sept. 3, 2024. The largest numbers came from Russia (19,850), and over 3,340 came from the United States and Canada, with support from Nefesh B'Nefesh. World Israel News, Sept. 29, 2024. For other examples, see Bret Stephens, "The Genius of Israel, Even Still," *Commentary*, Dec. 2023.

30 *Algemeiner*, June 19, 2024.
31 "The Second Coming" is a poem written by the famed Irish poet in 1919, first printed in the *Dial* in November 1920, depicting a world in disarray with a sense of approaching catastrophe and the breakdown of established order.
32 Daniel Gordis, *We Stand Divided: The Rift between American Jews and Israel* (New York: HarperCollins Publishers, 2019). The rift between those Israelis calling for the release of hostages now—even at the cost of a cease-fire or stopping the war—and those calling for fighting on until victory surfaced early on. One example of the latter was a strong statement by Hagai Lober, whose son Yonatan was killed in Gaza, addressed to the hostage families who sought to intensify the protests against the government, *Yisrael Hayom*, July 10, 2024. Also see Liel Liebowitz, "'Bring Them Home' is Bringing Us to the Brink," *Tablet*, Sept. 3, 2024.
33 *Jerusalem Post*, June 23, 2024; *Times of Israel*, July 21, 2024.
34 Monty Noam Penkower, *Awakening to Radical Islamist Evil: The Hamas War against Israel and the Jews* (New York: Touro University Press, 2024), Conclusion.

Appendices

1. "In Our Name: A Message from Jewish Students at Columbia University," May 8, 2024

Over 600 Jewish students at Columbia published this open letter to the Columbia community, which was posted by Prof. Shai Avidai on X.

We proudly believe in the Jewish People's right to self-determination in our historic homeland as a fundamental tenet of our Jewish identity. Contrary to what many have tried to sell you—no, Judaism cannot be separated from Israel. Zionism is, simply put, the manifestation of that belief. Our religious texts are replete with references to Israel, Zion, and Jerusalem. The land of Israel is filled with archaeological remnants of a Jewish presence spanning centuries. Yet, despite generations of living in exile and diaspora across the globe, the Jewish People never ceased dreaming of returning to our homeland—Judea, the very place from which we derive our name, "Jews." Indeed just a couple of days ago, we all closed our Passover seders with the proclamation, "Next Year in Jerusalem!" We connect to Israel not only as our ancestral homeland but as the only place in the modern world where Jews can safely take ownership of their own destiny. Our experiences at Columbia in the last six months are a poignant reminder of just that.

We were raised on stories from our grandparents of concentration camps, gas chambers, and ethnic cleansing.

The evil irony of today's antisemitism is a twisted reversal of our Holocaust legacy; protestors on campus have dehumanized us, imposing upon us the characterization of the "white colonizer." We have been told that we are "the oppressors of all brown people" and that "the Holocaust wasn't special." Students at Columbia have chanted "we don't want no Zionists here," alongside "death to the Zionist State" and to "go back to Poland," where our relatives lie in mass graves.

This sick distortion illuminates the nature of antisemitism: In every generation, the Jewish People are blamed and scapegoated as responsible for the societal evil of the time. In Iran and in the Arab world, we were ethnically cleansed for our presumed ties to the "Zionist entity." In Russia, we endured state-sponsored violence and were ultimately massacred for being capitalists. In Europe, we were the victims of genocide because we were communists and not European enough. And today, we face the accusation of being too European, painted as society's worst evils—colonizers and oppressors. We are targeted for our belief that Israel, our ancestral and religious homeland, has a right to exist. We are targeted by those who misuse the word Zionist as a sanitized slur for Jew, synonymous with racist, oppressive, or genocidal. We know all too well that antisemitism is shapeshifting.

We are proud of Israel. The only democracy in the Middle East, Israel is home to millions of Mizrachi Jews (Jews of Middle Eastern descent), Ashkenazi Jews (Jews of Central and Eastern European descent), and Ethiopian Jews, as well as millions of Arab Israelis, over one million Muslims, and hundreds of thousands of Christians and Druze. Israel is nothing short of a miracle for the Jewish People and for the Middle East more broadly.

Our love for Israel does not necessitate blind political conformity. It's quite the opposite. For many of us it is our deep love for and commitment to Israel that pushes us to object when its government acts in ways we find problematic. Israeli political disagreement is an inherently Zionist activity; look no further than the protests against Netanyahu's judicial reforms—from New York to Tel Aviv—to understand what it means to fight for the Israel we imagine. Yet we all come from a place of love and an aspiration for a better future for Israelis and Palestinians alike. We came to Columbia because we wanted to expand our minds and engage in complex conversations. While campus may be riddled with hateful rhetoric and simplistic binaries now, it is never too late to start repairing the fractures and begin developing meaningful relationships across political and religious divides. Our tradition tells us, "Love peace and pursue peace." We hope you will join us in earnestly pursuing peace, truth, and empathy. Together we can repair our campus.

2. President Isaac Herzog's address at the annual ceremony at the Western Wall in Jerusalem marking the beginning of Israel's Memorial Day for its fallen soldiers on May 12, 2024

Ministry of Foreign Affairs, May 12, 2022, www.gov.il

Every year, after the sounding of the Shofar, there reigns here in the expanse of the Western Wall Plaza a sacred, special silence, preserved only for this moment of the year. But tonight, we have no peace, and there is no silence. Because this year is not like any other year. This year, in addition to the mourning siren that commemorates our fallen since the beginning of our struggle, a new, prolonged, continuous siren has been added. A siren that began at 6:29 in the morning of the terrible national disaster on October 7, at the height of the joyous holiday of Simchat Torah. And it has continued alongside us ever since. A cry, sharp, piercing. The cry of a nation, the cry of national mourning. "My God, my God, my soul laments, cry out Daughter of Israel, eulogise and weep bitterly. Israel has been devoured by fire."

I stand here, next to the remnants of our Temple, in torn garments. This tearing—a symbol of Jewish mourning, it is a symbol of the mourning and sorrow of an entire people in this year—a year of national mourning. A symbol of a blood drenched rend in the heart of the people. A tear in the heart of the State of Israel—shattered, bereaved, crying bitter tears, refusing to be comforted for its sons and daughters—soldiers and civilians, civilians and soldiers. Our voices do not refrain from weeping, and our eyes from shedding tears. A great tragedy has befallen us.

I turn from here, in this holy moment, to our brothers and sisters held hostage, and to their families: throughout these national days, we never forget that there is no greater commandment than redeeming captives. The entire nation is with you. We must summon courage and choose life. Not to rest and not to be quiet until they all return home.

Beloved and dear families, those wounded in Israel's battles against its enemies, the Defense Minister, the Chief of Staff and the heads of the security forces, ministers and Knesset members, former President of Israel, Rabbis, Mayor of Jerusalem, ambassadors and diplomats, heads of the representative organizations of the bereaved families, citizens of Israel.

A year ago, I spoke here about Section 9 of Area A in the Mount Herzl National Cemetery—the section of fallen from the War of Independence. Since then, between last Memorial Day and this Memorial Day, the graves on the mountain have increased—one hundred and thirty new graves; and hundreds more graves have been added throughout the country—changing its face. Our face. The pain strikes with force. Just a few hours ago, we brought five of our beloved to their eternal rest. "From Dan to Beersheba, from Gilgal to the sea, no spot of our land has been atoned for without blood."

A few nights ago, I ascended once again to Mount Herzl. I found myself walking among the graves, in grateful recognition and sacred awe. I felt with unusual intensity the intergenerational connection among the resting places. A connection of longing and heroism, of pain and resilience. A connection of a fighting spirit—"from generation to generation." A connection between the fallen of the Yom Kippur War, in the Lebanon and Metula, in Givat Hatachmoshet, in Sinai and the Golan Heights, in Beaufort, in Bint Jbeil, in the many battlefields, in intelligence and combat operations, and in the victims of terror since the dawn of Zionism and from there to the new and numerous graves on Mount Herzl—which have been added to and unfortunately continue to be added to—in sections—yes, many sections—of this heavy, heavy campaign.

Believe me, my sisters and brothers, I would—with all my heart—like to tell about each and every one of our fallen loved ones—from all of Israel's wars, from all the security forces, from all over the country. About their goodness, their beauty, their bravery. But the fracture is so great, and our losses are too many, too many indeed. And so, I stand here, in my mind's eye what a grieving father said to me a few weeks ago: "I hear they're talking about one of the fallen sons, and I feel as if they're talking about my son." That's what he said. Therefore, in my words tonight, I, in humble supplication, ask to return with you to that same night-time visit to Mount Herzl, to kindle candles of remembrance, and tell a few stories, a few—of some of this year's fallen. Each one of them represents in some way the eternal figure of all the fallen of Israel's wars and hostile actions against us. Each one of them—a mirror of thousands of stories. We will remember, and love, and cherish in our hearts—all of them, all of them.

"My soldiers are there and I need to be there," Brigade Commander Col. Yehonatan Steinberg said to his wife, on the morning of October 7. Yoni, the commander of the Nahal Brigade, encountered terrorists on his way south. He was killed fighting courageously and was buried in the new section on Mount Herzl. "The greatest thing one can do is to protect the people of Israel," Yoni left recorded words for his son. Right next to him, I see the grave of Col. Roi Levy, 44, commander of the Multidomain Unit. Roi, who was seriously injured in Operation Protective Edge, recovered, returned to combat, and even got engaged on Israel's 70th Independence Day.

On that black Saturday morning, he left, like Yoni, from his home, and headed to Kibbutz Re'im. He fought against the enemy until he was shot and killed. Yoni and Roi are examples of commanders leading from the front, like pillars of fire before the camp. When I saw their graves side by side, I could not help but think of so many heroic commanders we lost in Israel's wars. Commanders who stormed the front lines and paid the terrible price.

And there, not far from them, lies the grave of Eitan Hadad, a member of the pre-military academy from Kibbutz Be'eri where he grew up and lived.

He is now also buried on the mountain. I stand there—in the darkness of the night, in the heart of the mountain—and reflect with astonishment on the long hours of heroic battles in all the towns and communities of the western Negev. Incredible civilian heroism. About all the members of the pre-military academies. About the commanders, lieutenants, and ordinary citizens who leaped into the heart of battle, with real courage, and fought—sometimes alone—on the front line, until the last bullet.

Hundreds fell on October 7th and throughout the entire campaign. And in the spirit of the prayer "Unetaneh Tokef" recited on Yom Kippur—a few days before the terrible disaster—we gather on this Memorial Day to remember all the victims and fallen—civilians and soldiers who perished: some by fire and some by suffocation, some by sword and some by beast. Some at the doorstep of their home, and some in armored personnel carriers, some in the warmth of their bed and some in the streets, some at a guardpost and some in the battlefield, some at a bus stop and some at a police station. Some in a car and some in an armored vehicle, some on the kibbutz pathways, some in the pasture and some at a party, some in the shopping mall and some in missiles and rockets, some in tunnels, and some in hiding. Forever, forever we remember them.

"Generations dreamed of reaching Jerusalem; we have the honor of defending it," said Bella Levin a year ago—a combatant from the Border Police and a lone soldier. On that black Saturday morning, Bella participated in defending Kibbutz Sa'ad. A month later, she fell when fighting a terrorist in the Old City of Jerusalem. The police section of the Mount Herzl cemetery where Bella is buried, is a section of courage, dedication, and heroism—the essence of the Israeli police force, both men and women. I see Bella's grave—and remember all those brave women, soldiers, and police officers, observers, fighters, and commanders, the heroines of Israel—who sacrificed themselves, stood guard, saved lives, and paid with their lives. And like Bella, in the Heroism Section of our Mount, there are so many immigrants from the Diaspora and so many lone soldiers. Heroes who embarked on a journey from their homeland to the homeland, and took part in "the great campaign to fulfill the aspirations of the generations for the redemption of Israel." And now they are buried among the hills in the sacred ground of Mount Herzl, and throughout the country.

"The loved ones have carried us without words," and now grief carries us—and breathes a spirit of battle on the front line and beyond. For example, among the fallen heroes are Major General of Golani, Lieutenant Colonel Tomer Greenberg, a native of Kfar Saba and a man of the Jordan Valley communities, whose grave I see on Mount Herzl; and Major General Sharion, Lt. Col. Salman Habaka, buried near his home in the Druze village of Yanuh-Jat. On the

October 7, both of them, Salman and Tomer, fought bravely in the kibbutzim—Tomer in Kfar Aza and Nahal Oz, and Salman in Be'eri. Both fell in battles in the Gaza Strip. "This is Salman, I'm here . . . Can I help you evacuate urgently?" Salman's voice was heard moments before he fell. "Cover me with fire," Tomer requested from him. This grief is a covenant—an Israeli covenant. A covenant that transcends faiths and religions, perceptions, and ideologies. I cry out here the cry of the Druze and Bedouin bereaved families: who demanded from me and demand from all of us to recognize the right and the privilege to be part of the Israeli story—equal among equals, in the fullest sense of the word.

Every name is a shattered world. Every name is a sacrifice. A void that will never be filled. Here is the grave of Lavi Lifschitz from Modi'in, who did not want, in his words, to be "an animal of war," and not far from him—on the same mountain of memory—the grave of Oriya Ayimalk Goshen, born into a dedicated Zionist family that immigrated from Ethiopia; and Roi Daoui of Jerusalem—who enlisted in Givati following Liel Gidoni—who fell in Operation Protective Edge and is also buried on Mount Herzl. The three of them, Roi, Oriya, and Liel—and so many other fallen—"worldly heroes, with smiles of angels," left behind final words, including one directive: to smile. Just smile.

And there are moments—there, in the new plots—where one's breath is taken away, and one's heart shattered to pieces. Grave next to grave. Noam and Yishai Slutzky. On October 7, the Slutzky brothers left their wives and children, and although no one commanded of them—hurried to come and fight in Kibbutz Alumim. Together they stormed and killed dozens of terrorists. Together they fell in battle. "The beautiful and the pleasant in their lives and in their deaths is that they were not separated." I see their graves and think of so many families that have lost more than one loved one. Of worlds that have been destroyed again and again. And the letters of the verse float in the air—on Mount Herzl, and throughout the land: "Why should you also be cut off, both of you in one day."

If I could stand here tonight and tell the story of each and every one of our fallen, this year, and over the years, I would. And reluctantly, in pain, I would speak of their portion. Because behind every story, and every candle, burn immense flames of heroism, strength, life, and many more.

Citizens of Israel, at this sacred moment, I remind us and the entire world: we never wanted nor chose this terrible war. Not this one nor its predecessors. All we wanted was to return to Zion from which we were forcibly expelled, and to renew our freedom there—in a Jewish and democratic state. To build a life here. A future. A hope. We always dreamed of peace and good neighborliness with all the peoples and countries in the region, and no less than that forever. But as long as our enemies seek to destroy us, we will not lay down our sword.

The past few months have been very painful. But in them, we learned about the strength of a wonderful and awe-inspiring people, who rose from the terrible destruction and fought as lions. We discovered fighters—of the IDF and the security forces, aged 18 to 96; in all branches, on all fronts—in the south, in the north, in Judea and Samaria, and in every place. They, who endanger themselves for us, ask simply at all times—that we remember that we are one people. That we be worthy. Only be worthy.

This tear in the fabric, the bleeding rend that we all feel in our hearts this year, cannot remain meaningless. The bereaved families tell me this again and again. The tear in the heart of the people must heal the tear in the nation. This rend is also a call and a cry. A call to action, a call to rise up. Rise up as one people.

From here, I pray for the swift and full recovery of all the wounded, in body and soul. We must support them and their families in the difficult and painful battles for rehabilitation, and in treating their wounds—physical and psychological. I offer strength and embrace—on behalf of all of us—the women and men of the IDF—soldiers and reservists who left everything behind and went to the front lines for long months. I offer strength and embrace—on behalf of all of us—the police, the Border Police, the ISA, the Mossad, the Prison Service, the intelligence units, and all the security forces and internal security—the firefighters, the emergency and rescue services. I thank them and their families, who sacrifice so much for the sake of the country. The right to defend the security of Israel, the right to serve in the IDF—is a tremendous right. It is not a privilege. It is a right. A tremendous one. A sacred right. May the Lord keep them from now and forever.

Bereaved families, beloved and dear. On behalf of the entire people, I am grateful to you. I bow my head in the face of your loss and your courage, and pray that days of light and grace, of comfort, and even joy, will come upon you. We draw so much faith and hope from you.

Two months before Yishai Slutzky fell, his first daughter was born, and her name: Shachar Be'eri. Now the name of the little baby girl has taken on a new meaning. "A new dawn will rise over Kibbutz Beeri and all the surrounding communities," said Rabbi Shmuel Slutzky—the father of Yishai and Noam—who is here with us today. And beside the grave of his beloved sons on Mount Herzl, added, "The name "Shachar Be'eri" expresses the hope that we will not be destroyed and ruined."

People of Israel, my sisters and brothers. Even today, deeply within the national mourning, I know, I believe with all my heart: a new dawn will rise over all of Israel. By their merit, for their sake, and for ours. May the memory of the fallen of the Israel Defense Forces and victims of enemy hostility against us, be preserved in the heart of our nation for generations to come.

3. *Kinot* for Tish'a B'Av 5784 (August 13, 2024)

A Lament for Be'eri
By Yagel Harush
Translated by Sara Daniel

Eicha
How did Be'eri / turn into my tomb
The day of my light / to the day of my gloom
Its songs silenced / trampled fruit and leaf
My eyes well with tears / from the depth of my grief

Eicha
How did the Torah / arranged and arrayed
In all her glory / not rush to their aid
On the day of her beauty / my countenance stained
My eyes well with tears / from the depth of my pain

Eicha
How could Yisrael / when they call out to God
Asking for life / receive nothing but blood
Elder and child / till their blood overflow
Their joy violated / by bloodthirsty foe
My eyes well with tears / from the depth of my woe

Eicha
How could mothers and daughters / torn from their home
Be led away, blood-soaked / like days of pogrom
Our dancing has ceased / our bodies are numb
Their fences breached / dragged through the dirt
My eyes well with tears / from the depth of my hurt

Eicha
How we stagger and reel / Creator Above
For how long can a nation / bleed with love
Rise up now, shine forth / we will dance again
In Your great mercy / please heal our pain
Heal our hearts / dispel our fears
Let us water Be'eri / from the well of our tears

4. Statement on the Execution of Hostages by Hamas Terrorists

Issued by the Global Imams' Council (GIC) at the Islamic Seminary of Najaf, Iraq, Sept. 1, 2024, https://imams.org/gic-statement-on-the-execution-of-hostages-by-hamas-terrorists/.

In the name of God, the Most Compassionate, the Most Merciful.
The Global Imams Council condemns in the strongest possible terms the barbaric actions of Hamas, which have resulted in the brutal execution of six innocent hostages, among them a dual American citizen, Hersh Goldberg-Polin, in a tunnel in the Gaza city of Rafah. We are deeply saddened and outraged by these heinous murders, which violate all principles of humanity, religious teachings, and international law.

The targeting and brutalization of civilians, especially those who are defenseless and held against their will, are acts of unmitigated evil. These actions represent a gross violation of the sacred laws of conflict as ordained by all major faith traditions, including Islam, which categorically prohibit the harming of innocents. Furthermore, these atrocities contravene international humanitarian laws, including the Geneva Conventions, which are designed to protect civilians during times of war.

We hold Hamas directly responsible for the deaths and suffering of all innocent lives lost since October 7, as their actions have not only brought death and destruction upon the region but have also led to immense suffering for the Palestinian people. Hamas's reckless and inhumane tactics, using civilians as shields and exploiting their plight, have only escalated the cycle of violence and undermined the cause of justice and peace.

Moreover, we recognize that the regime in Iran shares equal responsibility for these tragedies, as its continued support and endorsement of Hamas's actions perpetuate violence and instability in the region.

We stand with all victims of this conflict, regardless of nationality, ethnicity, or religion, and we extend our deepest condolences to their families. Our prayers are with those who have lost loved ones and with those still living under the shadow of fear and uncertainty. It is our hope and prayer that justice will prevail and that the dignity and sanctity of human life will be upheld above all else.

We call upon the international community, all religious leaders, and people of conscience to unite against these acts of terror and to work tirelessly towards a future where peace, justice, and respect for all human life are the foundations of our shared existence.

May God guide us to a path of peace and grant solace to the hearts of the bereaved.

5. Rachel Goldberg-Polin, eulogy for her son Hersh at his funeral in Jerusalem on September 2, 2024

Times of Israel, Sept. 3, 2024

I have had a lot of time during the past 332 days to think about my sweet boy, my Hersh.

And one thing I keep thinking about is how out of all the mothers in the world, God chose to give Hersh to me. What must I have done in a past life to deserve such a beautiful gift? It must have been glorious.

Hersh and I watched some documentaries a couple of years ago together about young people who had died and he said, "How come everyone who dies young is always said to be, the funniest, the smartest, greatest, the handsomest? Why doesn't anyone ever say, 'I liked Max, but you know what? He was pretty stupid, his sense of humor was off and had bad breath?"

I am honest. And I say, it is not that Hersh was perfect. But, he was the perfect son for me. And I am so grateful to God, and I want to do *hakarat hatov* and thank God right now, for giving me this magnificent present of my Hersh. . . . For 23 years I was privileged to have this most stunning treasure, to be Hersh's Mama. I'll take it and say thank you. I just wish it had been for longer.

Hersh, for all of these months I have been in such torment worrying about you every millisecond of everyday. It was such a specific type of misery that I have never experienced before. I tried hard to suppress the missing you part. Because that, I was convinced, would break me. So I spent 330 terrified, scared, worrying, and frightened. It closed my throat and made my soul throb with 3rd degree burns.

Part of what is so deeply crushing and confusing for us is that a strange thing happened along this macabre path upon which our family found itself traveling for the past 332 days. Amidst the inexplicable agony, terror, anguish, desperation and fear....we became absolutely CERTAIN, that you were coming home to us ALIVE. But it was not to be.

Now I no longer have to worry about you. I know you are no longer in danger. You are with beautiful Aner*; he will show you around. You will hopefully meet my grandparents, who will adore you, and start to play chess with Papa Stan. But now my worry shifts to us: Dada, Leebie, Orly and me. How do we do the rest of this life without you?

I also pray that your death will be a turning point in this horrible situation in which we are all entangled. I take such comfort knowing you were with Carmel, Ori, Eden, Almog and Alex. From what I have been told, they each were delightful in different ways, and I think that is how the 6 of you managed to stay alive in unimaginable circumstances for so very long. You each did every single thing right to survive 329 days in what I can only call Hell.

I send each of the families my deepest sympathies for what we are all going through and for the sickening feeling that we all could not save them. I think we all did every single thing we could. The hope that perhaps a deal was near, was so authentic it was crunchy. It tasted CLOSE. But it was not to be so. Those beautiful 6 survived together and those beautiful 6 died together. And now they will be remembered together forever.

Hersh, like most parents, Dada and I often would talk about who you would become, what you would be like when you 'grew up', what you would do, what you would look like, what kind of parent you would be. But now you will be forever our beautiful boy. You will stay energetic, kind, patient, curious, funny, irreverent, pensive. Forever handsome. Forever young. Forever my sweet boy.

You squeezed into your young life a lot of experiences. And that gives me relief and comfort. You made true and deep friendships, you traveled each summer and started to explore the world, you worked, you learned, you read, you taught, you served, you listened, you even fell in love and had a deep true relationship for more than 2 years. And you shared the excitement of that new experience with us. You charmed everyone you ever talked to, old or young. You promoted justice and peace in a way only a young pure, wide-eyed idealist

---

* "Staff Sgt. Aner Elyakim Shapira, 22: Unarmed, He Fended Off 7 Grenades. Slain inside a Bomb Shelter near the Supernova Music Festival on October 7," *Times of Israel*, Oct. 18, 2023.

can. You never raised your voice to me in your life. You treated me respectfully always, even when you chose a different path.

When you wrote to us from the bomb shelter you had just seen Aner get killed. You had lost your arm, and you thought you were dying. You wrote to us, "I'm sorry" because you knew how crushing it would be for us to lose you, so you fought to stay alive . . . all this time. But now, you are gone.

At this time I ask your forgiveness. If ever I was impatient or insensitive to you during your life, or neglectful in some way, I deeply and sincerely request your forgiveness. If there was something we could have done to save you and we didn't think of it, I beg your forgiveness. We tried so very hard. So deeply and desperately. I'm sorry.

Now, my Hersh, I ask for your help.

As we transform our hope into grief and this new unknown brand of pain, I beg of you, please do what you can to have your light shine down on me, Dada, Leebie and Orly. Help shower us with healing and resilience. Help us to rise again. I know it will take a long time, but please may God bless us that one day, one fine day, Dada, Leebie, Orly and I will hear laughter, and we will turn around and see . . . that it's us. And that we are ok. You will always be with us as a force of love and vitality, you will become our superpower.

To Dalya, Matt, and Richard who came to be with us every single day during this Odyssey of torture, there will never be enough time or words to express my gratitude to each of you.

And I want to say now the sincerest and most heartfelt thank you to the countless people in our extended community who have held us, cared for us, prayed for us, cooked for us, and carried us when we could not stand up.

I'm so thankful to you, and I apologize deeply, but we will need continued help to get through this sickening new chapter too. I am so sorry to ask, because we have given you nothing, and you have already given so profoundly and completely. But I beg of you all, please don't leave us now.

Ok, sweet boy, go now on your journey, I hope it's as good as the trips you dreamed about, because finally, my sweet sweet boy, finally, finally, finally, finally you are FREE!

I will love you and I will miss you every single day for the rest of my life. But you are right here. I know you are right here, I just have to teach myself to feel you in a new way.

And Hersh, I need you to do one last thing for us. . . . Now I need YOU to help us to stay strong. And I need YOU to help us to survive.

6. *October Rain*

October Rain was the original song to be sent as an Israeli entry to the 2024 Eurovision Song Contest. After multiple rejections of different versions of the song, claiming that it contained references to Hamas's October 7 massacre in Israel, the European Broadcasting Union confirmed the participation of Israel with the song *Hurricane*. The song, which hinted at that massacre, then qualified for the Finals and ended off in fifth place, with the second-highest public televote. The Israeli singer Eden Golan released *October Rain* in March 2024. The lyrics and music were written by Avi Ohayon, Keren Peles, and Stav Beger.

[Verse 1]
Writers of the history
Stand with me
Look into my eyes and see
People go away but never say goodbye

[Verse 2]
Someone stole the moon tonight
Took my light
Everything is black and white
Who's the fool who told you boys don't cry?

[Pre-Chorus]
Hours and hours and flowers
Life is no game for the cowards
Why does time go wild
Every day I'm losing my mind
Holding on in this mysterious ride

[Chorus]
Dancing in the storm
We got nothing to hide
Take me home
And leave the world behind
And I promise you that never again
I'm still wet from this October rain
October rain

[Verse 3]
Living in a fantasy
Ecstasy
Everything's meant to be
We shall pass but love will never die

[Pre-Chorus]
Hours and hours and flowers
Life is no game for the cowards
Why does time go wild
Every day I'm losing my mind
Holding on in this mysterious ride

[Chorus]
Dancing in the storm
We got nothing to hide
Take me home
And leave the world behind
And I promise you that never again
I'm still wet from this October rain
October rain
October rain

[Outro]
לא נשאר אוויר לנשום
אין מקום
אין אותי מיום ליום
כולם ילדים טובים אחד אחד

[No air left to breathe
No place
I disappear day by day
They're all good children each and every one]

7. Benjamin Netanyahu's speech at the seventy-ninth session of the UN General Assembly, Sept. 27, 2024

Times of Israel, Sept. 27, 2024

Mr. President, ladies and gentlemen, I didn't intend to come here this year. My country is at war, fighting for its life.

But after I heard the lies and slanders leveled at my country by many of the speakers at this podium, I decided to come here and set the record straight. I decided to come here to speak for my people.

To speak for my country, to speak for the truth. And here's the truth: Israel seeks peace. Israel yearns for peace. Israel has made peace and will make peace again. Yet we face savage enemies who seek our annihilation, and we must defend ourselves against them.

These savage murderers, our enemies, seek not only to destroy us, but they seek to destroy our common civilization and return all of us to a dark age of tyranny and terror. When I spoke here last year, I said we face the same timeless choice that Moses put before the people of Israel thousands of years ago, as we were about to enter the Promised Land. Moses told us that our actions would determine whether we bequeath to future generations a blessing or a curse.

And that is the choice we face today: the curse of Iran's unremitting aggression or the blessing of a historic reconciliation between Arab and Jew. In the days that followed that speech, the blessing I spoke of came into sharper focus.

A normalization deal between Saudi Arabia and Israel seemed closer than ever. But then came the curse of October 7th. Thousands of Iranian-backed Hamas terrorists from Gaza burst into Israel in pickup trucks and on motorcycles, and they committed unimaginable atrocities. They savagely murdered 1,200 people. They raped and mutilated women. They beheaded men. They burned babies alive. They burned entire families alive—babies, children, parents, grandparents, in scenes reminiscent of the Nazi Holocaust.

Hamas kidnapped 251 people from dozens of different countries, dragging them into the dungeons of Gaza. Israel has brought home 154 of these hostages, including 117 who returned alive. I want to assure you, we will not rest until the remaining hostages are brought home too, and some of their family members are here with us today. I ask you to stand up.

With us is Eli Shtivi, whose son Idan was abducted from the Nova music festival. That was his crime—a music festival. And these murderous monsters took him. Koby Samerano, whose son Jonathan was murdered, and his corpse was taken into the dungeons, into the terror tunnels of Gaza—a corpse held hostage.

Salem Alatrash, whose brother Mohammad, a brave Arab Israeli soldier, was murdered. His body, too, was taken to Gaza. And so was the body of Ifat Haiman's daughter, Inbar, who was brutally murdered at that same music festival.

With us is Sharon Sharabi, whose brother Yossi was murdered, and who prays for his older brother Eli, who is still held hostage in Gaza. And with us too is Yizhar Lifshitz from Kibbutz Nir Oz, a kibbutz that was wiped out by the terrorists.

Thankfully, we achieved the release of his mother, Yocheved, but his father, Oded, is still languishing in the underground terrorist hell of Hamas. I again promise you, we will return your loved ones home. We will not spare that effort until this holy mission is accomplished.

Ladies and gentlemen, the curse of October 7th began when Hamas invaded Israel from Gaza, but it didn't end there. Israel was soon forced to defend itself on six more war fronts organized by Iran.

On October 8th, Hezbollah attacked us from Lebanon. Since then, they have fired over 8,000 rockets at our towns and cities, at our civilians, at our children. Two weeks later, the Iran-backed Houthis in Yemen launched drones and missiles at Israel, the first of 250 such attacks, including one yesterday aimed at Tel Aviv. Iran's Shiite militias in Syria and Iraq have targeted Israel dozens of times over the past year as well.

Fueled by Iran, Palestinian terrorists in Judea and Samaria perpetrated scores of attacks there and throughout Israel. And last April, for the first time ever, Iran directly attacked Israel from its own territory.

Firing 300 drones, cruise missiles, and ballistic missiles at us. I have a message for the tyrants of Tehran: If you strike us, we will strike you. There is no place—there is no place in Iran—that the long arm of Israel cannot reach. And that's true of the entire Middle East.

Far from being lambs led to the slaughter, Israel's soldiers have fought back with incredible courage and with heroic sacrifice. And I have another message for this assembly and for the world outside this hall: We are winning.

Ladies and gentlemen, as Israel defends itself against Iran in this seven-front war, the lines separating the blessing and the curse could not be more clear. This is the map I presented here last year. It's a map of a blessing.

It shows Israel and its Arab partners forming a land bridge connecting Asia and Europe. Between the Indian Ocean and the Mediterranean Sea, across this bridge, we will lay rail lines, energy pipelines, and fiber optic cables, and this will serve the betterment of 2 billion people.

Now look at this second map. It's a map of a curse. It's a map of an arc of terror that Iran has created and imposed from the Indian Ocean to the Mediterranean. Iran's malignant arc has shut down international waterways.

It cuts off trade, it destroys nations from within, and inflicts misery on millions. On the one hand, a bright blessing—a future of hope. On the other hand, a dark future of despair. And if you think this dark map is only a curse for Israel, then you should think again.

Because Iran's aggression, if it's not checked, will endanger every single country in the Middle East, and many, many countries in the rest of the world, because Iran seeks to impose its radicalism well beyond the Middle East.

That's why it funds terror networks on five continents. That's why it builds ballistic missiles for nuclear warheads to threaten the entire world. For too long, the world has appeased Iran. It turned a blind eye to its internal repression. It turned a blind eye to its external aggression. Well, that appeasement must end. And that appeasement must end now.

Nations of the world should support the brave people of Iran who want to rid themselves of this evil regime. Responsible governments should not only support Israel in rolling back Iran's aggression, but they should join Israel. They should join Israel in stopping Iran's nuclear weapons program.

In this body and the Security Council, we're going to have a deliberation in a few months. And I call on the Security Council to snap back UN Security Council sanctions against Iran because we must all do everything in our power to ensure that Iran never gets nuclear weapons. For decades, I've been warning the world against Iran's nuclear program. Our actions delayed this program by perhaps a decade, but we haven't stopped it. We've delayed it, but we haven't stopped it. Iran now seeks to weaponize its nuclear program. For the sake of the peace and security of all your countries.

For the sake of the peace and security of the entire world, we must not let that happen. And I assure you, Israel will do everything in its power to make sure it doesn't happen.

So, ladies and gentlemen, the question before us is simple: Which of these two maps that I showed you will shape our future? Will it be the blessings of peace and prosperity for Israel, our Arab partners, and the rest of the world?

Or will it be the curse in which Iran and its proxies spread carnage and chaos everywhere? Israel has already made its choice. We've decided to advance the blessing. We're building a partnership for peace with our Arab neighbors while fighting the forces of terror that threaten that peace.

For nearly a year, the brave men and women of the IDF have been systematically crushing Hamas's terror army that once ruled Gaza. On October 7th, the day of that invasion into Israel, that terror army numbered nearly 40,000 terrorists. It was armed with more than 15,000 rockets. It had 350 miles of terror tunnels—an underground network bigger than the New York subway system—which they used to wreak havoc above and below ground.

A year later, the IDF has killed or captured more than half of these terrorists, destroyed over 90% of their rocket arsenal, and eliminated the key segments of their terror tunnel network.

In measured military operations, we destroyed nearly all of Hamas's terror battalions—23 out of 24 battalions. Now, to complete our victory, we are focused on mopping up Hamas's remaining fighting capabilities.

We are taking out senior terrorist commanders and destroying remaining terrorist infrastructure. But all the while, we remain focused on our sacred mission: bringing our hostages home, and we will not stop until that mission is complete.

Now, ladies and gentlemen, even with Hamas's greatly diminished military capability, the terrorists still exercise some governing power in Gaza by stealing the food that we enable aid agencies to bring into Gaza.

Hamas steals the food, and then they hike the prices. They feed their bellies, and then they fill their coffers with money they extort from their own people. They sell the stolen food at exorbitant prices, and that's how they stay in power. Well, this too has to end, and we're working to bring it to an end.

And the reason is simple: because if Hamas stays in power, it will regroup, rearm, and attack Israel again and again and again, as it has vowed to do. So, Hamas has got to go.

Just imagine, for those who say Hamas has to stay, it has to be part of a post-war Gaza—imagine, in a post-war situation after World War II, allowing the defeated Nazis in 1945 to rebuild Germany? It's inconceivable. It's ridiculous. It didn't happen then, and it's not going to happen now.

This is why Israel will reject any role for Hamas in a post-war Gaza. We don't seek to resettle Gaza. What we seek is a demilitarized and de-radicalized Gaza. Only then can we ensure that this round of fighting will be the last round of fighting.

We are ready to work with regional and other partners to support a local civilian administration in Gaza, committed to peaceful coexistence.

As for the hostages, I have a message for the Hamas captors: Let them go. Let them go. All of them. Those alive today must be returned alive, and the remains of those whom you brutally killed must be returned to their families.

Those families here with us today and others in Israel deserve to have a resting place for their loved ones. A place where they can grieve and remember them.

Ladies and gentlemen, this war can come to an end now. All that has to happen is for Hamas to surrender, lay down its arms, and release all the hostages. But if they don't, we will fight until we achieve victory. Total victory. There is no substitute for it.

Israel must also defeat Hezbollah in Lebanon. Hezbollah is the quintessential terror organization in the world today.

It has tentacles that span all continents. It has murdered more Americans and more Frenchmen than any group except Bin Laden. It's murdered the citizens of many countries represented in this room. And it has attacked Israel viciously over the last 20 years.

In the last year, completely unprovoked, a day after the Hamas massacre on October 7th, Hezbollah began attacks against Israel, which forced more than 60,000 Israelis on our northern border to leave their homes, becoming refugees in their own land.

Hezbollah turned vibrant towns in the north of Israel into ghost towns. So I want you to think about this in equivalent American terms. Just imagine if terrorists turned El Paso and San Diego into ghost towns.

Then ask yourself: How long would the American government tolerate that? A day, a week, a month? I doubt they would tolerate it even for a single day.

Yet Israel has been tolerating this intolerable situation for nearly a year. Well, I've come here today to say enough is enough.

We won't rest until our citizens can return safely to their homes. We will not accept a terror army perched on our northern border, able to perpetrate another October 7th-style massacre.

For 18 years, Hezbollah brazenly refused to implement UN Security Council Resolution 1701, which requires it to move its forces away from our borders. Instead, Hezbollah moved right up to our border. They secretly dug terror tunnels to infiltrate our communities and indiscriminately fired thousands of rockets into our towns and villages.

They fire these rockets and missiles not from military sites—they do that too—but they fire those rockets and missiles after they place them in schools, in hospitals, in apartment buildings, and in the private homes of the citizens of Lebanon. They endanger their own people. They put a missile in every kitchen.

A rocket in every garage. I said to the people of Lebanon this week: Get out of the death trap that Hezbollah has put you in. Don't let Nasrallah drag Lebanon into the abyss. We're not at war with you. We're at war with Hezbollah, which has hijacked your country and threatens to destroy ours.

As long as Hezbollah chooses the path of war, Israel has no choice. And Israel has every right to remove this threat and return our citizens to their homes safely, and that's exactly what we're doing.

Just this week, the IDF destroyed large percentages of Hezbollah's rockets, which were built with Iran's funding for three decades. We took out senior military commanders who not only shed Israeli blood but American and French blood as well.

And then we took out their replacements. And then the replacements of their replacements. And we'll continue degrading Hezbollah until all our objectives are met.

Ladies and gentlemen, we're committed to removing the curse of terrorism that threatens all civilized societies. But to truly realize the blessing of a new Middle East, we must continue the path we paved with the Abraham Accords four years ago. Above all, this means achieving a historic peace agreement between Israel and Saudi Arabia.

And having seen the blessings that we've already brought with the Abraham Accords, the millions of Israelis who have already flown back and forth across the Arabian Peninsula over the skies of Saudi Arabia to the Gulf countries, the trade, the tourism, the joint ventures, the peace—I say to you, what blessings such a peace with Saudi Arabia would bring.

It would be a boon to the security and economy of our two countries. It would boost trade and tourism across the region. It would help transform the Middle East into a global juggernaut.

Our two countries could cooperate on energy, water, agriculture, artificial intelligence, and many, many other fields. Such a peace, I am sure, would be a true pivot of history. It would usher in a historic reconciliation between the Arab world and Israel, between Islam and Judaism, between Mecca and Jerusalem.

While Israel is committed to achieving such a peace, Iran and its terror proxies are committed to scuttling it. That's why one of the best ways to foil Iran's nefarious designs is to achieve the peace.

Such a peace would be the foundation for an even broader Abrahamic alliance, and that alliance would include the United States, Israel's current Arab peace partners, Saudi Arabia, and others who choose the blessing of peace.

It would advance security and prosperity across the Middle East and bring enormous benefits to the rest of the world. With American support and leadership, I believe this vision can materialize much sooner than people think. And as the Prime Minister of Israel, I will do everything in my power to make it happen. This is an opportunity that we and the world should not let go by.

Ladies and gentlemen, Israel has made its choice. We seek to move forward to a bright age of prosperity and peace. Iran and its proxies have also made their choice. They want to move back to a dark age of terror and war.

And now I have a question, and I pose that question to you: What choice will you make? Will your nation stand with Israel? Will you stand with democracy and peace? Or will you stand with Iran, a brutal dictatorship that subjugates its own people and exports terrorism across the globe?

In this battle between good and evil, there must be no equivocation. When you stand with Israel, you stand for your own values and your own interests. Yes, we're defending ourselves, but we're also defending you against a common enemy that, through violence and terror, seeks to destroy our way of life. So there should be no confusion about this, but unfortunately, there is a lot of it in many countries and in this very hall, as I've just heard.

Good is portrayed as evil, and evil is portrayed as good.

We see this moral confusion when Israel is falsely accused of genocide when we defend ourselves against enemies who try to commit genocide against us. We see this too when Israel is absurdly accused by the ICC Prosecutor of deliberately starving Palestinians in Gaza. What an absurdity. We help bring in 700,000 tons of food into Gaza. That's more than 3,000 calories a day for every man, woman, and child in Gaza.

We see this moral confusion when Israel is falsely accused of deliberately targeting civilians. We don't want to see a single innocent person die. That's always a tragedy. And that's why we do so much to minimize civilian casualties, even as our enemies use civilians as human shields.

And no army has done what Israel is doing to minimize civilian casualties. We drop flyers. We send text messages. We make phone calls by the millions to ensure that Palestinian civilians get out of harm's way. We spare no effort in this noble pursuit.

We see yet another profound moral confusion when self-described progressives march against the democracy of Israel. Don't they realize they support the Iranian-backed goons in Tehran and in Gaza, the goons who shot down protesters, murder women for not covering their hair, and hang gays in public squares? Some progressives.

According to the US Director of National Intelligence, Iran funds and fuels many of the protesters against Israel. Who knows, maybe some of the protesters or even many of the protesters outside this building now?

Ladies and gentlemen, King Solomon, who reigned in our eternal capital, Jerusalem, 3,000 years ago, proclaimed something that is familiar to all of you. He said: There is nothing new under the sun.

Well, in an age of space travel, quantum physics, and artificial intelligence, some would argue that's a debatable statement. But one thing is undeniable: there is definitely nothing new at the United Nations.

Take it from me. I first spoke from this podium as Israel's ambassador to the UN in 1984. That's exactly 40 years ago. And in my maiden speech here, I spoke against a proposal to expel Israel from this body. Four decades later, I find myself defending Israel against that same preposterous proposal.

And who's leading the charge this time? Not Hamas, but Abbas.

Palestinian Authority President Mahmoud Abbas. This is the man who claims he wants peace with Israel, yet he still refuses to condemn the horrific massacre of October 7th. He's still paying hundreds of millions to terrorists who murdered Israelis and Americans.

It's called Pay for Slay. The more you murder, the more you get paid.

And he still wages unremitting diplomatic warfare against Israel's right to exist and against Israel's right to defend itself. And by the way, they amount to the same thing, because if you can't defend yourself, you can't exist. Not in our neighborhood, certainly. And maybe not in yours.

Standing at this podium 40 years ago, I told the sponsors of that outrageous resolution to expel Israel: Gentlemen, check your fanaticism at the door. Today, I tell President Abbas and all of you who would shamefully support that resolution: Check your fanaticism at the door.

The singling out of the one and only Jewish state continues to be a moral stain on the United Nations. It has made this once-respected institution contemptible in the eyes of decent people everywhere. But for the Palestinians, this UN house of darkness is home court. They know that in this swamp of antisemitic bile, there's an automatic majority willing to demonize the Jewish state for anything. In this anti-Israel flat-earth society, any false charge, any outlandish allegation can muster a majority.

In the last decade, there have been more resolutions passed against Israel in this hall, in the UN General Assembly, than against the entire world combined. Actually, more than twice as many. Since 2014, this body condemned Israel 174 times.

It condemned all the other countries in the world 73 times. That's more than 100 extra condemnations for the Jewish state. What hypocrisy. What a double standard. What a joke.

So, all the speeches you heard today, all the hostility directed at Israel this year—it's not about Gaza; it's about Israel. It's always been about Israel. About Israel's very existence. And I say to you, until Israel, until the Jewish state, is treated like other nations, until this antisemitic swamp is drained, the UN will be viewed by fair-minded people everywhere as nothing more than a contemptuous farce.

And given the antisemitism at the UN, it should surprise no one that the prosecutor at the ICC, one of the UN's affiliated organs, is considering issuing arrest warrants against me and Israel's defense minister, the democratically elected leaders of the democratic state of Israel.

The ICC prosecutor's rush to judgment, his refusal to treat Israel with its independent courts the way other democracies are treated, is hard to explain by anything other than pure antisemitism.

Ladies and gentlemen, the real war criminals are not in Israel. They're in Iran. They're in Gaza, in Syria, in Lebanon, in Yemen. Those of you who stand with these war criminals, those of you who stand with evil against good, with the curse against the blessing, those of you who do so should be ashamed of yourselves.

But I have a message for you: Israel will win this battle. We will win this battle because we don't have a choice.

After generations in which our people were slaughtered, remorselessly butchered, and no one raised a finger in our defense, we now have a state. We now have a brave army, an army of incomparable courage, and we are defending ourselves.

As the book of Samuel says in the Bible: "נֵצַח יִשְׂרָאֵל לֹא יְשַׁקֵּר"—"The eternity of Israel will not falter." In the Jewish people's epic journey from antiquity, in our odyssey through the tempest and upheavals of modern times, that ancient promise has always been kept and it will hold true for all time.

To borrow a great poet's phrase: Israel will not go gently into that good night. We will never need to rage against the dying of the light because the torch of Israel will forever shine bright.

To the people of Israel and to the soldiers of Israel, I say: Be strong and of good courage."חִזְקוּ וְאִמְצוּ אַל־תִּירְאוּ וְאַל־תַּעַרְצוּ מִפְּנֵיהֶם כִּי ה' אֱלֹקִיךָ הוּא הַהֹלֵךְ עִמָּךְ לֹא יַרְפְּךָ וְלֹא יַעַזְבֶךָּ".

"עם ישראל חי"—"The people of Israel live now, tomorrow, forever."

Index

A
a-Srag, Samah, 157
Abadhu, Abu, 139
Abbas, Mahmoud, 28, 55, 61, 78–79, 129, 135, 146–147, 225, 276
Abdallah, Alim, 63, 109, 119, 145, 207, 213, 222, 248
Abdul Hadi, Ahmad, 172
Abdullah II, 11
Abdullah, Sami Taleb, 89
Abed Ali, Nazih, 158
Abraham Accords, 30, 34, 132, 151
"Abu Alhilu" school, 81
Abu Aljidian, Hatem, 207
Abu Allahyani, Ayman Khaled Ahmed, 213
Abu Ashak, Wissam, 103
Abu Atiya, Muhammad, 214
Abu Dalal, Walid Abd, 79
Abu Daqqa, Azmi, 56
Abu Daqqa, Samer Ismail Khadr, 210
Abu Dhabi, 38
"Abu Hamed," 56
Abu Hamza, 77
Abu Ma'ad, 98
Abu Marzouk, Mousa, 167
Abu Nada, Taha, 181
Abu Obaida, 119, 212
Abu Reala, Abdallah, 213
Abu Rudeineh, Nabil, 64
Abu Salmiya, Mohammad, 113
Abu Seidu, Muhammad, 138
Abu Sha'ab, Ra'af Omar Salman, 208
Abu Sharar, Ibrahim, 214
Abu Toameh, Khaled, 196
Abu Zuhri, Sami, 35, 41, 83, 88, 129, 142
Abusada, Mkhaimar, 91
Abyar, Sayeed, 80
Acre, 22, 79, 162
Acta Paediatrica, 167
Adar, Tamir, 15
Adas Torah synagogue, 102
Adraee, Avichay, 68, 215

Afghanistan, 13, 108, 128, 164, 202, 209
Afula, 106
Agam Labs, 117
Aharon, Yogev, 247
Ahimas, Tomer, 143
Aitaroun, 208
Al Busaidi, Sayyid Badr, 59
Al Jazeera, 1, 13, 31, 33, 81, 108–9, 139
Al Mughayyir, 14
Al Saud, Faisal bin Farhan, 73, 224
Al Sharq, 174
Al Thani, Mohammed, 51
Al Udeid, 38
Al-Ahli Arab Hospital, 1
Al-Ain media, 1
Al-Akhbar, 36, 38, 121, 162, 175
Al-Ansari, Majed, 59
Al-Aqsa compound, 5–6
Al-Aqsa Martyrs Brigade, 137, 233
Al-Aqsa Mosque, 156, 194–95
Al-Arabiya, 134, 225, 227
Al-Araby Al-Jadeed, 19, 23, 184
Al-Asad airbase, 160
Al-Atar, Meitam Mustafa, 118
Al-Din, Abbas Ibrahim Sharaf, 225
Al-Din, Amin Badr, 162
Al-Furqan Battalion, 160
Al-Habbash, 239
al-Hassouni, Amina, 16, 33
Al-Hayek, Munzer, 11
al-Jama'a al-Islamiya, 27
Al-Jarida, 171
Al-Khair Foundation, 130
Al-Khalil, Mumeen, 1
Al-Manar, 36, 226
Al-Mawasi area, 210
Al-Mayadeen media, 206
Al-Nasser Salah al-Deen Brigades, 196
Al-Qaeda, 108, 201
Al-Qaradawi, Yusuf, 29
Al-Qarara school, 140
Al-Risheq, 209

Al-Saeed, Najat, 29
Al-Shaer, Muhammad Kassem, 211
Al-Shati refugee camp, 98, 129
Al-Shifa Hospital, 1, 113
Al-Taba'een school, 166, 170
Al-Wadiya, Fadi, 103
Al-Zayani, Abdullatif bin Rashid, 34
Al-Zeriei, Abed, 160
Alal, Nadal Abdel, 229
Albado, Salah, 214
Alfoneh, Ali, 241
Algeria, 170, 204
Ali, Ahmed, 9, 45
aliya, 179, 194, 249–50
Aljamal, Abdallah, 109
Allan, Muhammad, 185
Almasri, Ahmad, 133
Alon, Nitzan, 62
Alsauarka, Ahmed Hassan Salame, 96
Alsharafa, Deya Aldin, 63
Alshubaki, Yusuf, 63
"Am ha-netzach lo mefached mi-derech aruka," 246
Amad, Saleh Jamil Muhammad, 39
Amal terrorist organization, 208
Amer, Arafat, 189
Amini, Mahsa, 57, 73, 220
Amir-Abdollahian, Hossein, 20, 56
Ammar, Ali, 147, 220
An-Dur, Admed, 211
Andor, Ahmed, 191
antisemitism, 3, 28, 37, 46, 57, 70, 102, 121, 126, 226, 228, 243–44, 251
Aqabat Jabr, 138
Aqil, Ibrahim, 221
Arab Gulf States Institute, 241
Arab Israelis, 4, 240
Araghchi, Abbas, 220, 228
Arbel, Moshe, 156
Ardestani, Ahmad Bakhshayesh, 168
Argamani, Noa, 86, 201
Ariel, Yaakov, 151
As-Sultaniyeh, 9
Asa-El, Amotz, 196
Asharq Al-Awsat, 25, 27
Ashdod, 5, 69, 99
Ashkelon, 215, 233
Aspaklaria theater company, 150
Asserson, Trevor, 243
Atarot, 199
Atiyeh, Mohammad Khalil, 22
Austin, Lloyd, 14, 41, 90, 136
Australia, 2–3

Awad, Ziad, 191
Axios, 40, 104, 153, 195, 236
Ayoub, Muhammad Mustafa, 93
Ayta ash Shab, 24
Azzun, 8

B
Baalbek, 19
Bach'ri, Eden, 247
Bachar, Amit, 198
Badran, Husam, 128
Baerbock, Annalena, 148, 152
Bagheri, Mohammad, 16
Baharav-Miara, Gali, 2, 214
Balata refugee camp, 81
Bar-David, Arnon, 198
Bar-Gil, Evyatar, 51
Bar, Ronen, 3, 48, 127, 172
Bar, Tomer, 169
Baraka, Ali, 202
Baraka, Salame, 79
Baram, Amir, 120
Baranes, Noa, 124
Barghouti, Abdulah, 191
Barghouti, Jasser, 192
Barnea, David, 41, 115, 172, 184
Baruch, Tzvika, 246
Basal, Mahmoud, 126
Basiuk, Oded, 96
Bat Hefer, 68, 98, 106–7
Bava Batra, 246
Baz, Ismail Yusef, 18
BBC, 32, 73, 144, 196, 206, 233, 235, 252
Bedouin, 16, 35, 185, 196
Beirut, 99, 105, 115, 146–47, 157, 168, 172–73, 218, 221–22, 225–29, 236, 241
Beit Hanoun Battalion, 19, 63
Beit Lahia, 47, 54
Beita Junction, 211
Beitar Illit, 158
Beitin, 85
Beizer, Nik, 211
Ben-Gvir, Itamar, 4, 46, 53, 60, 79, 81, 93, 134, 180, 188, 193–95, 212, 224
Bendjama, Amar, 204
Beqaa Valley, 82, 98, 114, 145
Bergen-Belsen, 127
Berri, Nabih, 172
Biale, Tamar, 253
Bialik, Chaim Nahman, 245
Bibas, Ariel, 160
Biden, Joe, 3–7, 12–14, *passim*
bin Zayed Al Nahyan, Sheikh Abdullah, 215

Bir Zeit University, 137
Bitar, Maher, 71
Biton, Yuval, 15
Blinken, Anthony, 12–14, 18, *passim*
blood libel, 205, 233
Bob, Yonah Jeremy, 101, 122, 150, 191, 194, 235, 237, 251
Boko Haram, 108
Bou Habib, Abdallah, 145, 222
Brodski, Kiril, 143
"broken heart syndrome," 253
Bron-Harlev, Efrat, 204
Brooklyn Museum, 102
Brown, Charles, 100
Bureij Battalion, 39
"butcher of Tehran, the," 57

C

Caban, Edward, 36
Cameron, David, 12, 22, 77
Canada, 2–3, 17, 67, 71, 245, 250, 253
Caspian Airlines, 173
cease-fire, 5, 8–13, 17, *passim*
Central Camps Brigade, 187
ChaiFlicks, 253
Channel 14, 11, 122, 206
Chebaa, 145
Chidon HaTanakh, 51
China, 13–14, 17, 27, 59, 73, 82–83, 103, 148, 151, 164, 251
CIA, 46, 83, 118, 131, 186, 207
CNN, 5, 13, 31–32, 44, 47, 60–61, 68, 73, 97–98, 131, 144, 157, 165, 167, 173, 187–88, 190, 201
CNN Arabic, 187
Cohen, David, 186
Cohen, Eli, 30, 175
Cohen, Gilad, 164
Cohen, Itzik, 178
Cohen, Meir, 134
Cohen, Yosef, 192
Colombia, 168
Columbia University, 27, 30, 33–34, 37, 70, 95, 249
Commando Brigade, 92, 148
Commando Division, 7, 113
confirmed dead, 198
Coons, Chris, 49
Corriere della Sera, 65
Cotton, Tom, 46
Crosetto, Guido, 66
Cullison, Alan, 80, 108
Cyprus, 27
Czech Republic, 59, 126, 234

D

Daeb, Saeed Mahmoud, 180
Dagan, Yossi, 173
Dagestan, 102
Dahieh, 157, 169, 218, 226, 241
Dangor, Zane, 65
Danino, Ori, 210, 234
Danon, Danny, 186, 224
Daraj Tuffah Battalion, 200
Darwish, Tariq, 79
Davar, 195
David's Sling, 222, 241
Davidovich, Moshe, 90
Dayan, Dani, 27
Deif, Mohammed, 57, 77, 129, 135, 156, 202, 213
Denmark, 68, 126
Dermer, Ron, 200, 233
Dhaifallah, Hayil, 213
Dib, Samir Tawfiq, 236
"disengagement law," 61
Druze, 82, 144–46, 201, 240, 248
Dudin, Musa, 191
Dura, 1

E

Edri, Moshe, 92
Egypt, 6, 14, 17–18, 25, 27, 33, 37, 42, 48–49, 52–53, 60–62, 65, 67, 71, 84, 87, 89, 97, 107–8, 114, 122, 124–25, 127–29, 131, 134, 142, 148–49, 167–69, 175, 178, 183–84, 199, 201, 211, 223
Eide, Espen Barth, 66, 73
Eilat, 136, 140
Ein al-Hilweh, 182
"Ein lanu eretz acheret," 248
Einstein, Albert, 246–47
Eisenkot, Gadi, 28, 84, 87, 205
El-Sisi, Abdel Fattah, 11, 25, 29, 177, 181
Eli community, 206
Eliyahu, Shmuel, 151
Eliyasam, Gideon, 123
Ellison, Keith, 194
Emanuel, Rahm, 164
Engelman, Matan, 105
Entebbe raid, 86
Erdan, Gilad, 163, 171, 252
European Commission, 18, 230
Eurovision, 47, 72
Eygi, Aysenur Ezgi, 207, 214

F

F-35 jets, 82
Fadl, Osama Bani, 206

Fahd, Ahmed Muhammad, 228
Faki, Rami Khalil, 56
Fakih, Mohamed, 191
Faraj, Adam, 81
Faraj, Majed, 10
Fatah, 10, 25, 27, 61, 82, 103, 133, 139, 151, 178, 205, 224, 229
FBI, 62
Fiad, Hussein, 63
Fidan, Hakan, 28
Filant, Yitzhak Levi, 186
Finer, Jonathan, 71
Finkelman, Yaron, 91
Fisher, William Arms, xi
Fox, Yehuda, 24
France, 9, 17–18, 32, 59, 61–62, 70, 74, 83, 121, 125–26, 139, 169, 181, 201, 233, 244, 249
Frank, Anne, 127, 244
Frankel, Naftali, 192
Frazier, Vanessa, 4
"Free Palestine," 102, 142
Friedman, Thomas, 37
friendly fire, 31

G

Gadallah, Osama, 187
Gallant, Yoav, 8, 14, 18, *passim*
Gan Ner, 68
Gan Yavne, 1
Ganim, 51, 61
Gantz, Benny, 3, 26, 53–55, 66, 82, 84, 92, 113, 197, 205
Gardos, Yogev, 131
Gat, Carmel, 234
Gaza, ix–xiii, 1–15, *passim*
Gaza City, 1, 13, 24, 45, 63, 105, 119–120, 123–24, 133, 166, 181, 200, 207, 211, 213, 215
Gazans, 9, 15, 23, 25, 27, 38, 42, 47, 53, 63, 67, 74, 91, 97, 107, 132, 140, 150, 152, 198, 220, 239
genocide, 44, 54, 59, 64–65, 68, 74, 113, 142, 164, 225, 244
Georgia, 169
Germany, 6, 9, 18, 30, 59, 62, 71, 74, 83, 102, 105–6, 126, 136, 169, 172, 233, 244
Geva, Mano, 191
Gezer, 216
Ghatma, Ayman, 98
Givat Asaf, 213
Golan, Eden, 72
Goldberg-Polin, Rachel, 9, 25, 157, 178, 197–98, 207, 231, 234

Goldfus, Dan, 215
Goldich, Haim, 95
Goldin, Oren, 143
Gordin, Ori, 84, 96, 216
Gordis, Daniel, 195, 253–54
Goren, Maya, 143
Gottheimer, Josh, 156
Graham, Lindsey, 44
Grandi, Filippo, 229
Grassley, Chuck, 62
Griffiths, Martin, 36
Grossi, Rafael Mariano, 57, 245
Guardian, 130, 211, 216, 235
Guterres, António, 50, 53, 84, 186, 198, 211, 218–19, 228

H

Haaretz, 5, 15, 30–34, 59, 68, 70–75, 85, 99, 105, 108–111, 113–14, 121, 142, 145–46, 148–53, 160, 168, 174, 181, 184, 186, 189–96, 209, 211–12, 215, 224–25, 231–36, 248, 252–53
Habeck, Robert, 65
Hadad, Sarit, 246
Hagari, Daniel, 14, 16, 45, 48, 64, 67, 87, 92–93, 95, 110, 119, 128, 135, 145, 221
Haim, Bella, ix
Haines, Avril, 124, 152
Haj-Hassan, Tanya, 194
Hajir region, 9, 134
Hala organization, 97
Halal, Omar Abu, 9
Halevi, Herzi, 21, 24, 39, 49, 82, 90, 93, 129–30, 132, 146–47, 163, 167, 172, 203, 215, 222, 226
Haliva, Aharon, 21, 214
Hamad, Ghazi, 174
Hamas, ix–xiii, 1–3, 5–14, *passim*
Hamdan, Mahmoud, 211
Hamdan, Osama, 36, 91, 177
Hamida, Nimer, 129, 137
Hanegbi, Tzachi, 68
Hanghal, Geri Gideon, 213
Haniyeh, Ismail, 13, 21, 52, 57, 70, 84, 86, 88, 103, 147–48, 153, 155–59, 160–64, 168, 170, 178, 190, 202, 215, 240
Har Dov, 26
haredim, 2, 90–91, 93, 102–3, 120, 131, 137, 162
Hariri, Rafic, 162
Harris, Kamala, 141–44, 152, 167, 180, 188, 194, 214, 243, 253
Harris, Simon, 60
Hashemi, Nader, 190

HaShomer Yosh, 186
Hassan Salame school, 160
Hassan, Eid, 229
Hassan, Kawa, 242
Hassin, Ali Ahmed, 9
Hatikva, xi
Hazem, Wassem, 189
Healey, John, 148
Hemo, Ohad, 163
Hennis-Plasschaert, Jeanine, 145
Hermesh, 56
Herzog, Isaac, 16, 35, 40, 46, 48, 51, 57, 72, 78, 94, 116, 137, 173, 175, 179, 185, 197, 201, 210
Hezbollah, x–xiii, 1, 5–8, 11, 18–20, *passim*
High Court of Justice, 2, 4, 63, 102, 105, 114, 152
Hijazi, Hala, 194
Hirsch, Gal, 211
Histadrut, 198, 201
Hitler, Adolf, 163
Hiyun, Shai Biton, 248
Hochstein, Amos, 94–95, 97, 172
Hodeidah port, 135–136, 166, 229
Holit, 42, 184
Hollanders, Eliakim, 40
Holocaust, ix, 37, 39–41, 43, 46–47, 56, 58, 74, 109, 127, 141, 163, 234, 244
Holon, 158
"Hostage Square," 116
hostages, 4, 7, 9–14, 17, *passim*
Houthis, 8, 134–36, 143, 156, 166, 171, 216, 229, 242, 245
Huli, Zaher, 56
Hurfeish, 82
Huwara, 206

I
Ibrahim, Fadel, 96
Ibrahim, Raymond, 29
Ignatius, David, 58
Im Tirtzu organization, 200
Indonesia, 252
intifada, 134, 233
Iran, x–xiii, 1–5, 7–23, *passim*
Ireland, 4, 60–61, 67
Iron Dome, 15, 44, 97–98, 105, 182, 241
Ish-Ran, Amiad Israel, 192
Islamic Revolution, 85
Islamiya, Jamaa, 98
Israel, ix, xi, 1–55, *passim*
Israel Bonds, 253
Israelis, ix, 1, 4, 9, 11, 13–15, *passim*
Israeloff, Assi, 246

Issa, Marwan, 202
Italy, 71, 74, 126, 244, 250

J
J Street, 142
Jabal Safi, 106
Jabaliya, 47, 49–52, 63–64, 69, 207
Jabarah, Mohammed, 133
Jaber, Adnan Ayser, 185
Jabotinsky, Ze'ev, 159
Jadeh Iran news outlet, 10
Jan, Almog Meir, 86
Jazini, Ibrahim Hussein, 236
Jenin, 4, 24, 27, 56, 63, 98, 105–6, 115, 162, 185, 187, 189, 200, 205–6, 233
Jerusalem, x–xv, 3–4, 6, 8, 13, 15, *passim*
Jewish Chronicle, 111, 153, 196
Jewish Federations of North America, 46, 137
Jibril, Jibril Ghasan, 185
Jit, 173, 179, 186
Johnson, Mike, 141
Johnson, Ron, 62
Jordan, 11, 14, 16–18, 22, 66, 87, 93, 106, 125, 129, 133, 149, 160, 167, 176, 187, 191–92, 206, 208, 213, 223, 240
Jouaiya, 163
Juneau, Thomas, 242

K
K'sheh ha-lev bocheh, 246
Kadim, 61
Kalkilya, 115
Kan Radio, 83
Kan Reshet Bet, 36
Kanaani, Nasser, 144, 161, 230
Kanbari, Issam, 4
Karbala, 89, 109, 151, 195
Karki, Ali, 226
Karmei Tzur, 188–89
Karmiel, 114
Karr, Jean-Baptiste Alphonse, 148
Karsh, Efraim, xi
Kashlan, Mansur Adel Mansur, 79
Kasseb, Hassin Ibraheem, 174
Kataib Hezbollah, 147
Katif Bloc, 35
Katrouy, Muhammad, 187
Katz, Israel, 19, 28, 37, 191
Katz, Ravid Aryeh, 143
Katz, Yaakov, 108, 151, 196
Katzir, Elad, 6
Katzrin, 79, 178
Kauders, Refael, 82
Kedem, Gadi, 54

Kemp, Richard, 202
Kerem Shalom Crossing, 5, 39, 41, 44, 48, 65, 67, 85, 92, 107
Kessler, Paul, 111
Kfar Ganim, 51
Khala, Mosab, 27
Khamayseh, Islam, 56
Khamenei, Ali, 2, 57, 69, 79, 155, 184, 241
Khan, Karim, 38, 57
Khan, Muhammad Shahzeb, 245
Khatib, Abdallah, 207
Khodaei, Hassan Sayad, 32
Kibbutz Be'eri, xi, 11, 45, 83, 86, 128, 177, 184, 193, 245
Kibbutz HaGoshrim, 217
Kibbutz Kfar Aza, ix
Kibbutz Magen, 185
Kibbutz Meirav, 98
Kibbutz Nahal Oz, 32, 86, 132, 210
Kibbutz Neot Mordechai, 206
Kibbutz Nir Oz, 15, 32, 63, 81, 196
Kibbutz Nirim, 187
Kibbutz Ortal, 124
Kibbutz Shamir, 172
Kibbutz Sufa, 38
Kintsugi, 246
Kirby, John, 28, 41, 79, 96, 164, 205, 222
Kiryat Gat, 32
Kiryat Ono, 201
Kiryat Shmona, 24, 39, 96, 172, 204, 208
Kissufim, 11
Klein, Sayde, 246
Knesset, 2–3, 53, 57–58, 61, 77, 80, 90, 100, 120, 123–24, 133–34, 146, 160, 240, 252
Kobi, Micah, 24
Kol Ha'am, 31
Koss, Andrew, 232
Kozlov, Andrey, 86
Kramer, Martin, 74
Kuperwasser, Yossi, 85
Kurilla, Michael, 14

L

La France Insoumise, 121
La Vanguardia, 4
Lahham, Mariam Majdouline, 204
Lammy, David, 148, 167, 193
Lapid, Yair, 4, 180, 203, 224
Larnaca port, 2
Le Monde, 39
Le Parisien, 226
Lebanon, 1, 5, 7, 9, 16–18, *passim*
Leiter, Yechiel, 141
Levanon, Elyakim, 151

Levin, Andy, 194
Levin, Yariv, 198
Lew, Jack, 49, 198
Limon, Gil, 103, 171
Lior, Dov, 151
Lis, Jonathan, 30
Litani River, 38, 110, 145, 147, 170, 230
Lobanov, Alexander, 234
Lober, Hagai, 122, 254
Lober, Yehonatan, 122
Lodhammar, Pehr, 26
Los Angeles, 102, 111, 247
Lubnov, Alex, 198

M

Ma Kashur trio, 246
Ma'aleh Efraim, 206
Ma'ariv, 24, 53, 67, 232
Maatuk, Ali Jaafar, 134
Mabhouh, Ayman, 210
Macron, Emmanuel, 11, 41, 66, 77, 146, 163–64, 187, 223
Magash HaKesef, 195
Maglan, 148
Mahasneh, Mohammed, 161
Mahmoud, Osama Mahmoud Abdelkhalek, 213
Maifadoun, 162
Majali, Ziad, 42
Makki, Hussein Ibrahim, 53
Malachei Shalom, 14
Malkieli, Michael, 97
Malta, 4
Mansour, Hossam, 129
Mansour, Muhammad, 222
Mansour, Riyad, 4, 19, 213, 219
Marciano, Noa, 213
Margoliot, 24
Marmorstein, Oren, 145
Maroun El Ras, 208
Mashaal, Khaled, 163, 187, 202
Masharqa, Misra, 189
Mashiach, Oriel, 118
Mast, Brian, 156
Masyaf, 209
Matar, Iyad, 214
McCain, Cindy, 38
McColl, John, 251
McGraw, Phil, 47
McGurk, Brett, 13, 124
Medan, Yaakov, 173
Mehanna, Naser, 126
Meir, Golda, 137, 246
Merwede Square, 127

Meshaal, Khaled, 218
Metula, 41, 96, 221
Michaelshvili, Shalom, 246
Midgam Research and Consulting, 140
Miller, Jonathan, 213
Miller, Matthew, 59, 101, 140
Milo, Rafi, 158
Milwidsky, Hanoch Dov, 2
Mishkenot Sha'ananim, 72
Mishmar HaEmek, 32
Mitzpeh Ramon, 47
Mitzpeh Yosef, 188
Mizrachi, Baruch, 191
Modarres military base, 121
Montenegro, Luis, 64
Moore, Richard, 207
Morocco, 34, 52, 151
Morris, Benny, xi
Moshav Ya'ara, 176
Mossad, 17–18, 41, 47, 60, 68, 115, 117, 128, 130, 132, 153, 172, 177, 182, 184, 203, 235, 241
Mousavi, Abdolrahim, 163
Mousawi, Nawaf, 217
Mu'arrajat, 217
Muchtar, Amnon, 98, 158
Mughniyeh, Imad, 1, 236
Muhammad, prophet, 109, 151
Murad, Anas, 133
Mushtaha, Rawhi, 157
Mushtaha, Warchi, 191
Muslim Brotherhood, 29, 98
Mustafa, Mohammad, 66
Muwasi refugee camp, 99
Myanmar, 108, 164

N

Nabi Ilyas, 8
Nablus, 8, 85, 115, 173, 185, 188, 207, 211, 214
Nagar, Khaled, 66
Naim, Bassem, 61, 183
Najar, Ahmas, 191
Nashabat, Mahmoud, 133
Nasrallah, Hassan, 1–2, 6, 90, 96, 99, 115, 123–24, 132, 155, 162–63, 173, 183, 195, 215, 221, 226–28, 231, 236, 241–42, 252
Nasser, Muhammad Nimah, 114
Natal, 138
Natanz nuclear site, 20
NATO, 59, 127, 251
"Naval Iron Dome," 13
Nazer, Hassan, 229
Nazzal, Jamal, 239

Nebenzahl, Avigdor, 193
Nefesh B'Nefesh, 179, 253
Negm, Muhammad Mahmoud, 180
Netanyahu, Benjamin, 1–5, 7, *passim*
Netiv HaAsara, 11, 138, 162, 200
Netzarim axis, 175
New York City, 9, 36, 102–3, 201, 253
Nicaragua, 30
Nigrekar, Shai Silas, 206
Nilforoushan, Abbas, 236
Nimra base, 118
Nir, Nimrod, 117
Nisenbaum, Michel, 64
Nissim-Emanuel, Gal, 248
Nitzana Crossing, 13
Noam, Gilad, 53
Nof HaGalil, 213
Nofal, Ismail, 158
Norway, 60–61, 67, 166
Nur Shams refugee camp, 20, 123, 184
Nuseirat, 21, 35, 56, 79, 83, 86–87, 158, 214
Nusseibeh, Lana, 136

O

Obama, Barack, 32, 75, 252
Obaida, Abu, 22, 119, 212
Ocasio-Cortez, Alexandria, 194
Odeh, Ammar Razek Kamel, 158
Olmert, Ehud, 236
Oman, 30, 59
Oren, Michael, 31, 53, 71, 253
Oslo Accords, xi, 98, 122
Oster, Eitan Yitzhak, 247
Otzma Yehudit, 180
Oz Zion, 85

P

Pa'atei Modi'in train station, 216
Pahlavi, Mohammad Reza, 85
Palestine, 19, 25, 31, 34, 39, 60, 68, 71, 102, 106, 149, 181, 196, 205, 212, 229, 234, 239, 243–44, 252
Palestinian Arabs, 149, 195
Palestinian Chronicle, 109
Palestinian Red Crescent, 97, 123
Palestinian State, 4, 25, 30, 36–37, 49, 52–53, 55–56, 60–61, 67–68, 73, 78, 99, 106, 113, 133, 149, 165–66, 207, 215–16, 230, 234
Palestinian terrorists, 98, 188–89, 191, 243, 245
Paris, 102, 139, 187, 212, 244
Passover, 21–22, 233
Pasternak, Anne, 102

Pearl Harbor, 31
Pelosi, Nancy, 6, 13
Pentagon, 14, 26, 40, 63–64, 74, 90, 97, 104, 158, 169, 174, 184, 195, 214, 220, 230
Petro, Gustavo, 37
Petropoulos, Georgios, 47
Pezeshkian, Masoud, 124, 164, 240
Phillips, Melanie, 71, 75, 252
Phillips, Moshe, 98
Planet Labs, 121
Poilievre, Pierre, 198
Poland, ix, 2–3, 47, 59, 126, 233
Politico, 63, 164, 172, 178
poll, 11, 13, 28, 31, 43, 53, 91, 116, 122, 191, 220–21, 232
Polyanskiy, Dmitry, 205
Pope Francis, 33, 231
Portes, Thomas, 139
"Protest Seder," 22
Putin, Vladimir, 18, 173

Q
Qabatiya, 221
Qalqilya, 98, 158, 185
Qaouk, Nabil, 228
Qarawi, Mohanad Kamal, 185
Qasim, Faris, 186
Qassem, Naim, 81, 114, 217, 229
Qatar, 6, 13, 17, 20, 22, 29–30, 33, 38, 42, 44, 60, 66, 74, 81, 84, 115, 130–31, 139–40, 142, 148, 156, 165, 167–68, 172–75, 178, 189, 199, 201–3, 223, 232
Qatash, Amin, 138
Qawasameh, Mahmoud, 191
Qubaisi, Ibrahim, 222

R
Rabia, Yassin, 66
Radi, Jamal Hussein Ahmad, 63
Radwan Force, 22, 134, 136, 161, 174, 211, 216, 221–22
Rafael, 57, 99, 245
Rafah, 7–8, 11–13, 19, 21–22, 24–29, 31, 35–45, 47–59, 61–69, 71, 73–75, 79, 82–83, 88, 91–95, 97, 99–101, 103, 107, 113, 117–19, 121–22, 134, 138, 162, 171, 175, 178, 184–85, 187–88, 197, 200, 213, 215, 218, 220, 243, 253
Rafat, 213
Rahat, 185
Raisi, Ebrahim, 17–18, 56–57, 59, 73
Ramadan, 5–6, 13
Ramallah, 14, 58, 63, 176, 209, 213
Ramle, 130

Ramon, Ilan, 109
Rasmussen, Lars Løkke, 68
Rav Huna, 246
Ravid, Barak, 95
Raz, Ze'ev, 85
Regev, Miri, 179, 186, 196
Reuters, 4, 13, 20, 24, 32, 36, 41, 44, 74, 83, 89, 95, 99, 103–4, 108–9, 111, 170, 177, 207, 226–27
Risch, Jim, 96
Rizkov, Maxim, 214
Rodriguez, David, 238
Rogers, Michael, 238
Rohingya, 13
Rosenfeld, Avi, 88
Rosenfeld, Malkachi, 191
Rosengarten, Shai, 201
Russia, 17–18, 21, 62, 64, 73, 83, 89, 102, 108–9, 121, 136, 161, 209, 213, 216, 233, 249, 251, 253
Ryder, Patrick, 63

S
Sa-Nur, 61
Sa'ad, Ra'ad, 98
Sa'ar, Gideon, 146
Sabri, Sheikh Ekrima, 156
Safadi, Ayman, 54, 61, 64, 125, 206, 228
Safed, 90, 105, 151, 215
Sagi, Ada, 81
Sagiv, Assaf, 195
Sakhl, Nael, 166
Salah, Muhammad, 99
Salameh, Rafa'a, 129, 135
Salami, Hossein, 17, 221, 240
Salem military outpost, 27
Salfit, 158
Salman, Mustafa Hassan, 118
Sanchez, Pedro, 4, 60
Saposnik, Arieh, 249
Saqlawi, Qassem, 62
Saree, Yahya, 136
Sariel, Yossi, 214
Sarna, Igal, 245, 253
Sarusi, Almog, 234
Saudi Arabia, 13, 17–18, 30, 36–37, 47, 55, 68, 88, 115, 160, 167, 223–24
Scholz, Olaf, 64, 141
Sde Teiman detention center, 63
Sdeh David, 86
Sderot, 32, 231
Sebutinde, Julia, 74
Second Lebanon War, 5, 84, 169
Segal, Amit, 125

Seibert, Steffen, 217
settler violence, 135
Seyedah Zeinab, 218
Shabak, 113
Shabat, Yussef Rafik Ahmed, 19
Shadi al-Zaytun school, 215
Shaer, Gilad, 192
Shafik, Minouche, 27
Shahadeh, Imad, 214
Shahar, Meirav Eilon, 246
Shakir, Omar, 31
Shalit, Gilad, 15, 151, 191
Shamir-Borer, Eran, 125
Shamni, Gadi, 218
Sharansky, Natan, 249, 253
Sharia law, 85
Shas Party, 134, 193
Sheikh Khalil, Izzadin, 191
Sheikh Yussef, Muhammad, 185
Sherzer, Adi, 249
Shiite Muslims, 109, 132, 151
Shikaki, Khalil, 176
Shoidach, Aiman, 128
Shoshani, Nadav, 185
Shujaiyeh, 114, 120, 128
Shukr, Fouad, 147–48, 155, 162, 182
Shura Council, 44, 162
Sidon, 166, 178
Singh, Sabrina, 90
Sinwar, Yahya, 15, 71, 77, 119, 128, 162, 202, 225
Slovenia, 4
Smith, Lee, 244, 252
Smotrich, Bezalel, 44, 79, 166, 198
Sohlberg, Noam, 103
Soleimani, Qasem, 1, 131, 151
Somalia, 108
Soroka Hospital, 16
Spain, 4, 17, 60–61, 67–68, 74, 113, 126, 136, 233
Stamford Hill, 102
Starmer, Keir, 187, 252
Stein, Alex, 103
Støre, Jonas Gahr, 60
Suad, Sharif, 26
Sudan, 34, 209, 213
Sufa, 38, 42
Sullivan, Jake, 3, 58, 126, 166, 198
Sunak, Rishi, 9
Susya, 181
Sweden, 47, 69, 126
Switzerland, 19, 250
Syria, 1, 6–8, 13, 16, 18, 20, 25, 31, 72, 80, 108, 147, 149, 157, 162, 164, 173, 181, 209, 214, 218, 228, 230, 233, 236, 241–242

T

Taasa, Gil, 200
Tablet, 34, 75, 151, 191, 242, 249, 252–54
Tajani, Antonio, 65
Taliban, 13
Tamari, Meir, 56
Tarif, Sheikh Mowafaq, 145, 248
Tariq, Mohammed, 138
Tehran, 6, 14, 10, 17–18, 20–23, 25, 32, 59, 62, 68, 71, 75, 83, 85, 106, 108–9, 121, 124, 147, 153, 155, 159–61, 163–64, 168, 170–71, 178, 215–16, 230, 240, 242, 245, 252
Tekuma Authority, 32
Tel al-Sultan, 58, 93, 138, 204, 211
Tel Aviv, 8, 14, 25, 35, 65–67, 70, 78, 87, 93, 98, 116, 124, 134–35, 157–59, 162, 166, 172, 175–76, 182, 193, 199, 216–17, 222, 229, 240
Tel HaShomer base, 12
Tel-Hai, 106
Telegraph, 99, 148, 166, 226
Temple Mount, 156, 180, 190, 193–95, 251
The New Arab, 45
Third Jewish Commonwealth, x
Thomas-Greenfield, Linda, 19, 89, 104, 179, 219, 228
Tibon, Amir, 253
Tish'a B'Av, 170, 193
Torres, Ritchie, 158–59, 201, 244
Trudeau, Justin, 198
Trump, Donald, 30, 32, 34, 46, 62, 135, 151
Tulkarm, 9, 20, 24, 38, 68, 81, 98, 107, 115, 123, 139, 158, 184–87, 189, 214
Tulkarm Battalion, 186
Türk, Volker, 41, 209, 222
Turkey, 17–18, 21–22, 30, 39, 51, 68, 81, 137, 148, 157, 163
Tuwaitha, 85
two-state solution, 11, 19, 26, 37, 53, 56, 60–61, 64, 73, 88, 99, 176, 224, 230, 234, 251
Tyre, 53, 145, 174, 180

U

Uganda, 74, 86
Ukraine, 17, 23, 46, 64, 109, 121, 209, 213, 216, 249
Umayyad dynasty, 109
UN, 4–6, 9, 12, 17–20, *passim*
United Kingdom, 3, 18, 32, 62, 71, 169, 172, 201–2, 250
United States, 2–3, 6, 10, 12, 14–19, *passim*
United Torah Judaism, 2, 120
UNRWA, 54, 69, 71, 83, 103, 105, 114, 140, 148, 162, 214, 243

Upper Galilee, 96, 114, 161, 171–72, 177, 182
US Congress, 121, 136, 139
US House of Representatives, 20
US Justice Department, 201
US Senate, 4, 23
US State Department, 30, 59, 62, 104, 137, 140
USAid, 87, 126, 134
USS Abraham Lincoln, 169, 214
USS Cole, 161
USS Laboon, 161
USS Theodore Roosevelt, 161, 214
USS Wasp, 105
Uyghurs, 13

V
Vatik, Ozel, 173
von der Leyen, Ursula, 18

W
Wahbi, Ahmed, 222
Wald, Charles, 238
Walla, 40, 117, 131
Walz, Tim, 207
West Bank, 1, 5–7, 14, 22, 25, 27, 37–38, 51, 53, 55, 61, 66–68, 70, 74, 79, 81, 83, 85, 91, 98–99, 103, 106–7, 115, 123, 126, 128–29, 135, 137, 149, 158, 162, 165, 173, 178–79, 181, 184–89, 196, 199, 204, 206–9, 211, 213–14, 217, 219, 234
Western Sahara, 34, 151
White House, 3–5, 22, 27–28, 30–32, 34, 36, 40–41, 46–47, 50, 52, 59, 62, 64, 67, 69, 71, 80, 94–96, 108, 114, 124, 136, 143–44, 151, 155, 164, 166, 168, 173, 179, 181, 199, 252
Wicker, Roger, 11
Widodo, Joko, 155
Wikiran, 173
Wood, Robert, 12, 245

Y
Yablonka, Hanan, 64
Yad Vashem, 26
Yahav, Yona, 169
Yahya, Ali Mohammed, 145
Yamour, Jihad, 191
Yanuh-Jat, 248
Yaron, Lee, 253
Yaroun, 208
Yated, 42, 195
Yated Ne'eman, 195
Yediot Achronot, 21, 45
Yellen, Janet, 126
Yemen, 16–17, 38, 109, 121, 134–36, 164, 216, 225, 242, 245
Yeni Safak, 231
Yerushalmi, Eden, 157, 234
Yevul, 42
Yiftach, Eyal, 192
Yinon, Bilha, 162
Yisrael Hayom, 10, 29, 53, 97–98, 116, 122, 149–50, 160, 170, 173, 190, 216, 254
Yom HaAtzmaut, 51
Yom HaShoah, 39
Yom HaZikaron, 45, 48, 51, 245
Yosef, Yitzhak, 193
Yosef, Yuval Mor, 192
Yudkin, Yisrael, 249

Z
Zaarab, Aiman, 38
Zahedi, Mohammad Reza, 1
Zakarana, Shadi, 221
Zeitoun area, 209
Zelenskyy, Volodymyr, 17, 46
Zimel, Dov, 19
Zionist rabbis, 138, 151
Ziv, Shlomi, 86
Zubeidi, Muhammad Zakaria, 205
Zubeidi, Zakaria, 205, 233

www.ingramcontent.com/pod-product-compliance
Lightning Source LLC
Chambersburg PA
CBHW052057300426
44117CB00013B/2173